THE SHADOW WAR

The Shadow War:
Michael Collins and the Politics of Violence

Joseph E.A. Connell Jnr

Eastwood

First published in 2019
Eastwood Books,
an imprint of the Wordwell Group.
Unit 9, 78 Furze Road, Sandyford Industrial Estate, Dublin 18
www.eastwoodbooks.com
www.wordwellbooks.com

Cover image—The Four Courts, 30 June 1922—moments after the 'great explosion', a massive plume of smoke rises into the air. (Irish Architectural Archive)

ISBN 978-1-9161375-0-9

British Library Cataloguing-in-Publication Data.
A catalogue record for this book is available from the British Library.

Typeset in Ireland by Wordwell Ltd
Copy-editor: Emer Condit
Cover design and artwork: Wordwell Ltd
Printed by Gráficas Castuera, Pamplona

Contents

To the memory of
Constance Cowley and Bob Fuquea.
Each inspired me.
May they rest in peace.

Acknowledgements

I must thank my parents for everything; without them I would have had no such love for Ireland. My brothers and sister and their families supported me at all times.

I am most grateful to Eastwood Books, and it has been a pleasure to work with Nick Maxwell, Una MacConville, Ronan Colgan, Helen Dunne and everyone at the Wordwell Group. Emer Condit is a wonderful editor and I cannot thank her enough. Everyone at Eastwood has given polish to my efforts and all their assistance is most appreciated.

Clare Cowley started helping with research, and helped on everything thereafter.

I thank Michael Kennedy of the Royal Irish Academy. This book would not have been contemplated without his encouragement.

I am always grateful to Anthony Tierney for his continuing advice and suggestions.

Dr Patrick Geoghehan and Susan Cahill have given me the privilege of a recurring spot on their NewsTalk radio show, *Talking History*. I have been a guest several times on Myles Dungan's RTÉ Radio show, *The History Show*. Dónal Ó hUallachain always finds time to have me on his show, *Looking Back*, on Radio Dublin. Carol Dooley has given me many opportunities to talk on her show, *Saturday Live*, on Sunshine Radio. It has been a joy to work with them all over the years and I am most grateful.

Mícheál Ó Doibhilín, the editor of www.kilmainhamtales.ie, has let me submit articles for his site and has published my books under his imprint. I am always pleased with his editing and guidance.

Tommy Graham of *History Ireland* has been most encouraging and helpful. I am indebted to him for allowing me to write a column, *100 Years Ago*, in *History Ireland*.

All of them have a respect for those men and women of the revolutionary years, and have given me great assistance and support.

Everyone knows that I am technologically illiterate. I simply could not have prepared a manuscript without the gracious help of Lou Yovin.

I have always been welcomed throughout Ireland with the greatest kindness and hospitality, and I thank everyone with whom I've spoken. I assure you that those feelings are returned with the deepest and most lasting affection.

Those who have helped and encouraged me are too numerous to mention and I thank them all. Everyone I asked always gave me assistance, reassurance and direction; all heartened me when I needed that most, and from time to time most fed me when I needed that most, too. At the risk of offending someone I omit, I must especially mention Ray Bateson, Áine Broy, Bob Clarke, Marie Coleman, Lorcan Collins, C.B. Connell, Briny M. Connell, Molly Connell, Revd Paul Connell, Carla Cowley-Ralph, John Dorney, Tom and Mary Duffy, Sgt Wayne Fitzgerald, Col. David Fuquea, Liz Gillis, Marcus Howard, Lar Joye, Peggy Keating, Dermot McEvoy, Frank MacGabhann, Jim McIlmurray, Mary Mackey, Brenda Malone, Barbara and Dominic Montaldi, Gregory O'Connor, Pól Ó Murchú, Lord Mayor Nial Ring, Detta and Seán Spellissy, and Padraic Yeates.

And Pam Brewster for all things.

While I have been given a great deal of assistance, all mistakes are mine alone.

Overview: From Frongoch to the Truce

Ireland's story from 1918 to 1921 may be summed up as the story of a struggle between our determination to govern ourselves and to get rid of British government and the British determination to prevent us from doing either. It was a struggle between two rival Governments, the one an Irish Government resting on the will of the people and the other an alien Government depending for its existence upon military force—the one gathering more and more authority, the other steadily losing ground.

—**Michael Collins**

The Irish struggle of 1917–21 has been called many things: the Anglo-Irish War, the 'Tan' War and the War of Independence. The War of Independence was fought to bring to Ireland a native government deriving its authority from the Irish people, and militarily was mostly a guerrilla war. Guerrillas go by many different names: rebels, irregulars, insurgents, partisans and terrorists. Such wars are now characterised as asymmetrical or unconventional warfare.

There was very little public support for the rebels during the 1916 Easter Rising.[1] For the most part, the Irish supported the British war effort in World War I. Moreover, many civilians were killed or lost their property in the fires that ravaged Dublin. When the rebels were marched off to boats bound for prisons in Britain, many were pelted with vegetables, bottles and even the contents of chamber-pots. Nothing that these men and women had done during the week led the people to take their side, though the bitterness of the public was tinged with a little admiration—the Irish had fought well against the regular British troops.

Immediately after the Rising this view had not changed. Soon, however, admiration for the rebels who fought well and honourably against the British began to move closer to approval, and the public would increasingly come to support their position and their political objectives, if

1

still disapproving of their methods. Shortly after the Rising, one woman wrote in her diary:

> Of course this is not Ireland's rebellion—only a Sinn Féin rising … The Sinn Féin leaders were such good men. They died like saints. Oh! the pity of it! And Ireland wanted them so much. They were men of such beautiful character, such high literary power and attainments—mystics who kept the light burning … But as sure as God's sun rises in the east, if England does not get things right … if there's not immediately conciliation and love and mercy poured out on Ireland—all the Sinn Féin leaders will be canonized … Already the tone is changing.[2]

Britain, still engaged in World War I, determined that the Rising was an act of 'treason' for which the participants and leaders should suffer the fate of traitors in wartime, and executed sixteen of them. Moreover, the Irish had enlisted German support, a move that prompted outright vilification.[3] The Rising had hardly been the work of a massive conspiracy, but the British acted as if it were.[4] Over 3,000 men and women were imprisoned after the rebellion, many in jails in England and Wales. Like Michael Collins, most of those imprisoned were never charged, and there were certainly many who had not participated at all. Ironically, it was in the British detention centres that less ardent nationalists came under the influence of more radical comrades who converted them to the principle of resistance to British rule. These mass arrests and the increased British military presence demonstrated bluntly that Ireland was under the control of an oppressive and alien government that could only rule the country by force. Though it was never enforced outside Dublin in 1916, when General Sir John Grenville Maxwell declared martial law throughout the country the people realised that they were being treated as second-class citizens by a British government no longer in touch with Ireland.[5]

The War of Independence could not have occurred without the conversion of the Irish people from supporting Home Rule to advocating an open and, shortly, violent revolution. The Easter Rising should have been an adequate warning to the British that events and forces in Irish society were slipping out of the grasp of the Dublin Castle administration and its police. Further, the same influences that inspired many of the rebels—the GAA, the Gaelic League and Irish nationalism/separatism—also appealed to the younger members of the clergy. The last words of the executed leaders, reported in a religious vein, contributed to the slow change in clerical attitudes.[6] As time passed, a measure of support for nationalist ideals appeared in the younger priests who came forward at nationalist rallies and on Sinn Féin platforms, while the conversion of some priests into more outspoken nationalists was vital to the growth of the movement. A police report noted of the priests: 'They exercise an immense influence over the youth in their parishes and unless some means can be used to make them abstain from interference in politics I fear that disaffection will be dangerously spread'.[7]

Some in Ireland began to feel a spiritual kinship with past fighting generations, and the words of James Fintan Lalor were often quoted, 'that somewhere, and somehow, and by somebody a beginning must be made'. Patrick Pearse, the idealist, and James Connolly, the Lalor disciple, had begun the rebellion, in Lalor's words, 'even if [it was] called premature, imprudent or dangerous—if made so soon as tomorrow—even if offered by ten men only—even if offered by men armed only with stones'.

While Collins was imprisoned in Frongoch, he was consolidating his position within the IRB as well as setting up for the future. Richard Mulcahy, in his notes on Frongoch, noted of Collins:

> In Frongoch 'he was very consciously pulling the threads of the IRB together with a view to the situation which would develop politically and organizationally when all the prisoners, including the Lewes prisoners, were back at home and political life was beginning again in Ireland'.[8]

The failure of the Rising and the execution or internment of so many of the senior personnel of both the Volunteers and the IRB made it appear, on the surface at least, as if the Irish underground had been virtually destroyed. However, the work of two men in particular—Collins, operating amongst his IRB contacts, and Cathal Brugha, working through the Volunteers—began quickly and effectively to reconstitute it. Brugha, very seriously wounded in the 1916 fighting, escaped execution, and when discharged from medical care in late 1916 immediately began recruiting for the Volunteers.

In 1917–18 there were parliamentary by-elections in Roscommon, Kilkenny and Longford. Count George Plunkett was elected under the Sinn Féin banner in North Roscommon, and Joseph McGuinness, who was in Lewes Jail in England, won the by-election in Longford in 1918 with the campaign slogan 'Put him in to get him out'. Collins was involved in the organisation and campaigning for these by-election candidates, and it was he who convinced the prisoners in England that Irish opinion had undergone such a change that McGuinness's election to parliament was possible. In 1917, too, following the Sinn Féin annual convention in October and a reorganisation convention of the Volunteers that same month, national co-ordination of the IRA began in earnest.[9] Later in 1917, the death of Thomas Ashe from being forcibly fed while on hunger strike aroused tremendous passion. His funeral led to massive defiance of the orders against uniformed marches, and Volunteers from all over Ireland gathered in Dublin to pay their last respects. Collins's funeral oration gave some hint of things to come when he said merely, 'Nothing additional remains to be said—the volley we have just heard is the only speech it is proper to make above the grave of a dead Fenian'.[10]

These, then, were the major antecedents of the War of Independence: an increasingly ineffective British administration faced by Irish men and women fired with revolutionary zeal and convinced that they could attain their ends by violence. A set of contingent events was to provide the final catalyst, as there was yet to come another imperious decision that would harden Irish attitudes against the British. Although about 210,000 men from Ireland, of whom some 35,000 died, served in the British army during World War I, not one had been conscripted.[11] Most entered the army for financial reasons, because they were poverty-stricken and employment opportunities were so few in Ireland. Others, particularly the Irish National Volunteers who heeded the call of John Redmond, believed that enlisting 'to fight for small nations' would lead to Home Rule for Ireland. In 1918, however, a conscription crisis provided the springboard for the change in Irish opinion and the transfer of political allegiance from the Irish Parliamentary Party to Sinn Féin.

So it was that within two years of the Easter Rising Ireland abandoned the Irish Parliamentary Party and its goal of Home Rule and went marching forward resolutely under what was then described as the Sinn Féin banner but was in reality Collins's IRB standard. For the first time in Irish nationalist history, the advocates of physical force and those of political agitation would work together rather than against each other.

There was, then, a gradual change of political allegiance on the part of the Irish in the period between the end of the 1916 Rising and the onset of the War of Independence in 1919. The perceived legitimacy of the incumbent British administration dwindled in almost inverse proportion to the growing support of the underground government of the Irish Republic proclaimed in front of Dublin's GPO at Easter 1916 and endorsed through a series of elections culminating in the Dáil Éireann election of 1918. The most tangible change that occurred in Ireland after the Rising was this power shift in Irish politics from the Irish Parliamentary Party to the newly unified Sinn Féin.

On 21 January 1919 the First Dáil met in the Round Room of Dublin's Mansion House and at 3.30 p.m. Count Plunkett called the meeting to order, nominating Cathal Brugha as Ceann Comhairle (speaker/chairperson) for Dáil Éireann, a proposal seconded by Padraig Ó Maille. Brugha presided thereafter, and following the reading of the Declaration of Independence he told the cheering assembly: 'Deputies, you understand from what is asserted in this Declaration that we are now done with England. Let the world know it and those who are concerned bear it in mind. For come what may, whether it be death itself, the great deed is done.'

From 1919 to the end of 1921, the Irish waged the War of Independence with strong reliance on intelligence, propaganda, politics and guerrilla tactics, co-ordinated by Collins in Dublin, Florence O'Donoghue in Cork and the Volunteer GHQ to make up an orchestrated plan of campaign.[12] The Irish forces evolved in both scale and purpose, though in a haphazard manner. The British forces, on the other hand, at no time fought their campaign in all these arenas. Their approach was piecemeal: they had no overall strategy and no conception of a co-ordinated counter-insurgency. During the summer and autumn of 1920 they began to reorganise and develop in the intelligence, political and military fields, but by this time it was perhaps too late to put down the revolt. Collins's intelligence ring and his ruthless killers were the linchpin of the war effort in Dublin, and he sent directives across the country to co-ordinate the campaign.[13] The IRA won the battle for the hearts and minds of the Irish people and the IRA/Volunteers became the fighting arm of an underground, alternative government.[14]

In the early years of the war, Collins set about reorganising the Volunteer movement as Director of Organisation.[15] In 1918 both Collins and Richard Mulcahy were considered for the position of Chief of Staff of the Volunteer GHQ. Dick McKee, Director of Training, who went on to be the O/C of the Dublin Brigade, agreed beforehand that Mulcahy and not Collins should be Chief of Staff. Mulcahy later noted:

> McKee, as he came away from the meeting with me, expressed satisfaction and relief that Collins was not being recommended. The main reason for that was that in the light of what he knew about Collins' temperament … McKee—like others—was a little bit wary of entrusting him with anything like complete control. In fact he did want time to disclose himself and his qualities.[16]

In one of his rare personal remarks about Collins in his annotation of Piaras Béaslaí's books Mulcahy wrote:

> If, internally, he [Collins] had grown in power, strength of will and flexibility, as he had, he had done it by tireless, vigorous, almost turbulent hard work, applied to his office work as much as to his widespread and general personal contacts.[17]

During this period Collins developed the morale and discipline of the fighting men to the very high level that characterised the Irish for the next four years. He recognised that guerrilla warfare was the only way forward, both in Dublin and in the countryside. In fact, it was the sheer efficiency of Collins's planning that was his most valuable asset. Physical fighting against the British was of a rather different character in the country than in Dublin, Cork or Belfast. In rural areas, attacks on RIC barracks were first undertaken by men who assembled at night and who resumed their ordinary civilian lives after an operation. Later, small bodies of men in flying columns remained on full-time active service in the countryside, obtaining shelter and food from the country people, using assistance from local IRA men and Cumann na mBan women and civilians in their activities, and operating in a hit-and-run manner.

As the Volunteer Director of Intelligence, Collins masterminded an Irish intelligence network that successfully countered British intelligence in Ireland. It did so by making a mirror image of the British system and then improving upon it. Collins was the first to understand the necessity for an intelligence service that would penetrate the British military and civil administration in Dublin Castle, and the success of the revolutionary movement was largely due to this effort. Inexperienced personnel, who had no rigid ideas about the kind of organisation needed, helped build up the intelligence system from nothing. Collins, through the dual areas of intelligence and operations, co-ordinated the active side of the IRA/Volunteers with the same concentration that he expected of all who worked for him. He knew that the fundamentals of intelligence were acquisition, analysis, implementation and counter-intelligence, and he was entirely clear about what results he wanted from any organisation. In this sphere, success or failure depended largely on his vision and energy, as well as on the efficiency of his operatives. Slackness and inertia, the failure to put weapons to good use and failure to file reports produced harsh rebukes. Collins did not just attend meetings or send out memos; he lived his motto and 'got on with the work'.

Though Collins often walked and cycled throughout Dublin after the Dáil met in January 1919, he was never arrested despite the fact that the head of the British army in Ireland, General Nevil Macready, wrote to his superiors in London in March 1921 recommending that the British government offer £10,000 for his capture.[18] (The average worker's wage at the time was £2 2s per week, yet no one seriously thought of betraying Collins. The story of a £10,000 price on Collins's head is not strictly true. After Detective Inspector W.C. Forbes Redmond was killed on 21 January 1920, a £10,000 reward was offered by Dublin Castle for information leading to the arrest and conviction of the person(s) responsible for his death, 'especially the man who issued the order'. This is where the story of the bounty on Collins probably originated, as he was the one who ordered Redmond's killing. Rewards of £5,000 had previously been offered in regard of the deaths of other DMP detectives,

Smith, Hoey and Barton, and these offers were now doubled, but there was never a specific reward for Collins's actual capture.)

Collins recognised at an early stage that his twin enemies were the spy and the informer, the enemies of any revolutionary movement, and he systematically removed both as a crucial element of IRA tactics. As late as the spring of 1921 they were still being shot. Between January and April 1921 seventy-three bodies, with placards around their necks announcing the removal of an informer or spy, were taken from the Irish streets. The secrecy of IRA operations was rigorously maintained and Collins's intelligence agency could act with a considerable feeling of security.

While this internal sanction of eliminating British agents had been institutionalised, the weapon was also turned, with great effect, on the special branches of both the Dublin Metropolitan Police (DMP) and the Royal Irish Constabulary (RIC) outside of Dublin. (The DMP had always been an unarmed force, while the RIC had been armed. However, the command structure of the RIC had never been designed to deal with a war situation.) Collins's view in 1920 was simple:

> a man might have been murdered in broad daylight (and many were) in the Dublin streets, and not one policeman have lifted a finger. The uniformed men on point duty would have gone on waving traffic this way and that ... The attitude of the police was reasonable—while they stayed neutral they were safe; as soon as they interfered they became marked men.[19]

The intelligence network was organised on two distinct levels—the civil and the military. The military side, the more important of the two, operated mainly through the underground cells of the IRB that Collins commanded. Formally, the IRA/Volunteers were organised along British military lines. Each company and battalion had an intelligence officer whose reports were passed through a brigade intelligence officer to the central office in Dublin. This, however, was an adjunct to Collins's own network of IRB spies operating separately in most Irish communities. On the civil side Collins had men and women in post offices, and the Irish Post Office was certainly one of Collins's most useful sources. In addition, he had men on the railways, on Channel ferries, in every prison in Ireland and in many in England. The trade unions were mobilised to hamper police and military movements by road, rail and sea. Collins had many operatives who worked in all the various telephone exchanges, whether military or civilian, as in hotels. Men and women in hotels and restaurants throughout Ireland were especially helpful sources. Similarly, dockers in all parts of Europe and the USA served in what Collins referred to as his 'Q' Division.

Collins studied previous Irish risings and recognised the extent to which espionage had been responsible for their failure. Throughout the centuries, spies had infiltrated every Irish revolutionary organisation—a relatively easy task in a small country like Ireland, where a careless word spoken at a fair or in a pub travelled quickly to the headquarters of the British spy network, Dublin Castle. The eyes and ears of this network, especially in villages and the countryside, were the members of the RIC, who reported all snippets of information to Dublin Castle or to the DMP's political section, 'G' Division, based at Great Brunswick Street police station. Some 'G' Division detectives roamed freely around the city, following those suspected of disloyalty to the Crown or meeting informants and taking notes. Other G-men were positioned at railway stations or docks to watch arrivals and departures. At the end of each working shift, all the G-men would transfer their notes and reports into a large ledger-type book held at the police station, so that all members of the division would have access to the same information. This served as a communal cross-reference and also avoided unintentional encroachment on the work of a colleague, which might jeopardise months of intelligence-gathering. All important reports were dispatched to Dublin Castle for sifting and correlation. The system was simple—crude, even—but very effective.

By far the most important amongst Collins's agents were the men and women working for him in military intelligence and the civilian Special Branches. They were at the heart of the British administration, with access to restricted information, all British military and government codes and the like. In particular, three Dublin policemen, Éamon (Ned) Broy, Joseph Kavanagh and James MacNamara, as well as Dave Neligan in Dublin Castle, helped to turn what had been Britain's greatest security asset in Ireland against itself. In 1916 Kavanagh was assigned to pick out the Rising's leaders when they were assembled in Richmond Prison. Even then, however, his loyalty was clear, as he walked among the prisoners and asked, 'Is there anything I can do for you?' or 'Can I take a message for you?'. Kavanagh was a key Collins spy for about a year until he succumbed to cancer, but by then he had recruited another valuable agent for Collins in James McNamara, who worked in Dublin Castle. Broy gave Collins a detailed, inside knowledge of the British police system in Ireland. Collins learned how the system worked and how the police were trained—Broy turned him into an intelligence master.

A realist like Collins knew that it was necessary to shut down the British sources of knowledge and blind the Dublin Castle administration. The information obtained enabled him to identify G-men, who were warned to stop their intelligence activities or the IRA would kill them. Collins realised that in order to defeat Britain they would have to take out their spies, as they would be unable to replace them. 'I am a builder, not a destroyer. I get rid of people only when they hinder my work,' he told Broy. He warned the detectives to look the other way or suffer the consequences. Those detectives who scoffed at the warnings paid the price.

Collins's passion for secrecy was so intense that for many months none of these men knew of the existence of any of the others. On occasion they actually followed one another. Broy was godfather to Kavanagh's oldest son before he knew that they were both working for Collins.

> One evening, we were walking in St Stephen's Green, and we both made the discovery that we were in contact with Michael Collins. I told him about Mick's visit to No. 1 Great Brunswick St. He nearly fell, laughing, knowing the mentality in the G. Division office and knowing Mick. He got me to tell it to him a second time, and he laughed so much that people looked at him as if he were drunk or mad. He asked me what did Mick look like in the office, and I said: 'He looked like a big plain–clothes man going out on duty, with a stick'. Shortly afterwards, when I met Mick, he apologised for not having told me about Kavanagh. I told him that that was what I had been preaching to him since I met him, not to tell anything, that the Irish people had paid too big a price for carelessness like that, in the past. Michael similarly apologised to Joe the next time he met him, but Michael was glad the two of us knew and understood each other.[20]

Collins, Broy and Richard Mulcahy agreed that the war had to be taken to the DMP detectives and that pre-emptive strikes were necessary.

> The authorities were apparently biding their time to have certain preparations made before the Dáil was suppressed. The work of men like Smyth, Hoey, and Barton ['G' Division detectives], and the G Division generally was being effectively snowballed to increase the information regarding the persons who were particularly active and important both on the political and volunteer side. To allow it to have developed any way effectively would have been disastrous. The initiative against the detectives was only begun in time.[21]

Although he knowingly embarked upon his ruthless path, Collins was also aware of a possible public backlash. Republican newspapers and those sympathetic to the ideals of Sinn Féin were fed with appropriate propaganda. This policy of killing G-men led in turn to suppression and censorship by Dublin Castle. Such a knee-jerk reaction, together with the obvious alarm caused by the killings of the G-men, confirmed to Collins that he was hurting the British intelligence system, and he realised that London and Dublin would increase their efforts to smash his organisation. The first killings were carried out by Volunteers, but he reasoned that a specialist unit was needed, a killing unit (the 'Squad'), who would react to orders efficiently and, most importantly, without qualms of conscience.

Collins's intelligence system was a crucial asset in the War of Independence. In all the important military centres throughout the country, on the railroads, and on the docks and ferries Collins succeeded in planting someone who kept him well supplied with information. Nevertheless, he decried the need for it: 'This damn spying business plays hell with a man. It kills the soul and the heart in him. It leaves him without pity or mercy. I am fed up with the whole rotten business … Look how the poor girls are ruined by us. There is no softness in them anymore!'[22] There was, however, one serious drawback in his intelligence organisation: Collins never knew what was happening in the inner circles of power in Westminster. Although he had a first-rate military intelligence system, he had no political intelligence organisation whatsoever. Ultimately, this was a major flaw, particularly since there is strong evidence to suggest that the British had a fairly good idea of the thinking within the Dublin cabinet, and it became a grave defect as the Treaty negotiations ensued in late 1921. Still, the British intelligence war was widely acknowledged as being ineffective, with Collins and his men and women operatives consistently out-spying His Majesty's secret services.[23]

The streets of Dublin were the front line in Collins's conflict between the police and the IRA. Well known to their putative targets, the G-men who specialised in political work proved particularly vulnerable to IRA attacks. Collins's decision to assassinate these men was partly pragmatic. Their elimination would remove a vital source of intelligence from the British administration in Ireland, allowing the IRA vital breathing space. But there were also political and symbolic motives. The G-men were the most hated symbols of the British regime, particularly despised for their role in picking out the leaders of the rebellion for execution in 1916. Their killings could be depicted as justifiable, while the British response to them would escalate the conflict. Between July 1919 and May 1920 a dozen DMP men were assassinated. By the end of Collins's brutal but effective campaign, the DMP's intelligence-gathering capabilities had been destroyed and the force was on the verge of collapse. The DMP was compelled to withdraw from direct involvement in the conflict, its members refusing to carry arms or assume any responsibility for political crime.[24] When the new Secret Service men were assigned to Dublin, there were few policemen of the old persuasion who could or would help them. Collins forced each man to start from scratch, and the British intelligence system was never the same.[25]

The leading edge of the terror campaign of Collins's Squad was selective assassination, involving groups of three to ten men.[26] Collins recognised the ever-present possibility that public and international opinion would react against such killings, so precautions were taken. (This is not to say that the killings were always of the correct person but that a serious attempt was made to identify the person and the activity that had to be targeted.) The selection of targets reflected Collins's and the Irish concern for legitimacy and the prevention of wanton violence. The aim was not to kill massive numbers of people but to limit the killing, where possible, to targets that could be justified as legitimate objects of military or political resistance.[27] Collins set out to undermine the morale and effectiveness of the police in order to knock out the eyes and ears of the British administration. Policemen, magistrates, informers and men prominent in public life were shot. Assassinations ran the gamut from the police killings and military killings (such as that of an officer in the British army, Captain Percival Lea-Wilson, who severely mistreated Tom Clarke and other combatants of the Rising) to those arising from necessity. W.C. Forbes Redmond, Chief Inspector of the DMP, had to be removed because he was pressing Collins too hard. Similarly, the magistrate Alan Bell, taken in daylight from a Dublin tram and shot without anyone interfering, was assassinated because he was carrying on a most successful investigation into the origin and whereabouts of the Dáil Loan deposits.[28] Collins regarded assassinations such as these, and particularly the removal of spies, as essential to the success of the IRA campaign. Police intelligence reported in 1919 that 'according to information received from various sources the Irish Volunteer HQ has directed all county commanders to hold a certain number of men armed and in readiness to execute orders to attack barracks and assassinate police'.[29]

The War of Independence was a guerrilla campaign mounted against the British government in Ireland by the IRA/Volunteers from January 1919 until the truce in July 1921, under the proclaimed legitimacy of the First Dáil. Military operations remained limited during 1919, although raids for arms became a regular occurrence. Even though the Irish abandoned the idea of Home Rule and embraced separatism, the violence was at first deeply unpopular with the broader Irish population. Attitudes gradually changed, however, in the face of the terror of the British government's campaign of widespread brutality, destruction of property, random arrests, reprisals and unprovoked shootings. The small groups of IRA/Volunteers on the run were extremely vulnerable. Their success could make or break the activity of the IRA in a particular district—losing them often meant the end of operations. The local populace provided more than just moral support; in many cases they provided logistics, intelligence, and men and women for local actions. In September 1919 the Dáil was banned by the British, which served to make it easier for IRA/Volunteers to carry out attacks, because their more moderate politicians no longer had a public platform from which to restrain them.

For the remainder of 1919 and into 1920 the level of violence throughout Ireland increased. The British had to exert effective control over much of the countryside or lose the war. Nearly all the Irish lived in the country, on farms or villages, and various quasi-official bodies like the Dáil/Republican Courts or the IRA police effectively neutralised loyalists throughout Ireland. The IRA benefited from the widespread support given to them by the general Irish population, which regularly refused to pass information to the British. Much of the IRA's popularity was due to the excessive reaction of British forces to insurgent activity. An unofficial government policy of reprisals began in September 1919 in Fermoy, Co. Cork, when 200 British soldiers looted and burned the main businesses of the town after a soldier was killed when he refused to surrender his weapon to the local IRA. Actions such as these increased local support for the IRA and international support for Irish independence.

The British government was unwilling to admit that a rebellion existed that had to be countered with military methods. The conflict was never defined as a war, and the issue was obscured by attempting to distinguish between war and insurrection, summed up by British Prime Minister David Lloyd George's comment, 'You don't declare war against rebels'.[30] The struggle was never a conventional war; it was rarely more than a police action. The British army was used only sparingly, and the soldiers greatly resented the blame that accrued to them from the actions of the police, the Black and Tans and the Auxiliaries.[31] In fact, with some exceptions, the military enjoyed a more civil relationship with the civilian population. The Black and Tans were not all prisoners released from English jails, as has been claimed, but they were too ignorant of the law to be useful at police work, and too undisciplined to have any military value.[32] The British were never able to distinguish properly between the role of the army and that of the Auxiliaries and Black and Tans, who were attached to the police. Good policemen don't shoot first. They provide order. They protect. They reduce chaos. The Auxiliaries and the Black and Tans did none of these things.

The arrival of the Black and Tans in March 1920 changed the entire complexion of the war.[33] The 'Tans' were established as a section of the RIC and first appeared in the village of Upperchurch, Co. Tipperary. The British government needed more troops in Ireland to maintain its position, and turned to demobilised soldiers from World War I who were unemployed. The name came from their uniforms, which were black tunics and dark tan or khaki trousers, some with civilian hats but most with the green caps and black leather belts of the RIC.[34] Collins viewed the Black and Tans and the terror that came with them (and with the Auxiliaries who soon followed) as a sort of mixed blessing, which clearly drove any doubting nationalists into the arms of Sinn Féin. 'Apart from the loss which these attacks entail, good is done as it makes clear and clearer to people what both sides stand for.'[35] The Black and Tans were a force calculated to inspire terror in a population less timid and law-abiding than the Irish. There was no question of discipline: they robbed and killed on a daily basis. Collins took advantage of the public's reaction and knew that the terror backfired on the British. By late 1920 General F.P. Crozier, the O/C of the Black and Tans, had dismissed or imprisoned over fifty of them for indiscipline or criminal acts.[36]

Their appearance in Dublin altered the whole view of the city. Kathleen Napoli McKenna, who worked on *The Irish Bulletin* and saw Collins almost daily, wrote of what a Sunday morning in Dublin looked like. Instead of empty streets with only Mass-goers about,

> ... citizens were thronging to hear Mass through the streets filled with British Regulars carrying rifles with fixed bayonets, Auxiliary Cadets, Black and Tans and here and there, broad-shouldered plainclothesmen distinguishable as members of the 'G' Division of the Dublin Metropolitan Police engaged in political espionage. A tank was ambling along Bachelor's Walk, military lorries, filled with armed-to-the-teeth troops, their rifles at the ready, were racing through O'Connell St., and military cordons were drawn with barbed wire around entrances from Grafton St. from Nassau St. and College Green.[37]

A British army private, J.P. Swindlehurst, stationed in Dublin from January to February 1921, concurred:

> Dublin seems to be a rotten place to be ... people hurry along the streets, armoured cars dash up and down, bristling with machine guns ... The men who style themselves as Black and

Tans walk about like miniature arsenals … They dash about in
cars with wire netting covering at all hours of the day bent on
some raid reprisal or capture of some Sinn Féiners … One can
sense the undercurrent of alarm and anxiety in the faces of the
passers-by.[38]

That was the Dublin that resulted from Collins's plans and actions from
March 1920 onward.

Between November 1920 and the Truce in July 1921 the pace of the
war intensified, and bitterness increased on both sides. No description of
guerrilla warfare can fully convey the horror of a situation in which soldier
and civilian occupy the same area and are turned with hatred on each other.
In Ireland, the sole purpose of the police and the military was to subjugate
the IRA/Volunteers by whatever means they could. The purpose of the
civilians was to support the Irish forces arrayed against the British. The
civilian population inevitably suffered the most, emotionally as well as
physically. They were in a constant state of trauma.[39] The British were clearly
out of touch with the temper of the Irish people, as was evident from some
of the ideas proposed in the British Cabinet. In 1920, the General Officer
Commanding the British Army in Ireland, General Sir Nevil Macready,
proposed to take on the IRA with more mobile forces, but Field Marshal
Sir Henry Wilson said that Macready's plan was useless. Wilson pressed the
British 'to collect the names of Sinn Féiners by districts; proclaim them on
church doors all over the country; and shoot them whenever a policeman
is murdered; pick five by lot and shoot them!'[40]

General Macready refused to take responsibility for the RIC, the Black
and Tans or the Auxiliaries and openly condemned their acts of indiscipline.
This friction between the military and the police was a major factor in
Britain's failure to implement an effective security policy during 1920. By
October 1920 the 'King's Writ' no longer ran in the countryside. The Irish
strategy of making Ireland ungovernable by Britain was beginning to work.
British rule in Ireland had virtually collapsed, and the Dáil made astonishing
strides in setting up the counter-state. Some people dutifully paid their rates
to local republican authorities and ignored the tax demands of the British.
The wholesale destruction of tax offices made the British tax-gathering
system unworkable. In addition, the Dáil/Republican Courts proved far

more effective and prompt than the old system ever was. All British forces were now being concentrated in the towns, or at least in very strong barracks, obviously with a view to shortening the front. The IRA/Volunteer forces opposing them were becoming stronger and highly organised, albeit with little overall co-ordination from Dublin. Collins had begun to exert some control over matters outside Dublin but still concentrated his efforts within the city.[41]

Further complicating matters for the British, there was usually little co-ordination between the Royal Irish Constabulary, the Black and Tans, the Auxiliary Cadets and the regular British Army. The lack of control over the Tans and the Auxiliaries caused widespread hostility throughout Ireland, often directed at any British official. Consequently the British military and civil administration was torn between those who thought it best to ride out the storm, letting politicians negotiate a settlement, and those who advocated sterner measures to stamp out the IRA/Volunteers completely.

Neither the Black and Tans nor the Auxiliaries exhibited much in the way of military discipline, and the levels of their violence and reprisals mounted daily. Their arrival and the brutality of their tactics drove more and more Irish to support the IRA. The Irish, ruled by the British for so long, now began to think of their resistance as patriotism. By late 1920 public opinion had swung wildly against the British presence in Ireland. The Dublin execution of an eighteen-year-old medical student, Kevin Barry, for killing a British soldier,[42] the shooting of the lord mayor of Cork, Tomás MacCurtáin, in front of his wife, and the arrest and death on hunger strike of the succeeding lord mayor of Cork, Terence MacSwiney, were events that made the British position in Ireland ever more untenable.[43] Terence MacSwiney's death on 25 October 1920 seemed the most important event that occurred in the country at that time. Ireland went into mourning when he died on the seventy-fourth day of his fast.[44]

The IRA had shot 182 policemen and fifty soldiers by the end of 1920. In response to the growing violence, the British government introduced the Restoration of Order in Ireland Act. This Act, passed in August 1920, allowed for the internment and court-martial of civilians and led to the arrest of a large number of IRA officers. The level of public support for the IRA, however, continued to rise. The British government initially asserted that it was dealing with civil disorder rather than war, but by this stage it had realised otherwise. The struggle was embittered by successive acts of violence and terror, and the reprisals and counter-reprisals that followed. In December 1920 the British sanctioned official reprisals, raising the level of violence to new levels and further alienating the local populations.

The condemnation of British reprisals was not limited to the Irish, nor expressed just in quiet British government communications. It was open on the part of the British, as well. General Sir Hubert Gough wrote to the *Manchester Guardian* in early October:

> In Ireland at the moment murder and destruction are condoned and winked at, if not actively encouraged. The murder of policemen and others by the 'Irish republicans' have been inexcusable. As you say the leaders of Sinn Féin and the Irish priesthood are very greatly to be condemned for not having taken a far more active part against such methods, but that is no excuse for any government, and especially a government of the great British empire, adopting such methods.[45]

And so rebellion continued in Ireland, not with a great take-over of Dublin or with pitched battles but with brutal city and country ambushes designed to demoralise representatives of the British government and the British people themselves. The war was primarily between the British Secret Service, the DMP and the RIC and Collins's network in Dublin, a similar war led by Florence O'Donohue's intelligence operatives in Cork, a war of harassment and reprisal in the country, and a war of propaganda. Collins's plans for urban and rural guerrilla warfare kept the British from exerting control over the country and inexorably turned the tide of opinion against British rule in Ireland.

In an effort to placate those in the North who were still opposed to any movement in the direction of Home Rule in Ireland, the Government of Ireland Act was passed in the British House of Commons on 11 November 1920 and was enacted on 23 December. It proposed separate parliaments for Southern Ireland and for Northern Ireland. A Council of Ireland was to be set up with members from each parliament in a move to one day remove partition and potentially reunite the two entities. Both parliaments would be subject to Westminster. The Parliament of Northern

Ireland came into being in 1921. At its inauguration in Belfast City Hall on 22 June 1921, King George V made his famous appeal for Anglo-Irish and north–south reconciliation. The speech, drafted by David Lloyd George's government on recommendations from Jan Smuts, Prime Minister of the Union of South Africa, with the enthusiastic backing of the king, opened the door for formal contact between the British government and the Republican administration of Éamon de Valera.

The Parliament of Southern Ireland never became a reality. Both it and the Parliament of Northern Ireland were to be bicameral legislatures as part of 'Home Rule'. The Second Dáil was elected on 19 May 1921 in the Twenty-Six Counties of the South and on 24 May in the Six Counties of the North. This election became known as the 'Partition Election' because it was the first time in which an election in the Six Counties was held at a different time from that for the Twenty-Six Counties. All 128 MPs elected to the House of Commons of Southern Ireland were returned unopposed, and 124 of them, representing Sinn Féin, declared themselves TDs and assembled as the Second Dáil of the Irish Republic. James Connolly had predicted that a partition previously proposed in 1914 by British Prime Minister H.H. Asquith and agreed upon by John Redmond, leader of the Irish Parliamentary Party, would be a disaster for Ireland. In the *Irish Worker* he wrote of partition:

> It is the trusted leaders of Ireland that in secret conclave with the enemies of Ireland have agreed to see Ireland as a nation disrupted politically and her children divided under separate political governments ... Such a scheme as that agreed by Redmond and Devlin—the betrayal of the national democracy of industrial Ulster—would mean a carnival of reaction both north and south, would set back the wheels of progress, would destroy the oncoming unity of the Irish Labour Movement and paralyse all advanced movements while it endured. To it Labour should give the bitterest opposition, against it Labour in Ulster should fight even to the death if necessary.[46]

Those 1920/21 partition actions again backfired on the British government because they infuriated the IRA/Volunteers, but they did establish the partition that exists to this day.[47]   Nevertheless, as Connolly had foreseen, the British had agreed partition with the North long before 1920. On 29 May 1916 (just a month after the Rising), David Lloyd George, at the time Britain's Minister for Munitions, wrote to Edward Carson:

> My Dear Carson
> I enclose Greer's draft resolutions.
> We must make it clear that at the end of the provisional period Ulster does not, whether she wills it or not, merge in the rest of Ireland.
> Ever sincerely
> D. Lloyd George
> P.S. Will you show it to Craig?[48]

Éamon de Valera returned to Ireland from an eighteen-month sojourn in the United States in December 1920, and the continued British and US newspaper references to the IRA/Volunteers as 'murderers' led him to press for a full-scale engagement with the British as opposed to the guerrilla tactics used by the IRA. Soon after he returned from America, de Valera told Richard Mulcahy: 'You are going too fast. This odd shooting of a policeman here and there is having a very bad effect, from the propaganda point of view, on us in America. What we want is, one good battle about once a month with about 500 men on each side.'[49] De Valera overruled Collins's objections to the strategic error of attacking the British in large numbers in a single battle, and plans were discussed for a large-scale attack. On 25 May 1921 the IRA burned down the Custom House, the centre of British administrative rule in Ireland. The attack was calamitous for the IRA/Volunteers in Dublin and a disaster as a military operation, with over one hundred men captured and five killed. The venture into conventional warfare was a setback, and Collins knew it. As worldwide propaganda, though, it was a huge success, demonstrating to the wider world how strong the IRA was and how weak the British position now was in Ireland. That Irish 'strength' was illusory, however, and most IRA leaders, especially Collins, recognised that the organisation's desperate shortage of weapons and ammunition would soon allow the British to wear it down.

Throughout the war, IRA propaganda, like its intelligence, was highly efficient. It was planned to reach, and did reach, all the major European capitals and the US. *The Irish Bulletin* was its main organ and was distributed free to press correspondents and liberal-minded men of political influence in England.

Of the intelligence and propaganda war, Collins himself wrote:

> Ireland's story from 1918 to 1921 may be summed up as the story of a struggle between our determination to govern ourselves and to get rid of British government and the British determination to prevent us from doing either. It was a struggle between two rival Governments, the one an Irish Government resting on the will of the people and the other an alien Government depending for its existence upon military force—the one gathering more and more authority, the other steadily losing ground.[50]

As British hopes of controlling the country faded, they began to wonder whether Ireland was worth the price: it now cost more to defend and control than it was worth. On the Irish side, morale was deteriorating with the escalating British reprisals and raids. The IRA/Volunteer numbers had been greatly reduced by imprisonments and internment. In the rural areas, the need for intelligence had not really been understood, and Collins did not have the same sources throughout the countryside as he had in Dublin.[51] Although their positions were greatly different, both sides began to realise their own shortcomings.

At that time, as president of Dáil Éireann, de Valera authorised members of the government to open negotiations with Britain. 'Peace feelers' were extended progressively throughout the first half of 1921, until a truce was agreed which went into effect at noon on 11 July. Frank Thornton, one of Collins's most important lieutenants, wrote that the Truce came with dramatic suddenness:

> Whether the truce was a good thing or not remains for historians to record, but, in my humble opinion, had it not taken place we would have found ourselves very hard set to continue the fight with any degree of intensity, owing to that very serious shortage of ammunition, because men, no matter how determined they

may be or how courageous, cannot fight with their bare hands.[52]

Collins, too, emphasised that suddenness of the Truce. 'When we were told of the offer of a truce, we were astounded. We thought you [the British] must have gone mad.' But there was trepidation as well. Mulcahy agreed that to drive the British from anything more substantial than a police barracks was beyond them.[53] Further, Collins said, 'once a Truce is agreed, and we come out into the open, it is extermination for us if the Truce should fail. ... We shall be ... like rabbits coming out from their holes.'[54] It has been said that Collins was an extremist, but the evidence of history shows that he was really more moderate than de Valera.

> Unlike the President [de Valera] who tended to portray a moderate public image while advocating a more hardline approach, Collins tended to do the opposite. Privately he was much more moderate than generally believed.[55]

The Truce was formal and was reported to the League of Nations, giving *de facto*—and possibly *de jure*—legitimacy to the IRA, since one can only conclude a truce with an equal.[56]

Following the Truce, de Valera and British Prime Minister David Lloyd George engaged in meetings in London to determine how negotiations should proceed. Both had reputations as skilled negotiators, and they probably possessed the shrewdest political minds in Europe at the time. De Valera continually pressed his interpretation of the meetings in correspondence through the next few months, but Lloyd George just as firmly made it clear that Britain would not enter negotiations on the basis that Ireland was 'an independent sovereign state'.[57]

The basis of the conference was the 'Gairloch Formula' proposed by Lloyd George. According to this formula, the status of a republic as previously demanded by de Valera was unacceptable, and instead the purpose of the Irish delegation was to ascertain 'how the association of Ireland with the community of nations known as the British Empire may best be reconciled with Irish national aspirations'. It was said that de Valera's difficulty was that Lloyd George 'offered the Irish what they don't want [a dominion], and the one thing they do want—unity with Ulster—he had no power to give them'.[58]

On 18 September 1920 Lloyd George wrote:

> From the very outset of our conversation I told you that we looked to Ireland to own allegiance to the Throne, and to make her future as a member of the British Commonwealth. That was the basis of our proposals, and we cannot alter it. The status which you now claim for your delegates is, in effect, a repudiation of that status.

Finally, after more correspondence between the two over the next two weeks, on 30 September de Valera chose to write:

> Our respective positions have been stated and are understood and we agree that conference, not correspondence, is the most practical and hopeful way to an understanding. We accept the invitation, and our Delegates will meet you in London on the date mentioned 'to explore every possibility of settlement by personal discussion'.[59]

The 'date mentioned' was 11 October, and on that date treaty negotiations began in London. Arthur Griffith, Collins, George Gavan-Duffy, Robert Barton and Éamonn Duggan represented the Irish, as plenipotentiaries.

The day before he left for London, Collins wrote presciently:

> At this moment there is more ill-will within a victorious assembly than ever could be anywhere except in the devil's assembly. It cannot be fought against. The issue, and persons, are mixed up to such an extent as to make discernability [sic] an impossibility except for a few. ... the trusted ones, far from being in accord, are disunited. ... This is a time when jealousy and personal gain count for more than country.[60]

Although Griffith was the top-ranking delegate, Collins was recognised as the *de facto* leader. Collins was extremely uncomfortable with being chosen as a delegate. It was not his field of expertise, but it was his duty and he accepted it grudgingly.[61] Batt O'Connor, a close friend, described how Collins bitterly complained that, 'It was an unheard-of thing that a soldier who had fought in the field should be elected to carry out negotiations. It was de Valera's job, not his.'[62]

On 6 December 1921 the British negotiating team and the Irish plenipotentiaries signed the Articles of Agreement for a Treaty, and the Irish delegation returned to Ireland for ratification. De Valera was much opposed to the Treaty, though it has been said that he was more affronted that he had not been consulted on the final day before signature in disregard of his 'instructions'. On learning of the details of the Treaty, de Valera announced that it was a matter for the Cabinet. At an acrimonious Cabinet meeting the Treaty was approved by a four-to-three majority. When the Cabinet approved the agreement, de Valera said that it was a matter for the Dáil. It was then presented to the Dáil for ratification, where the divisions of ideology and personality that had always existed were put on public display.

The 'Treaty debates' in the Dáil took place between 14 December 1921 and 7 January 1922, when the Dáil voted 64–57 in favour of the Treaty. Those debates were considered by some as the most vituperative in Irish history. Invective was hurled at and by both sides, personality conflicts that had simmered for many years degenerated into name-calling and *ad hominem* insults, and the vote was considered a 'betrayal of the ideals of 1916' by those who felt that the only acceptable treaty would be one unequivocally recognising an Irish Republic. Accusations of bad faith filled the air. Most importantly, the Treaty called for an oath of fealty to the British Crown, and Republicans considered that traitorous. Finally, the Treaty called for partition of the North, and although partition was an established fact after 1920 the conflict in the South only served to further undermine any possibility of reunification. Partition, however, was hardly mentioned in the Treaty debates.

Terence de Vere White described the debates and their descent into eccentricity:

> ... much latent hysteria; the calm, courteous, but unsound reasoning of Childers; the restless, sometimes effeminate emotionalism of de Valera; the moderation of Collins; the firm manliness of Griffith; the withering blight of Mary MacSwiney;

the naivety of the other women; the weakness and candour of Barton; the sterile bitterness of Brugha; the incorrigible idealism of Mellows; the cynicism of J.J.Walsh; and the intelligence of two young men, Kevin O'Higgins and Patrick Hogan.[63]

Finally, that democratically elected body of Irish men and women had spoken, but de Valera led the anti-Treaty contingent from the assembly. De Valera claimed to know 'in his heart' the wishes of his Irish countrymen, and refused to accept the Dáil vote as binding. Collins led the fight for Treaty ratification in the Dáil and in the country, and was vilified by the most hard-case republicans for selling out to the British.

The armed resistance of the Irish was strong enough to make reconquest prohibitively expensive, militarily and politically, for Britain, but not to achieve complete victory. Once again, nationalist Ireland split on the issue of compromise.

There was bitterness among the men and women of both sides, and the seeds of the Irish Civil War were sown.

Notes

[1] Ironically, Patrick Pearse's play, *The Singer*, written in autumn 1915, foretold this 'quietness' in the country:
'Cuimin: We've no one to lead us.
Colm: Didn't you elect me your captain?
Cuimin: We did; but not to bid us rise out when the whole country is quiet.'
Patrick Pearse, *Collected Works of Patrick H. Pearse: Plays, Stories, and Poems* (5th edn) (1922).

[2] Letter from Margaret Ashton, 16 July 1916. NLI 20 MS II,016, Bryce Papers 1915/16 (i).

[3] C.P. Curran, 'Griffith, MacNeill and Pearse', *Studies: The Irish Jesuit Quarterly Review* (Spring 1966).

[4] Cyril Falls, 'Maxwell, 1916, and Britain at war', in F.X. Martin, OSA (ed.), *Leaders and Men of the Easter Rising: Dublin 1916* (London, 1967), p. 203 *et seq.*

[5] Major-General Sir S. Hare, KCMG, CB, 'Martial law from the soldier's point of view', *Army Quarterly*, vol. 7 (October 1923 and January 1924).

[6] One prayer-card for the executed leaders read: 'O Gentlest Heart of Jesus, have mercy on the souls of thy servants, our Irish heroes; bring them from the shadows of exile to the bright home of Heaven, where, we trust, Thou and Thy Blessed Mother have woven for them a crown of unending bliss'. TCD MS 2074, 'Prayer cards for the repose of the souls of the following Irishmen who were executed by English law, 1916'.

7   PRO CO 904/102, January 1917.
8   Risteard Mulcahy, *My Father the General: Richard Mulcahy and the Military History of the Revolution* (Dublin, 2009), p. 35.
9   Michael Laffan, 'The unification of Sinn Féin in 1917', *Irish Historical Studies*, vol. 17 (1971).
10 Florence O'Donoghue, 'The reorganisation of the Volunteers', *Capuchin Annual*, vol. 34 (1967).
11 There is no agreement on the total number of Irish men who served in the British army and navy in the First World War. There appears to be a consensus on the figure of 210,000, of whom at least 35,000 died, although the figure on the National War Memorial is 49,400.
12 Charles Townshend, 'The Irish Republican Army and the development of guerrilla warfare, 1916–1921', *English Historical Review*, vol. 94 (1979).
13 Calton Younger, *Ireland's Civil War* (New York, 1969), p. 93.
14 Tom Bowden, 'The Irish underground and the War of Independence 1919–1921', *Journal of Contemporary History*, vol. 8, no. 2 (1973).
15 Risteard Mulcahy, 'The development of the Irish Volunteers, 1916–1922', *An Cosantóir*, vol. 40 (February 1980). The paper was read to the Irish Historical Society on 9 November 1978.
16 Ulick O'Connor, *Michael Collins and the Troubles* (New York, 1996), p. 127.
17 Richard Mulcahy, notes on Piaras Béaslaí's *Michael Collins*, vol. I, p. 56. Mulcahy Papers, UCD.
18 Tim Pat Coogan, *Michael Collins, the Man Who Made Ireland* (London 1992), p. 209.
19 See J.M. Nankivell and S. Loch, *Ireland in Turmoil* (London, 1922).
20 Éamon Broy, Witness Statements 1280, 1284, 1285.
21 Letter from Richard Mulcahy to Broy, Mulcahy papers, P/7b/184.
22 Patrick J. Twohig, *Blood on the Flag* (Ballincollig, 1996), p. 155.
23 John McGuigan, 'Michael Collins on file?', *History Ireland*, vol. 19, no. 4 (July/August 2011).
24 Fearghal McGarry, 'Keeping an eye on the usual suspects: Dublin Castle's "Personality Files", 1899–1921', *History Ireland*, vol. 14, no. 6 (November/December 2006).
25 Seán MacAodh, 'IRA wipe out "G" Division', *An Phoblacht*, 6 September 2001.
26 Since Collins's time, there has been historical, military and legal debate on 'targeted killings'. See Samuel Issacharoff and Richard H. Pildes, 'Targeted warfare: individuating enemy responsibility', *New York University Law Review*, no. 1521 (2013); John Borgonovo, 'Revolutionary violence and Irish historiography', *Irish Historical Studies*, vol. 38, no. 150 (1996).
27 Maryann Valiulis, *Portrait of a Revolutionary: General Richard Mulcahy and the Founding of the Irish Free State* (Blackrock, 1992), p. 53.
28 PRO CO 904/177/1.
29 Michael Collins, *The Path to Freedom* (ed. T.P. Coogan) (Cork, 1996 [1922]), pp 69–70. At first the 'Squad' numbered only four but was later expanded to include some twenty men. There is some confusion over the O/C. Some claim that it was Paddy Daly (O'Daly) from the start, whereas others claim that Mick McDonnell first led the Squad until medical issues forced him to emigrate to the US. See Donal O'Kelly, 'The Dublin scene', in D. Nolan (ed.), *With the IRA in the Fight for Freedom* (Tralee, 1946). See also PRO CO 904/109 (3), Inspector General's Monthly Report,

September 1919.

[30] Maurice Walsh, *The News from Ireland: Foreign Correspondents and the Irish Revolution* (Dublin, 2008), p. 70.

[31] A.D. Harvey, 'Who were the Auxiliaries?', *The Historical Journal*, vol. 35, no. 3 (1992).

[32] Martin Petter, '"Temporary gentlemen" in the aftermath of the Great War: rank, status and the ex-officer problem', *The Historical Journal*, vol. 37, no. 1 (March 1994).

[33] D. Leeson, 'Imperial Stormtroopers: British paramilitaries in the Irish War of Independence, 1920–1921', unpublished Ph.D thesis, McMaster University (2003); 'The "scum of London's underworld"? British recruits for the Royal Irish Constabulary, 1920–1921', *Contemporary British History*, vol. 17, no. 1 (Spring 2003).

[34] 'This day, 25 March, Feast of the Annunciation, 1920, marked the arrival of the first Black and Tan in Limerick, *en route* to Newcastle West. To the late Christopher O'Sullivan, a local journalist/editor/proprietor of the old *Limerick Echo*, goes the credit of having given the new police force their colourful name, due to their manner of dress: a black tunic, as worn by the Royal Irish Constabulary, and khaki or tan trousers of the British soldier', *The Limerick Leader*, 25 March 1980. See Richard Bennett, *The Black and Tans* (London, 1964; 2001); David Leeson, *The Black and Tans: British Police and Auxiliaries in the Irish War of Independence, 1920–1921* (Oxford, 2012).

[35] Letter from Collins to Donal Hales, 13 August 1920.

[36] *Daily News*, 18 October 1920.

[37] Kathleen Napoli McKenna, 'The Irish Bulletin', *Capuchin Annual* (1970).

[38] William Sheehan, *British Voices of the Irish War of Independence* (Doughcloyne, 2007), pp 13–17.

[39] Eoin Neeson, *The Life and Death of Michael Collins* (Cork, 1968), p. 42.

[40] Diary of Thomas Jones, Lloyd George's personal secretary, 31 May 1920.

[41] Dublin GHQ recognised that a 'war zone' existed in counties Kerry, Limerick, Tipperary and especially Cork. Other than some activities under Seán MacEoin in County Longford, those were the areas in which most fighting occurred. Charles Townsend, 'The Irish Republican Army and the development of guerrilla warfare, 1916–1921', *English Historical Review*, vol. 94 (1979), quoting the Richard Mulcahy papers.

[42] Martha Kearns, 'Mary (98) recalls her vigil the day Kevin Barry was hanged', *Irish Independent*, 13 October 2001.

[43] Art Mac Eoin, 'Terence MacSwiney', *An Phoblacht*, 25 October 2001.

[44] *The Times*, 29 October 1920; *New York Times*, 28 October 1920; *Irish Bulletin*, 28 October 1920. Seán MacAodh, 'Terence MacSwiney', *An Phoblacht*, 25 October 2001.

[45] *Manchester Guardian*, 10 October 1920.

[46] *Irish Worker*, 14 March 1914.

[47] See Denis Gwynn, *The History of Partition, 1912–1925* (Dublin, 1950).

[48] Tim Pat Coogan, *Michael Collins, the Man Who Made Ireland* (London 1992), p. 67.

[49] Tim Pat Coogan, *De Valera: Long Fellow, Long Shadow* (London, 1995), p. 215 *et seq.*

[50] *Ibid.*, p. 65.

[51] Collins was involved in all aspects of the war throughout the country, though he did not visit those other commands often. For example, when the Cork No. 3 Brigade was formed at Caheragh, Drimoleague, on 16 August 1919, Collins presided at the meeting, but that was the last time he visited that particular brigade until mid-1921.

[52] Frank Thornton, Witness Statement 615.

[53] Commanders in the field mostly disagreed. They thought that the IRA was 'winning' and would soon have a military victory. See Liam Deasy, *Brother Against Brother* (Cork, 1998), p. 11 *et seq.*; Ernie O'Malley, *The Singing Flame* (Dublin, 1978), p. 13.

[54] Rex Taylor, *Michael Collins* (London, 1970), p. 110.

[55] T. Ryle Dwyer, *Michael Collins and the Treaty* (Dublin, 1981), p. 31.

[56] Charles Townshend, *Political Violence in Ireland. Government and Resistance since 1848* (Oxford, 1983), p. 359.

[57] Frank Pakenham (Lord Longford), *Peace by Ordeal* (London, 1935; 1972), p. 77.

[58] Calton Younger, *Ireland's Civil War*, p. 162.

[59] Pakenham details at length the correspondence between de Valera and Lloyd George leading up to the Treaty negotiations. He takes pains to note that there were two separate 'debates' entangled in the correspondence: (1) whether England had any right to restrict Ireland's form of government and (2) on what basis could a conference be held in light of the first issue. He opines that discussion on the first issue favoured Ireland while that on the second issue favoured England. He further points out that in de Valera's eyes the position of a Republic 'had been preserved', but the British position was clearly that Ireland would remain a member of the Empire. He concludes: 'On abstract rights De Valera had secured an agreeable academic triumph. On the question of status at the Conference he had, formally at least, held his own. But in the race to secure opinion favourable to the settlements that they respectively contemplated, De Valera was still waiting for the pistol while Lloyd George was half-way home.' Packenham, *Peace by Ordeal*, pp 77–9. For a contrasting view to Pakenham's, see Desmond FitzGerald, 'Mr Pakenham on the Anglo–Irish Treaty', *Studies: The Irish Jesuit Quarterly Review*, vol. 24 (1935). FitzGerald contends that de Valera's correspondence with Lloyd George was coloured by his need to placate Cathal Brugha (and to a lesser extent Austin Stack), who was 'a convinced irreconcilable' to whom the truce was only a period to re-arm. As a result, in de Valera's correspondence 'it will be seen that the word "Republic" is never used, while nothing is said that directly implies a readiness to accept the Crown'. FitzGerald asserts that 'Mr Pakenham has failed to understand the situation at the time. This is probably due to the fact that documents were not available to him. Indeed, there is no documentation of that time.' FitzGerald concludes: 'Mr Pakenham's book reveals much that was not known to the public, and it is a valuable contribution to the history of our time. But the author omits vital facts and wrongly interprets others. In the absence of documents this may have been more or less inevitable. There are questions to which no answer perhaps can be given … His narrative, however, is eminently readable.'

[60] Neeson, *The Life and Death of Michael Collins*, p. 50.

[61] Pakenham, *Peace by Ordeal*, p. 266.

[62] Batt O'Connor, *With Michael Collins in the Fight for Independence* (London, 1929), p. 171.

[63] Terence de Vere White, *Kevin O'Higgins* (London and Tralee, 1948; 1986), p. 69.

1. Moving Towards War, 1916–18

There must be a hidden and malevolent influence somewhere in the government of Ireland, whether in the War Cabinet or the Castle, determined that Ireland shall not have peace in freedom and that there shall be no reconciliation between the British and Irish peoples.
—*Freeman's Journal*, **26 September 1917**

The Irish Volunteer organisation was practically obliterated by the Rising. As a result, open political or military activity by those who survived the Rising was almost impossible. There was no central organisation and all public activity was banned.[1] Following the publication of Piaras Béaslaí's book *Michael Collins and the Making of a New Ireland* in 1927, many contested Béaslaí's views. In the 1950s Dr Risteard Mulcahy asked his father, General Mulcahy, to read the book and to annotate it. General Mulcahy's descriptions of Collins show the latter's development as a leader and how their relationship ripened. In a review of his father's notes, Dr Mulcahy categorised, analysed and commented on the General's involvement from the Rising through his later years as leader of the Fine Gael political party. Specifically, Dr Mulcahy presented a table that outlined the sequence of development of the Volunteers following the Easter Rising of 1916:

- End of 1916 rebellion and the deportation of the prisoners to Frongoch and elsewhere, May 1916.
- The return of the Frongoch prisoners, Christmas 1916.
- Return of leaders from Lewes, June 1917.
- Ashe's death on hunger strike, 26 September 1917.
- Sinn Féin Convention 25/26 October 1917.
- Volunteer Convention, 27 October 1917.
- Conscription threat and formation of General Headquarters, March 1918.

- General Election and first Dáil, December 1918–January 1919.
- Suppression of the Dáil, September 1919.
- Truce, July 1921.
- Ratification of the Treaty, January 1922.[2]

Dr Mulcahy wrote that the Volunteers were clearly in disarray after the Rising. Many were imprisoned. The country people were demoralised, and some were humiliated by their failure to take part. For these reasons, and because there was no clear public vision of the Rising, there was no outward Volunteer activity. There was little evidence of formal organisation and there was no central leadership.

Collins was one of the prisoners sent to Frongoch Prison Camp, near Bala, North Wales. Until 1916 it had housed German prisoners of war in an abandoned distillery and crude huts, but in the wake of the Rising the German prisoners were moved and it was used as a place of internment for approximately 1,800 Irish prisoners—800 in the North camp and 950 in the South camp. Frongoch was the largest of the prisons housing the 1916 prisoners and became a fertile seed-bed for the spreading of the revolutionary gospel, with inspired organisers such as Collins giving impromptu lessons in guerrilla tactics. Later the camp became known as the 'University of Revolution', or sometimes 'Sinn Féin University'.[3]

After his release from Frongoch, Collins assumed a leadership role in all three nationalist organisations: he was Director of Organisation for the Volunteers, Minister for Finance for the Dáil and President of the Irish Republican Brotherhood. In addition, he was on the Executive of Sinn Féin, and was a central figure in the leadership of the clandestine government after the departure of Éamon de Valera to the United States in 1919. In view of the degree of mythology that developed around Collins, it should be noted that he did not start or prosecute the Anglo-Irish war by himself. Nevertheless, no other person held such positions concurrently and that put him at the centre of action in all areas. Moreover, not content with formal titles or positions, Collins would encroach on any area where he thought 'something should be done'. In 'exceeding his brief' he antagonised other cabinet members and stepped on many toes owing to his brusque and seemingly uncaring attitude as regards organisational boundaries. His manner, which led some in Frongoch to dub him 'the Big Fellow', would lead to conflict throughout the war and culminated in the many *ad hominem* comments made about him in the Treaty debates of 1921–2.

The outlook and attitude of the released prisoners changed when they reached Ireland.

> The returning prisoners found a country waiting for leadership and organisation. The prisoners themselves had been transformed. Internment had produced intense rage and resentment among those affected, prisoners and extended families alike. It had brought together men from all parts of the country and bonded them, even those innocent of any involvement in political conspiracy, into an organic unit. A chain of command had been established. The men learnt about ideas and policies and techniques which became common to them all, instead of innovations devised in one place only. Everyone knew everyone else. If they had been in different jails, they had heard on the grapevine about other men from other districts. They emerged from prison as members of an organisation with a sense of belonging and a sense of purpose.[4]

Volunteer reorganisation began during the summer following the Rising.[5] Seán Ó Muirthile and Diarmuid O'Hegarty toured the country, establishing contact between the few leaders who had not been arrested.[6] These two were members not only of the Volunteers but also of the secret, oath-bound Irish Republican Brotherhood. The IRB had infiltrated most nationalist organisations founded in the twentieth century and had planned the 1916 Rising.[7] Ó Muirthile's and O'Hegarty's contacts within this secret society helped them to reconstitute the broken remains of the Volunteer organisation. Under cover of the Gaelic League Ard Fheis on 7 August, they gathered enough Volunteer delegates in Dublin to form a Provisional Committee.[8] Reorganisation continued in earnest with Cathal Brugha's release from hospital in November 1916. Brugha had been an active member of the IRB, but after his release he met with Ó Muirthile and O'Hegarty and told them that in his opinion the society had outlived its usefulness.[9] Despite Brugha's objections, the Provisional Committee was dominated, as the early Executive of the Volunteers had been, by members of the IRB.[10] The IRB reorganised itself at the same time, electing a new Supreme Council in February 1917. The officers were Seán McGarry, Michael Collins and Diarmuid Lynch; other important figures included Con Collins and Tomás Ashe, who was still in prison. All had taken part in the Easter Rising and spent time in British jails.[11] Participation in the rebellion served as a form of political capital in republican circles.

Collins was in a position, through the IRB, the Volunteers and Sinn Féin, to have a great effect on all aspects of the war. Moreover, his job as secretary of the Irish National Aid and Volunteers' Dependants' Fund, which was his first employment after returning from Frongoch, gave him a vital role in bringing the prisoners together, particularly in advancing the policies they had discussed in the camps.[12] The bulk of them were ready to force the issue of Irish independence onto a different plane.[13] Collins was firm in his determination to make the Irish understand the concepts of guerrilla warfare: to stage unconventional hit-and-run attacks to inflict as many casualties as possible and then disappear into the countryside, keeping the British off guard and demoralised. Not every Irish leader accepted this strategy; Cathal Brugha disagreed and their conflict would escalate throughout the war, ending in violent clashes at the end and in the Treaty debates.[14] Éamon de Valera, for all his political skill, tended to think in conventional military terms, and when he sought an attack on the Custom House in 1921 it was at the expense of Collins's guerrilla tactics.

Like other guerrilla warriors before them, the Irish perfected their own strategy and tactics. Each such conflict brings its own unique requirements; all insurgents modify previous wars, and there are no hard and fast models. The first wars were guerrilla wars—tribal wars. There were no 'conventional wars' until there were city-states to raise armies, arm them and support them in the field. Throughout history there have been more guerrilla wars than conventional ones. In particular, the Irish drew inspiration from the Boer War, in which a few Volunteers had served in the Irish Brigade. Of course, the term 'guerrilla' comes from the Spanish partisans during the Peninsular Campaign of the Napoleonic War. They were often called the 'Spanish Ulcer' and it was said that they 'bled Napoleon's troops white'.[15]

Guerrilla war always pits the weak against the strong, and it would be foolhardy for the guerrilla to attack the enemy's strength. Republican field commanders necessarily adapted to their local situations, but Collins and the other leaders recognised a number of historical precedents and theoretical influences at work. The potential for such a war in Ireland had been considered decades earlier. For example, in 1847 James Fintan Lalor wrote to D'Arcy McGee, offering advice to the Young Irelanders:

> The force of England is *entrenched* and *fortified*. You must draw it out of position; break up its mass; break its trained line of march and manoeuvre, its equal step and serried array.[16]

As the war developed, the IRA did exactly this by utilising small units to divide the strength of the Crown forces, spreading them thinly over the whole country in a system of patrols. The republican campaign benefited in both the military and the political sense from another piece of advice from Lalor:

> You cannot organize, or train, or discipline your own force to any point of efficiency. You must therefore disorganize, and untrain, and undiscipline that of the enemy, and not alone must you unsoldier, you must unofficer it also; nullify its tactique [*sic*] and strategy, as well as its discipline; decompose the science and system of war, and resolve them into their first elements. You must make the hostile army a mob, as your own will be.[17]

That defined what the Irish had to do in their guerrilla war to come.

The British had seen and fought a series of such wars before this time. Colonel C.E. Callwell collected a number of lessons from these campaigns in his book *Small Wars*, which dealt with fighting against armies who would not meet the British in the open field. Callwell stressed the difficulty for a British commander:

> No amount of energy and strategic skill will draw the rebels into risking engagements, or induce them to depart from the form of warfare in which most irregular warriors excel and in which regular troops are seen at their worst … it is the difficulty of bringing the foe to action which forms, as a rule, the most

unpleasant characteristic of these wars. Having drawn out an
enemy, a superior force will almost always prevail in combat, but
it is the prelude which frustrates the regular commander. ...
... an adept guerrilla leader will avoid confrontation ... [18]

With this principle in mind, Callwell called guerrilla warfare a type of
operation to be avoided by the conventional commander above all things.

The writers of *An t-Óglách*, the newspaper of the Irish Volunteers, also
drew guerrilla inspiration from the Spanish resistance to Napoleon's
invasion, the Cuban insurgency against Spain, and the campaigns waged
against the British by Boer General Christiaan de Wet[19] and German
General Paul-Emil von Lettow-Vorbeck.[20] Despite variations in time and
place, all of these examples preceding the Irish War of Independence stressed
the importance of mobility, of choosing the terrain for combat, of avoiding
unsustainable casualties and of winning the active support of the local
population. That was exactly how the Irish pursued the guerrilla war against
Britain.

T.E. Lawrence, a contemporary guerrilla leader, wrote:

The guerrilla army resembles a gas—able to disperse as molecules
to prevent a counter-strike—but able to coalesce for its own
operations.

British responses to the Irish demand for their own government were
unimaginative and foolish, starting with the executions and mass
imprisonments after the Rising. Arthur Griffith, a nationalist who was most
in favour of constitutional action, spoke of the executions after the Rising
by General Sir John Maxwell: 'I knew the English were brutal enough to
do it; I did not think they were stupid enough. Had I foreseen that, perhaps
my views on the whole matter might have been different.'[21] With such
displays of brutality the British attempted to strike terror into the hearts of
any remaining nationalists in Ireland. Maxwell's executions were meant to
create a fear that would resonate throughout the country, thereby preventing
any further rebellions. The British acted as if all the Irish were against them,
so they did not bother to differentiate: to be Irish was to be guilty. Nothing
could have brought the Irish to the nationalist/separatist side more

completely. Tom Kettle once wrote: 'Dublin Castle, if it did not know what the Irish people want, could not so infallibly have maintained its tradition of giving them the opposite'. General Nevil Macready, ultimately O/C of British troops in Ireland, wrote in 1920 that 'whatever we do we are sure to be wrong'.[22]

As in all guerrilla wars, the Irish were the weaker side and as such were dependent for strategic and tactical successes on the errors committed by the British. A military maxim is that 'when your opponent is doing stupid or foolish things, don't interfere'. Collins followed this assiduously, and encouraged the British to continue their ways. Perhaps apocryphally, Collins is quoted as saying, 'Tell Winston we could never have done it without him'.[23] The people were driven into the arms of the IRA, exactly as Collins had hoped. Collins is the prototype of the urban guerrilla. He wrote the blueprint for subsequent revolutionary movements from Malay to Israel and from Cuba to Vietnam and Afghanistan. His plans worked well and the British continued to make mistakes.

Collins's views on violence were carefully considered. He said that he had 'strong fighting ideas, or I should say I suppose ideas of the utility of fighting'. Above all, Collins was a realist. He was always concerned about shaping public opinion and about the political impact of violence. He stressed the use of the minimum force necessary to achieve the objective in a politically acceptable and productive way. Nevertheless, he was a believer in the principle of getting your retaliation in first.

The Prussian Carl von Clausewitz wrote:

It is dangerous—but necessary—to try to predict the actions of the enemy. To do that, one must see the battle like your enemy.

Insurgent and counter-insurgent commanders must ask:

- How can I get the advantage?
- What is the opponent thinking/going to do?
- What do I need to do to outguess him—to out-play him on this field?

Collins and the Irish were better than the British at answering these questions. Among Clausewitz's lessons pertinent to the Irish situation between 1917 and 1921 was his insistence on the subordination of military strategy to political authority and objectives, as well as the advantages (and disadvantages) of surprise in combat.

The Irish War of Independence contributed four concepts that we see in later insurgencies:

• The Irish could only fight a guerrilla war. It must be noted that the British greatly contributed by overreacting—part of the Irish strategy.
• It is not necessary to wait until all the conditions exist for the war to start. The war can create them. That was one of the guiding principles used by Che Guevara in Cuba.
• Use of roadside explosives—Improvised Explosive Devices (IEDs).
• The countryside was the usual arena for guerrilla fighting in wars prior to the Irish War, but Collins showed that guerrilla principles worked well in Dublin. The Irish War was probably the first urban guerrilla war to succeed.

To accomplish these objectives, Collins, Florence O'Donoghue and the other Irish leaders relied on:

• Intelligence
• Propaganda
• Politics
• A loosely co-ordinated military campaign

In current worldwide counter-insurgency manuals, insurrections are defined as a violent competition between a State and a rival political group to control a population or to establish an alternative political order. That is what separates them from bandits, and *that* defined the Irish War of Independence. The insurgent challenges the status quo; the insurgent initiates. The counter-insurgent seeks to reinforce the State and so defeat the challenge. Before fighting begins, moderates are in charge. Radicals sideline the moderates and resort to violence against the enemy. That is how the war began. In any conflict, whatever the cause, at the start there will be:

• An active minority for the cause

- An active minority against the cause
- A passive neutral majority

The Irish had to convince those who were neutral to become supporters. To turn the IRA campaign into a success, it was imperative to convince a majority of the Irish population of the necessity and legitimacy of the use of violence. In 1773 Samuel Adams said, 'It does not require a majority to prevail, but rather an irate, tireless minority'.

When Clausewitz published *On War* in 1832, he posited his most famous military principle: 'War is the continuation of politics by other means'. The political view is the object; war is the means. Clausewitz's dictum had as its central tenets:

- Military action without a clear political objective is useless, and vice versa.
- A guerrilla war event must include propaganda and politics alongside military action.
- All events must recognise a military purpose.

T.E. Lawrence didn't think that many of Clausewitz's principles applied to a guerrilla war, but he agreed with this one: bad government drives insurrections. Recognition of an Irish civilian authority was an absolute necessity for Irish and international perceived legitimacy, and that was the main objective of the Irish leaders.

The release of the prisoners was extremely important for reorganisation in all areas, and when they returned they were more determined than ever to further the cause of Irish freedom. The ecstatic welcome given to the returning prisoners should have been a clear warning to the British, who thought that the Easter Rising would be soon forgotten. Shortly after their return, they began drilling and training. Displays of strength were mostly limited to demonstrations at by-elections and funerals, but following the death of Thomas Ashe after force-feeding while on hunger strike in September 1917 such displays became more common, and more violent clashes with the authorities ensued.

Until the end of 1917 the Volunteers remained a relatively small and inactive organisation in most counties.[24] The conscription crisis that followed in early 1918 changed this, and afterwards Volunteer membership and public displays of disregard for the law were widely accepted and established Sinn Féin as the main representative of public opinion. Joost Augusteijn notes that several aspects influenced the further development of the Volunteers:

- Action of any kind was a strong impetus to further activity, both to the men involved and others who were inspired by what took place.
- Diverse experience of action led to an increasing differentiation between areas.
- The dominance of those among the leaders who saw the Volunteers as a political instrument over those who felt that a military conflict was necessary meant that military operations were not led from above but by the most radical of local leaders.[25]

Because many of the most radical Volunteers were young and wanted to protect their livelihoods and families, only a few were prepared to engage in open activities that would jeopardise both. As a result, many of the regional differences became more apparent: development towards violent confrontation with the British occurred most often in Dublin and Munster, particularly in Tipperary in 1918. Even in Dublin, however, the Volunteers did little up to 1920. Activities were limited to a few in Collins's 'Squad', rendering most companies militarily inactive. The entire work of an average Dublin company during that year consisted of three arms raids.[26]

Richard Mulcahy wrote that the Volunteers were the hard core of the emerging political organisation of Sinn Féin, and that much of the continuing reorganisation of the Volunteers in 1917–18 took place under cover of the by-elections of that time.[27] Shortly after the release of the prisoners held in British jails, a parliamentary seat opened up in the Roscommon North constituency. The Irish Parliamentary Party (IPP)— the moderate nationalists who supported Home Rule—ran Thomas Devine. A consortium of radical nationalists decided to run George Noble Plunkett, father of the executed 1916 leader Joseph Mary Plunkett. The sixty-five-year-old, a papal count, had been inducted into the IRB in April 1916,[28] and on 3 February 1917 he won the seat by a landslide, receiving in excess of 1,300 votes more than the Irish Parliamentary Party candidate.[29] The Sinn Féin party founded by Arthur Griffith in 1905 advocated abstention from the Westminster parliament as a means of achieving political independence, but Plunkett did not subscribe to this stance until after the election.

This success encouraged the radical nationalists to take an even bolder step, and when a seat opened in South Longford in May the Sinn Féin nomination was definitely made by a group of IRB members. A series of covert negotiations between Michael Collins in Dublin and Thomas Ashe in Lewes Gaol resulted in the nomination of Joseph McGuinness, a prisoner in Lewes Gaol.[30] The election slogan was 'Put him in to get him out'. McGuinness won the seat by a mere thirty-seven votes.[31] The first count indicated a win for the IPP candidate, Patrick McKenna, but those thirty-seven votes were found—or were manufactured 'by some skilful vote rigging', as some later contended—and McGuinness gained the victory.[32] The South Longford result was described in the *Manchester Guardian* as 'the equivalent of a serious defeat of the British Army in the field'.[33]

Later that year Sinn Féin nominated another prisoner for the vacant East Clare seat.[34] Their candidate was Éamon de Valera, who had commanded Dublin's Third Battalion during the Rising. At Mount Street Bridge over the Grand Canal, troops under his command had decimated the British Sherwood Forester reinforcements entering the city, and his reputation from then on relied on this action. *The Times* noted a more violent tone in the East Clare election speeches than in previous Sinn Féin campaigns. De Valera and speakers on his behalf continued to use internationalist rhetoric, insisting that Ireland should be recognised at a peace conference at the close of the European war. They tinged these optimistic pronouncements with aggressive oratory, claiming that they were in favour of the violent overthrow of British government if a suitable opportunity presented itself.[35] Following de Valera's victory, the lord lieutenant of Ireland, Ivor Churchill Guest (Lord Wimborne), in a secret report for cabinet not released until 1978, wrote that 'The Sinn Fein victory in East Clare is a fact of cardinal importance … [I]t marks the definite failure of the policy to rehabilitate constitutional nationalism or disarm Sinn Féin defiance of English rule … [I]n a remarkably well conducted political contest … the electors, on a singularly frank issue of self-Government within the Empire versus an Independent Irish Republic, have overwhelmingly pronounced for the latter.'[36]

The assertion that Sinn Féin would gain independence via an international peace conference was an attempt to capitalise on a deep reservoir of goodwill towards the Allied Powers, now joined by the United States. US President Woodrow Wilson's Fourteen Points, which endorsed democracy and national self-determination, resonated powerfully in nationalist Ireland. The republican speakers at de Valera's rallies emphasised this but made it clear that they were willing to use force if the peace conference failed them. De Valera told a crowd at Creeslough, Co. Donegal, that 'winning freedom internationally was infinitely preferable to any attempt to win it from England … Sinn Féin will use every means that common sense and morality would admit of to achieve its goals'.[37] He was more explicit later when he said that '… they were prepared and organised and they could be in such a position, if a suitable opportunity presented itself to secure their demand by force of arms'.[38] The mixture of peaceful and violent rhetoric resulted in an overwhelming victory for de Valera, and presaged his future ambivalence in his speeches. He was elected by a wide margin on 10 July 1917.

In addition to the rhetorical escalation in de Valera's campaign, there was an increase in actual clashes with the RIC officers observing them. Constables regularly attended Sinn Féin meetings to make notes of what they claimed to be seditious speeches, and their reports reveal overt hostility from republican crowds. These early conflicts with the police seemed to validate Sinn Féin's most incendiary rhetoric, which was reserved for the RIC itself. Many speakers called them the 'eyes and ears' of the British government in Ireland, while Peter Clancy of Ennis went so far as to call them 'murderers'.[39] Gearóid O'Sullivan called the police 'their principal enemies' and advised no one to even speak to them.[40] Martin Walton noted the prevalence of the RIC throughout the country and their capacity for intelligence: 'the country was studded at the time with small police barracks every few miles … they were the eyes and ears. You couldn't travel from Dublin to Swords—that's a distance of about seven miles—without going into three RIC outposts, and everybody passing up and down the road was noted carefully.'[41]

Though the IPP did recover somewhat and win two by-elections in February and April 1918, in South Armagh and East Tyrone respectively, it must be noted that both IPP candidates, Patrick Donnelly in South

Armagh and T.J.S. Harbison in East Tyrone, benefited from long-time IPP organisation, and at least as much from the fact that the demographics of the constituencies were largely Protestant. Further by-elections in Offaly (then King's County, where Patrick MacCartan was elected in April), East Cavan (where Arthur Griffith was elected in June) and Kilkenny City (where William Cosgrave was elected in August) later cemented the view of the Irish people that the IPP was out of touch with the southern Irish electorate's wishes. In Kilkenny, Peter de Loughry clearly staked out the Sinn Féin position against the IPP: 'it was time to get rid of diplomacy because deep down in the hearts of everyone was the idea of independence'.[42] (Any real prospect of an IPP recovery was shattered by the conscription threat of early 1918, as discussed in Chapter 3.)

Throughout the period, republicans debated whether the organised use of force was necessary or was the best means of achieving Irish independence.[43] P.S. O'Hegarty was of the opinion that

> after 1916, there should not have been a shot fired in Ireland, nor a gun bought. They were totally unnecessary. We had the Sinn Féin policy, the men who made it, the enthusiasm and the support of the people. Without firing a shot we could have forced from England anything that we forced from her and more. We would at the same time have maintained our solidarity, escaped Partition, and avoided the irreparable moral disaster [the Civil War] which has overtaken us.[44]

He was equally cynical regarding Ireland's efforts at international recognition: 'So far as the Peace Conference was concerned, it was all waste labour, and might just as well have been recognised as such at the beginning. We never had a chance of getting into the Peace Conference.'[45] Fr Pat Gaynor, an early Sinn Féin convert, claimed that the only benefit of violent action was the international exposure it gave the republican cause: 'The one solid argument in favour of our war was that the shootings were news and received world-wide publicity'.[46] In the light of some later guerrilla actions, some remarkably pacifist statements were made on the republican platforms as well. An RIC sergeant recorded that, while sharing the platform with de Valera on New Year's Day 1918, Revd J.W. O'Meehan said that 'It was not by lying in wait for a victim behind a ditch, or attacking a man's house at night that they would obtain their independence. Such outrages were said to be the work of cowards, were un-Irish and foreign to the methods of the men of Easter Week.'[47] At the time, even the most active Sinn Féin supporters viewed physical force with great apprehension, but the fact that these types of statements did not stop the violence shows the determination of those who committed it. It is possible that denunciations of physical force restrained aggressive attacks at that early time, but by and large members of the growing IRA engaged in whatever activities they felt would strengthen their organisation in local areas.[48] Despite the mounting disorder, British officials were reluctant to deal with the Irish situation while the European war continued. Further, the British parliament was divided on the question of publicly recognising what was happening in Ireland.

Beginning in 1917, the prisoners who had been charged and taken to jails in Britain returned to Ireland, and there was a resurgence of political violence. One of the earliest shooting incidents presaged what would become standard IRA operating procedure: a unit created a reason for the RIC to leave their barracks and then ambushed them as they went to investigate. On the night of 17 February 1917, local RIC received a report that shots had been fired into a farmer's house outside Portumna, Co. Galway. A patrol left the barracks, and five people opened fire on them as they neared the house, wounding one constable.[49]

The first fatality among government forces since the Rising occurred in Dublin. On 10 June 1917, Cathal Brugha and Count Plunkett led a group of several thousand Sinn Féin supporters into Beresford Place, where Brugha began to address them. Dublin Metropolitan Police Inspector John Mills and a detail of officers approached and declared the meeting illegal. As Mills was escorting prisoners to Store Street Police Station, a man leapt from the crowd and fractured his head with a hurley. As early as mid-1917 the IRA was beginning to be organised and aggressive, though its weapons were crude.

During 1917 and 1918 great progress was made in the recruitment and training of Volunteers, and in the reorganisation of the military command with the formation of General Headquarters (GHQ) in Dublin in March 1918.[50] By early 1919 the country had a force that was very loosely organised under a GHQ command structure, and there was a 'unity of purpose, a high standard of voluntary discipline, and a growing eagerness to serve'.[51] As Charles Townshend points out, however, from the point of view of the Irish Republican Brotherhood, the national movement had passed out of their hands and into the control of non-IRB men like Griffith, de Valera and Brugha.[52] It was this, rather than any theorising about future military possibilities in the wake of the Rising, which led to the guerrilla initiative of 1919. The means were dictated by circumstance. Slender resources created the style of warfare, rather than a conviction that it held a real hope of ultimate military success. The campaign of violence, which occurred sporadically in the first six months of 1919, was unattractive to most 'political' Sinn Féiners. And although the Volunteers after January 1919 claimed that they were the legally constituted army of a lawful state and began to call themselves the IRA, their connection with the Republic represented by Dáil Éireann was tenuous. They resisted the oath of allegiance to the Dáil which Brugha, as Minister of Defence, sought to impose; they tended to resist all central control, especially political control; and there was a long delay (until April 1921) before the Dáil took public responsibility for their actions. In reality the physical-force men acted independently, compelling moderates to move towards their extreme position and so regaining their grip upon the independence movement as a whole.[53]

At this early stage of the conflict the Volunteers undertook actions based on their own initiative or that of local leaders, but GHQ in Dublin began directly encouraging arms raids and defensive violence from the first issue of *An t-Óglách* on 15 August 1918. This bi-monthly journal published General Headquarters orders, gave tips on technical aspects of weapons and equipment, and constantly encouraged Volunteer units to engage in operations. *An t-Óglách* ('The Young Warrior/Soldier') was 'The official newspaper of the Irish Volunteers'. It was conceived by Collins in 1918 and edited by Piaras Béaslaí. Collins played an active role in guiding editorial policy and finding writers. He also contributed its 'Organisation Notes' until May 1919. In this column he laid out the official formula for unit organisation and the duties of officers. The paper was a 'secret' internal journal printed in Dublin and distributed to the Volunteers throughout the country by the IRA, clandestinely circulated in flour sacks and by other means. It was not only a 'military journal' but also contained much of the

Sinn Féin ideology and had a great influence on the IRA/Volunteers. Throughout the war, *An t-Óglách* took the most aggressive military stance against the British.

The inaugural issue appeared on 15 August 1918 and declared:

> The Volunteer does not talk, but acts … Whenever and however an opportunity occurs of offering effective resistance to an attack of the enemy, that resistance must be offered. Volunteers with weapons in their hands *must never surrender without a fight.*
>
> We will strike in our own way, in our own time. If we cannot, by force of arms, drive the enemy out of our country at the present moment, we can help to make his position impossible and his military activities futile.[54] [Emphasis in original]

Clearly, even at this very early stage, the Irish intent was to make the country ungovernable by the British—and ultimately they did. *An t-Óglách* also took on the issue of the peace conference. Predicting that the European war would soon end, the journal stated on 29 October that 'the freedom of Ireland depends in the long run not upon the play of politics, nor international dealings, but upon the will of the Irish people to be free and maintain their freedom … [They should] leave no stone unturned in the effort to arm and equip themselves thoroughly.'[55] Instead of preaching the politics of a party or of any particular leader, it always emphasised that the Volunteer's allegiance was to the Irish nation.

The first editorial by Piaras Béaslai included:

> Volunteers are not politicians; they were not created for the purposes of parades, demonstrations, or political activities; they follow no particular leader as such; their allegiance is to the Irish Nation. To their own chosen leaders they render the obedience that all soldiers render to their officers. Their obedience to their officers is not affected by personal considerations. It is the office, not the man, to whom deference is due.
>
> The Irish Volunteers have chosen in open Convention those leaders in whom they have confidence to control the public

policy of the organisation. It is the duty of those leaders to conform that policy to the national will, by co-operating on the military side with those bodies and institutions which in other departments of the national life are striving to make our Irish Republic a tangible reality.[56]

Though GHQ staff were united in their call for decisive action, different views existed as to what form the conflict would take. In an early edition of *An t-Óglách* Collins emphasised the importance of the company as the basic Volunteer unit, but wrote: 'forget the Company of the regular army. We are not establishing or attempting to establish a regular force on the lines of the standing armies of even the small independent countries of Europe.' Instead, Collins described the Volunteers as a 'body of riflemen scouts, capable of acting individually or in units'.[57]

Later in 1918 *An t-Óglách* went further, calling on the Irish to

acknowledge no limit and no scruple in resistance to the British … we must recognize that anyone, civilian or soldier, who assists directly or by connivance in this crime against us, merits no more consideration than a wild beast, and should be killed without mercy or hesitation as opportunity offers … the man who voluntarily surrenders when called for … the man who drives a police car or assists in the transport of army supplies, all these having assisted the enemy must be shot or otherwise destroyed with the least possible delay.[58]

The paper continued publication throughout the war, and always addressed the 'official' response to British announcements. For example, in September 1918 Lord Lieutenant French indicated that the English 'Government's policy toward Conscription for Ireland remains unchanged'. In response, *An t-Óglách*, the mouthpiece for the most violent opposition to conscription, editorialised:

It is desired that we should eliminate all talk and all thought of passive resistance [against conscription], because passive resistance means, in effect, no resistance at all.

We must fight with ruthlessness and ferocity …[59]

The article went on to quote George Bernard Shaw: 'Nothing is ever done in the world unless men are willing to kill each other if it is not done'. Collins liked the article, had many copies distributed and asked its author, Ernest Blythe, for more of the same.

Whether the Irish were prepared to take the next step is arguable, but politics, in the election of 1918 and the establishment of Dáil Éireann on 21 January 1919, was to make the leap to the War of Independence.

Notes

[1] Intelligence notes 1916: PRO CO 903/19.

[2] Dr Risteard Mulcahy, MD, 'The development of the Irish Volunteers, 1916–1922', *An Cosantóir*, vol. 40 (Part 1: February 1980). When Piaras Béaslaí's book, *Michael Collins and the Making of the New Ireland*, was released, General Richard Mulcahy did not comment publicly but did make voluminous notes on the book. His son, Dr Risteard Mulcahy, compiled those notes and referred to the two volumes in books and lectures. They are cited as Richard Mulcahy, Béaslaí Notes, vol. –, p. –.

[3] See W.J. Brennan-Whitmore, *With the Irish in Frongoch* (Dublin, 1917). See also Lyn Ebenezer, *Fron-Goch and the Birth of the IRA* (Llanrwst, 2006); Seán O'Mahony, *Frongoch, University of Revolution* (Killiney, 1987; 1995).

[4] Brian Feeney, *Sinn Féin—A Hundred Turbulent Years* (Dublin, 2002), pp 60–1.

[5] Florence O'Donoghue, 'The reorganisation of the Volunteers', *Capuchin Annual* (1967).

[6] Eileen McGough, *Diarmuid Lynch: A Forgotten Irish Patriot* (Cork, 2013), p. 82 *et seq.*

[7] Diarmuid Lynch, *The IRB and the 1916 Insurrection* (Cork, 1957), pp 21–32; Geraldine Dillon, 'The Irish Republican Brotherhood', *University Review*, vol. 2, no. 9 (1960).

[8] Padraig McCartan, 'Extracts from the papers of Dr Patrick McCartan', *Clogher Record*, vol. 5, no. 2 (1964).

[9] Lynch, *The IRB and the 1916 Insurrection*, pp 21–32.

[10] Tomás Ó Maoileoin, in Uinseonn MacEoin (ed.), *Survivors: The Story of Ireland's Struggle as Told Through Some of Her Outstanding Living People. Notes 1913–1916* (Baile Átha Cliath, 1966), p. 83.

[11] Lynch, *The IRB and the 1916 Insurrection*, p. 30.

[12] From the time the Irish prisoners returned from Frongoch the British were tracking them, and the DMP detective notes of 29 May 1917 indicated that 'Collins was the general secretary' here. A.T.Q. Stewart, *Michael Collins: The Secret File* (Belfast, 1997), document 7, p. 48.

[13] Francis Costello, *The Irish Revolution and its Aftermath, 1916–1923* (Dublin, 2003), p. 23.

[14] J.B.E. Hittle, *Michael Collins and the Anglo-Irish War: Britain's Counter-Insurgency Failure* (Chicago, 2011), p. 49.

[15] See David Gates, *The Spanish Ulcer: A History of the Peninsular War* (New York, 1986).

[16] James Fintan Lalor (ed. L. Fogarty), *James Fintan Lalor, Patriot and Political Essayist (1807–1849)* (Dublin, 1919), p. 73.

[17] *Ibid.*

[18] C.E. Callwell, *Small Wars: Their Principles and Practice* (London, 1903), p. 1.

[19] *An t-Óglách*, 1 March 1920.

[20] An indication of just how von Lettow-Vorbeck's campaign was viewed can be seen in *An t-Óglách* (13 April 1920): 'General Lettow-Vorbeck's campaign in East Africa affords perhaps more valuable instruction for the employment of the Irish Republican Army in its present circumstances than any other campaign that was ever fought'. In general, analyses of guerrilla conflicts from a variety of eras and different locations were a frequent subject of *An t-Óglách* articles.

[21] Piaras Béaslaí, *Michael Collins and the Making of the New Ireland* (London, 1926), vol. 2, p. 124.

[22] Charles Townshend, *The British Campaign in Ireland, 1919–1921* (Oxford, 1975), p. 85.

[23] Robert R. James, *Churchill, a Study in Failure, 1900–1939* (London, 1972), p. 119.

[24] Joost Augusteijn, *From Public Defiance to Guerrilla Warfare* (Dublin, 1996), p. 84.

[25] *Ibid.*, p. 86.

[26] *Ibid.*, p. 115.

[27] Dr Risteard Mulcahy, 'The development of the Irish Volunteers, 1916–1922', *An Cosantóir*, vol. 40 (Part 2: March, 1980).

[28] Geraldine Plunkett Dillon, 'The North Roscommon election', *Capuchin Annual* (1967).

[29] *Ibid.*

[30] Béaslaí, *Michael Collins and the Making of a New Ireland*, pp 153–4.

[31] *The Times*, 13 June 1917.

[32] Russell Rees, *Ireland 1905–25. Volume I, Text and Historiography* (Newtownards, 1998), pp 226–7.

[33] Edgar Holt, *Protest in Arms* (New York, 1960), p. 140.

[34] 'The East Clare election', *An Phoblacht*, 12 August 1999.

[35] *The Times*, 11 June 1917.

[36] Ivor Churchill Guest to Cabinet, 20 July 1917.

[37] *The Times*, 4 July 1917.

[38] 'Summary of speeches made by Mr de Valera and other Sinn Féin leaders, during his tour in the North', in *Sinn Féin and Other Republican Suspects 1899–1921: Dublin Castle Special Branch Files CO 904 (193–216)*, United Kingdom Colonial Office Record Series 1 (Dublin, 2006), CO 904/198/105.

[39] *The Times*, 16 July 1917.

[40] RIC Joseph McCarthy, 'Meeting at Skibbereen', in 'Summary of speeches made by Mr de Valera and other Sinn Féin leaders, during his tour in the North', *Sinn Féin and Other Republican Suspects*, CO 904/198/105.

[41] Martin Walton, in Kenneth Griffith and Timothy O'Grady, *Ireland's Unfinished Revolution: An Oral History* (London, 1982), p. 132. In fact, most of the participants used the term 'eyes and ears' to describe the RIC, and historians have followed suit.

[42] *Kilkenny Journal*, 21 July 1917.

[43] See Aodh De Blacam, *What Sinn Féin Stands For* (Dublin, 1921).

[44] P.S. O'Hegarty, *The Victory of Sinn Féin* (Dublin, 1924; 1998), p. 120.

[45] *Ibid.*, p. 23.

[46] Eamonn Gaynor (ed.), *Memoirs of a Tipperary Family: The Gaynors of Tyone, 1887–2000*

(Dublin, 2003), p. 103.

[47] RIC J. Clark, RIC Joseph McCarthy, 'Meeting at Galway', in 'Summary of speeches made by Mr de Valera and other Sinn Féin leaders, during his tour in the North', *Sinn Féin and Other Republican Suspects*, CO 904/198/105.

[48] Marie R. Cremin, 'Fighting on their own terms: the tactics of the Irish Republican Army 1919–1921', *Small Wars and Insurgencies*, vol. 26, no. 6 (2015), 912–36.

[49] *The Times*, 20 February 1917.

[50] As will become evident, GHQ exercised only a loose control over the units throughout the country, though it did have more and more effect as the war progressed. Richard Mulcahy stated: 'During the War of Independence, decisions about the organisation and strategy of the Irish resistance were made by the GHQ staff'; Risteard Mulcahy, *My Father the General: Richard Mulcahy and the Military History of the Revolution* (Dublin, 2009), p. 42.

[51] *Ibid.*

[52] See Richard P. Davis, *Arthur Griffith and Non-Violent Sinn Féin* (Dublin, 1974).

[53] Charles Townshend, 'The Irish Republican Army and the development of guerrilla warfare, 1919–1921', *English Historical Review*, vol. 94 (1979).

[54] *An t-Óglách*, 15 August 1918.

[55] *An t-Óglách*, 29 October 1918.

[56] *An t-Óglach*, 15 August 1918.

[57] *An t-Óglách*, 14 September 1918.

[58] *An t-Óglách*, 28 September 1918.

[59] *Ibid.*

2. Guerrilla war—war in the shadows

The guerrilla army resembles a gas—able to disperse as molecules to prevent a counter-strike—but able to coalesce for its own operations.

—T.E. Lawrence

At the outset it should be emphasised that rebels do not 'win' a guerrilla war by military action alone.[1] Most guerrilla wars of the twentieth century failed, and those that did 'succeed' did so by an intentional combination of military, political and propaganda action. Military action is a means to an end but it is not an end in itself. In the most basic sense, a guerrilla war is a competition for power—ultimately not military power but rather political power in the country. History has borne out the idea that confrontation between power and those who are subject to power is the only way that anything changes. There are certain conditions under which a particular insurgency has a chance of succeeding even against the professional armed forces of a *status quo* government, because for one reason or another the government cannot utilise its full resources.[2] Given these considerations, and in retrospect, the Irish leaders were justified in planning a strategy of insurrection that would bring them up against the armed forces of Britain because those forces would be hamstrung to a considerable extent. The Irish War of Independence falls into that 'successful' category. This does not happen often, but any revolutionary triumph is generally rare.

In his 1963 article 'Guerrilla warfare in Ireland, 1919–1921', Florence O'Donoghue (who ran intelligence and military operations in Cork that rivalled those of Michael Collins in Dublin) wrote:

> The type of guerrilla warfare evolved and operated by the Army of the Irish Republic in the years 1919–1921 was a *complete* departure from the policy of all earlier armed efforts in modern times to regain national freedom. It was *original* and *unique* and

has no *exact* parallels, either in the history of the Irish or any similar struggle before its time, or in the numerous guerrilla campaigns which have been fought since then. [Emphasis added][3]

The emphasised words *may* make O'Donoghue's statement acceptable, especially if only applied to Ireland, because all wars are unique in one way or another, but it misleads one into thinking that guerrilla war did not exist before the Irish War of Independence and that nothing was taken from the Irish war for use in later guerrilla conflicts. Neither assertion is true.

John MacBride, who was 51 when he was executed after the Rising and led the Irish Brigade in the Boer War, poignantly said:

Liberty is a priceless thing and anyone of you that sees a chance, take it. I'd do so myself but my liberty days are over. Good luck, boys. Many of you may live to fight another day. Take my advice, never allow yourselves to be cooped inside the walls of a building again.[4]

All guerrilla wars—both prior to and after the Irish War of Independence—are fought by mobile, small-unit bands, usually in conjunction with a larger political–military strategy. Such wars are 'wars of skirmishes'. The word *guerrilla* (the diminutive of Spanish *guerra*, 'war') stems from the Peninsular campaigns of the Duke of Wellington in the Napoleonic Wars, in which Spanish and Portuguese irregulars, or *guerrilleros*, helped drive the French from the Iberian Peninsula. Long before that time, the general and strategist Sun Tsu in *The Art of War* (sixth century BC) was one of the first proponents of the use of guerrilla warfare:[5] 'All warfare is based on deception … Every battle is won or lost before it is ever fought. Attack the enemy where he is unprepared and appear where you are not expected. It is vital to undermine the enemy, subvert and corrupt him, sow internal discord among his leaders, and destroy him without fighting him.' His dictum that 'The supreme art of war is to subdue the enemy without fighting' presages the use of intelligence and politics to bring a war to the best conclusion. The earliest description of guerrilla warfare is an alleged battle between Emperor Huang and the Miao in China.[6] Guerrilla warfare was not unique to China; nomadic and migratory tribes and Huns used elements of guerrilla warfare to fight the Persians, Alexander the Great and the Romans. Quintus Fabius Maximus, known as Cuncator, widely regarded as the 'father of guerrilla warfare' of his time, devised the so-called 'Fabian strategy' that was used to great effect against Hannibal's army in 218 BC.[7] Guerrilla warfare was also a common strategy of the various Celtic, Iberian and Germanic tribes that the Romans faced. Caratacus, the British war chief, employed guerrilla warfare against the Romans for approximately eight years, mixed in with occasional set-piece battles. Although he was ultimately captured by the Romans, the historian Tacitus wrote that many Romans respected him while detesting his tactics. In the classical ancient world, this kind of warfare was indirectly mentioned by the Greeks in Homeric stories but usually as hit-and-run acts of foraging for booty in enemy territory, pretty much like later Viking piracy.[8] Fighting irregular warfare has been part and parcel of our history for a very long time. Most often, the Irish referred to tactics used in South Africa's Boer War of 1899–1902.[9]

Over the centuries the practitioners of guerrilla warfare have been called rebels, irregulars, insurgents, partisans and mercenaries. Frustrated military commanders have consistently condemned them as barbarians, savages, terrorists, brigands, outlaws and bandits. The Prussian general and theorist Carl von Clausewitz reluctantly admitted their existence by picturing partisans as 'a kind of nebulous vapoury essence'. Other writers called their operations 'small wars'.[10] T.E. Lawrence, a guerrilla contemporary with Michael Collins and the Irish, held that, if certain factors existed, guerrilla warfare could be an exact science. He required an unassailable guerrilla base, a regular opposing army of limited strength with the task of controlling a wide area, and a sympathetic population.[11] Lawrence knew that the goal of a guerrilla war is to make action a series of single combats. He held that 'irregular war is far more intellectual than a bayonet charge'.[12] But war, like politics, is not an exact science. While all of these factors did not exist at all times and in all places for the Irish, the Irish understood the necessity of each and moved to accomplish all of them. All events, most especially revolutions, have deep roots, but the Irish roots are particular, extending far into the past and greatly determining the course of present events. The fact that revolutionary fervour did not exist at the outset was not an impediment to the revolution, as Che Guevara understood later: 'It is not necessary to wait until all conditions for making revolution exist: the insurrection can create them'.[13] Lawrence's conceptualisation also moved away from the notion of guerrilla warfare as a purely military phenomenon and laid far more stress on the political aspects of such a conflict. Guerrilla operations must flow from a clearly defined political goal, which in turn must flow from the aspirations of the people. Mao Zedong's 'Long March' and his writings contributed much to the concept of guerrilla war. 'When the enemy advances, we retreat. When the enemy halts and encamps, we harass him. When the enemy seeks to avoid battle, we attack. Whenever the enemy retreats, we pursue.' Always attack, and quickly disperse. Popular support is not only necessary for the success of the struggle but also determines the nature and location of guerrilla operations. 'The guerrilla must move among the people as a fish swims in the sea.' And good planning depends on superior intelligence, which can only be gleaned from the people.[14]

Charles Townsend continued to place military action in a guerrilla war alongside political (and, by extension, propaganda) effects:

> The purely military effects of guerrilla warfare will usually be seen as subordinate to its political and psychological effects. Victory is achieved not so much by knocking the enemy's sword from his hand, as by paralysing his arm. On the question whether guerrilla war can by itself be the means of defeating a strong and determined enemy, views differ.
>
> Eastern theory, exemplified by Mao [Mao Zedong, in China] and Giáp [Võ Nguyên Giáp, in Vietnam], has tended to see it as no more than a transitional phase, which must give way by degrees to conventional open war. Westerners have perhaps been more inclined to believe that the moral effect of guerrilla struggle can be sufficient to overcome governments, at least those dependent on public opinion.[15]

A comprehensive description of guerrilla warfare, used interchangeably with insurgency, is:

> Guerrilla warfare is a form of warfare by which a strategically

weaker side assumes the tactical offensive in selected forms, times, and places. Guerrilla warfare is the weapon of the weak. It is never chosen in preference to regular warfare; it is employed only when and where the possibilities of regular warfare have been foreclosed.[16]

An insurgency—and, in response, counter-insurgency action (COIN)—is primarily a political struggle in which both sides use armed force to create space for their political, economic and propaganda activities to be effective.[17]

Following World War II, such *revolutionary warfare* (asymmetrical or unconventional warfare) became a staple, as did *insurgency, rebellion, insurrection, people's war* and *war of national liberation*. Thereafter, 'wars of national liberation' proliferated, and most were fought using guerrilla principles. As noted, most guerrilla wars are unsuccessful, but the ones that do succeed combine politics and propaganda along with military action. Regardless of terminology, the importance of guerrilla warfare has varied considerably throughout history. Traditionally, it has been a weapon of protest employed to rectify real or imagined wrongs inflicted on a people either by a ruling government or by a foreign invader. As such, 'guerrilla war' has scored remarkable successes and has suffered disastrous defeats. Throughout the war, the British may have had the power to dominate the Irish militarily but the Irish succeeded in achieving their goal—their own governance.

With that in mind, O'Donoghue continued:

> The accepted definition of guerrilla warfare is an armed struggle carried on by organised forces in territory occupied by the enemy. Within that definition it has taken many forms but its object is, invariably, to inflict as much loss and damage to the enemy while evading engagements that could result in the annihilation of the guerrilla forces. The common attribute of all guerillas is a material weakness in relation to the army opposed to them. They cannot fight positional warfare; they cannot afford losing battles; they must fight only when there is a prospect of success.[18]

O'Donoghue's words define precisely how the Irish modified and adapted well-known guerrilla principles to the Irish terrain, as well as fighting in the cities. All guerrilla activity is conditioned by local circumstances, and the measure of success is influenced by the extent to which maximum use is made of those conditions that are favourable to its operation. There was hardly a single conventional battle. The Irish War of Independence was a 'shadow war': that shadow war was the essence of the conflict. Broadly speaking, the IRA waged guerrilla war in the countryside, targeting police barracks and patrols, while in the cities its soldiers operated more as terrorists, killing off-duty policemen or civil servants.

The growing Volunteer army experienced many of the problems that plague nascent armies, and training and organisation were not completed in a uniform manner nationwide. Over most of the country officers and men had undergone such elementary training as it was possible to give them under the conditions of arming and organising *sub rosa*. While many tactical ideas and innovations were born in the field, the IRA GHQ in Dublin set a policy of guerrilla war and began to guide the Volunteers as early as spring 1918. The policy was intended to be a nationwide one but never accomplished that aim. The IRA in the field, for most of the war, acted on its own initiative and made its own decisions.[19] In some ways this proved valuable to the Irish, as inactivity or setbacks in one area did not affect the morale or operations of other areas. Nevertheless, the slow development of a GHQ policy, restraining some of the more belligerent among the rank and file outside Dublin, was to be one of the keys to prolonging the struggle and ultimately forced the British to negotiate a truce. When Séamus Robinson[20] led Seán Treacy, Dan Breen, Seán Hogan, Paddy O'Dwyer, Tadhg Crowe, Patrick McCormack, Michael Ryan and Seán O'Meara in an ambush of the constables escorting a load of gelignite in Soloheadbeg, Co. Tipperary, on 21 January 1919 (the same day as the first meeting of Dáil Éireann in Dublin) it was without any sanction from GHQ.[21] Two RIC men, James McDonnell and Patrick O'Connell, were killed. At the time, the Irish press headlined the events as 'New Era of Terrorism Begins'.[22] There is little doubt that Treacy fired the first shot,[23] and he was quoted as saying that the intent of the Tipperary Volunteers was clear: 'If this is the state of affairs, we'll have to kill someone, and make the bloody enemy organise us'.[24] In describing the action at Soloheadbeg, Breen wrote that, without any authorisation, they set out to fire the shots that 'would begin another phase in the long fight for the freedom of our country'. Breen felt that 'we had to kill and can't leave anyone alive afterward'. He was only sorry that there had not been more policemen: 'If there had to be dead Peelers at all, six would have created a better impression than a mere two'.[25] Like many members of the IRA (particularly in Munster), Breen, Treacy and their comrades were afraid that the whole movement was drifting into politics, and in danger of becoming just another 'political party'. They felt that action was required to turn their men into an army.[26] Breen wrote that 'The Volunteers were in danger of becoming merely a political adjunct to the Sinn Féin organisation'.[27]

Despite all the action in 1917–18,[28] most accounts attribute the start of the war to that attack.[29] Following de Valera's election victory in East Clare in June 1917, Breen had led a protest of uniformed Volunteers in Tipperary:

> Our military display in Tipperary town did not cause a bigger shock to the enemy than it did to the local Sinn Féiners, many of whom were not in favour of any stronger weapons than resolutions. They were exasperated by our audacity. We should not have acted until the matter had been solemnly discussed in advance. A formal long-winded proposition would then be put before the meeting and a decision arrived at by majority vote. Such timid souls often hampered our line of action, but we were not prone to worry. The political wing of Sinn Féin criticised us severely. We just listened to all the orations and prognostications and made up our own minds.[30]

According to Treacy, they had had 'enough of being pushed around and getting our men imprisoned while we remained inactive'. Breen argued that the republicans needed the explosives, but said of the expected six RIC guards: 'If they put up an armed resistance, we had resolved not merely to capture the gelignite but also to shoot down the escort'.[31]

At the start of the war, it was not clear that the Irish had any definite plan beyond militarily attacking representatives of the British government. The Soloheadbeg ambush made very little impression on the immediate political situation, and both *The Times* and the *New York Times* reported the event as a double murder. The idea that the perpetrators were Irish Volunteers or that the crime might have had a political intent was not mentioned.[32] Soloheadbeg did not change the course of the Irish struggle, but the British government's response and GHQ's reaction to the Dáil opening did alter the situation. Tipperary was proclaimed a disturbed district by the British and subject to martial law. Before the month was out, arms raids took place in at least three different County Cork towns, and grenades were thrown at a Londonderry prison.[33] On 31 January *An t-Óglách* reinforced the Dáil's assertion that a state of war existed between Ireland and England. It added that IRA members were justified in treating the armed forces of the enemy, whether soldiers or policemen, exactly as a national army would treat the members of an invading army. They were to 'use all legitimate methods of warfare against the soldiers and policemen of the English usurper'.[34] Piaras Béaslaí, who wrote the editorials, asserted that they were approved by Brugha and the GHQ staff and therefore reflected Volunteer policy.

Fintan O'Toole points out: 'In retrospect, Soloheadbeg was shaped as a mythic point of origin. In reality, it looks more like a local coup—not against British rule but against those in Sinn Féin who favoured a non-violent path to revolution.'[35] Richard Mulcahy went on to discuss Breen and Treacy in detail:

> It pushed rather turbulent spirits such as Breen and Treacy into
> the Dublin arena from time to time, where their services were
> not required and their presence was often awkward.[36]

Such impetuous activities had to be controlled for the Irish to maintain the pace of the war, which had to be set by GHQ. Politics, propaganda and military actions needed to run approximately in step with one another.

It is important to understand the reaction to the attack at Soloheadbeg in considering the need to 'pace' a guerrilla war. The attack was generally condemned throughout Ireland.[37] The newspapers condemned it, as did the Catholic Church and many of the TDs who had been sworn into office that very day. The shocked reaction underlined the danger of the population's being alienated by excessive military aggression and brutality.

Not only was Collins concerned about public reaction but he was also personally affected by a curious tension whenever a 'job' was planned or ordered to be carried out. He did not view assassinations and killing as the first resort but only as a necessary last resort.

When Breen, Treacy and Robinson were summoned to Dublin, Collins met them in the street, not in an office—an expression of the official displeasure with the attack. Robinson remembered that Collins asked them whether they were ready to go to the US. Robinson answered that 'to kill a couple of policemen for the country's sake and leave it at that by running away would be so wanton as to approximate murder'. Collins asked what they intended to do and was told that they intended to fight it out. He replied, 'That's all right with me'. Clearly, Collins started out by giving the official Volunteer policy but then saw that they intended to continue and left it at that. Even in early 1919 Collins was playing a very dangerous political game.[38]

The Irish war was like many insurrections in that, at least initially, a small group of militants used violence while much of the population was uneasy with the means, even if supporting the political ends. How the war developed was determined by several factors:

- The British government's need to provide military forces to garrison and protect a worldwide empire while the Irish war was ongoing. 'Imperial over-stretch' prevented the British from massing sufficient forces to overwhelm the insurgents. Britain was required to garrison a far-flung empire, as well as to provide forces for the newly Mandated Territories and an occupation force for the German Rhineland. In addition, the British government faced public pressure to reduce the unprecedented size of its army and to control costs in the wake of a very expensive global war.
- The ability of the Irish to create a variety of threats to the British security forces. The flying columns, the full-time irregular field troops of the IRA, were just large enough to require military as opposed to only paramilitary forces to deal with them.
- The impact of world opinion on British policy. (See Chapter 4 on Propaganda.)
- The self-imposed restrictions on action by British security forces. Being

a democratic state supposedly dedicated to the rule of law and the freedom of the press, the British government limited its actions to those that Parliament and the British people would support and accept.[39] (Extraordinary measures, especially those that could be perceived as illegal or immoral, would be difficult to justify and thus impossible to take in the light of an open press and public opinion, which is just what happened in the case of the 'Terror', as treated in Chapter 6.)

At the beginning of 1919, Irish politicians feared that incidents such as Soloheadbeg would turn the people against the separatist movement in general. Collins realised that he would have to wait until the shock and anger abated somewhat. He could not risk assaulting the detectives of 'G' Division for a time, and so there was a lull in Irish activities. Early on, Collins knew the importance of public reaction to the Irish political position. He did not authorise an attack on policemen for some weeks while he gauged the public mood, and when the attacks came the reaction was muted compared to that after Soloheadbeg. As the time for action neared, Éamon Broy saw Collins becoming 'extremely anxious as to what effect the shooting of detectives would have on the Volunteers themselves and on the Sinn Féin movement generally, and how it would be taken by the public'.[40] Collins was always aware of the ultimate political and propaganda effects.

General Richard Mulcahy defended this policy, stating that the killings were a matter of conscience but that they were also

> matters of political expediency, of common sense, and in accordance with the spirit in which the Volunteers were founded as a defence force.[41]

Like Collins, Mulcahy always kept an eye on the ultimate goal—removal of British governance—and always deemed it 'prudent' to be especially careful about taking any action that could alienate the local population.

The Soloheadbeg attack indicated how little control Dublin's GHQ exercised over the IRA in the countryside early in the war. Every act orchestrated by GHQ was designed, however, to contribute to the political and psychological demoralisation of the British, even though local initiatives were another matter. It would be misleading to attribute to GHQ control or co-ordination of all actions; until the end of the war there was a great deal of local action which took place without GHQ control, and often without even GHQ knowledge.[42] Autonomy was the byword for all units outside Dublin. Moreover, GHQ, which superseded the old Volunteer Executive in March 1918, expected payment for such supplies as field equipment and training manuals. Right up to the Truce, units were expected to be financially self-sufficient, though their sources of money became less spontaneous as their needs mounted. It was only in late 1919 that GHQ began to show greater skill in its command and control of the IRA. They began to offer more and demand less.

General Mulcahy felt that GHQ was willing to compromise and to be tolerant of what he deemed to be the 'intransigence' of country units and leaders, but there is no doubt that attempts at central control by GHQ became more manifest as the war continued.[43]

> During 1918 and 1919, however, headquarters began to show greater adeptness at directing and supervising the Volunteers.
>
> …
>
> Headquarters provided advice, instruction, a little equipment and a welcome sense of national togetherness. In return, provincial units accepted the dismissal and appointments of commandants, provided [that] the families of local influence were not seriously inconvenienced; and to some extent they modified their military activities to accord with headquarters' preferences.[44]

Mulcahy felt that GHQ played a large (and often misunderstood) part in imposing a national policy and attempting further control of the army.[45] Although many actions were initiated without consultation with GHQ, Mulcahy felt that they usually received approval (albeit belatedly) because they conformed to the military, ethical and political policies of the army and the Dáil. He related:

> Without the stabilising influence and prudent policies of the GHQ staff, which were sometimes resented by the fighters in the field, military initiative during the war could not have been maintained and expanded, nor would the subservience of the

army to parliament and the people have been so certain, if and when independence was achieved.[46]

Still, there always seemed to be an underlying conflict between commanders in the country and GHQ in Dublin. Personality clashes were common, and in that the Irish War of Independence was no different from other guerrilla wars. The gulf between HQ and field officers is a common problem and is usually remedied by some 'cross-fertilisation' of the two. With the commitment to guerrilla war, a training programme and exchange of information became essential. It often seemed, however, that GHQ was not aware of the needs of the men and women in the country and did not really understand the kind of war that guerrilla tactics entailed. To leaders like Liam Lynch, it sometimes seemed that GHQ was too 'squeamish' in the instructions that there should be no casualties.

At the outset of organisation, GHQ sent Andy Cooney, Seán MacBride, Ernie O'Malley and others to more fully organise and teach. They were to show the country Volunteers how to set up outposts, how to run patrols, how to deploy the units and escape. Many of the country units had been doing these things for some time, however, and resented the 'Dublin interference'. Persuasion and goodwill always worked better than direct exercise of authority.[47]

Moreover, some of those sent 'to the country' did not fit in with the units they were to teach. Ernie O'Malley, for example, was an intellectual and raised eyebrows among the rural men when he said that he knew of their ways because his grandmother used to churn butter in their Dublin home. O'Malley's reports to Dublin indicated his near-disdain for some of the country units. He reported in December 1919 that

Officers or men have not the faintest idea or at most only a very faint idea of military work in general. They know very little of the organization and systematic training necessary to turn out an efficient soldier. Military propaganda is necessary. Already I have instructed officers to court-martial men who have missed more than three consecutive parades.[48]

Moreover, when the men would retire to a pub for a few pints at the end of a day's training, O'Malley would sit in a corner, as he did not drink. The fact that he read a book, possibly in Greek, and did not really socialise with the men separated him still further.[49] To compound the problems, when the Dublin instructors recommended the replacement of many of the local leaders, who had been elected to their positions, there was further resentment in the ranks. These attempts at GHQ control alienated many local leaders, and the antipathy of some of the local commanders towards what they felt was interference and micro-managing was to have repercussions throughout the war, and especially in the lead-up to the Civil War.

There was frequent disagreement between the strategy and tactics recommended by GHQ and those of field commanders. On 2 August 1919, representatives of the Cork, Kerry, Waterford and West Limerick brigades met with Collins and the other members of GHQ staff in order to co-ordinate IRA activity in the countryside. The representatives were Terence MacSwiney (Cork No. 1 Brigade), Liam Lynch (Cork No. 2 Brigade), Liam Deasy (Cork No. 3 Brigade), Paddy Cahill (Kerry No. 1 Brigade), Dan O'Mahoney (Kerry No. 2 Brigade), Jeremiah O'Riordan (Kerry No. 3 Brigade), Pax Whelan (Waterford West) and Revd Dick McCarthy (West Limerick). Mulcahy outlined GHQ policy with regard to ambushing:

> General ambushing was to be the principal form of attack against the British, but 'in all cases the enemy should first of all be called upon to surrender'.

Clearly this would defeat the purpose of an ambush. Brugha supported Mulcahy, but Collins and the men in the field objected strenuously that this was impractical. In the end, the principle of surprise as set forth by the brigade officers won the day. Conflicts like this continued throughout the war.

The Irish military effort in the War of Independence differed from previous Irish rebellions and risings in three significant respects:

- Previous insurrections committed the whole available force at the first blow and stood by the result.
- Previous efforts had been much influenced by the hope of foreign aid.

61

- The IRA had an advantage not possessed before—the approval of a national government constitutionally elected in the 1918 election.[50]

The Irish guerrilla war was waged on three fronts: (1) the urban terrorist campaign waged by Michael Collins against the intelligence system of Dublin Castle; (2) the small-scale warfare by part-time guerrillas attacking the RIC and outlying British posts; and (3) the larger-scale but still guerrilla war conducted by the flying columns of the IRA.

In assessing its development even up to the war's end in 1921, it would seem that the IRA was marked by the irregularity and separation of its units, many of which never became ready for serious action. Fortunately for the Irish, the British were slow to recognise the growing power of Sinn Féin; when the violence started in 1919 they failed to understand or exploit the divisions between Sinn Féin and the IRA, and that lack of understanding increased later after the conflict exploded into full-scale guerrilla warfare in 1920. The notion of a unified popular nationwide uprising, combining political and military elements, was a fiction. GHQ 'command and control', dealing with an army that was in large measure self-created and self-sustaining, made constant and strenuous efforts to break down local independence and to regularise the hierarchy of control. Beyond a certain point, however, central operational control of guerrilla warfare is impossible, and the Irish never had a complete command and control structure imposed from Dublin. Mao Zedong wrote later: 'In guerrilla warfare, small units acting independently play the principal role and there must be no excessive interference in their activities'.[51] Whether by design or because of circumstances, much Irish activity was independent of Dublin control and was accomplished in autonomous actions. Within the IRA it was evident that there was 'tension between the strong centrifugal tendency of the local units and the growing centripetal drive of GHQ'.[52] The latter impulse culminated in 1921 and gave rise to most of the IRA's theories of guerrilla action, but until then the major evolutionary stages of the campaign were spontaneous and unplanned. Nobody was more conscious of local inconsistencies in the IRA's performance than GHQ in Dublin, and in 1921 strenuous efforts were made to translate into reality the image of a single, unified insurgent nation. While Collins continued to build up the muscle of the IRA, dealing out praises and rewards for success and fulminating against failure, Mulcahy laboured to regularise and integrate its multiform, disparate components and to elaborate a total strategy.[53]

At this time *An t-Óglách* began to print more articles of encouragement to the Volunteers:

the enemy is feeling the strain on his resources …

. . .

the Republic of Ireland IS and WILL BE …

. . .

We are carrying out a well-considered plan of campaign in which the object is to harass and demoralize the enemy without giving them an opportunity to strike back effectively. We realize that it is far more profitable to *kill* for Ireland than to *die* for her.[54] [Emphasis in original]

The initial goal of the IRA was to arm itself. Each unit was supposed to take care of this individually, and that, of course, led to a great disparity of arms throughout the country. Further, GHQ provided little support and the lack of arms was a constant complaint throughout the conflict. From 1919 Headquarters attempted to enforce a monopoly on arms acquisition. GHQ was constantly reminded that the small core of active Volunteers necessarily had to be limited because of this lack of arms and ammunition. Major actions involving large numbers of men and arms had to be avoided at all costs.[55] Most early actions had but one aim: to get arms and to use them to get more arms. The whole development of the war depended on captured arms.

Local units were encouraged to raid in their local areas, but arms purchases outside the local territories were forbidden. For example, Michael Brennan of Clare seized £1,500 during a raid on the Limerick post office, and then came to Dublin to buy arms. He bought a number of revolvers before being informed that Collins was unhappy that he was spoiling the market. GHQ ordered him to stop his activities.[56] Thomas Kettrick, the quartermaster in Mayo, went to buy arms in England and arranged to transport weapons and explosives to Mayo. Collins was enraged at his going independently to England without permission and told him that his activities would upset the market.[57] 'Spoil the market'; 'upset the market'—

one has to ask whether this was Collins the businessman, the Minister for Finance, or Collins the commander talking. Collins was a naturally accomplished businessman and he always approached his duties in a businesslike manner.

In addition to stifling independent attempts to acquire weapons, GHQ closely monitored the distribution of arms from its stockpile to country units. It had a habit of only supplying weapons to units that were already active. Collins wrote to a brigade commander in May 1919:

> When you ask me for ammunition for guns—which have never fired a shot in this fight—my answer is a simple one. Fire shots at some useful target or get to hell out of it.

In time, these differences became so acute that Cork, for example, would act largely on its own with little regard to the Dublin GHQ. Many units made use of the old saw that it's easier to ask for forgiveness than to ask for permission. Michael Brennan in Clare said:

> During the election [in December 1918] my brother Paddy worked out a completely new policy which I'm afraid he didn't submit to GHQ for approval. He was pretty certain it wouldn't be approved, but on the other hand he thought if it worked, GHQ would accept it and issue it as their own policy. This was in fact what happened a few weeks later.[58]

That policy continued throughout the war, and in Dublin as well as the country. Martin Walton related that in late 1919 he was asked to go on a raid with four Volunteers whom he met in Drumcondra. 'Now raids at that time were more or less forbidden officially by our headquarters staff. If you got away with it you got a pat on the back, and if you didn't get away with it you were disowned.'[59] In military slang, 'ground truth' describes the reality of a tactical situation as opposed to intelligence reports and mission plans. The closer one is to the fight, the more 'real' it is. On the other hand, the further one is from it, the more abstract it is. The IRA leaders throughout the country always felt that they understood the ground truths of the situation much more clearly than did GHQ in Dublin, and they proceeded accordingly.

O'Donoghue listed three distinctive features of guerrilla war as waged by the Irish in 1919–21:

- They had no external military aid or direction.
- They acquired their arms primarily from the occupation forces by fighting for them, at first almost with bare hands. [Though Collins pursued many chances to import arms for the Volunteers, arms captured from the British were the primary source for the Irish.]
- The whole force was never committed to the struggle at the same time. The policy was rather a piecemeal attack by limited numbers on successive, selected objectives.[60]

The overwhelming numerical and arms superiority of the British army, later augmented by the Black and Tans and Auxiliaries, raises the question of how the Irish were able to avoid annihilation and succeed to the degree that the British were willing to negotiate a treaty in 1921.[61] It is accepted that there are three major reasons. First, the explosive upsurge of national vitality at the time demanded a widespread outlet for action. For the Volunteers it could be nothing less than a military fight in arms. Second, the democratic organisation of the Volunteers and the impossibility in the circumstances of any tight control by GHQ permitted and encouraged the development of local initiatives on a scale that would have been inconceivable in a regular army, enabling local commands to harass the British in myriad actions. Third, these individualised initiatives generated the dispassionate study by local commanders, each in his own area, of the relative strengths of his own and the opposing forces, and they determined that a new approach to the military problem was necessary— hence the need for guerrilla tactics, constantly being adapted as circumstances changed.[62]

While the British army, like every other actor in the conflict, became brutalised by the cycle of attack and retaliation, it was the British paramilitary police forces who became the most feared and hated by the Irish public, and it was their paramilitary police, with their indiscipline and hostility to the general population, who did most to turn the civilian population against the Crown forces.[63] The Black and Tans and the Auxiliaries are often confused; both introduced an atmosphere of stark terror throughout Ireland but they were distinct entities.[64] The Black and Tans were deployed to Ireland in March 1920, and the Auxiliaries followed in July. About 7,000 men served as Black and Tans, while another 2,200 were Auxiliaries.[65] The guidance to both units did not 'advocate lenience for the Irish rebels, and encouraged the meanest form of warfare'.[66] On arrival they began to engage in wholesale intimidation and violence against civilians without any provocation. It was said of the Black and Tans that

> ... they had neither religion nor morals, they used foul language, they had the old soldier's talent for dodging and scrounging, they spoke in strange accents, called the Irish 'natives', associated with low company, stole from each other, sneered at the customs of the country, drank to excess, and put sugar on their porridge.[67]

While both units were undisciplined and were despised by the population, the Auxiliaries were by far the more feared.[68] They were overwhelmingly former British army officers who were demobilised after World War I, but there were also former officers from British Empire regiments—Canadians, New Zealanders, Australians, South Africans and some Americans who had served in British regiments during the war. They were intended to serve as adjuncts to the RIC but, although they were supposed to undertake police functions, they were only nominally part of the RIC and were actually employed as separate paramilitary divisions.[69] It was the Auxiliaries who perpetrated most of the notorious outrages between July 1920 and the Truce in July 1921. The Auxiliaries have been described as

> cunning, intelligent and better armed than an ordinary military unit and with the conviction that might makes right, the Auxiliaries resembled a sort of English *Freikorps*, a close fraternity of jobless veterans with few skills except the profession of arms, comfortable within a military structure, fiercely loyal to the government, and out for adventure. ... Significantly, they were not generally held accountable for their actions to either military or police authority. Ostensibly, their mission was to restore law

and order, but instead of attempting to stabilize the situation, or pacify the people, they were employed to punish the Irish and damage the local economy in an effort to destroy the IRA's base of support.[70]

Tom Barry differentiated between the Black and Tans and the Auxiliaries:

> The Black and Tans and the Auxiliaries came from two different strata of life, and the general feeling even here in Ireland at the time was that the Black and Tans were the worst. I don't accept that at all. The Black and Tans included good and bad, like every armed force you meet and quite a number of them were rather decent men.
>
> But the Auxiliaries were something else … They were far worse than the Black and Tans … I have no doubt that a few of them could pass as ordinary decent men, but the vast majority were the worst the British produced at any time … They were sent over here to break the people and they were a far more dangerous force than the Black and Tans.[71]

Seán O'Casey expressed his opinion: 'The Tans alone would make more noise, slamming themselves into a room, shouting to shake off the fear that slashed many of their faces. The Auxies were too proud to show a sign of it. The Tommies [British army troops] would be warm, always hesitant at knocking a woman's room about.'

Considerations of propaganda and politics were never very far away from military action during the war. The outrageous behaviour of the 'Tans' and 'Auxies' captured the attention of the press in Ireland, Britain and overseas, especially in the US, with the British government being accused by its critics of 'conniving in a systemic program of barbaric reprisals against the Irish people'.[72] Among the many critics of the Black and Tans was King George V, who told Lady Margery Greenwood, wife of Chief Secretary Hamar Greenwood, that 'he hated the idea of the Black and Tans'.[73]

As the war evolved, there was a growing feeling among IRA members that they needed a standing force to carry out a sustained series of attacks. The 15 May 1919 issue of *An t-Óglách* called for 'intensive, persistent, and widespread guerrilla warfare'.[74] In fact, many of the men on the run were a burden on the local population, and the formation of 'flying columns' was thought to solve the problem. Donal O'Hannigan wrote of the men in Limerick: 'fully armed we had traveled over 30 miles cross-country in daylight without any great difficulty ... What we had in mind was an efficient, disciplined, compact and swift-moving body of men which would strike at the enemy where and when a suitable opportunity arose.'[75] The unit carried out its first operation on 9 July, disarming four constables at Ballinahinch. Its first action under fire in an engagement occurred four days later, when the Volunteers ambushed a military patrol at Emly.[76] In addition to taking the fight to the British, the bolder daylight raids were designed to win the PR battle and show the world the IRA's strength.

Most of the Black and Tans were young, unemployed, former enlisted men in the British army, and products of Britain's working class. Records and their statements indicate that they were attracted by promises of upward mobility, steady work, good pay and a comfortable pension. The Auxiliaries were all former officers in the army but they, too, were attracted by a wage of '£1 per week, all found'. Contrary to some Irish propaganda that the groups were just British convicts, about 20% of the Black and Tans and 10% of the Auxiliaries were Irish-born.[77]

It was to counter these British forces that the flying columns were established and the idea has been attributed to several individuals.[78] Dan Breen credited his Tipperary comrade Seán Treacy with the concept: 'We wanted full-time soldiers who were prepared to fight by night or by day, ready for any adventure. They would constitute a mobile force capable of striking at a given moment in one district and on the next day springing a surprise thirty miles away.'[79] Others, including Dublin Volunteer Joe Good and British General Nevil Macready, wrote that Michael Collins invented the units.[80] This reflects a tendency to attribute every republican initiative to the seemingly ubiquitous Collins. As late as June 1920 there was still a difference of opinion about the columns. GHQ discussed them in a meeting that month:

> Dick Mulcahy was not too keen on the idea, but Michael Collins was very keen on it. 'We'll have to get these bloody fellows doing something' said Collins referring to the men on the run. (At that time and for some time later, they were a bloody nuisance, for

they lounged around, slept late, ate people's food, and did no work for the Company or Battalion in which they happened to be.)[81]

Each might have had theories about full-time mobile republican units, but that ambush of the military patrol at Emly is the first recorded use of a flying column. Small actions such as that illustrated the beginning of a new pattern in the mode of Irish warfare.[82] At this early stage there was no real designation from GHQ as to what the pattern was to be, and it would take several months for GHQ to exercise severe restraint on the actions of individual Volunteer units.[83] Guerrilla warfare in Ireland was constantly evolving, as it must for all successful guerrillas.[84]

Michael Brennan had another reason for men to combine in the columns:

As the year wore on the pursuit became tougher and we were inclined to drift together, partly for company, but mainly because the 'safe areas' were now fewer and we usually met in them. The local Volunteers always posted men at night to warn of raids, and it was as easy to warn four as one and much easier than to send a message to four widely separated men. We very quickly discovered that moving around in a group gave greater security and without any actual orders being issued other men on-the-run drifted to us and our numbers grew.[85]

By later in 1920 all of the Dublin officers had encouraged GHQ staff to adopt flying columns as a policy, and on 4 October GHQ issued an order for all brigades to start columns. The 'official' column was to consist of twenty-six men and four squads. They were to function as individual units but were to co-ordinate with their battalions. The tactical innovations took place in the field, but Headquarters adopted the idea and sought to facilitate its spread to other areas. The column commander received clear instructions:

- To gain experience for himself and his men by planning and then carrying out simple operations.
- By harassing smaller and quieter military and police stations.

- By interrupting and pillaging all stores belonging to the enemy.
- By interrupting all communication.
- By covering towns threatened by reprisal parties.[86]

In addition to providing a standing body of troops, the columns helped to alleviate the arms situation.[87] Brigades and battalions forming a column pooled their weapons on the understanding that they would be more effective in the hands of a compact striking force than scattered in dumps across the countryside. Even so, the East Limerick column began with five Lee-Enfield service rifles, one old Winchester, seventy rifle rounds, three shotguns, three revolvers and a few cartridges for each.[88] This was hardly a formidable arsenal and it is no wonder that their first action was to seize arms from a police patrol.

At the beginning of the war, little thought was given to guerrilla tactics in the local units; the emphasis was on acquisition of arms in all areas. Collins was acutely aware of this. Joe Good recounts that he was having a meeting with Collins when a visitor from America interrupted them:

> I was speaking to Mick when an American visitor flourished a cheque-book and was offering Collins a cheque or cash if he preferred. But Mick replied, angrily and rudely, 'We don't need your bloody money, we want guns—and more guns'. I said later that surely the money could have been used to buy guns, but Mick insisted that supply of arms (and not the means to pay for them) was our great problem.[89]

In a review of Maryann Valiulis's biography of Richard Mulcahy, C.C. Trench wrote:

> The main feature of the guerrilla war—the use of mobile, full-time active service units and attacking soft targets rather than hard army targets—were [sic] not invented by the chief of staff [Mulcahy] but were devised perforce by the field commanders such as Liam Lynch. All Mulcahy did was to order the others to do likewise.[90]

Risteard Mulcahy contested this strenuously:

> This rather dismissive remark conceals a considerable degree of ignorance about the organisation and evolution of the Irish army. Many of the successful strategies which were adopted during the War of Independence were, of course, initiated by those who were fighting in the field and who were face to face with the realities of the conflict. But the extension of those tactics to achieve an orderly strategy, the burning of the three to four hundred police barracks, and the organisation and training of the flying columns and the active-service units could not have taken place without the guidance and control of the GHQ staff.[91]

Local Volunteers were often called up to provide support for an ambush or attack in a given area. They would normally make use of shotguns or revolvers, while the column men used rifles. GHQ organised camps all over the country to facilitate the growth of the new units.

Whatever their origin, the columns do represent the essence of the war: live to fight another day; attack and disperse; attack and disengage and move to another position to attack again.[92] Each column must attack constantly, and from all and unexpected directions. Guerrilla tactics have to be changed constantly: it could be said that 'if it works, it is obsolete, try something else'.[93] Fire and movement formed the basis of all the Irish tactics. When conditions were not favourable, the Irish learned to disengage and develop a new plan; no attack would be started unless conditions were very much in their favour. The plans of action had to be simple, understood by all in the column and, if possible, well rehearsed. The guerrilla is always on the offensive, always takes the initiative. The Irish moved in small units and prevented the British from moving in small units. Each column was 'an army in itself', self-contained and prepared to fight on its own.

There are several characteristics to any guerrilla war, and the Irish War of Independence illustrated them.

- The guerrilla cannot have a fixed base: T.E. Lawrence wrote that 'bases are targets'.
- The Irish used attack and retreat—hit and run—to preserve their

fighting ability.

- The function of the individual Volunteer, and even their military leaders, was not to defeat the British militarily. Collins and the Irish wanted to wear out and drain the British army, and render the British government ineffective.
- The principal task of the Irish was to distract the British government from their ability to govern. That permitted the emergence of the Sinn Féin political government in contrast to the British government.
- In general, the Irish objective was to inflict as much loss and damage upon the British as possible while avoiding a fight to a finish.

The regular commander seeks decisive methods but a guerrilla leader will avoid direct confrontation. It is important to remember that the IRA had distinct goals in mind that justified their strategy and tactics. The function of the Irish guerrilla war was to use attrition in exactly the same way as in the guerrilla wars that followed worldwide. The Irish intent was

> not to destroy the enemy, for that is utopian, but it is indeed to force him, through a prolonged war of psychological and physical attrition, to abandon our territory due to exhaustion and isolation'.[94]

All guerrilla wars are wars amongst the people—in the Irish war and the guerrilla wars of today. Such warfare is largely one of evasion, and the Irish war was characterised by a ceaseless and relentless offensive against the weak points of the British in Dublin and Cork, and in the countryside, and then a withdrawal to attack somewhere else. As Lawrence defined them, 'Most wars are wars of contact, ours [a guerrilla war] is one of detachment'. Collins and the Irish were fighting a war of erosion of the British military: their long-term goal was to wear down the British in the field, but more importantly to break the British will to continue the military fight in the knowledge that the Irish would never quit.

The columns tied down and embarrassed the British, especially in international opinion. The very existence of armed men in an area, even if they never attacked, was a continuous challenge to the British and forced them to maintain large garrisons to meet the threat and for the security of civil administration. What the British most wanted was for the Irish to have another Rising like that in 1916, which they could quickly put down and destroy. Instead, they got a guerrilla war. As Henry Kissinger wrote so cogently fifty years later about the US role in Vietnam (and which could be adapted to any guerrilla war),

> We fought a military war; our opponents fought a political one. We sought physical attrition; our opponents aimed for our psychological exhaustion. In the process, we lost sight of one of the cardinal maxims of guerrilla warfare: the guerrilla wins if he does not lose. The conventional army loses if it does not win.[95]

In Cork Tom Barry followed classic guerrilla tactics: fighting only when the odds looked particularly good, and focusing his efforts on keeping the column away from the enemy. His men travelled light and chose difficult terrain and weather, exhausting and wearing down the British. The British tried to fight a military war; the Irish fought a political one. To continue to exist meant the IRA were 'succeeding'—not winning, but succeeding. They were a threat to the British. Barry wrote:

> It was accepted in West Cork that the paramount objective of the Flying Columns, in the circumstances then prevailing, should not be to fight, but to continue to exist. The very existence of such a column of armed men, even if it never struck a blow, was a continuous challenge to the enemy and forced him to maintain large garrisons to meet the threatened onslaught on his military forces and for the security of his civil administration. Such a column moving around must seriously affect the morale of garrisons, for one day it would surely strike.[96]

In the final analysis, the Irish strategy and tactics did not beat the British militarily nor win the war, but they did prevent defeat. That, in itself, was a triumph.[97]

As the war began, many units outside Dublin wanted to begin operations on a much larger scale than was envisioned by GHQ. The Volunteers from Munster, in particular, were dangerously enthusiastic. They were spoiling to get into the fight and were apt to be reckless. For example, Cork Brigade Commandant Tomás MacCurtáin proposed a plan to Collins, who refused to sanction the project and referred him up the chain of command. Vice-Brigadier Terence MacSwiney met with Mulcahy early in November seeking approval to attack ten different constabulary barracks in one night. Michael Leahy, commander of the brigade's Fourth Battalion, later wrote that, owing to casual security measures in the rural outposts, the capture of most of the RIC barracks in the brigade area would involve little more than walking in and capturing all arms, supplies and records.[98] MacSwiney proposed the barrack assaults as a prelude to a general uprising of Volunteers in Cork City. Mulcahy later quoted him as saying that 'they could hope to last about a fortnight anyway before they would be wiped out, but the flag would have been raised and in six months time the same could be done in Galway'.[99]

The idea of Volunteer risings in urban areas was a departure from GHQ strategy, even at that early stage of the war. The Cork plans, and others in the south-west, indicated a willingness to incur heavy casualties. Moreover, implementing the idea of urban uprisings would ruin several of Ireland's largest cities and towns, and such human and material sacrifices were antithetical to GHQ plans. Florence O'Donoghue, intelligence officer in the First Cork Brigade, wrote that two essential keys to GHQ plans were 'the governing policy of not committing the whole force to the conflict at the start, and though severe damage was done to the economic life of the country ... no part of the country was completely devastated'.[100] Mulcahy offered a compromise by allowing the Cork Brigade officers to select and attack three barracks in one night.[101] Michael Leahy wrote that a further condition was to await the outcome of a particularly sensational attack that was in the works for Dublin, and it was January 1920 before the attacks could proceed.

During a November 1919 meeting, MacSwiney accused Mulcahy and GHQ officers of not understanding the mind-set in the rest of the country. Long years of drilling and arrests, as well as a feeling of having missed out during 1916, were frustrating country Volunteers.[102] Demoralisation was a serious threat to the IRA. Periods of inaction, mass arrests, a lack of arms, and constant accusations of cowardice and murder in the press took a toll on rank-and-file morale. Moreover, these incidents show that tension existed between GHQ and the most active republican units from the beginning of the war.

Collins has been called the 'founder of modern guerrilla warfare' but, as noted earlier, all guerrillas have followed in the footsteps of previous insurrectionists. Nevertheless, Collins did bring to the Irish war some guerrilla concepts adapted to a city, and for that he should be remembered. There were few deliberate large-scale attacks in the cities (the burning of the Custom House, addressed later, is the most notable example in Dublin), but there were so many small-scale attacks and ambushes that one area of Aungier Street was known as 'the Dardanelles'. Guerrilla warfare is difficult in cities, for both sides, and most IRA actions there were intelligence operations and arms-gathering, intimidation of civilians, patrolling, disruption of transportation and assassinations. In Dublin, Cork and Belfast most actions were single actions of chance or of design, with a small group sent out on an assassination mission. (While Dublin was the centre of police assassinations, Belfast was the more dangerous. There were more attacks there than in other cities, and this continued throughout the war.) Some have claimed that this is not 'war', but it was the reality on the streets of Dublin at the time.[103] As with British actions in the country, Irish assassinations and bombings in the cities served political and propaganda roles as well as military ones, and press reports in the British and international papers indicated just how dangerous the city streets were to the British.

The continued unfettered enthusiasm of the country units required GHQ to head off several attempts to escalate the conflict or even to redirect it from the emerging system of guerrilla war. The first such proposed action emanated from the Tipperary Volunteers, soon after the Soloheadbeg action. On 23 February officers of the Third Tipperary Brigade drafted a proclamation against the constabulary in their county. It stated that 'by the end of the month, any members of the Force remaining in the county will be deemed to have forfeited his life'. The document extended the threat to 'anyone paid by the British government, or whoever helps England to rule this country ... Civilians giving information to the Constabulary and doctors who assisted them were also threatened with execution.'[104] The brigade officers sent the draft to Dublin, where the Dáil and GHQ forbade its publication. Richard Mulcahy later wrote that 'such an initiative would disrupt the minds and lives of a whole people, undercutting the IRA's support'.[105] Rather than directing the entire war, GHQ often saw its role as that of preventing excesses of violence that might undermine support of the IRA.[106] (See Chapter 6 for a discussion of British and Irish use of terror.)

'Pace' continued to be of great importance throughout the war. Collins and GHQ knew that they were aiming not for a military victory but to bring the British to the bargaining table. They could not let any part of the war get ahead of the military/political/propaganda pace that they determined was the best way to accomplish that. It was necessary to control the factors that made that possible:

- The governing policy of not committing the whole force to the conflict at the start.
- The slow build-up of activity from 1919 to 1920 that allowed the Volunteers and the people to become acclimated gradually to the atmosphere of war.
- The fact that over a large part of the country the IRA retained the initiative.
- The IRA maintained high standards of morale and discipline.
- The fact that though severe damage was done to the economic life of the country through reprisals, destruction of creameries, factories and shops, no part of the country was completely devastated. There was no aerial bombing.[107]

GHQ increasingly imposed its control in Dublin and sanctioned larger and more frequent attacks in the country. At the same time, Collins and other GHQ leaders did not want to escalate the conflict out of control, so they kept a steady and constant pressure on the true target: British governance. Setting the 'pace' was always the key. By the end of 1919, in the final issue of that year, *An t-Óglách* editorialised:

> A year ago we compared the Irish Volunteers to any army in the
> trenches whose activities were confined to occasional trench raids
> and sniping. Since then the raids and sniping have greatly

increased in frequency; in fact a situation has been created which more resembles guerrilla warfare.[108]

The drift toward 'organised' guerrilla warfare depended on an extremely small segment of the Volunteers, most of whom were concentrated in the south-west.[109] The restraints imposed by GHQ had most of the Volunteers confined to activities regarding the Dáil Loan and Dáil Courts. Sporadic and unsanctioned attempts to procure arms led to more confrontations with the British, and when the Volunteers were identified they were forced to go on the run. Overall, the numbers of active Volunteers remained very small. It was only in January 1920 that attacks on the British forces were sanctioned by the Dáil.

Over the course of the war, rifts continued to develop between GHQ and the local commanders. In Cork, for example, Tom Barry (arguably the most successful column leader) and his immediate superiors believed that maintaining momentum against the British was of utmost importance, even though GHQ preferred the Cork IRA to manoeuvre on its timetable.[110] In the end, however, all concerned determined that the local commander knew best.[111]

By 1920 the RIC had abandoned or closed most of the smaller barracks and those that remained occupied were reinforced, making barracks attacks increasingly difficult by the summer of 1920. The change from barracks attacks to ambushing, causing many more casualties on both sides, made the conflict more vicious and hardened attitudes. Such a change in attitude on the part of the Irish became self-sustaining as the IRA became ever more active, and the ambushes became more frequent and more lethal for the British. Activity increased everywhere in 1920. Flying columns were a logical and realistic extension of the basic tenets of guerrilla war. Moreover, the components of the columns were already in existence:

- The men on the run had taken up full-time service.
- Usually they were the most experienced and active men in each unit.
- Invariably they were the men who had pioneered the earlier local activities.

By early 1920 there was a sufficient supply of rifles to arm small columns, and those on full-time service could better defend themselves in organised groups than as individuals. The basic organisation envisioned by GHQ had been brought to a state of efficiency that made it capable of undertaking the vital roles of providing intelligence, billeting and a pool of trained reserves to utilise the columns.[112] The essential purpose of the columns remained the same thereafter. The basic idea was capable of being adapted to a wide range of activities, from ambushes to barracks attacks, thus putting a premium on local initiative and enterprise. The Irish drew the British forces into terrain most advantageous to the Irish—choosing the battlefield on which the battle was to be fought—then retreating into hiding and shelter. (That was the intent of the Irish in their small attacks and assassinations in the cities as well.) The IRA's strength lay not in large, conventional military power but in speed, mobility and intelligence that made possible the columns' swift, concentrated blows at selected British objectives. The fundamental characteristic was mobility: in a few minutes the columns could move from a specific location, and in a few hours far from the region. Che Guevara wrote that 'the essential task of the guerrilla fighter is to keep himself from being destroyed'.[113] Another fundamental for the guerrilla is flexibility, the ability to adapt to all circumstances and to work in all areas of the region. Good intelligence breeds good morale for all guerrillas and is vital. The Irish utilised all facets of guerrilla warfare.

Although writing of another theatre of war, Lawrence could have been precisely defining the Irish columns and their use:

> Our tactics were always tip and run, not pushes, but strokes. We never tried to maintain or improve an advantage, but to move off and strike again somewhere else. We used the smallest force, in the quickest time, at the farthest place. If the action had continued till the enemy had changed his dispositions to resist it, we would have been breaking the spirit of our fundamental rule of denying him targets.[114]

The British reports after the war came to a different conclusion regarding the establishment and function of flying columns:

> In October 1920, so many of the Irish were 'on the run' that they

were grouped together to form 'flying columns'. ... This was an astute move on the part of Sinn Féin. It provided organisations to which all *rapparees* could go when they could not stay in their own areas with safety and in almost all areas it created a small force which stirred the sluggish Sinn Féiners into some sort of activity and ensured terror among the remainder.

...

Whatever it may have been called by the IRA, [they were] neither more nor less than a murder gang ...[115] [Emphasis in original]

Their reports also minimised the military effects of the Irish columns:

In the country by a system of military drives organised whenever any objective was reported and by strong [British] mobile columns, the IRA forces were continually hunted from place to place and were undoubtedly becoming tired and somewhat dispirited. These drives and their mobile columns [Irish] did not achieve any tangible or sensational results, beyond improving our knowledge of the country and training the troops and police to a new system of tactics that were quite new to them after their experience of the war in Europe.[116]

In June 1920, *An t-Óglách* provided not only a rationale for why the RIC were targeted by the IRA but also a generally accurate assessment of the state of the RIC at that time.[117] This assessment was an indication that the tactics of the IRA were working.

The English front line in Ireland, his chief instrument of executive power, was the R.I.C., an armed force of Irish mercenaries with elaborate local knowledge, situated in strongholds in every part of the country, even the wildest and remotest. The R.I.C. were his eyes and ears and his strong right arm in Ireland. A relatively small body of men as compared to the people of Ireland, they were able by their organisation and elaborate system of intelligence to dominate the unarmed citizens. ... To-day the first line of the enemy, the chief instrument of executive power has broken down and ceased to be effective. The R.I.C. have been driven from their outposts, nearly five hundred of their strongholds have been evacuated and destroyed, and they have been forced to concentrate only in certain strong centres, where, in some parts of the country, they are in the position of beleaguered garrisons. They are no longer effective for the purpose for which they were intended. ... Demoralisation has set in their ranks. ... There are lists of resignations from the force daily, and the effort of the enemy to fill up the gaps by English recruits [Black and Tans] is a confession of failure. The English recruits will not be effective for the purpose for which the R.I.C. were established. ... English soldiers have not the local knowledge of the Irish constables ... They are not likely to succeed where the R.I.C. failed.[118]

The British approach to the deteriorating situation in Ireland continued to be conducted in a haphazard manner which took little account of the prevailing political and social conditions. In general, an IRA action was followed by a British show of strength that only increased the popular feeling of British oppression. Even so, in August 1920 Hamar Greenwood complained to the House of Commons that the Irish were operating under advantageous conditions that were not available to the British. The columns, though recently started, were certainly having an effect.

[The Irish] are conducting warlike operations against us and we are not permitted to do so against him. He also enjoys the usual advantages of guerrilla warfare without suffering any of the penalties attached to it. We have to fight largely on the defensive, for we have no-one to take the offensive against. As far as we possibly can we take the offensive but our blows fall on empty air, and the enemy forces at once take up the role of innocent peasants whom we must not touch.[119]

Greenwood's rant in the Commons underscores the political restraints placed on the British military by both their politicians and the British public, and the frustration caused by such restraints.

There were two distinct types of action that developed during the war: the ambush in the country, and the revolver and bomb attack in the cities and towns.[120] These required different tactics and different arms. Shotguns, rifles, light machine-guns (Lewis guns) and land-mines (later in the war) were the main ambush weapons. Revolvers, pistols and hand-grenades were essential for street fighting. Columns in the country could occupy a position and wait for the British; on the streets, the IRA had to keep on the move, the only cover available to them being the ordinary street traffic. Though fighting in different venues and ways, each unit made it clear that there were no safe areas for the British. Because of the closeness of the IRA and the British, there often seemed to be more intense fighting in Dublin and Cork than in other parts of the country. Both in the cities and the country, hand-grenades were effective weapons against unarmoured vehicles. They were so effective that by the end of the war the British could use no vehicles unless covered with wire netting. This gave rise to the saying that 'The Boers put them in khaki, the Germans put them in helmets, and the Irish put them in wire cages'.[121]

As the war progressed, the British learned to spread out their columns so that, if the first lorry was ambushed, additional elements could move up from the rear as reinforcements. Although the IRA in their flying columns lacked experience, their discipline was good and they fought on familiar ground, as all guerrillas must do. They struck suddenly and without warning, and then disappeared just as suddenly, moving cross-country on foot to evade pursuit by the road-bound British. Dumping their arms in well-hidden caches, the Volunteers took refuge on farms and in 'dugouts', hide-outs literally dug into the ground. The Irish could depend on support from the local population, and some who were not actual combatants acted as spies, scouts and couriers, and brought food and medical supplies. By 1920 the Irish had perfected the art of guerrilla warfare on their home ground.

At that time the British instituted guerrilla warfare classes at the Curragh. (The 5th Division had its own guerrilla warfare school in County Cork, which all officers assigned to the Division were required to attend before reporting to their assignment.) The Curragh camp school issued a set of instructions to the British officers:

Orders

All Officers and NCOs require practice before commencing an operation.

Secrecy

The leakage of information in Ireland is very great and it may be generally assumed that no inhabitant or civilian employee is to be trusted.

Rebel Tactics

The tactics of the enemy are those of ambush. Ambushes are dependent for their success on surprise and fire effect at close range, and do not aim at further offensive action, the rebels having no stomach for fighting at close quarters or suffering heavy casualties.

Individuals cutting peat in a bog may not be as harmless as they appear.

Our Tactics

... the idea of taking the active offensive will be in the minds of all ranks.

Lorry patrols will always consist of at least two motor vehicles.

Reconnaissance

Much practice is required by Officers and NCOs in the making of reconnaissance of buildings, especially at night.

Bicycle patrol

Bicycle patrols have been found most useful—especially where quietness is required ...

Bicycles must be kept in good condition.

Cyclist patrols will not allow civilian bicycles or motor cycles or motors to pass for fear of information being given away on the approach of the patrol.

Lorry patrols

Lorries are particularly easy to ambush and the greatest vigilance is required.

Lorries should be disposed in depth ... There are officers who consider 300 yards to be the minimum.

... lorries should be in good working order before starting out.

The success of lorry raids is dependent on speed rather than secrecy. The Commandant should never be in the lead lorry.

Dress

All patrols will be as lightly equipped as possible.

Armoured lorries

... care must be observed in ascertaining the armour on lorries is bullet proof or only against long range pistol fire and slug.

Armoured cars

As soon as any portion of a column is attacked, the armoured car should move to the ambushers and pin them down.

Searches

Places to be searched

Pedestrians—man wearing a hat, under the hat.

In animal's ears, under the cow horn ...

Houses

Whenever a house is to be searched a receipt should be obtained from the inhabitants to the effect that no damage has been done and nothing taken away with the exception of the arms or documents seized.

General

... It must be remembered that the rebels are not highly disciplined troops and a threat to their line of retreat usually makes them bolt. In short the one essential condition for success in raids, searches and drives is *surprise* and every ruse by which surprise can be obtained must be studied and practised.[122]

It is not known how much day-to-day effect the Curragh classes had on the British officers, but it is clear that these comprehensive 'orders' brought much mirth to the Irish who captured them and learned that no damage was to be done on raids, that receipts were to be 'obtained from the residents', and that the British thought that they were 'not highly disciplined' and that a threat 'would make them bolt'.

The dramatic increase in British operations by the end of 1920 changed conditions nationwide. The fighting increased so much that by early 1921 the positions of most columns throughout the country were untenable. The greater numbers of British forces, the increased use of effective counter-insurgency tactics, the use of reconnaissance aircraft, better knowledge of guerrilla warfare as more British officers underwent training, combined with the lengthening days of spring and summer, all made the columns' existence increasingly dangerous and Irish successes more unlikely. The war was not going well for the Irish with the increased British pressure into mid-1921; there were more casualties, more men were captured and there was difficulty in finding replacements.

The Dublin units felt increasing pressure as well. Up to then the use of violence had been confined to an extremely small group of Volunteers, who only engaged with those pursuing them. (Collins's 'Squad' was mostly employed in targeted assassinations and usually did not engage the British in any other operations.) At the end of 1920 there were many more indiscriminate attacks on British forces throughout the city, resulting in more random searches by the British military and Auxiliaries, which again increased substantially the number of men who were arrested. The growing availability of arms contributed to this, but the inevitable losses made the continuing acquisition of even more weapons and ammunition vital.

Although there was a disparity of forces throughout the country during most of the war there was no shortage of Volunteers for action, but there was a persistent and perilous arms problem. (This is always a problem for guerrilla armies.) As in most guerrilla wars, the primary purpose of the Irish ambush was to acquire weapons. Che Guevara stated the principle that 'all attacks should recover the same amount of ammunition as that expended'. When the war started in 1919, Britain became a vital source of arms for the IRA. Two things are needed for any guerrilla war— arms and money—and Michael Collins took the lead in providing both. He did business with gunsmiths in London, German arms dealers, British members of the IRA who worked at collieries in Scotland, criminal gangs in the British midlands—in effect, anyone who would take the Irish money. Liverpool Volunteer Paddy Daly recalled that 'we found the Englishman always willing to do business'.[123]

The British command at the Curragh camp required that all lorries on patrol carry a 'box of 1000 rounds of .303 ammunition' to supplement that carried by each soldier. (The .303 ammunition was used in British rifles as well as in Lewis and Maxim machine-guns, and was the most prevalent ammunition size used by weapons in the war on both sides.) Taking a lorry's spare ammunition was a prime motive for all Irish ambushes. In fact, at the end of the war in July 1921, it was apparent that the Irish didn't run out of weapons but they were running out of ammunition.

It was primarily for arms that the Irish looked outside the country for sources and assistance. When Collins conceived the Dáil Loan, it was to be used to fund the Dáil's administrative activities. On 19 June 1919 the Dáil launched the National Loan prospectus, which it was hoped would raise £250,000. This money would enable the Dáil to function. The bonds were to be issued in denominations of £1, £5, £10, £20, £50 and £100, and the general population were invited to subscribe. The purpose of this range of certificates was to enable individuals on small incomes to subscribe. Each certificate would qualify for a five per cent rate of interest paid half-yearly. The appeal for subscriptions was published 'in national newspapers'. The National Loan was marketed as the means by which the general population could contribute to and have control of the future of Ireland. From the outset, its purpose was to finance the operation of the government, not to finance the war effort or arms purchases. An unpublicised exception was for the purchase of Thompson machine-guns from the US.

While a dribble of small arms continued to be smuggled in from England and Scotland, there was no importation of arms of any quantity during the war with the exception of one small lot of Thompson machine-guns from the US in 1920. As in all successful guerrilla wars, the IRA not only adapted their tactics to give them the greatest advantage but also sought out the latest technological weapons of which they could avail themselves. The Irish were the first to use the new Thompson guns that would change the guerrilla wars that followed, but they did not just purchase the guns as they became available; the remnants of Clan na Gael in the US were the ones to whom General John T. Thompson turned for major investment. Thompson's partner was Thomas Fortune Ryan, an American entrepreneur with close ties to the Clan. Upon the gun's development and availability for sale in late 1920, Ryan placed an order for 100 of the weapons, but funds were lacking. Then Harry Boland took over the financial end and began channelling Dáil funds for the purchase.[124] Only the first few weapons of the initial consignment made it to Ireland, with two former US Army officers, Major James J. Dineen and Captain Patrick Cronin, as instructors.

The Thompson guns were introduced in November or December 1920. The first introduction of these guns followed the arrival of two ex-officers of the American Army, one was Major Dineen and the other, whose rank I forget, was named Cronin. These two men were made available to the Brigade for the purpose of giving lectures and instructions in the use of the Thompson sub-machine guns. The lectures, which were given to selected men of the Dublin Brigade, consisted in the main of taking the gun asunder, becoming acquainted with the separate parts and securing a knowledge of the names of these parts, the clearance of stoppages, as well as the causes of these stoppages. In the early stages it was not possible to give practical demonstrations of the shooting powers of these weapons, but the handling of the guns, together with the methods of sighting, made the men reasonably proficient.[125]

The first few Thompson guns arrived in late autumn 1920, and to try them out Collins and others went to the Marino Casino in Clontarf, where there was a disused, wide, dry tunnel leading to Charlemont House. The interconnecting chambers and tunnels run underneath the grounds surrounding the Casino. On 24 May 1921 Collins, Boland, Gearóid O'Sullivan and Tom Barry[126] fired and practised with the Thompson guns that Clan na Gael had purchased in America.[127] The tunnels are only a few feet below the ground, however, and the neighbouring local Christian Brothers alerted the rebels that the supposedly secret target practice could be heard all over Marino and further afield. Nearby was an orphanage run by the Christian Brothers, who allowed Collins's men to use the grounds for drilling, but the Brothers warned Collins that any further firing of the guns would attract attention. After this demonstration, Collins enthusiastically ordered another 500 of the machine-guns, but the ship *East Side* carrying them was raided in New York harbour. The guns and a sizeable amount of money were lost.

The Thompsons were first used in combat on 16 June 1921, when the IRA ambushed a trainload of soldiers from the West Kent Regiment in Drumcondra, wounding three of them. In its rather typical hyperbole, *An t-Óglách* heralded their use and called them 'our latest ally'. The paper told the Volunteers that 'with such a superb weapon available to us it is up to the individual soldier to lose no opportunity of learning all he can about the construction, use and care of it'.[128] The guns were used in several Dublin ambushes and had a psychological effect on both the Irish and the British, but there were too few of them, and too late, to materially affect the war.[129]

On 13–14 December 1920 a meeting of GHQ was held in Barry's Hotel on Great Denmark Street to finalise plans to import arms from Italy. Donal Hales, whose brothers Seán and Tom were both in the IRA, lived in Genoa and was the contact trying to buy the weapons. Cathal Brugha, Collins, Liam Mellows, Joe Vize, Liam Deasy and O'Donoghue attended. Michael Leahy, second-in-command of Cork No. 1 Brigade, and Seán O'Shea left Dublin for Italy on 2 January 1921.[130] Arms were to be distributed throughout the south-western counties of Kerry, Cork, Limerick and Tipperary. Leahy and O'Shea soon returned to Dublin, however, after the project failed.

> About three or four months before the Truce a messenger came from Ireland to Italy for arms. We were requested by an Italian General to accompany him down to Rome to the military department. The man who came over first was a Mr O'Shea, I think. O'Shea had gone over to France to buy arms, being commissioned to do so by Collins. He failed to get them there. He was merely a messenger. I think he lives in Dublin but I do not know his Christian name. He was sent by Michael Collins to get in touch with me for the acquisition of arms in Italy. ... Another man was also sent out from Cork called Leahy. They both came for arms ...
>
> ...
>
> I approached the Italian General who accompanied me to Rome for the arms. At that time contact would not be difficult. In fact, through the good offices of the general we found we had no difficulty in getting the guns. We could get as many rifles as we wished—up to 100,000. These rifles were Italian rifles which had been used in the previous war; they were in good condition and only required cleaning. We could also get ammunition. There was some talk as to what ammunition would fit these rifles.

Things were in such a position in Ireland that we could not get quickly in touch with it.

O'Shea had returned to Ireland to report to Collins regarding the position and I did not hear anything further about sending the arms.

Just on his return to Dublin many raids and burnings, effected by the Black and Tans, took place in the city which may have been the reason I could not have any news from him or from Michael Collins for some time after. I believe the truce came on shortly after this. These rifles were not removed. However, the British Consul-General must have been told by someone that I had hidden these arms in Genoa. He was informed probably by his Intelligence officer, that the guns were in Genoa awaiting shipment. That was not true because they were in Rome. They were not paid for and were never called for. My sister spoke to Collins then who said the money would present no difficulty at all. He mentioned the sum of £100,000 which she thought would be sent immediately. No money was sent and they were never removed.

My opinion is that the arrangements to procure the arms may have been to bluff England. If the Irish were fully armed they could hold out longer and kill most of the British soldiers here. The idea of getting the arms, I believe, would be to influence England to come to terms with Ireland. Collins may also have had the idea of trying to get in Ulster. Ulster would come in if there was a final settlement. There would have been some difficulty in shipping these arms to Ireland, now the British got the knowledge of them.[131]

Collins continued to seek arms from abroad as the war progressed, and large quantities were *en route* from Hamburg but had not arrived at the time of the Truce.[132] Robert Briscoe, later lord mayor of Dublin, was a major gunrunner for the IRA, and purchased boats in Germany to run the guns to Ireland. Charles (Charlie) McGuinness was the captain of these vessels, and it was actually after the Truce that the largest single shipments were imported from Germany. In November 1921 McGuinness piloted the *Frieda* with a load of weapons from Germany; she was originally scheduled to land at Ballinagoul, Co. Waterford, but was forced by fog to offload at Cheekpoint on the Suir River. Her cargo consisted of rifles, Luger pistols and 1,700,000 rounds of ammunition. He also piloted the *Hanna* to Ballinagoul on 2 April 1922 to deliver another load of weapons, including machine-guns, which were picked up and used by the anti-Treaty forces of the IRA.[133]

In addition to the widespread use of machine-guns, the Irish War of Independence was the first guerrilla war in which there was a significant counter-insurgency use of mechanised and armoured vehicles.[134] The Irish had to develop tactics, techniques and procedures to disrupt and disable the more mobile British forces.[135] To limit their mobility in the country, roads were trenched and bridges were demolished. It is important to note that many of the British vehicles had wheels with wooden spokes, and a blow to the wheel in a road trench was most likely to completely disable the vehicle. Such deep trenching could not be undertaken extensively because it would cripple the economic life of the country. The selective use of road-cutting and bridge demolition forced the British onto fewer routes, forced them to carry repair materials and slowed their movements through constant fear of encountering fresh obstacles or an ambush while in the process of repair.

It is notable that modern insurgencies have gone through the very same stages in terms of tactics as the IRA did from 1920 to 1921—from massed assaults on barracks to ambushes with small arms, and finally more sophisticated ambushes using what are now known as Improvised Explosive Devices (IEDs). The remotely detonated IED, in modern terminology, combines the advantage of relatively low risk for the guerrillas with the potential for causing mass casualties among troops or police even in armoured vehicles. The British started out using high driving speeds to avoid an ambush. In response, the Irish would dig a shallow trench in the roads to disable the British lorries. As guerrilla wars are always evolving, the Irish found that their simple answer was soon unsuccessful, so by autumn 1920 their ambush tactics began to change. To counter the use of armour, the IRA began to rely on interdicting the roads particularly by the use of IEDs.

While the IED is sometimes described as a new technology, it actually has a lengthy history, but the use of such weapons in the past was fairly limited and certainly without strategic consequences. The very name 'improvised' was originally meant pejoratively: an IED was used 'when you couldn't get something better', not something to be widely emulated. Ships loaded with explosives were used as far back as the 1500s, while various jury-rigged bombs and mines were used in the American Civil War, such as at the naval battle of Mobile Bay and the land battle of Petersburg. Captain Gabriel Rains became infamous for 'booby-trapping' dead Seminole Native Americans with explosives—when the bodies were collected after the battle they would explode, killing more Native Americans—and used similar tactics as a Confederate general in the Civil War.[136] Further, the Irish were not the first to use explosives in ambushes; the first recorded roadside assassination effort by explosives was an attempt on Napoleon in 1803. Irish revolutionaries used explosive devices in the mid-nineteenth century, as did the Fenians in the latter part of the century, but mostly in attacks on barracks and other buildings, not in ambushes.[137] The Volunteers/IRA were really the first to manufacture explosives, casings, springs and all the other necessary bomb components from raw materials, and to use them as tactics changed with the advent of armoured vehicles.

An IED is a bomb fabricated in an improvised manner incorporating destructive chemicals and designed to destroy or incapacitate personnel or vehicles. In some cases IEDs are used to distract, disrupt or delay an opposing force, facilitating a follow-up type of attack. Irish IEDs incorporated military or commercially sourced explosives, and often combined both types, and they were otherwise made with home-made explosives. Any IED designed for use against armoured targets such as armoured cars or lorries will be designed for armour penetration. The Irish IEDs were extremely diverse in design and contained many types of initiators, detonators, penetrators and explosive loads, and their effectiveness varied greatly because they were not uniformly manufactured. At the outset of their use, the IRA 'mine' was usually made of civilian explosives such as gelignite, placed in a petrol tin or milk churn and detonated using an electrical charge via a cable.

The IRA IEDs came from three sources:

- stolen from civilian companies, particularly Scottish quarries and mines;
- stolen from the British military;

- manufactured in Irish munitions factories.

At the beginning of the war the most common explosive used was gelignite (a nitric-based explosive) stolen from quarries, along with detonators customarily used in collieries. Gelignite, however, was susceptible to freezing and could not be left in the ground for long periods in cold weather, and as a commercial explosive was simply not powerful enough unless used in very large quantities. The supply was insufficient and became more difficult to obtain, so the Irish turned to chemists and others with military experience from World War I to develop home-made explosives.

Irish units throughout the country tried making explosives, and many were *ad hoc* combinations made by a Volunteer with little or no experience in explosive or bomb manufacture. Joe Good worked as an electrician at the Phoenix Park Works on Dublin's Parkgate Street, and in 1918 the British used part of the building as a shell works. In his work he learned a little bit about the construction of explosive devices, and was asked to pass that on to his fellow Volunteers. Good described his knowledge as dangerous:

> Richard Walsh of Balls, Co. Mayo, brought many of his officers to the house where I lived. I instructed them in the elementary use of explosives. My knowledge was very elementary. I used and demonstrated only with batteries, that is, accumulators. I had not the necessary technical knowledge to make exploders, and I believe at that period we lacked technical knowledge from those who were competent to give instructions. In retrospect I dread to think of the possible consequences of my ignorance.[138]

Some of the stories are almost unbelievable and had tragic consequences.

> On one occasion while grenades were being made, we received a quantity of gelignite to be used in their manufacture from the 3rd Battalion area [Castlecomer, Co. Kilkenny]. This particular lot had been taken from the coal mines near Castlecomer and was frozen when we got it. To thaw it out Joe [McMahon] put it into the stove of a gas oven in [Peter] De Loughry's workshop and lit the gas on full. Missing the gelignite, I asked him where

he had put it and when he told me, I went to the stove and I was shaking as I turned the gas off. Poor Joe! He was subsequently killed when giving a demonstration of those same grenades in Cavan.[139]

The need for 'experts' to make explosive devices was apparent.

James (Séamus) O'Donovan was the primary 'chemist/inventor' of explosives for the IRA, and the person most responsible for developing and establishing Irish-centred explosive manufacturing. A postgraduate chemistry student at UCD, he worked directly for Collins.[140] In 1918 he began producing explosives from fulminate of mercury, a notoriously unstable compound. In 1919 Collins directed him to develop an explosive that was more powerful but that 'men with no technical skill could produce it in a farmhouse kitchen … They have to be fairly foolproof because we can't have people all over the country having their heads blown off!' *Irish War Flour* was O'Donovan's first original explosive, named after its appearance; a nitrated resin using the ingredients of resin, flour, acid and potassium chlorate, it was quite unstable and didn't have the explosive power he wanted, so he kept experimenting. His second explosive compound, nicknamed *Irish Cheddar*, again because of its looks, was a form of cheddite, an explosive used quite extensively in the early twentieth century. Its ingredients were paraffin, potassium chlorate, nitrobenzene and castor oil.

The first use of a road-mine in the war occurred at Annascaul on 18 August 1920.[141] The IRA detonated a small charge in the roadway, a lorry was upset, the British surrendered and the Irish took their weapons. The attack utilised a very small mine, the first to be used against a vehicle, but an IED was not the norm in ambushes at that time. In autumn 1920 and thereafter there was an increase in IRA anti-road and anti-bridge attacks, and they also began to use IEDs in ambushes with regularity. In the British War Diaries there were reports of 172 ambushes from then until the Truce in July 1921, and 109 of them involved explosive devices of some sort. The British records of their use are the most accurate, and they indicate that of the 109 attempts there were about 23 instances in which the bombs did not cause much damage.

British tactics taught at the Curragh directed that 'Lorries should be so disposed in depth that it becomes difficult for the ambushers, without employing a large force, to ambush the whole column'. The IRA quickly learned the trick of laying multiple roadside IEDs at the same spacing as the British vehicles in a convoy, which usually travelled 300 yards apart. From their first use, the British regarded improvised explosive devices as a weapon of shame, atrocity and cowardice. Today's IEDs have the same reputation as their early ancestors and are used in precisely the same way as the Irish used them in wars from Iraq to Afghanistan.

Having the explosives was not enough; proper placement of IEDs was difficult for the inexperienced Irish—they had little enough training in how to conduct ambushes and placement of men, much less in how to use explosives in these attacks. As the war progressed, they found that their IEDs were best initiated not by pressure/contact detonators but by electrical detonators attached to hidden wires buried in the road and exploded just when they were crossed by a lorry or armoured car.

The first major IRA ambush that used what we would now recognise as an IED with sufficient explosive power to bring the fight to a quick end took place on 2 February 1921 at Clonfin, Co. Longford.[142] Under the command of Seán MacEoin, the IRA attacked two lorries of Auxiliaries, disabled one, killed four (including the O/C Lieutenant Commander Francis Craven) and wounded nine. After a short fire fight the Auxiliaries surrendered; the Irish recovered twenty rifles and over 1,200 rounds of .303 ammunition. Towards the end of the war the IRA showed increasing proficiency with explosives, in part because they were so short of infantry weapons. Although on many occasions they failed to explode, 'mines' could be devastating when they did. In May 1921 a remotely detonated bomb at Youghal, Co. Cork, killed seven military bandsmen and wounded 21. By the end of the war the 'mine' was one of the IRA's most utilised weapons.

O'Donovan also developed what he called

[p]articular compositions made up for certain jobs; one of these that I remember was quantities of a solution of Phosphorus in Carbon bi-Sulfide. This was packed in small bottles of grenade size and was used in the attack on the L.N.S premises [London North Western Railway Hotel] on the North Wall, at that time an enemy outpost.[143]

The hotel was used as a barracks by 'Q' Company of the Auxiliaries and was attacked on 11 April 1921. This was one of the first uses of grenade-sized, throwable chemical weapons.

By the time of the Truce in July 1921 the IRA had eleven foundries making bomb components. Collins also had his engineers working on armour-piercing ammunition, because his sources could not buy them at any price; however, the Irish were never able to manufacture their own. (It is of note that the IRA's use of explosives did not stop with the end of the War of Independence. During the Civil War, on 18 August 1922, a fuel delivery lorry was packed with explosives and exploded in Dundalk by the anti-Treaty IRA in order to stop the Free State army who were marching on Dundalk barracks, which had been taken over by anti-Treaty forces under Frank Aiken on 14 August.) Although Collins wanted to utilise IEDs as much as possible, he knew that their primitive explosives were unreliable and that the Irish were inexperienced in their use. As a result, there were few ambushes in which the IEDs were crucial, rather than ancillary, to the attack itself.

Guerrilla wars that followed have consistently utilised IEDs; while the technology has changed drastically, their strategic and tactical use remains vital to guerrillas. Che Guevara wrote:

> One of the weakest points of the enemy is transportation by road and railroad. It is virtually impossible to maintain a vigil yard by yard over a transport line, a road, or a railroad. At any point a considerable amount of explosive charge can be planted that will make the road impassable; or by exploding it at the moment that a vehicle passes, a considerable loss in lives and materiel to the enemy is caused at the same time that the road is cut.
>
> ...
>
> The technique of lying in ambush along roads in order to explode mines and annihilate survivors is one of the most remunerative in point of ammunition and arms. The surprised enemy does not use his ammunition and has no time to flee, so with a small expenditure of ammunition large results are achieved.[144]

Since the Irish war, IEDs have radically altered counter-insurgency actions. They have forced patrols to move down the centre-line of roadways, disrupting traffic and alienating the population. Further, they usually cause civilian casualties, making locals wary of patrols and frightened to be near them. Far from finding such 'presence patrols' reassuring, the public finds them threatening and a source of danger.[145] Thus the intelligence value of patrols is reduced, along with their ability to disrupt insurgents. As a result of the use of IEDs by the Irish, and adaptations by the guerrillas who followed, classic patrol tactics have required substantial modification.

As regards its influence on future guerrilla actions, in addition to tactical innovations in the field the Irish War of Independence also introduced the Thompson machine-gun, the IED and the car bomb to the catalogue of guerrilla weapons.

Following the war, A.E. Percival, who served as an intelligence officer in Cork and was one of the most hated British officers, wrote:

The rebel campaign in Ireland was a national movement backed by a large proportion of the population and was not conducted by a few hired assassins as was often supposed.[146]

An t-Óglách editorialised thus:

The Volunteers of Ireland have made history both from a political and military point of view. They have brought the practice of guerrilla warfare from a casual thing to a science, and in that science have exercised a trained and disciplined skill which has revealed unsuspected possibilities to the student of the science of war.[147]

By spring 1921 the IRA had become a force in Dublin and its flying columns had become feared throughout the counties of Cork, Kerry and Clare. The columns were still mobile units of from ten to a hundred men, who could strike in devastating ambushes and then melt into a hinterland that they knew far better than the British military units who were deployed to fight them. Most IRA units, however, were chronically short of both weapons and ammunition.

> At this particular time things were so bad with all the units that
> it was a question of how long they could last, would we last a
> month, a fortnight? The only reason was we had little left to fight
> with. We had no ammunition; we had a few guns. So bad was it
> that they cut down Winchester ammunition to fit .45 and several
> members of the A.S.U. and other units met with serious accidents
> as a result.[148]

Earlier in the war, Collins had said that 'without guns you might as well be
dead'. Now the emphasis was on a lack of ammunition. By spring 1921,
though a formidable opponent, the IRA had not been able to dislodge the
British forces, and it became clear to Collins that the Irish could not defeat
those forces in the field.

The IRA's guerrilla war was a curious compound of the admirable
and the unpleasant—the chivalrous soldier and the cruel killer, the selfless
patriot and the swaggering jack-in-office, the devout Catholic and the self-
conscious martyr.[149] In the end, its campaign overcame all practical failings.
As O'Malley remarked, the folk imagination could give the smallest action
a 'heroic and epical' quality, and the saga concealed many acts of cold-
blooded violence, cowardice and betrayal.[150] The IRA was heir to a tradition
of agrarian terrorism, a succession of secret societies to which it remained
akin, and its elemental quality of political change was one of its main sources
of strength.[151]

On 11 July 1921 the Truce was agreed. It was a product of exhaustion
and did not signify a military victory for either side. Nevertheless, the IRA
had achieved a great deal in forcing the British government to meet the
representatives of the republican movement in formal peace talks, although
the decision of the republican leadership to negotiate inevitably meant that
the demand for an Irish Republic would be compromised. The Truce, and
the follow-on Anglo-Irish Treaty of December 1921, had to be based on
the extant facts and circumstances of the situation—*realpolitik*. Many Irish
commanders felt that since the British 'agreed to' a Truce, they had been
fairly beaten. They thought the treaty negotiations to follow would be those
of a victorious Irish and a supplicant British delegation. However much the
British commanders and politicians dismissed the Truce, or however some
of the Irish viewed their position as victors, that cannot negate the essential

truth of the situation. Regardless of what the positions on the battlefield were thought to be by either side, the fact was that the IRA fought the conflict until British politicians were ready to negotiate with them.

It is dangerous to mix ideology and operations. It clouds one's thinking and makes one see only what one wants to see. So often we see that people make their decisions based on what the facts mean to them, not on the facts themselves. The fact that many IRA volunteers were unaware of the limitations of what could be achieved through physical force and political pressure would become an intractable problem after the Truce.

Notes

[1] Andrew Mack, 'Why big nations lose small wars: the politics of asymmetric conflict', *World Politics* (January 1975).

[2] Colin S. Gray, 'The Anglo-Irish War 1919–1921: lessons from an irregular conflict', *Comparative Strategy*, vol. 26, issue 5 (8 January 2008).

[3] Florence O'Donoghue, 'Guerilla warfare in Ireland', *An Cosantóir*, vol. 23 (1963).

[4] Peadar Kearney, 'Reminiscences of Easter Week', TCD MS 3560.

[5] Thomas M. Leonard (ed.), *Encyclopedia of the Developing World* (1989), p. 728.

[6] Western Political Science Association, *The Western Political Quarterly*, vol. 15 (1962), p. 180: 'We might note that the first guerrilla war had been carried on in 360 BC in China, when Emperor Huang was fighting the Miao race under Tsi Ya'.

[7] Walter Laqueur, *Guerrilla Warfare: A Historical and Critical Study* (London, 1977), p. 7.

[8] See I.W.F. Becket, *Modern Insurgencies and Counter-insurgencies: Guerrillas and their Opponents since 1750* (London/New York, 2001).

[9] See Christiaan Rudolf de Wet, *Three Years' War* (New York, 1902), and Arthur Conan Doyle, *The Great Boer War* (New York, 1902).

[10] C.E. Callwell, *Small Wars: Their Principals and Practice* (London, 1903), p. 1.

[11] T.E. Lawrence, *Seven Pillars of Wisdom* (1926), p. 104.

[12] T.E. Lawrence, *The Evolution of a Revolt* (1920), p. 20.

[13] Che Guevara, *Principles of Guerrilla Warfare* (New York, 1961), p. 15.

[14] Mao Zedong, *On Guerrilla Warfare* (Westport, CT, 1961), pp 56–8, 75.

[15] Charles Townshend, 'The Irish Republican Army and the development of guerrilla warfare, 1919–1921', *English Historical Review*, vol. 94 (1979). See Võ Nguyên Giáp, *People's War, People's Army: The Military Art of People's War* (New York, 1971).

[16] See Samuel Huntington, *Modern Guerrilla Warfare* (New York), 1962).

[17] R. Johnson, M. Whitby and J. France (eds), *How to Win on the Battlefield* (London, 2010), p. xxvii.

[18] O'Donoghue, 'Guerilla warfare in Ireland'.

[19] There was also a feeling in the country that GHQ was out of touch with the local leaders and columns. Throughout the war few GHQ officers, except trainers, visited the local commands. The country brigades felt that decisions were being made without any consultation or regard for their input. This feeling was especially prevalent in Munster.

[20] Ronan McGreevy, 'What really happened at Soloheadbeg?', *The Irish Times*, 17 January

2019. Robinson's daughter, Dimphne Brennan, contends that 'it was accidental and should never have happened. There was never any intention of killing them.' Robinson was from Glasgow and after the Rising he was sent to Tipperary 'to organise a group of men who were enthusiastic but not experienced in the ways of warfare. They were misbehaving and not doing things properly. He was to go down and try to put some discipline on them so he was unpopular from the start.'

21 T. Ryle Dwyer, 'A momentous day as Dáil meets and first shots of War of Independence occur', *The Irish Examiner*, 20 January 2019.

22 *The Irish Times*, 22 January 1919.

23 Kevin Haddock Flynn, 'Soloheadbeg: what really happened', *History Ireland*, vol. 5, no. 2 (1997).

24 Richard Mulcahy, Béaslaí Notes, vol. I, p. 89.

25 Dan Breen, *My Fight for Irish Freedom* (Dublin, 1964), pp 7–35.

26 Peter Hart, *Mick: The Real Michael Collins* (London, 2006), p. 215. See Mark Coalter, *Rebel With a Cause: Dan Breen and the IRA* (Cork, 2006).

27 Breen, *My Fight for Irish Freedom*, p. 30.

28 Florence O'Donoghue, 'Volunteer "actions" in 1918', *Capuchin Annual*, vol. 35 (1968).

29 Some historians have argued that it is a mistake to view the Soloheadbeg ambush in January 1919 as the starting point of the conflict. The first IRA Volunteer whose death is attributed to the war was Daniel Joseph McGandy from Derry city, who was killed on 20 January 1919, a day before the Soloheadbeg ambush. He was found drowned in the River Foyle. His father claimed that he had been attacked by Crown forces, who had drugged him and thrown him into the river. Many historians, however, claim that later stages represent a more realistic beginning. See, for example, Joost Augusteijn, 'Review of M. Hopkinson: *War of Independence*', *American Historical Review*, vol. 108, no. 4 (2003). See also Peter Hart, *The IRA at War, 1916–1923* (Oxford, 2003), pp 201–2; John Dorney, 'Did the ambush at Soloheadbeg start the War of Independence?', http://www.theirishstory.com/2019/01/21/opinion-did-the-ambush-at-soloheadbeg-begin-the-irish-war-of-independence/#.XEyCQFVKjcs.

30 Breen, *My Fight for Irish Freedom*, p. 30.

31 *Ibid.*, p. 31.

32 *The Times*, 22 January 1919; *New York Times*, 23 January 1919.

33 *The Times*, 28 January 1919.

34 *An t-Óglách*, 31 January 1919.

35 Fintan O'Toole, 'The first shots of the "Tan War" in 1919', *The Irish Times*, 16 January 2019.

36 Richard Mulcahy, Béaslaí Notes, vol. I, p. 89.

37 Fr Séamus Murphy, 'War of Independence seen as Catholic war on Protestants', *The Irish Times*, 15 January 2019.

38 Hart, *Mick*, p. 218.

39 John T. Broom, 'The Anglo-Irish War of 1919–1921, "Britain's Troubles—Ireland's Opportunities"', final draft, published in *That Fatal Knot: Compound Warfare* (Fort Leavenworth, Kansas: US Army Command and General Staff College Press, 2002).

40 Éamon Broy, Witness Statement 1280.

41 Risteard Mulcahy, 'The development of the Irish Volunteers, 1916–1922', *An Cosantóir*, vol. 40 (Part 2: March 1980).

42 Townshend, 'The Irish Republican Army and the development of guerrilla warfare,

1916–1921'.

43 David Fitzpatrick, *Politics and Irish Life, 1913–1921: Provincial Experience of War and Revolution* (Dublin, 1977), p. 93.

44 *Ibid.*, pp 206, 208.

45 Mulcahy, 'The development of the Irish Volunteers' (Part 2).

46 Risteard Mulcahy, *My Father the General: Richard Mulcahy and the Military History of the Revolution* (Dublin, 2009), p. 61.

47 Townshend, 'The Irish Republican Army and the development of guerrilla warfare'. Townshend comments that 'O'Malley never seems to have fully integrated into his area'.

48 O'Malley to Capt. G. Plunkett, 5 December 1919. O'Malley papers, UCD Archive.

49 See Richard English, *Ernie O'Malley, IRA Intellectual* (Oxford, 1998).

50 Florence O'Donoghue, *No Other Law* (Dublin, 1954; 1986), p. 70.

51 Mao Zedong, *Guerrilla Warfare*, p. 54.

52 Townshend, 'The Irish Republican Army and the development of guerrilla warfare'.

53 *Ibid.*

54 *An t-Óglách*, August 1920.

55 Mulcahy, 'The development of the Irish Volunteers' (Part 2).

56 Michael Brennan, *The War in Clare, 1911–1921: Personal Memoirs of the Irish War of Independence* (Dublin, 1980), pp 38, 41, 103.

57 Annie Ryan, *Comrades: Inside the War of Independence* (Dublin, 2006), p. 122.

58 Fitzpatrick, *Politics and Irish Life*, p. 124.

59 Martin Walton, quoted in Kenneth Griffith and Timothy O'Grady, *Ireland's Unfinished Revolution: An Oral History* (Boulder, CO, 2002), p. 187.

60 O'Donoghue, 'Guerrilla warfare in Ireland'.

61 John Ainsworth, 'The Black & Tans and Auxiliaries in Ireland, 1920–1921: their origins, roles and legacy', paper presented to the Queensland History Teachers' Association, Brisbane, Queensland, 12 May 2001.

62 O'Donoghue, 'Guerilla warfare in Ireland'.

63 Paul O'Brien, 'Masters of chaos: British Special Forces during the Irish War of Independence', *An Cosantóir* (March 2019).

64 D. Leeson, 'Imperial stormtroopers: British paramilitaries in the Irish War of Independence, 1920–1921', unpublished Ph.D thesis, McMaster University (2003).

65 *Cabinet Weekly Survey of the State of Ireland Memorandum*, 29 July 1921, PRO CAB 24/126/72.

66 Thomas R. Mockaitis, *British Counterinsurgency, 1919–1960* (London, 1990), pp 9–11; G. Dangerfield, *The Damnable Question: A Study in Anglo-Irish Relations* (Boston, 1976), p. 323.

67 M.R. Fierro, 'British counterinsurgency operations in Ireland 1916–1921: a case study', unpublished MA dissertation, US Naval War College (Newport, RI, 1997).

68 Martin Petter, '"Temporary gentlemen" in the aftermath of the Great War: rank, status and the ex-officer problem', *The Historical Journal*, vol. 37, no. 1 (March, 1994).

69 Such operations are now classified by the world's military as 'Military Operations Other than War' (MOOTW). See Fierro, 'British counterinsurgency operations in Ireland 1916–1921'.

70 J.E.B. Hittle, *Michael Collins and the Anglo-Irish War: Britain's Counter-insurgency Failure* (Chicago, 2011), pp 115–16.

71   Griffith and O'Grady, *Ireland's Unfinished Revolution*, p. 154.
72   Richard Bennett, *The Black and Tans* (London, 1964; 2001), pp 95–6; Francis M. Carroll (ed.), *The American Commission on Irish Independence 1919. The Diary, Correspondence and Report* (Dublin, 1985), pp 162–5.
73   Mark Sturgis (ed. Michael Hopkinson), *The Last Days of Dublin Castle: The Mark Sturgis Diaries* (Dublin, 1999), p. 176.
74   *An t-Óglách*, 15 May 1920.
75   Donal O'Hannigan, 'The origin of the IRA flying column', *An Cosantóir*, vol. 6, no. 12 (1946).
76   *Ibid.*; Major-General Donnocha Ó Hannigan, 'The flying column originated in east Limerick', in The Kerryman, *Limerick's Fighting Story, 1916–1921* (Tralee, 1948).
77   W.J. Lowe, 'Who were the Black and Tans?', *History Ireland*, vol. 12, no. 3 (2004).
78   Michael Brennan claimed that the columns were 'a purely spontaneous development which arose from prevailing conditions'. David Fitzpatrick (*Politics and Irish Life*, pp 329–32) argues that the paramount reason was for self-preservation.
79   Breen, *My Fight for Irish Freedom*, p. 127.
80   Joe Good (ed. Maurice Good), *Enchanted by Dreams: The Journal of a Revolutionary* (Dingle 1946; 1996), p. 160; General Nevil Macready, *Annals of an Active Life* (2 vols), vol. I (London, 1925; 1942), p. 207.
81   Joost Augusteijn, *From Public Defiance to Guerrilla Warfare* (Dublin, 1996), pp 124–5.
82   'Organisation of Flying Columns': Organisation Memo No. 1, Óglaigh na hÉireann (4 October 1920); reproduced in John M. MacCarthy, Witness Statement 883.
83   Florence O'Donoghue, 'The reorganisation of the Volunteers', *Capuchin Annual*, vol. 34 (1967).
84   Thomas Ryan, 'One man's flying column', *Tipperary Historical Journal*, vol. 4 (1991); 'One man's flying column, part 2', *Tipperary Historical Journal*, vol. 5 (1992); 'One man's flying column, part 3', *Tipperary Historical Journal*, vol. 6 (1993).
85   Brennan, *The War in Clare*, pp 70–1.
86   O'Malley papers, P 17 b 127.
87   S. Fitzpatrick, *Recollections of the Fight for Irish Freedom and of the Part Played by the 3rd (South) Tipperary Brigade Irish Volunteers, More Colloquially 'IRA', as from Spring/Summer of 1920* (privately published, n.d.).
88   O'Hannigan, 'Origin of the flying column'.
89   Good, *Enchanted by Dreams*.
90   See Maryann G. Valiulis, *Portrait of a Revolutionary: General Richard Mulcahy and the Founding of the Irish Free State* (Blackrock, 1992). See also Richard Mulcahy, Béaslaí Notes, vol. 1, p. 20.
91   Mulcahy, *My Father the General*, p. 47.
92   Tadgh Crowe, 'Life with a flying column, 1919–1921', *Tipperary Historical Journal*, vol. 17 (2004).
93   Bernard Fall, 'The theory and practice of counterinsurgency', *Naval War College Review* (April 1965).
94   Ignacio Cuenca-Sanchez, 'The dynamics of nationalist terrorism: ETA and the IRA', *Terrorism and Political Violence*, vol. 19 (2007).
95   Henry Kissinger, 'The Viet Nam negotiations', *Foreign Affairs* (January 1969). Cited in Mack, 'Why big nations lose small wars'.
96   Tom Barry, *Guerilla Days in Ireland: A Personal Account of the Anglo-Irish War* (Dublin,

1981), p. 23.

[97] J. Bowyer Bell, *The Secret Army: The IRA* (Dublin, 1997), p. 41.

[98] Michael Leahy, 'East Cork activities—1920', *Capuchin Annual* (1970).

Richard Mulcahy, 'Chief of Staff, 1919', *Capuchin Annual* (1970).

[100] O'Donoghue, 'Guerrilla warfare in Ireland'.

[101] Leahy, 'East Cork activities—1920'.

[102] Mulcahy, 'Chief of Staff, 1919'.

[103] W.H. Kautt, *Ambushes and Armour: The Irish Rebellion 1919–1921* (Dublin, 2014), p. 186.

[104] Mulcahy, 'Chief of Staff, 1919'.

[105] *Ibid.*

[106] Valiulis, *Portrait of a Revolutionary*, p. 53.

[107] O'Donoghue, 'Guerrilla warfare in Ireland'.

[108] *An t-Óglách*, 15 December 1919.

[109] Augusteijn, *From Public Defiance to Guerrilla Warfare*, p. 121.

[110] See Ewan Butler, *Barry's Flying Column: The Story of the IRA's Cork No. 3 Brigade, 1919–1921* (London, 1971); Tom Barry, *The Reality of the Anglo-Irish War, 1920–21, in West Cork: Refutations, Corrections and Comments on Liam Deasy's 'Towards Ireland Free'* (Dublin, 1974).

[111] Michael Hopkinson, *The Irish War of Independence* (Dublin, 2004), p. 75; Barry, *Guerilla Days in Ireland*, p. 25.

[112] O'Donoghue, 'Guerrilla warfare in Ireland'.

[113] Che Guevara, *Principles of Guerrilla Warfare* (http://www3.uakron.edu/worldciv/pascher/che.html).

[114] Lawrence, *The Evolution of a Revolt*, p. 15.

[115] 'Record of the Rebellion in Ireland in 1920–1921 and the Part Played by the Army in Dealing with it,' Imperial War Museum, Box 78/82/2. The authors of this report knew that they had learned a great deal about fighting a guerrilla war during this conflict, and this knowledge would have come in handy in Palestine and other post-World War II insurgencies. Inexplicably, however, there were few references to 'lessons learnt' throughout the report.

[116] *Ibid.*

[117] Andrew Silke, 'Ferocious times: the IRA, the RIC, and Britain's failure in 1919–1921', *Terrorism and Political Violence*, vol. 27, issue 3 (19 April 2016).

[118] *An t-Óglách*, 15 June 1920.

[119] W. Alison Phillips, *The Revolution in Ireland: 1906–1923* (London, 1923), p. 185.

[120] O'Donoghue, 'Guerrilla warfare in Ireland'.

[121] *Ibid.*

[122] William Sheehan, *Hearts and Mines: The British 5th Division, Ireland, 1920–1922* (Cork, 2009), pp 280–4.

[123] Patrick G. Daly, Witness Statement 814.

[124] J. Bowyer Bell, *The Gun in Politics: An Analysis of Irish Political Conflict, 1916–1986* (New Brunswick, 1991), pp 35–44.

[125] Oscar Traynor, Witness Statement 340.

[126] Barry, *Guerilla Days in Ireland*, pp 189–90.

[127] J. Bowyer Bell, 'The Thompson submachine gun in Ireland', *The Irish Sword*, vol. 8, no. 31 (1967).

[128] *An t-Óglách*, 21 June 1921.

[129] P. Jung, 'The Thompson machine gun during and after the Anglo–Irish War: the new evidence', *The Irish Sword*, vol. 21, no. 84 (1998); P. Ó Snodaigh, 'The Thompson machine gun: a few notes', *The Irish Sword*, vol. 22, no. 89 (2001).

[130] Seán O'Shea, Witness Statement 760.

[131] Donal Hales, Witness Statement 292.

[132] Andreas Roth, 'Gun running from Germany to Ireland in the early 1920's', *The Irish Sword*, vol. 22, no. 88 (2000).

[133] Charles John McGuinness, *Sailor of Fortune: Adventures of an Irish Sailor, Soldier, Pirate, Pearl-fisher, Gun-runner, Rebel and Antarctic Explorer* (Philadelphia, 1935), p. 172; R. Briscoe, *For the Life of Me* (London, 1958), pp 95–6.

[134] 'Supply of Motor Transport', NAUK, WO 32/9539; 'Increase in Mechanical Transport in Ireland', WO 32/9540; 'Mechanical Transport, Armoured Cars and other forms of Protection for Troops in Ireland', WO 32/9541.

[135] Kautt, *Ambushes and Armour*, pp 152–80. For a full discussion of land-mines used in a specific ambush see 'Landmines used against lorry-borne Auxiliaries at Rathcoole', in Gabriel Doherty (ed.), *With the IRA in the Fight for Freedom, 1919 to the Truce: The Red Path of Glory* (Mercier edition, Cork, 2010), pp 421–37.

[136] G.J. Rains, 'Torpedoes', *Southern Historical Society Papers*, vol. 3 (May–June 1877); Norman Youngblood, *The Development of Mine Warfare: A Most Murderous and Barbarous Conduct* (Westport, 2006), pp 25–7.

[137] K.R.M. Short, *The Dynamite War: Irish-American Bombers in Victorian Britain* (Dublin, 1979), p. 55; Michael Burleigh, *Blood and Rage: A Cultural History of Terrorism* (New York, 2009), pp 1–26.

[138] Joe Good, Witness Statement 388.

[139] James Lalor, Witness Statement 1032.

[140] James O'Donovan, Witness Statement 1713.

[141] Kautt, *Ambushes and Armour*, p. 152.

[142] *Ibid.*, pp 165–9.

[143] James O'Donovan, Witness Statement 1713.

[144] Guevara, *Principles of Guerrilla Warfare* (http://www3.uakron.edu/worldciv/pascher/che.html).

[145] David Kilcullen, 'Counterinsurgency *Redux*' (undated opinion paper of the Chief Strategist in the Office of the Coordinator for Counterterrorism, US State Department, Washington DC).

[146] William Sheehan (ed.), *British Voices from the Irish War of Independence 1918–1921: The Words of British Servicemen Who Were There* (Cork, 2007), p. 100.

[147] *An t-Óglách*, 6 May 1921.

[148] Dan McDonnell, Witness Statement 486.

[149] Townshend, 'The Irish Republican Army and the development of guerrilla warfare, 1919–1921'.

[150] *An t-Óglách*, 6 May 1921.

[151] Townshend, 'The Irish Republican Army and the development of guerrilla warfare, 1919–1921'.

3. Politics is the goal—war is the means

Without a political goal, guerrilla warfare must fail—as it must if its political objectives do not coincide with the aspirations of the people— and their sympathy, cooperation, and assistance cannot be gained.

—Mao Zedong

Overshadowing the Irish Volunteers' strategic and tactical military record is their political record. Politics is about principle, persuasion and power, and persuasion is the foremost factor. Not only do the most successful guerrilla tactics stress the 'political' over the 'military' element but also the 'victory' they achieve gains meaning only when exploited politically—only when the ruler has put his own house in order, the despot has been overthrown or the invader has been displaced. The purely military effects of guerrilla war will usually be seen as subordinate to the political and psychological effects.[1] Political vision is crucial for a guerrilla campaign. The movement has to have a mobilising idea, one that is inspiring and inclusive. The 'idea' is to fuel the military campaign with inspiration.

This historical record is of utmost importance if one is to understand why and how guerrilla warfare evolved into the ideal instrument for the realisation of socio-political and economic aspirations through the centuries, for the Irish in the early twentieth century and in guerrilla wars of today.[2] Michael Collins was, above all, a realist: he knew his enemies and what was necessary to 'defeat' them. The Irish did not have to hold large swathes of territory or drive the British into the sea; they only had to outlast the British will to fight. Their long-term objective was a political goal, and to achieve that they had to destabilise the British government in Ireland. Collins was the pragmatic strategist: if the vision of a Republic was unattainable (as it turned out to be), then Collins was willing to push the British into negotiations and take the best he could get. To paraphrase Henry Kissinger's dictum, 'they succeeded by surviving'.

US Field Manual 3-07.22, *Counterinsurgency Operations*, defines insurgency as an

> organized movement aimed at the overthrow of a constituted government through use of subversion and armed conflict. It is a protracted politico–military struggle designed to weaken government control and legitimacy while increasing insurgent control. *Political power is the central issue in an insurgency.* [Emphasis added][3]

In any struggle for political power there are a limited number of tools that can be used to induce the population to obey, including:

- coercive force,
- economic incentive and disincentive,
- legitimating ideology, and
- traditional authority.

While these tools are often available to both insurgent and counter-insurgent forces, in the Irish War of Independence the British could have had a head start; from the perspective of the Irish population, however, neither side had an explicit or immediate advantage in the initial battle for 'hearts and minds'. The civilian population would support the side which it was in its best interests to obey. The regard for one's own benefit or advantage is the basis for behaviour in all societies, regardless of religion, class or culture. To win the support of the people, the Irish military—and the *de facto* government of the Dáil—had to selectively provide security, as well as persuading the population that the Irish could provide them with a better government than could the British. Governments are elected to exercise control and ensure public safety in what amounts to a contract with the public. When the British government failed to provide security for the Irish people, and actually became a threat to them in the case of the Black and Tans or Auxiliaries, it failed to fulfil that implicit contract of governance, and the Irish goal of their own governance became a reality. This goes back to the ancient idea of protecting the public good and ensuring the happiness of the greatest number of people. The Irish revolutionaries believed that ordinary people could rule their own lives better than the British were doing.

Charles Townsend noted: 'If the nature of the challenging "force" is misunderstood, then the counter-application of force is likely to be wrong'.[4] The British never seemed to understand that the goal of the Irish war was as much a political as a military one. For example, the IRA consistently viewed itself as the legitimate army of a legitimate state, and construed its activities as a 'war' against British occupation. Thus any British actions that implied that the conflict was a war provided effective propaganda for the IRA. According to the Record of the Rebellion in Ireland in 1920–1, 'recognition [by British military authorities] of the IRA as belligerents may *ipso facto* be said to involve the Imperial Government in the recognition of an Irish Republic'.[5] Identifying the conflict as a war would have legitimised Sinn Féin and threatened the political legitimacy of the British government—and of the Union itself. As Lloyd George said in April 1920, 'You do not declare war against rebels'.[6]

Throughout the period, the British government position was that this was a criminal enterprise on the part of the Irish and thus should come under the purview of police forces. There were several legal reasons for this position, beyond the issue of criminality. British common law did not recognise an internal state of rebellion and therefore did not accept the actions of rebels as legitimate. Further, the law and constitution did not permit the use of military force in support of civil power except in rare and unusual circumstances. British law did not envision an armed, organised and determined IRA threatening the government, and thus there were inadequate mechanisms in place to deal with the Irish.[7]

Throughout the twentieth century, most guerrilla attempts at overthrow have failed. It is only when the political aspects of the wars are recognised by the national guerrilla leaders and emphasised over the military aspects that the rebels have succeeded. Those guerrillas who have 'succeeded' often do not 'win' in a military sense. They are successful because the invader/oppressor/autocrat is obliged to recognise the guerrillas and accedes, at least partially, to their political demands. For example, in conjunction with Vietnamese forces the US military *might* have been able to exercise control over the rice paddies of Vietnam, but the US government could not achieve control over the demonstrators on the streets of Chicago.

The Tet Offensive of 1968 is still recognised in the US as the turning point of the Vietnam War.[8] Although the communists suffered massive losses, Tet precipitated the collapse of the American people's will to win in Vietnam. General Võ Nguyên Giáp and the Vietnamese were losing the military war but they won the propaganda war. It is accepted that after that series of battles the American public felt that they had been deceived and misinformed about how the war was proceeding. Within one year the American troops began to withdraw from Vietnam. Likewise, with a great infusion of more troops and *matériel* the British military *might* have been able to maintain some control over the cities and countryside of Ireland, but the British government could not control Parliament nor British and international opinion. Like Tet's US military 'victories', Lloyd George's claim to have 'murder by the throat' just ten days before Bloody Sunday (21 November 1920) rang hollow in the British press and encouraged the British government to seek a negotiated solution.[9] The reprisals and the stories of atrocities that were published in the worldwide press completely changed the British view of the war. The political will of the British was beaten more soundly than was the military will of the British military establishment. Collins recognised that a guerrilla's task is to draw the opponent into a battle he cannot win. The British could not win the political/propaganda war. Within a year they, too, began their withdrawal from Ireland.

In a counter-insurgency, no military effort can succeed for long if the *status quo* government does not enact sound policies. The British military could contain the IRA only until the British government enacted policies or legislation that pre-empted or usurped the particular issues of national freedom from the Irish. The British government did not do so, and therefore did not support its military actions. In the long run, the British had to grant the Irish some measure of autonomy. Instead, they responded at the outset with forceful military measures, further alienating the population, so that by late 1918 the Irish had finally given up on the legitimacy of the British government and were committed to Irish independence.

Insurgencies are weakest at the beginning, and a forceful British move against the Irish in 1919 would have required careful political and propaganda operations that the British were not sufficiently ready to perform at that time. A 'foreign' power is often tentative, even fearful, in employing force against the local population. Such action might have strengthened the 'physical force' wing of Irish separatism, and could have damaged the British relationship with the US. It might have been viewed as nothing more than political repression. If the British had extended martial law over the whole country from 1916 to 1918 it would likely have speeded up the process of bringing the Irish people over to the rebel side. The application of martial law would have played directly into Irish propaganda, as it strips away the rights of everyone. Mass arrests, as after the Rising, would have generated more recruits. Executions after 'show' trials like Roger Casement's, or trials *in camera* as after the Rising, would have made the situation worse. Martial law has very rarely been used in the UK, as its legal basis is not certain. The British establishment has a 'love/hate' relationship with the concept, but by 1919, and more so in 1920, the pressure to introduce it from the senior military staff in London and Dublin was strong.[10] Introduction of martial law in Munster had very little effect on the IRA campaign, which rose to the challenge and became more energetic. The inconvenience to local people was considerable, but the biggest problem was the legal basis.[11] Throughout the period, the British Cabinet was sensitive to the opinion of Parliament and the British public, as well as to international opinion, particularly in the US. These pressures precluded the British from taking actions that would have offended those groups. Without mobilising popular Irish, British and international support to take the strongest military action, the British failed at the outset of the war. That mobilisation did not turn out to be possible later, either.

The Irish claim to be a legitimate government was based on the 'Proclamation of the Irish Republic' of the Easter Rising. The Proclamation based the claim on the existence of an Irish nation prior to the first English settlements in Ireland. It further stated that the Provisional Government would administer Irish affairs until a permanent national government could be elected, and that took place in the election of December 1918.[12] Irish willingness to be ruled by others faded, and that 1918 election was seen as the chance to form the permanent government envisioned in the Proclamation. The election success of Sinn Féin was seen as an expression of the Irish people, which legitimised the existence of a separate Irish state. The elected Dáil ratified the Proclamation and ordained itself the sole legitimate governing power in Ireland. The IRA campaign of 1920–1 was made possible by the complete change of Irish political allegiance from constitutional to 'physical force' nationalism between 1916 and 1921. *An t-Óglách* described the Irish military/political combination of strategy clearly:

> We will strike in our own way, in our own time. If we cannot, by force of arms, drive the enemy out of our country at the present moment, we can help to make his position impossible and military activities futile.

As long as British conventional commanders failed to adapt organisation, policies and tactics to meet the Irish political challenge instead of trying to convert it into an orthodox military challenge, the revolutionary campaign prospered. The Irish War of Independence did not lend itself to an exclusive military solution, which is ephemeral at best. The words 'winning' and 'victory' diminished in meaning as the British faced the awesome political/economic challenge that in 1919–21 they seemed unable to comprehend. T.E. Lawrence summed up a volume of thought in fifty words: 'Granted mobility, security (in the form of denying targets to the enemy), time, and doctrine (the idea to convert every subject to friendliness), victory will rest with the insurgents, for the algebraical factors are in the end decisive, and against them perfections of means and spirit struggle quite in vain'. Every successful guerrilla leader in history has heeded this basic formula. The Irish knew what Lawrence meant when he said that 'rebellion must have an unassailable base', and that it is found not so much in terrain as 'in the minds of men converted to its creed'. 'Rebellions must have a friendly population', he wrote, 'not actively friendly, but sympathetic to the point of not betraying rebel movements to the enemy.' Lawrence wrote almost nothing new but he learned greatly from history. Not much was new, either, in what the Irish guerrillas in their time said and did. The Irish preached an extremely effective doctrine—that of national independence, of pride and dignity. The first stage of the Irish revolution was essentially a political process in which the advanced nationalism of Sinn Féin squeezed out the Irish Parliamentary Party and established itself as the voice of the Irish people.

Above all, Lawrence called for qualitative tactics, just as used by the Israelis, Mao Zedong, Che Guevara, Ho Chi Minh and other rebels throughout the twentieth century. There was nothing new about these, nor about terrorist tactics such as those used by the Vietcong and condemned by United States moralists—American guerrillas in the Carolinas used precisely those same vicious tactics in the American Revolution, and they were as horrible in 1780 and in 1920 as they are today—but they are selective, very effective and kill far fewer people than major battles and big guns.[13] What one must realise is that every tactic employed by the Irish guerrillas served a political purpose in that it helped to enlarge and consolidate the support base—the 'water', as Chairman Mao has it, in which guerrillas 'swim'.

The only valid counter-insurgency tactic is to steal the support base from the guerrilla, and that means fighting a predominantly political war, an immensely complicated war that has almost nothing to do with conventional strategy and tactics.[14] It is a low-level war and involves, among many other things, protecting loyal citizens while repairing errors of government, for the Irish insurgency could not have begun, much less grown, but for those errors.[15] For example, between 1916 and the Truce the RIC lost its legitimacy in the eyes of a majority of the population in many counties by a process of physical (because so many barracks were closed), political (because the RIC were ostracised) and psychological distance between the police and the community.[16] By late 1917 the RIC were reviled as the most obvious instrument of British rule in Ireland.[17] In October the County Inspector for Clare reported that

> The people appear to regard the police as their enemies and have ceased all friendly intercourse with them. Shops continue to supply provisions, but they would rather that the police did not come to them.[18]

One of the most prolific writers among modern guerrilla warriors was Mao Zedong. He consistently reverted to the theme that a guerrilla war is carried out among the people, and that one must always look to the political effects of any military action.

> There is no reason to consider guerrilla warfare separately from national policy. On the contrary, it must be organised and

conducted completely in accord with national policy ...

...

It is only who misinterpret guerrilla action [*sic*] who say, as does Jen Ch'I Shan, 'the question of guerrilla hostilities is purely a military matter and not a political one'.[19] Those who maintain this simple point of view have lost sight of the political goal and the political effects of guerrilla action. Such a simple point of view will cause the people to lose confidence and will result in our defeat.[20]

The changing attitude of the Irish towards the Rising and the prisoners taken to British jails also brought difficulties for the Irish Parliamentary Party (IPP), under the leadership of John Redmond and John Dillon. Dillon, who was in Dublin during the Rising, was the first to recognise this even while General Maxwell's executions were ongoing.[21] He grasped the key political problem, which was how to prevent the growing reaction *in favour* of the Irish rebels from becoming a reaction *against* the IPP. He addressed the House of Commons in May 1916 and denounced the secret courts martial and the executions. He conferred a sort of moral sanction on the rebels, who

... fought a clean fight, a brave fight, however misguided, and it would have been a damned good thing for you if your soldiers were able to put up as good a fight as did these men in Dublin.[22]

British Prime Minister H.H. Asquith visited Dublin in May 1916 and the executions were halted, but it was too late. Upon his return to London, Asquith decided to take a different approach and attempted to make a political settlement. Not only was he being pressured by Dillon and others within the British establishment but he also hoped that a political settlement would come at the expense of the more radical nationalists and would deflate the growing international criticism of the British reaction to the Rising, particularly that coming from the US (Sir Cecil Spring-Rice, British Ambassador in Washington, alerted Asquith that the executions had badly shaken American opinion). An 'Irish Convention' sat in Trinity College Dublin from 25 July 1917 to 5 April 1918 (there were also some sessions in

Cork and Belfast); Horace Plunkett was its chairman. Its ninety-five members included mayors and chairmen of public bodies, together with almost every prominent Irishman outside politics, but its weakness was on the political side: Sinn Féin had been allocated five seats but declined to take part.[23] William O'Brien's All for Ireland Party also declined.[24] The membership consisted of fifty-two Nationalists, twenty-six Ulster Unionists (headed by Hugh Barrie and George Clarke), nine Southern Unionists (headed by Lord Midleton), six Labour representatives and two Liberals.[25] British Minister of Munitions David Lloyd George proposed the conference to the Irish Parliamentary Party chairman John Redmond in order to moderate nationalist opinion. The British thought that the Irish could debate the future government of Ireland, particularly with regard to Ulster, although attempts to broker a settlement were dismissed by Sinn Féin as surrender. There was a moment's silence for those who perished in the Rising and a call for those still in custody to be treated like prisoners of war, but the most significant action was a call asserting 'Ireland's right to freedom from all foreign control'. The convention reaffirmed the measure of disagreement between the North and South, bogged down over the issue of fiscal control, and partition could not be resolved. The fact that Sinn Féin boycotted the convention meant, however, that it was doomed from the outset to achieve very little, if anything. It was destined to fail, as the wide diversity of views even among the moderates prevented any consensus, much less the unanimity demanded by the Conservative and Unionist elements in the British Parliament and government. Although discussions carried on for almost a year, the base positions of a united Irish State and a separate Protestant Ulster were incompatible. By May 1918, when the convention's final report was published, the British had already ruined any hope of success by passing primary legislation providing for Irish conscription, although not legally triggering its actual commencement.

Beginning in 1917, in addition to contesting the by-elections in North Roscommon, Longford, East Clare, Cavan and Kilkenny, the Irish began to set up their own political structures that would set their course for the next four years. It is necessary to look at the politics within Ireland as much as those international political overtures that came later to fully realise the development of Irish political aims and Collins's maturation on political goals during the war.

Women were among the most involved activists in the nationalist movement from the beginning, but that they stood in danger of being marginalised was recognised in the aftermath of an important meeting held on 19 April 1917, almost exactly one year after the Rising. Count George Plunkett, father of one of the executed leaders, Joseph Mary Plunkett, convened the meeting to determine whether Count Plunkett's 'Liberty Clubs' or Arthur Griffith's Sinn Féin would become the nucleus of the new nationalist political movement. It was clear that the nationalist movement was divided: Griffith's more peaceful view of constitutional efforts clashed with Plunkett's harsher view of militarist separatism. The issue was not resolved but it was agreed that negotiations would continue, and a number of people were selected for this purpose. One month after the 19 April meeting, the dissidents came together to discuss the situation. Those who attended included representatives of Cumann na mBan, the Irish Women Workers' Union and women from the Irish Citizen Army. All the different viewpoints within the women's united front were represented: Áine Ceannt was actively involved in recruiting for Cumann na mBan, Jenny Wyse-Power was a member of Cumann na mBan and the Irish Women's Franchise League, Helena Molony was working for the Irish Women Workers' Union and Fiona Plunkett represented the younger generation of women activists. At long last the women succeeded in extracting a significant concession: four 'ladies' would be co-opted onto the executive of Sinn Féin, on the understanding that none of them represented any organisation and that they were all members of a Sinn Féin branch. There was an obvious concern to prevent the possibility of the formation of an organised feminist caucus. Four months after the informal 'League of Women Delegates' had been formed, their efforts had met with success. Women were now on the executive of a regenerated Sinn Féin.

The Tenth Sinn Féin Ard-Fheis was held in Dublin's Mansion House on 25–26 October 1917.[26] It was a crucial watershed in the Irish struggle for national independence and was the culmination of a process of reorganisation that had begun almost as soon as the quicklime had settled on the bodies of the executed leaders of the Easter Rising. Those who had taken part in the Rising (the Irish Volunteers, the Irish Citizen Army and the women's organisation Cumann na mBan), together with Sinn Féin and other small nationalist groups, were faced with the daunting challenge of creating an entirely new political movement in the midst of disarray and military defeat. About 1,700 delegates attended, including members from 1,009 Sinn Féin Clubs.[27] The secretary stated that the total number of clubs was about 1,200, with a membership of almost 250,000.[28]

Women were a visible and vocal presence at the Sinn Féin Convention of 1917. They decided to Gaelicise their name to Cumann na Teachtaire and to work to ensure that women would be elected onto public boards and onto all institutions within the Sinn Féin organisation. They reluctantly had to drop the idea of producing a women's newspaper, but they agreed to produce leaflets and to try to link up with other women's societies. When the convention met, the women's resolution, originally drawn up by the League of Women Delegates, was proposed by Kathleen Lynn and seconded by Jenny Wyse-Power: 'that the equality of men and women in this organisation be emphasised in all speeches and leaflets'. It was passed by general agreement. The women's tactic in getting executive backing had paid off. A precedent had been set, and four women were elected to the new twenty-four-member executive, while considerable numbers of women were later co-opted onto the various organisations set up by Sinn Féin as it refined its machinery of civil resistance to British rule in Ireland.[29]

Éamon de Valera was elected president of Sinn Féin (and, a few days later, of the Irish Volunteers as well). The vice-presidents were Arthur Griffith and Fr Michael O'Flanagan. Secretaries elected were Darrell Figgis (later replaced by Harry Boland) and Austin Stack (who remained Hon. Secretary until his death in 1929). Laurence Ginnell and William Cosgrave were the treasurers. Eoin MacNeill was elected to the twenty-four-member Sinn Féin Executive Council. (There was controversy when MacNeill was proposed for the Executive—Éamon de Valera, Arthur Griffith and Seán Milroy voted for him, while Kathleen Clarke, Helena Molony and Countess Markievicz opposed him—but he received an outstanding majority of votes.[30] Griffith expressed the opinion that MacNeill could not have acted otherwise in attempting to call off the Rising and reiterated, 'I will not stand by and see one man whom I know, sentenced and put out of Irish public life'. De Valera's input to the row was to say that 'he understood MacNeill's reasons for his actions were honest and that he had done his duty for Ireland as he conceived it'.)

Irish political differences were apparent from the beginning of this convention. The meeting began with Cathal Brugha (a former IRB member) barely consenting to sit in the same room as Griffith, and with Collins and Rory O'Connor walking out and being brought back by de Valera. Early cracks in 'Republicanism' were clear even then and would widen until the Treaty split. Collins took a hard line, supported by the IRB, to block-vote de Valera into the presidency. (Though de Valera, too, was once a member of the IRB for a short while, he resigned after the Rising, and Collins's position was that in spite of this he should be leader of Sinn Féin, not Griffith. The IRB viewed Griffith as much too moderate because Griffith clung tenaciously to the notion that Ireland could achieve her ends by constitutional means alone.) Collins viewed Sinn Féin with mixed feelings: on the one hand he was entirely in agreement with its doctrine of self-reliance and separatism, while on the other hand he disagreed with achieving those goals by entirely political efforts rather than by military force. At one stage Collins walked out of talks with Griffith, but eventually a compromise was reached. Griffith agreed to abandon his lifelong aim of restoring the sovereignty of Ireland under a dual monarchy, and in return for these concessions the militants, led by Collins, agreed to accept Sinn Féin's economic policies and its strategy of abstention from parliament.

Prior to the meeting, Collins and the others planned a 'take-over' of Sinn Féin, but their plan failed miserably. Collins's hard line backfired badly for the IRB at the Ard-Fheis, as most of its delegates were not elected to the Executive. Even Collins suffered, as he was only elected on the second ballot, held the next day. The other members elected to the Executive were Piaras Béaslaí, Ernest Blythe, Harry Boland, Cathal Brugha, Kathleen Clarke, Dr Thomas Dillon, Dr Richard Hayes, David Kent, Diarmuid Lynch, Fionan Lynch, Dr Kathleen Lynn, Seán MacEntee, Countess Markievicz, Joseph McDonagh, Joseph McGuinness, Seán Milroy, Seán T. O'Kelly, Count Plunkett, Grace Gifford Plunkett, Fr Matt Ryan, Fr Thomas Wall and James J. Walsh—a majority of 'physical force' advocates over those favouring more political means.[31]

It is important to note that at this early stage many of the Irish, particularly members of the IRB, including Collins, were wedded 'only to physical force'. After the failure of the Rising it should have been apparent that a physical conflict—using only military force—was going to fail again. Any future conflict along the same lines would meet the same fate, and the

British knew that as well.[32] Just as Collins and the others had to grow into their roles in intelligence, they also had to learn to accept that the political view was going to be at least equal to the physical-force view.

Brugha proposed the Sinn Féin Constitution, and Seán Milroy seconded it on 25 October. The Constitution stated:

> Whereas the people of Ireland never relinquished the claim to separate Nationhood; and
> Whereas the Provisional Government of the Irish Republic, Easter 1916, in the name of the Irish people, and continuing the fight made by previous generations, reasserted the inalienable right of the Irish nation to Sovereign independence, and reaffirmed the determination of the Irish people to achieve it; and
> Whereas the Proclamation of an Irish Republic, Easter 1916, and the supreme courage and glorious sacrifices of the men who gave their lives to maintain it, have united the people of Ireland under the flag of the Irish Republic, be it
> Resolved that we, the delegated representatives of the Irish People, in convention assembled, hereby declare the following to be the Constitution of Sinn Féin.
> The name of the organisation shall be Sinn Féin.
> Sinn Féin aims at securing the international recognition of Ireland as an independent Irish Republic. Having achieved that status, the Irish people may by referendum freely choose their own form of government;
> This object shall be attained through the Sinn Féin Organisation which shall, in the name of the Irish People:
>> Deny the right and oppose the will of the British Parliament and British Crown or any other foreign government to legislate for Ireland;
>> Make use of any and every means available to render impotent the power of England to hold Ireland in subjection by military force or otherwise.[33]

De Valera devised the following formula to satisfy the various views at the

Ard-Fheis: 'Sinn Féin aims at securing the international recognition of Ireland as an independent Irish Republic. Having achieved that status, the Irish people may by referendum freely choose their own form of government.' He subsequently closed the Ard-Fheis by declaring, 'We are not doctrinaire Republicans'.[34]

In October 1917 another meeting was held in Gaelic League Headquarters in Rutland Square (now Parnell Square) to establish a National Executive of Óglaigh na hÉireann (Volunteers/IRA). It was decided to have the meeting at the same time as the Sinn Féin Ard-Fheis, which met on 25 October. Among the leaders present were Brugha, Collins, de Valera, Diarmuid Lynch,[35] Richard Mulcahy, Diarmuid O'Hegarty and Michael Staines.[36] The IRB was well represented with Collins, Lynch, O'Hegarty and Seán Ó Muirthuile.[37]

Dr Risteard Mulcahy gave four reasons for the success of the Volunteer Convention:

- The unity of spirit and purpose, which developed amongst the prisoners at Frongoch and the other British prisons, and the great boost their return and the reception they received gave to the former prisoners.
- Some of those left behind in Ireland stimulated a revival of interest in the IRB with the object of its reorganisation.
- Ó Muirthuile and O'Hegarty acquainted Brugha with their plans, and he encouraged them to make all possible contact with the Volunteers with the object of reorganisation.
- Thomas Ashe's death in September and funeral played an important part in quickening the reorganisation.[38]

The Volunteer Convention provided a formal control structure and leadership of the army through the election of Éamon de Valera as president and a National Executive with representatives from the four provinces. In addition, the fact that de Valera was elected as president of both Sinn Féin and the Volunteers ended the Volunteers' apolitical role. Although there were disagreements (and some personal animosity between the members of the executives of Sinn Féin and the Volunteers continued throughout the War of Independence), for the most part these conventions ended the conflict between the two organisations. Although the National Executive functioned in name at least through to 1920, real power over the army had passed by March 1918 to the GHQ Staff and then to the Ministry for Defence when Dáil Éireann was proclaimed in January 1919. Nevertheless, Collins and Mulcahy remained in effective command of the army as well as intelligence throughout the war. Finally, the Volunteer Convention ended John Redmond's National Volunteers.

It must be said that it was greatly due to de Valera that Sinn Féin and the Volunteers were reconciled. After these conventions, there was a clear and persuasive political objective.

> Éamon de Valera brought, and only Éamon de Valera could have brought, Sinn Féin and the Volunteers together, giving resurgent Ireland a single forceful organisation, the institution and the consensus Griffith had looked forward to.[39]

In April 1918 Westminster passed a compulsory Conscription Act to be applied in Ireland, a move that greatly solidified Irish public opinion against Britain.[40] Fear of conscription was never far from the minds of the Irish. Indeed, Collins and many others who were living in Britain might not have returned to Ireland well in advance of the Rising had not conscription been imposed in Britain on 15 January 1916—the very day Collins returned to Dublin. The 1918 conscription issue united in spirit, if only temporarily, the two strands of nationalism, militant and moderate. The proposed application of conscription to Ireland produced the kind of revolutionary situation that leaders can exploit in order to inflame smouldering popular discontent and provide the heat necessary for open insurgence. The issue dominated Irish life and roused the country to support more militant tactics. Nothing could have been better calculated to stiffen Sinn Féin and move its moderates aside in favour of the physical-force advocates. The Volunteers pledged themselves to resist by force any imposition of conscription. Thousands of people now joined the Irish Volunteers to resist any forcible call-up.[41] The reaction was nationwide; in the West Riding of County Cork when conscription was announced there was a serious outbreak of raiding of private homes for arms.[42] Although no Irishman was in fact conscripted during the war, the threat was such that a multi-party conference was convened as a protest against its possibility and issued the following pronouncement:'The attempt to enforce conscription will be unwarrantable aggression which we call upon all true Irishmen to resist by the most effective means at their disposal'.[43] As always in the period, women were in the forefront and they had their own protest, pledging that 'We will not fill the places of men deprived of their work through refusing the enforcement of military service'. The Catholic hierarchy concurred with this sentiment at their annual meeting at Maynooth, declaring in their own manifesto:

> An attempt is being made to force Conscription on Ireland against the will of the Irish nation and in defiance of the protests of its leaders. In view especially of the historic relations between the two countries from the very beginning up to this moment, we consider that Conscription forced in this way upon Ireland is an oppressive and inhuman law, which the Irish people have a right to resist by every means that are constant with God.[44]

By now even the opinion of the Church was moving closer to the emerging spirit of nationalism.[45]

In the anti-conscription campaign, Irish Labour occupied a pivotal position with Sinn Féin. The trade union movement followed objections by all parties and a 24-hour general strike was called for 23 April. Except in Belfast, the strike was solid throughout Ireland. (In some places employers paid their employees for the day off, and there was no resistance from employers. Still, it was an impressive display, indicating the importance of workers to the functioning of society.)[46] It was clear that southern Ireland had no intention of standing patiently by in the remote hope that conscription would be accompanied by Home Rule. Thus the threat to introduce conscription in Ireland led to widespread support for independence and greatly fuelled support for the Republican separatist movement and Sinn Féin. The lasting effect of the conscription scare was to turn the Volunteers from a political minority into a national army.

It must be noted that there was not unanimous agreement in the British Cabinet on the conscription policy.[47] On 3 June conscription for Ireland was at least temporarily abandoned and replaced by an alternative plan seeking a voluntary recruitment of 50,000 men from ten specially created districts. The level of concerted opposition in Ireland was doubtless a factor in this decision, but it was outweighed by the fact that by June there was a general improvement in the British military position in Europe in World War I. Yet another consideration was revealed by the internal debate within the Cabinet following the decision to extend conscription to Ireland: a serious concern that the inclusion of Irish conscripts within British ranks might be counter-productive to the British effort, and that would give the Irish another propaganda coup.[48] Similarly, the burgeoning unrest in Ireland that was likely to accompany conscription could have required the placement of additional British regiments in Ireland. Lionel Curtis, a key legal adviser to the Cabinet and an architect of the Commonwealth system, wrote that the decision to abandon conscription was 'due no doubt partly to the conviction that they could not spare the necessary troops and also to evidence that the Irish conscripts would not be trustworthy'.[49]

The conscription threat was second only to the execution of the Rising leaders in creating a substantial backing for Sinn Féin among the Irish. A heavy-handed attempt by the British viceroy, Lord Lieutenant John French, to quell this reaction to conscription claimed that there was evidence of a treasonable 'German Plot' between Sinn Féin and the German military.[50] On 17–19 May 1918, Sinn Féin leaders and others were arrested because of the bogus 'German Plot', which put most of the Sinn Féin 'moderates' in prison.[51] The pretext for this 'Plot' was the capture of Joseph Dowling, a member of Roger Casement's ill-fated 'Irish Brigade', on an island off the coast of Galway on 12 April. (On the day of Dowling's capture, Collins was still in Sligo jail. He was incarcerated until 18 April, when he returned to Dublin. Dowling, who was arrested immediately on landing, had been a lance-corporal in the Connaught Rangers. Captured by the Germans on the Western Front, he joined Roger Casement's Irish Brigade in 1915 while a prisoner of war in Germany. Two years after Easter Week 1916, he was sent to Ireland by the German general staff to report on the prospects for another Irish rising. Since this was wholly a German idea, it was hardly evidence of a plot involving Sinn Féin and the Volunteers. Dowling was court-martialled, sentenced to penal servitude for life and held in jail in England until February 1924 despite resolutions by the Irish Free State.[52]) The Germans landed Dowling from a submarine on their own initiative, and no one from Sinn Féin had ever contacted him, though Collins and some of the other GHQ staff were aware of the approach. Only the most specious evidence was offered by the British authorities to support French's contention that Sinn Féin leaders were engaged in treasonable contact with Germany. That evidence consisted largely of previously published contacts between the Germans and Sinn Féin leaders such as the late Roger Casement in 1914. Furthermore, for the better part of a year following the Easter Rising, the vast majority of the Sinn Féiners arrested during 17–19 May 1918 had been in English prisons and were unable to make contact with the Germans even had they wanted to. Acquisition of the information that raids were planned, and the Irish to be captured, was an example of the efficiency of Collins's network and how he seemed to have had information even before the Castle told the police. That series of raids on 17–19 May rounded up many, and these arrests were what brought Collins fully into the intelligence effort, especially since so many who were arrested were Sinn Féin moderates, leaving more 'physical-force' activists like Collins, Brugha and Harry Boland in charge. Seventy-three prisoners were deported to England immediately, followed by others later.

The winter of 1918/19 saw a 'flu pandemic that killed millions of people across the globe. In December, in Usk Prison, Wales, republican prisoner Richard Coleman of Dublin contracted the virus and died. In February the 'flu struck the prisoners in Gloucester, including Pierce McCann (Piaras Mac Canna), a Tipperary TD. A strong constitution and general good health were no defence against the virus, which quickly turned to pneumonia and took McCann's life. Following his death, the British government released the remaining Irish internees from English jails, and this tragic incident gave the Irish yet another propaganda coup.

The unfolding conscription issue allowed Sinn Féin to rise to the undisputed position of national leadership, a role that it would convert into overwhelming electoral success in the election later in 1918. In this case Collins took advantage of another opportunity handed to him by the British, as he was able to grow in importance in Sinn Féin affairs, as well as becoming an important figure in the Irish propaganda effort. It is striking that, in seeking to exploit the anti-war/anti-conscription sentiment, Sinn Féin was very careful not to be seen to dishonour the 200,000 Irish soldiers who had already fought in World War I and the tens of thousands who had died in British uniform.

In March 1918 a General Headquarters (GHQ) of the Volunteers was established. In his papers Richard Mulcahy referred to the excellent spirit that existed among the GHQ staff. He claimed that there was never the slightest disagreement and that the work 'dovetailed and interlocked in a satisfactory way—no suspicions, no withdrawings, no waste of time'.[53] In particular, he wrote about the close relationship between himself and Collins:

> I opened and kept open for him all the doors and pathways that he wanted to travel—our relations were always harmonious and frank and we didn't exchange unnecessary information. We each knew what the other was at, and in particular in his domain of intelligence—I had no occasion to be questioning him. Over many matters we exercised a constructive and practical Cistercian silence.
>
> …
>
> … Collins dealt particularly with the aggressive activities of urgent and spot intelligence in relation to enemy activity.[54]

More than once Mulcahy refers to Collins's enormous capacity for work, his genius for organisation and his ability to motivate others. As regards work outside Dublin, Mulcahy wrote that there was the closest consultation between himself and Collins.

Joe Good recorded that in April 1918 Brugha and Mulcahy chaired a meeting at which it was decided to send Volunteers to London to attempt to assassinate the British Cabinet.[55] Brugha led the team to London in May and it stayed there until August, but he never received approval for the assassinations. Those on the team included Tom Craven, Joe Good, Matt Furlong, Martin Gleeson, James 'Ginger' McNamara, James Mooney, Peter Murtagh, Sam Reilly and William (Bill) Whelan.[56] Collins disagreed with this course of action, along with several of Brugha's later, similar schemes. Collins said: 'Do you think the British can have only one cabinet?' Brugha, the Minister for Defence, was responsible for some of the most bloodthirsty proposals throughout the war and pursued them ardently and independently. He once proposed the bombing and machine-gunning of crowds in theatres and cinemas. At a Cabinet meeting Collins threw up his hands in horror and said, 'Ye'll get none of my men for that'. Brugha answered, 'I want none of your men, Mr Collins'. The Cabinet rejected the plans without question, but afterwards Brugha pursued Collins with unrelenting hatred, and was usually seconded by Austin Stack. The later Cabinet meetings began to degenerate into quarrels between Brugha and Stack on one side and Collins on the other.[57]

At times it seemed that Brugha's solution for everything was a campaign against the British Cabinet. He moved to London to oversee the massacre of the government's front bench by members of the Dublin IRA should conscription be enforced in Ireland, playing billiards and looking after his baby daughter while he waited. This phony war had two sides, as British police forces and intelligence services worked to ward off the attacks that never came. Reports and rumours of assassins being sent from Ireland frequently reached the British Cabinet and individual MPs, often through Basil Thomson, Assistant Commissioner of London's Metropolitan Police. Bodyguards were assigned to fifty people in London, and policemen were stationed behind newly erected barricades in Westminster and Whitehall. Collins thought it an embarrassment and a waste of resources.[58] Brugha continued to advocate sending men to Britain, and even sent several in November 1921 to raid for arms. (As the Anglo–Irish Treaty negotiations were already under way at that time, their arrest and imprisonment created a 'delicate' atmosphere for the negotiators.) Despite the 'cracks' in Republicanism, the Dáil and the Cabinet, the Irish were to hold their political aims together until the final split over the Treaty, enabling them to conduct their guerrilla war with some control from Dublin and the necessary political connection to a legitimate Irish government in the Dáil.

When given a chance to show the world their intent, Sinn Féin election tactics were also thought out in terms of providing the country with an entire system of government alternative to the British. And while Sinn Féin was clearly on the rise before the late 1918 election, that rise was not without setbacks: after winning three by-elections in a row in 1917, the new party lost three in a row in early 1918. Thus, while the Irish Parliamentary Party was expected to lose seats in the election called immediately after the end of World War I, it wasn't clear to voters just how overwhelming the Sinn Féin tide would turn out to be. In the December 1918 election the more obvious revolutionary election strategy might have been to boycott the polls, thereby showing that the Irish took no interest in the electoral activities of the British. Instead, Sinn Féin put up candidates in every constituency. The strength of Sinn Féin and its claim to represent the political feeling of the Irish people were plain to the world. A blow far heavier than a boycott of the polling booths had been struck against the British administration.[59]

It is thought that Harry Boland and Collins collaborated during the nomination process for the election to be held on 14 December, and ruthlessly went through each nomination, culling anyone they felt would disagree with them in the future. The candidates they chose were all staunch Republicans and had proved themselves unwilling to compromise. Collins felt it vital that the bloc to be elected was completely and unquestionably Republican to demonstrate a united front to the British. He left no room for political moderation or vacillation. The hotter the candidates talked, the more Boland and Collins liked them. (Ultimately, this was to Collins's disadvantage in the Treaty debates of 1921–2, when many were still not capable of seeing the value of compromise.[60]) It is not certain that Boland and Collins were so conspiratorially involved as to make a farce of the election, but many did believe that 'the two friends went on to rig the process for candidates'.[61]

In this election women had the vote for the first time and other restrictions on the universal right to vote had been removed; the widening of democracy helped to ensure a stunning victory for Sinn Féin on a Republican platform.[62] In August 1918 the electoral register had been revised to take account of the widened franchise. Women over thirty could vote and remaining property qualifications for men over twenty-one were removed. This meant that the number of people in Ireland entitled to vote in the general election grew enormously, from 683,767 in 1910 to 1,926,274 in 1918. Alone of the parties, Sinn Féin supported women's right to full franchise.

The election was a test of electoral strength between the moderate Home Rule Irish Parliamentary Party and the new revolutionary Sinn Féin with its aim of an Irish republic, independent of and separated from Great Britain and the British Crown. The swing to Sinn Féin was not only because of the executions and mass imprisonments after the 1916 Rising; there had also been growing opposition to Ireland's involvement in the war and its cost in lives, the inclusion in the British Cabinet of Tory Unionists who vehemently opposed any form of Home Rule, the threat of Partition and the ineffectiveness at Westminster of John Redmond's Irish Party, increasingly seen as collaborators with British imperialism, as well as ongoing repression and press censorship.

The Sinn Féin election manifesto reflected the republican position adopted by the Ard-Fheis a year previously, stating that the party 'gives Ireland the opportunity of vindicating her honour and pursuing with renewed confidence the path of national salvation by rallying to the flag of the Irish Republic'. The party was committed to establishing the Irish Republic by withdrawing Irish representation from Westminster, using 'any and every means available' to make British rule impossible, establishing a constituent assembly and appealing to the post-war Peace Conference to recognise Ireland as an independent nation. It roundly condemned the role of the Irish Party in collaborating with the British government and attempting to 'harness the Irish people to England's war chariot'. The manifesto endorsed the 1916 Proclamation, 'guaranteeing within the independent Nation equal rights and equal opportunities to all its citizens'. From the outset, Sinn Féin presented itself as a viable alternative to the Irish Parliamentary Party in every way, including the pledge to abstain from attending Parliament at Westminster. The manifesto was aimed at placing Sinn Féin at the fore of the movement from then on:

> Sinn Féin aims at securing the establishment of the Irish Republic …

That goal would be accomplished by

> the withdrawal of Irish representatives from Westminster and by denying the right and opposing the will of the British Government.
>
> …
>
> Sinn Féin will establish a separate constituent assembly which would act in the name of the Irish people and to develop Ireland's social, political and industrial life for the welfare of the whole of Ireland.

The manifesto flatly stated that the voters had a choice between an independent nation state or

'remaining in the shadow of a base imperialism'.

It supported the use of every means available to render impotent the power of England to hold Ireland in subjection by military force or otherwise.

The British authorities censored the manifesto when it appeared in the newspapers but the full version was widely circulated. The establishing of an independent Irish Republic was an overriding issue, and the manifesto was a clear attempt to bring Ireland's case as a republic to the Peace Conference in Paris.

Newspapers were split in their predictions. The *Freeman's Journal*, the newspaper most loyal to the IPP to the very end of its existence in 1924, blamed Sinn Féin for playing into the hands of the Unionists and Lloyd George in a way that 'will enable him utterly to defeat the cause of National Self-Government'.[63] The election would decide 'whether Ireland has the intelligence to penetrate the hot air rhetoric of Sinn Féin' or endure the consequences of as great a mistake as 'ever disgraced the history of a nation'. On the other hand, the *Irish Independent* was blisteringly critical of the Irish Parliamentary Party that day. 'The poor old tottering Irish Party do not know what exactly they want', the newspaper declared in its editorial. 'No independent Nationalist will be sorry if at last the Irish people rid themselves of the Party which, by blundering and stupidity, lost every opportunity presented to them and earned contempt not only for themselves but for the country.'[64]

Further, the *Cork Examiner* declared in its election-day editorial:

The Irish people, on the one hand, are invited to support a practical policy of Dominion Self-Government, which is the country's one chance of national salvation, and on the other, they are asked to seek a mirage Republic. Today they will be called upon to make their choice in the polling booths, and to say whether they prefer a policy of rainbow-chasing, or one which offers practical tangible advantages in the present and will ultimately secure for them the liberty that they so earnestly desire![65]

125

Following the election, *The Times* reported that the election 'was treated by all as a plebiscite'.[66]

The general election of 1918 had possibly the most profound impact on Irish politics of any general election. For decades Irish politics had been driven largely by nationalist constitutional policies, but these were suddenly discarded in 1918.[67] 'The one predictable outcome of the General Election', the *Irish Times* proclaimed, 'is the triumph of Sinn Féin in most of the Nationalist constituencies.'[68] Of course, this was not a prospect that the *Irish Times* welcomed, as it had always been seen as a Unionist newspaper.

In overwhelmingly replacing the Irish Parliamentary Party with revolutionary republicans, this was the most significant general election in twentieth-century Ireland, providing Sinn Féin with a democratic mandate both to establish Dáil Éireann and to proclaim a republic. Sinn Féin won 73 out of 105 seats, but this was more than an electoral landslide. It was an act of largely peaceful secession. The successful Sinn Féin candidates would not be MPs; each would be called a Teachta Dála or TD. They had asked to be elected, in effect, to a parliament that did not exist: an Irish parliament which they intended to establish in Dublin. This was, above all, an imaginative and constructive act—it proposed to call into being a new democracy, using the methods of democracy itself.

One must acknowledge the central place of the 1918 election in determining the future course of Irish history: as one looks down the names of successful candidates, the governments of Ireland for the next thirty or forty years emerge. This is what the election of 1918 did:

> It declared to the British that they had no claim to Ireland that was not rendered null and void by the Irish people's repudiation of such claim, and that the only just and constitutional government in Ireland was the Government of Dáil Éireann, which was elected by the people and represented the people. There is no gesture in Irish history quite so magnificent, quite so proud as that; and nothing that has happened can take away from it ... It brought the people to the point that they gave their allegiance to Dáil Éireann, obeyed it and recognized it, and helped it, suffered British government but did not recognize it and did not help it.[69]

A victorious Sinn Féin immediately claimed that they had democratically won the right, through an overwhelming national endorsement from the Irish electorate, to officially declare and establish an Irish Republic. The results of the election demonstrated the greatest single shift in Irish parliamentary representation and also foreshadowed divisions that would deepen on the island until the Treaty debates in late 1921 and thereafter.

Collins was one of the members of that first Dáil, representing the Cork South constituency, and he would represent that same constituency until his death in 1922. He became one of the most successful of the politicians and administrators elected at that time. It was Collins's multiplicity of roles—in politics, in the Volunteers and in the IRB—that makes his performance extraordinary. 'Unlike the other Volunteers-turned-politicians, Collins kept one foot firmly in "the army", as it was increasingly called. So he not only ran the most important Dáil department [Finance], and ran it well, he was also waging a secret war against the men who were trying to catch him.'[70]

Though the Irish clergy had endorsed the anti-conscription campaign earlier in 1918, the majority of the clergy still criticised Sinn Féin and not all were pleased with the results of this election. Catholic criticism of the party had become more muted, but even after this there were still occasional outbursts of criticism from the clergy. Fr Walter McDonald, a maverick Maynooth professor, wrote disapprovingly shortly after the 1918 election:

> Great numbers of the junior clergy, and a considerable body of their seniors, with some even of the bishops, supported the Sinn Féin candidates, or voted for them. Some of this, I know, was bluff—asking, as I have heard one man put it, for more than they had hoped to get. Others voted Sinn Féin as for the less of two evils. But many of the priests, and perhaps some of the bishops, seem to have acted on the conviction that Ireland is *de jure* a fully independent nation. Is this really their teaching?[71]

Nevertheless, this teaching was where the anti-conscription campaign had led.

Whatever ambivalence the Catholic clergy may have shown towards the rise of Sinn Féin, they were unequivocal in their condemnation of political violence in the years afterwards and in questioning the morality of the killings. The threat of excommunication and the refusal of the sacraments were also widely used by priests in an attempt to break the will of IRA prisoners in British custody. Todd Andrews remembered Catholic priests visiting the republican prisoners on hunger strike in Mountjoy and using their religious and social position to try and force them to end their strike: 'I had a visit from the prison chaplain … he warned me that I was wilfully endangering my life which was an immoral act totally forbidden by the Commandments … The chaplain was doing the dirty work required by his British employers'.[72] While the hierarchy condemned the gunmen, many of the priests were nationalists and supported the objectives and activities of the IRA. Squad member Vinnie Byrne recalled: 'I went to confession one day and told the priest I had shot dead a man. He asked me why and I told him, "Because he was a spy". The priest then asked me: "Did you believe you were right to do this?", and I said, "Yes, Father, because I was a soldier and the man was one of the enemy". The priest smiled and said, "Good man yourself".'[73]

None of this means that the election of December 1918 can be seen as a pure and untroubled moment at which a fully formed democracy was born. Labour's fateful decision to stand aside had consequences from which the Irish left never recovered. Furthermore, while Sinn Féin did target the first-time female voters with broad hints of political power in the new Ireland ('in the future the womenfolk of the Gael shall have a high place in the councils of a freed Gaelic nation'), just two of the Sinn Féin candidates were women and only one, Countess Constance Markievicz, was elected.[74] Winifred Carney, like Markievicz a veteran of the Rising, was defeated in Belfast. A pattern of male domination was laid down. And, of course, the outcome of the election—the creation of the first Dáil in January 1919—was a reflection of a bitterly divided 'nation', not a truly united one. The Irish Convention, which met between July 1917 and March 1918, had been unable to forge an agreement between nationalists and unionists on the implementation of Home Rule, and this effectively ended any hope of an all-Ireland settlement.[75] Moreover, just before the first Dáil met, Richard Burdon Haldane, 1st Viscount Haldane, KT, OM, PC, KC, an influential Scottish Liberal and later Labour imperialist politician, lawyer and philosopher, was summoned to Ireland by his old friend Lord Lieutenant

Sir John French. Haldane was one of the first British politicians to argue that the solution to the problems between Britain and the Irish lay in compromise rather than force. He arrived in Dublin on 16 January 1919 and rapidly constructed a proposal for Lord French, with the intention that the overture would be passed to the political leaders of Sinn Féin: Ireland would be offered 'self-government on the status of a dominion under the Crown'. To facilitate this, the British government would ensure that generous financial provisions would be forthcoming.[76] The Soloheadbeg ambush, however, put paid to all Haldane's advice and efforts.

Despite conditions of repression, the 1918 election changed the view and the activities of the reorganising Irish Volunteers immensely. Florence O'Donoghue summed it up thus:

> Despite the intimidating factors and the immense disparity in the relative strength and resources, there were some compensation sources of hope and encouragement. The effect of the general election of December 1918 was fundamental. A great majority of the people had expressed its will for national independence and separation from Britain. When the elected representatives of the nation formed a government, endorsed the Proclamation of the Republic [from the 1916 Easter Rising] and issued a solemn Declaration of Independence, the Volunteers were given, at a critical moment, a clear mandate and a definite mission. The moral right inherent in all revolts against unjust alien rule became thereafter also for them an explicit duty—the duty of defending national institutions set up by the free will of the people.[77]

As a basis for insurrectionary tactics, the alternative administration of the Dáil, both as a political concept and as a political fact, was extremely important. It gave the Irish struggle a national standing which it otherwise could not have claimed at that stage. The Irish Volunteers became the Irish Republican Army, the accredited force of a nation that was fighting for its life.[78] The Irish leaders were then able to apply the concept of a nation at war, an idea that enabled them to justify the killings that were to become an essential part of the campaign for undermining the British political hold on Ireland but which otherwise might have been seen as pointless acts of terrorism. *An t-Óglách* made the point:

> The state of war which is thus declared to exist, renders the
> national army the most important national service of the
> moment. It justifies Irish Volunteers in treating the armed forces
> of the enemy, whether soldiers or policemen, exactly as a national
> army would treat the members of an invading army. Every
> Volunteer is entitled morally and legally, when in the execution
> of his duty, to use all legitimate methods of warfare.[79]

On 21 January 1919 the First Dáil met at 3.30 p.m. in the Round
Room of the Mansion House.[80] Count George Plunkett called the meeting
to order and nominated Cathal Brugha as Ceann Comhairle
(speaker/chairperson) for Dáil Éireann. Padraig Ó Maille seconded this.
Brugha presided thereafter and, following the reading of the Declaration of
Independence, he told the cheering assembly: 'Deputies, you understand
from what is asserted in this Declaration that we are now done with
England. Let the world know it and those who are concerned bear it in
mind.' It must be said that the political ferment that resulted in the election
of the Dáil carried with it at least an acknowledgement of militancy. The
Dáil declared at this first meeting that a state of war existed between Britain
and Ireland, though many of its members had ambivalent feelings about
what that war should be like—or even if a 'war' would be necessary at all.
The Dáil's dilemma was plain: its members had been elected to secure an
Irish Republic, something that they all knew they could not wish into
being.

The Declaration of Independence was passed unanimously. Brugha
read it in Irish, Éamonn Duggan in English and George Gavan-Duffy in
French. Piaras Béaslaí, Conor Collins, George Gavan-Duffy, Seán T. Ó
Ceallaigh, James O'Mara and James J. Walsh drafted the Provisional
Constitution and Declaration of Independence. The 'Message to Free
Nations' was read by Robert Barton in English and by J.J. O'Kelly in Irish,
and was an international appeal for solidarity to support Ireland's demand
for independence.[81] When the documents were read in Irish, most of the
delegates listened eagerly but few understood a word of Irish. The simple
fact that the Irish language was used, however, underscored the separate and

distinct nature of Ireland as its own country with its own language and culture.

A Democratic Programme of Dáil Éireann was read and unanimously adopted, founded on the 1916 Proclamation. Even in its 'watered-down' form, the Programme was a radical document outlining social change in Ireland. At the request of the Dáil, Thomas Johnson,[82] secretary of the Irish Labour Party, and William O'Brien[83] prepared and submitted a draft for a social and democratic programme. Only about half of their draft was included in the programme as finally amended and submitted by Seán T. O'Kelly.[84] Many of the TDs, including Collins, were opposed to some of the socialist ideas in the Programme, and Collins was vocal in his opposition. It is not clear whether he was innately opposed to socialism or simply feared that any ideology other than nationalism would hinder the independence movement. He threatened (through the IRB) to suppress the Programme on the grounds that it was too radical.[85] Prior to its submission, at the direction of Sinn Féin leaders who were nervous about its socialist content, O'Kelly amended the Programme to meet the objections of Collins and other senior IRB members. They wanted the removal of explicit affirmations of socialist principles, such as the right of the nation 'to resume possession' of the nation's wealth 'wherever the trust is abused or the trustee fails to give faithful service'. O'Kelly also had to remove a reference that encouraged the 'organisation of people into trade unions and co-operative societies'.[86] Some think that if Collins had been present at the first sitting of the Dáil, rather than in England preparing for de Valera's escape from Lincoln prison, the Democratic Programme might not have been accepted. Even de Valera objected, though he was not in attendance; he warned that the priority had to be the overthrow of British rule in Ireland.[87] It must, however, be noted that, like the radical social principles embodied in the 1916 Proclamation, the Programme would have had little appeal anywhere in Ireland except Dublin.

Twenty-eight TDs attended this first session.[88] The answer to the roll-call for thirty-four absent deputies was 'Imprisoned by the foreign enemy', and for three others 'Deported by the foreign enemy'.[89] Answering 'Present' were twenty-eight Sinn Féin TDs out of a total of 104 names called, including all other parties. Even Ulster's Edward Carson received an invitation—in Irish. Some TDs were elected for two constituencies, so there were only sixty-nine persons elected. Two were ill, three had been deported, five were on missions abroad, but most were in jail in England. (Collins and Harry Boland were in England working on de Valera's escape from prison but were marked present to keep others from asking where they were.) Thirty-three per cent of Dáil members were under thirty-five years of age, and another forty per cent were between thirty-five and forty. There were only two Protestant members: Ernest Blythe and Robert Barton.

Since the Soloheadbeg attack in County Tipperary occurred on the same day, some point to 21 January as the start of the War of Independence.[90] While that military aspect is not certain as regards a 'beginning', it is clear that the first sitting of the Dáil should be accepted as the start of the political campaign for independence.[91] All of the documents presented and speeches made were directed not only at the domestic audience but also at the international audience. To that end, there were about one hundred journalists present, most of whom represented international publications. Keeping in mind that many of the TDs taking their seats that day opposed and condemned the Soloheadbeg ambush, it is clear that even at this early stage many of the Irish saw that the true route to independence was through politics, and it was only subsequently that violence became a more important element of the equation.

However much the election of the Dáil changed Irish perceptions, it would be a mistake to argue that the Irish possessed a clear military, political or propaganda strategy for the conflict that was smouldering slowly, ready to be lit in 1919. They did not. Indeed, beyond a pragmatic principle that a massed uprising with fixed defences was to be avoided at all costs (the painful lesson of Easter 1916), the IRA campaign would prove to be a constant work in progress in all areas, adapting to circumstances and resources but gradually gaining in both intensity and sophistication.[92] *An t-Óglách* sketched the outline of a strategy in broad brush-strokes:

> England must be given the choice between evacuating this country and holding it by a foreign garrison with a perpetual state of war in existence. She must be made to realise that that state of war is not healthy for her. The agents of England in this country must be made to realise that their occupation is not a healthy one. All those engaged in carrying on the English

administration in this country must be made to realise that it is not safe for them to try to 'carry on' in opposition to the Irish Republican Government and the declared wishes of the people. In particular, any policeman, soldier, judge, warder, or official, from the English Lord Lieutenant downwards, must be made to understand that it is not wise for him to distinguish himself by undue 'zeal' in the service of England in Ireland, nor in his opposition to the Irish Republic.[93]

The press in Ireland was generally sceptical of the Dáil; the *Irish Times* called it a 'stage play at the Mansion House' and said that the TDs 'lived in cloud cuckoo land'. It reported that

The press gallery witnessed a solemn act of defiance of the British Empire by a body of young men [*sic*; no mention was made of Countess Markievicz, who was in Holloway Prison] who have not the slightest notion of the Empire's power and resources. The quicker Ireland becomes convinced of the folly which elected them, the sooner sanity will return.[94]

The British press reaction was overwhelmingly hostile, and the reaction in Ulster even more so:

Thus Ireland is alleged to be a Celtic and Roman Catholic nation, and all who are not Celts and Romanists are regarded as foreigners. It is because Ulster knows that this is what Home Rule means that it will not have it.[95]

At first, the British government did not see the Dáil as a threat serious enough to warrant the taking of active steps against it, but in republican minds a significant change took place on its establishment. The Dáil claimed to be the *de facto* government of Ireland, despatched envoys across the world to obtain international recognition and attempted to set up a 'counter-government' by establishing rival police, judicial and administrative departments. Fighting for a government—though ridiculed and unrecognised—legitimised the Irish acts of aggression against Crown forces that were already taking place.[96]   Nevertheless, there were continuing conflicts between those who wanted to follow solely 'constitutional methods', led by Arthur Griffith, and the 'physical-force men', led by those in the Irish Republican Brotherhood, Collins and the more aggressive men who had graduated from British prisons after the Rising. Though some of the Volunteers were moving to an open guerrilla war, the political wing regarded its task in the struggle for independence as the formation of a viable alternative government. As a result, translating Sinn Féin's moral and legal endorsement into practical political change was going to prove difficult.[97]

Almost until the Truce in July 1921, Lloyd George refused to accept the situation as a war, primarily for political and public relations reasons; this did make some sense, however, because against whom was a war to be fought? A democratically elected, if errant, assembly? The British did not intend to conquer Ireland, so war was not the appropriate concept, but how, then, to restore law and order and give Home Rule a chance, with a police force that could not deal with the scale of the threat?[98] That lack of direction and confusion on the part of the British hampered them throughout the war and was blamed by many in their military or intelligence reports of military 'failures' in 1921 and thereafter. As with so much of the war, the British reactions, and over-reactions, were as important to the Irish as their own actions.

Early in 1919 the republican movement faced another crisis regarding the relationship between its political and military components. On 24 March a notice purporting to have been issued by Sinn Féin's general secretaries appeared in the press. It stated that de Valera would be welcomed into Dublin by the lord mayor, and that there would be demonstrations by Sinn Féin and the Irish Volunteers. Two Sinn Féin secretaries, Harry Boland and Tom Kelly, signed the notice. *The Times* noted that 'the arrangements for his [de Valera's] reception seem to be designed with the object of impressing the Peace Conference and American opinion with the supremacy of the Republican movement in Ireland'.[99]

When the Sinn Féin Executive gathered that day, none of them recalled sanctioning such a reception. Darrell Figgis asked Kelly why he had signed the notice. Michael Collins rose and declared that the reception plans had not been issued by Sinn Féin but by the Volunteers. He indicated that the public demonstration was meant as a provocation, declaring that Ireland was likely to get more out of a state of disorder than from a continuance of the situation as it then stood. Returning to the issue of the authority for the statement, Collins added, 'The proper people to take decisions of that kind were ready to face the British military, and were resolved to force the issue. And they were not to be deterred by weaklings and cowards.'[100] Collins was essentially telling the assembled political leaders that the 'physical-force' wing would decide the course of the republican movement, but his bombastic style did not cow Arthur Griffith, who told Collins that no body other than the Executive had authority to decide whether to go ahead with the reception.[101] The Sinn Féin leaders debated for two hours, and their debate carried over to the next day, when Griffith reported that de Valera also objected to the reception and the Executive cancelled it.[102]

Collins's view of the necessity of politics had yet to manifest itself, and he continued to regard politicians with disgust. He wrote to Austin Stack on 17 March 1919 that 'the policy now seems to be to squeeze out anyone who is tainted with strong fighting ideas. It seems to me that official Sinn Féin is inclined to be ever less militant and ever more political, theoretical.'[103] In May Collins still deplored the 'constitutional, moral force' wing and their ability to exclude from the Standing Committee of Sinn Féin those who believed 'in the utility of fighting'. He added: 'There is, I suppose, the effect or tendency of all revolutionary movements to divide themselves up into their components'.[104] Collins's meaning was clear: if the politicians would not accept revolution, the revolutionaries would have to bypass the politicians. The relationship between the two arms of the movement remained ambiguous but strengthened as the conflict deepened and each became dependent on the other.

In August 1919 Brugha, as the Minister for Defence, took measures to bind the IRA to the Dáil. Initially the Irish Volunteers were answerable to no authority except their own executive. On 20 August Brugha moved that every Dáil representative and Volunteer should swear an oath of allegiance 'to support and defend the Irish Republic and the Government of the Irish Republic, which is Dáil Éireann, against all enemies, foreign and domestic'.[105] The motion sparked much debate. Tom Kelly called it a species of coercion against the Volunteers. Arthur Griffith, acting president in de Valera's absence, spoke strongly in favour of the oath. Brugha said that he regarded the Irish Volunteers as a standing army, and that as such they should be subject to the government.[106] The motion passed by thirty votes to five.

The controversy over the oath to the Dáil speaks to the lingering distrust between various sections of the republican movement. Carl von Clausewitz insisted that military authority should be subject to civil authority and that wars cannot be conducted without the political ends in view.[107] In a war such as that being fought in Ireland, in which the sides were so unequal and many anticipated a negotiated settlement, this necessity was even more apparent. Nevertheless, the Volunteers were created as an independent organisation, and the Dáil's recognition that the IRA founded the Republic during the Easter Rising gave them a certain legitimacy for many of the rank and file. For these reasons the oath created some dissension. Todd Andrews later wrote: 'I was sorry we took the oath to Dáil Éireann. I thought, or rather felt, that no outside organization should have any say in the activities of the Volunteers.'[108] Neither the Dáil nor the Volunteers were eager to formalise their mutual bonds. The Dáil, for its part, was more dilatory in admitting, or asserting, its responsibility for military actions. In practice, the oath was unevenly administered to various republican units at the discretion of their officers, but theoretically it bound the IRA to the Dáil.

Notwithstanding the conflicts in views between those advocating 'constitutional means' and those of a more 'physical-force' bent, the combination of effort in the military and political spheres was well illustrated in the campaign against the RIC. The attacks on individual RIC men and on their barracks were co-ordinated with a national call for the constables to resign from the force, discouragement of enlistment in it and social ostracism of those who refused to comply. The Dáil announced the policy of ostracism of RIC men and their families on 11 April 1919. This proved successful in demoralising the police, as people turned their faces from a force increasingly compromised by association with British government repression. The rate of resignation went up and recruitment in Ireland dropped off dramatically. The RIC were often reduced to buying food at gunpoint, as shops and other businesses refused to deal with them. Some RIC men co-operated with the IRA through fear or sympathy, supplying the organisation with valuable information. (See Chapter 6 for a description of ostracism as a method of terrorism.) In the spring of 1920 the RIC numbered around 9,700 men. From the beginning of 1919 to the time of the Truce in July 1921, the police sustained more than 1,000 casualties, constituting two thirds of all those suffered by the Crown forces, including 370 dead.

The fourth public session of the First Dáil was held on 19 August 1919 and established the 'Dáil/Republican Courts'.[109] These were set up under Austin Stack, Minister for Justice, and had civil and criminal jurisdiction.[110] Young barristers from the Law Library in Dublin's Four Courts drew up the Rules of Court under the direction of James Creed Meredith, KC, a Protestant, who served as the president of the Dáil/Republican Supreme Court from 1920 to 1922. The judges on the courts were rarely trained or qualified as solicitors or barristers but had an innate sense of justice and fair play. Soon even loyalists were appealing to the courts to decide their cases. The *Irish Times* wrote that 'the Sinn Féin Courts are steadily extending their jurisdiction and dispensing justice, even-handedly between man and man, Catholic and Protestant … landlord and tenant'.[111] These courts took advantage of the malaise within the British administration in Ireland, and by directing its blows at the weak points of that structure the IRA hastened its collapse. So effective was their campaign of terror and intimidation on the British courts, the police, the magistrates and the local authorities that in time they abandoned their responsibilities and saw them assumed by the local officers and leading politicians of the underground government represented by Dáil Éireann. The British administration in Ireland thus failed to provide for a modicum of internal law and order. Once a government can no longer guarantee public security it has abdicated its mandate. By 1919, after the result of the Dáil elections was proclaimed to the world, the British administration was thus doubly illegitimate, and the Irish *de facto* government was gaining legitimacy in the eyes of the Irish people and internationally.[112]

Enough had occurred in the way of violent insurrection throughout 1919 to make it clear to Lloyd George that the use of force alone was not the answer if Ireland was to be pacified. By the start of 1920 the 'King's Writ' was no longer to be found in much of Ireland.

The alternative government of Dáil Éireann had blossomed in the summer of 1920.

...

Its success with the courts, the police, army and local government
created a demand for services far beyond those of administration.
It is now seen by many, if not most people as the defacto
government of the country. It was now viewed by many people
as being at least one of the governing forces in Ireland.[113]

A report by the British on its Irish administration of the time presented a
damning view to the Cabinet:

The Castle Administration does not administer. On the
mechanical side it can never have been any good and is now quite
obsolete: in the infinitely more important sphere of a) informing
and advising the Irish government in relation to policy and b) of
practical capacity in the application of policy it simply has no
existence.[114]

Concurrently with increased military action, the Irish engaged in more
direct political action in 1920, including an attempt to disorganise the entire
transport system of the country so far as carrying British troops or war supplies
was concerned. Dublin dockers were instructed to refuse to handle suspect
cargoes, and railwaymen throughout the country were ordered to refuse to
work on trains carrying men or *matériel* for the British. Attempts were also
made to derail trains.[115] The campaign succeeded to the extent that General
Macready called it an almost complete 'dislocation of transport'.

Whenever the necessity arises, soldiers and police present
themselves as passengers by train. If they are carried, well and
good; if not, the defaulting railwaymen are suspended, and a
shortage of staff ensues, resulting eventually in a curtailment of
services. It is obvious that sooner or later complete paralysis will
overtake the Irish railway system. When this occurs, it will be
impossible to institute an alternative road transport service. In the
first place the necessary lorries and drivers are not available; and
in the second, it is unlikely that the Republicans would allow
such service without interruption.[116]

Not all guerrilla activities involved weapons and ammunition. Some of the best political weapons were those used to disrupt the economy, especially since much of the economy involved British or loyalist owners of businesses.

Nevertheless, the Irish suffered setbacks as well. In June 1920 Collins proposed that all republicans, except publicans, public servants and various classes of businessmen 'highly susceptible to enemy distraint or seizure', be encouraged to send their income tax payments to the Dáil instead of the British Department of Inland Revenue. He hoped thereby to augment the Dáil's income by as much as £500,000 annually. The Dáil agreed, intending the funds to be used for the new Irish apparatus of local government, but it eventually abandoned the programme. Farmers and businessmen, fearing that their land or assets would be seized if they refused to pay the taxes and rates to the British, showed no inclination to send them to the Irish instead.[117]

Meanwhile the British did have military successes in the field, although these came at a great political cost. Patrols, raids, reprisals and arrests were indiscriminate measures that caused resentment among local communities. By 1921 many of these raids and reprisals were carried out by regular British army soldiers, and this played into the IRA's hands. One of the chief objectives was to incite a violent British reaction or reprisal, so that it could be exploited for propaganda and political purposes.[118]

Politics were just as important within the British Cabinet and parliament as within the Irish contingent. It was a common thread in the British government that the Irish situation in 1920 was 'one of disastrous failure on the part of a police force overmatched by a vicious and cunning foe and undermined by a weak government'. That view was a general one and was shared by the head of the British civil service, Sir Warren Fisher, who prepared a report for Lloyd George on the state of British intelligence and the general administrative situation in Ireland. His report revealed a Dublin Castle political administration mired in stagnation, bureaucratic intrigue and sectarian bigotry, whose bunker mentality had completely 'demoralised the civil service'. 'With the notable exception of General Macready who had fortuitously now been imported, the Government of Ireland strikes one as almost woodenly stupid and quite devoid of imagination.'[119] Fisher saw that the British government thought that it faced a straight choice between conciliation and massive force, though the military leaders could not guarantee success, especially as it would have to rely upon that 'demoralised civil service and police'. He knew that the British intelligence and governance problems went much deeper, and he felt that an alternative should be made available.

To achieve that end, Fisher installed a new 'team' in Dublin Castle, led by Sir John Anderson, widely regarded as the most talented administrator of the day.[120] Reporting to Anderson were Sir Alfred (Andy) Cope[121] and Mark Sturgis.[122] Fisher proposed many changes and thought that over time his policy and personnel alternatives would eventually culminate in negotiations with Sinn Féin, and if and when that happened he intended that the Dublin Castle administration should be ready. Cope was described as 'Lloyd George's special agent, charged with informally exploring avenues of settlement with Sinn Féin'.[123] The three men often acted without the sanction of Hamar Greenwood, their ministerial superior. In fact, their brief was a secret and confidential attempt by the British government to find someone in Sinn Féin with whom they could negotiate. Since the trio favoured conciliation and negotiations leading to Dominion Home Rule, Fisher and Lloyd George had shrewdly left open the option of an eventual compromise peace.

Towards the end of 1920 the British were wearing down the Irish militarily, though the British did not know it. Bloody Sunday, the Kilmichael ambush and other Irish successes obscured the fact that the Irish were desperately short of ammunition and that the British had captured or killed many of their leaders. As the war continued into 1921 those shortages of arms and men became acute across the country. Cooler and more realistic heads on both sides began to see the benefits of a political peace.

Long before Collins went to London in October 1921 to participate in the Treaty negotiations he was involved in responding to the peace feelers extended by the British.[124] Dr Robert Farnan, a prominent gynaecologist who lived at 5 Merrion Square, was attending the wives of two Auxiliaries at the time, and he attributed the fact that his house was never raided or searched to respect for his medical practice. At Prime Minister Lloyd George's behest, Archbishop Patrick Joseph Clune of Perth, Western Australia, met Collins there on 7 December 1920 to discuss early British peace overtures. (Archbishop Clune was an uncle of Conor Clune, who had just been tortured and killed on Bloody Sunday in November.) It was at this time that the British were showing the first signs of negotiating in earnest. Lloyd George began to send out feelers for talks, but he did so in a fashion calculated to produce the maximum amount of distrust and obstinacy on the part of the Irish.

Archbishop Clune, born on 6 January 1864 in Ruan, Co. Clare, was first asked to mediate on behalf of his native land by the Hon. Lord Morris, T.P. O'Connor MP and Joe Devlin MP at a luncheon in London on 30 November. That night there were severe Black and Tan reprisals at Lahinch, Co. Clare, with several people killed and many homes burned. Lloyd George condemned all reprisals and asked the archbishop to go to Dublin, interview the Sinn Féin leaders, attempt to arrange a temporary truce and prepare an atmosphere for negotiations. These negotiations were opposed by General Nevil Macready but favoured by much of the British Cabinet and government.[125] Lloyd George could not guarantee the safety of the archbishop, however, and would not consent to a safe conduct for the Sinn Féin leaders. In order to remain incognito, Archbishop Clune travelled to Ireland on the mailboat as 'Revd Dr Walsh'. On arrival in Dublin on 6 December, he first stayed at All Hallows College, Drumcondra.

Joe O'Reilly, Collins's prime messenger, was assigned to bring the archbishop to Collins:

My [O'Reilly's] next meeting with Dr Clune was the evening of the next day, Monday, 6th December, 1920, when about eight in the evening I called at the Gresham Hotel in O'Connell Street, met Dr Clune, and told him of the time and place where he would meet Michael Collins the next day. I again warned him to be very careful on leaving for the appointment, and to show no surprise if the driver of the car that I would send took a roundabout way. His Grace took me aside and expressed his uneasiness at the prospect of being followed by Dublin Castle. He then said to me: 'I will go to Dublin Castle and see if my movements have been watched. It would be better to drop the negotiations than risk the capture of Michael Collins'.

On 7 December, accompanied by Dr Michael Fogarty, Bishop of Killaloe, Clune was driven to Farnan's home to meet Collins.

The next day, Tuesday, 7th December, Dr Clune, accompanied by Dr Fogarty, Bishop of Killaloe, set out from All Hallows College, Drumcondra, for the first interview with Michael Collins. They were driving quite a time, not noticing where they were, too interested in their chat, when Dr Clune looked out as the car drew up before one of the fine residences in Merrion Square, a most unlikely hide-out for a man with a price on his head. The driver knocked at the hall-door and the two bishops were shown into the consulting room of Dr Robert Farnan, one of Dublin's leading gynaecologists. I called upon Dr Farnan in October 1935, and he told me that Dr Clune and 'Mick' Collins met in his house regularly during the negotiations. Mick usually came on a bike which he left at a tobacconist in Merrion Row, just round the corner. At that time, December 1920, Dr Farnan was attending the wives of two of the auxiliaries, and consequently his house was never suspected. He remembered the horrible feeling he had on one occasion as a lorry full of auxiliaries pulled up before the door while Mick and Archbishop Clune were upstairs. The doctor had a few bad minutes until the husband of one of the two patients handed him a message from his wife. Another day Mick came down the stairs arm-in-arm with the Archbishop. Both were laughing at some story as Mick opened the hall door, and stood behind it until Dr Farnan hailed a cab from across the street. As the Archbishop got into the cab a lorry full of 'Black-and-Tans' moved slowly past the house. Perhaps some one had recognised Mick on one of his many visits. Mick closed the door, drew his revolver and watched the lorry from a corner of the curtain. The lorry continued its beat up and down the street, so Mick decided to get out through the back garden. That his house was never once searched or suspected throughout the negotiations Dr Farnan attributes to his professional interest in the wives of the auxiliaries he was attending. Suspicion there undoubtedly was, probably through some policeman glimpsing Michael Collins on one of his visits, but, fortunately, the house escaped a search, luckily for all concerned.[126]

Following his discussions with Collins, Archbishop Clune assured the British Cabinet that Collins 'was the one with whom effective business could be done'.[127] Collins was on the run but Arthur Griffith was in Mountjoy Prison at this time, and on 8 December Dr Fogarty and Archbishop Clune met with Sir Alfred Cope, the Assistant Undersecretary for Ireland, at Mountjoy, and then with Griffith, who enthusiastically welcomed the prospect of a truce. They then met with Eoin MacNeill, who was not so enthusiastic but accepted it. The idea was presented to Michael Staines. Cope was told to present a draft of a truce agreement to Dublin Castle authorities, but this received a hostile reception from Chief Secretary for Ireland Sir Hamar Greenwood and the British military.[128]

Archbishop Clune returned to London and met Lloyd George on 10 December, had another meeting with him on 11 December and returned to Dublin that night. The British authorities in Dublin Castle agreed to meet with the Dáil, but Collins and Richard Mulcahy could not attend. Moreover, the proposed truce would require the IRA/Volunteers to surrender all their arms and the Dáil could not meet publicly. Clune again returned to London on 18 December, and though meetings continued until 28 December the negotiations were at an end. Archbishop Clune wrote to Bishop Fogarty, outlining the failure and his feelings:

Jermyn Court Hotel,
London,
New Year's Day, 1921.
My Lord, You have heard, I daresay, that I broke off negotiations on the morning of Christmas Eve and that in the afternoon the Prime Minister's Secretary was here begging me not to leave town till the New Year, as Cabinet was to consider the whole question, and important developments might take place. He came again last Tuesday evening and took back with him a memo at the points of the Truce. On Wednesday afternoon there was a long Cabinet meeting and another on Thursday, at which General Macready, Lord French and several others were present. The Secretary rang me up on Thursday morning to inform me that he would call that night late or Friday (yesterday) morning. He came at 11.30 a.m. yesterday, and here is a summary of his oral communications.

That Cabinet etc. had given long and careful consideration to my proposals: that the proposed Truce gave no effective guarantee for a permanent settlement: that consequently the Government had come to the conclusion that it was better to see the thing through as was done in the American and South African wars unless meanwhile the Sinn Féiners surrender their arms and publicly announce the abandonment of violent measures: that the Government felt sanguine that the new Home Rule Bill when studied and understood would be worked, in fact they felt sanguine that within six months all would be working in harmony for Ireland, etc., etc. He then added a few gracious personal compliments from the Prime Minister. My first comment was that I felt sure the Holy Ghost had nothing to do with such a decision which sent him off exploding with laughter.

What is the source of this strange optimism about all classes working the Home Rule Bill in harmony within a few months, I can't make out. (Greenwood repeats it in a speech quoted in to-day's paper), unless it is a deduction from the whining [sic] across the water. This Government determination to carry on the policy of frightfulness to the bitter end may be bluff. I think it is not, and hence I believe that the position needs further reconsideration in the light of this considered declaration of policy on their part.

The Secretary incidentally mentioned that from my conversations the Prime Minister had a higher idea of the gunmen: that there could be no humiliation before the world in yielding to vastly superior forces: that the Home Rule Act can be worked for Ireland, not for England, and that through the working of it practically every English official could be sent out of Ireland in a few months, etc., etc.

The point I am coming to is: Ought our grand boys allow themselves to be butchered to make a Saxon holiday? Ought they not rely on passive resistance? However, I suppose the advent of De Valera to Ireland will quickly solve these questions.

Though I am naturally sorry that my mission has not been successful, in another sense I am glad it has ended. I was beginning to feel the strain. It has done good, I think, indirectly. It has narrowed down the issues, and incidentally it has saved Your Lordship's life and All Hallows College from military occupation.

My programme is now to leave for the continent as soon as Father McMahon joins me, and to catch the boat at Naples on the 24th, I feel sure you need have no further apprehension about yourself. They have given me assurances that all necessary measures would be taken to safeguard your life.

Wishing Your Lordship a full measure of New Year graces and Joys.

I remain, with grateful memories of your kindness.

Yours very sincerely in Xt.

P. J. Clune Archbishop of Perth.

A peace agreement might have been reached following Clune's mission along much the same lines as agreed a year later but for the British Cabinet's refusal to grant any form of dominion status and the demand that the Irish turn in their weapons before talks were initiated—and the most bitter and bloody period of the war could have been avoided.[129] If it had been up to Collins, a truce would have been declared in December 1920.[130] Unofficially, by that time it was clear to some British policy-makers in Dublin and London that many Irish leaders would accept a ceasefire followed by negotiations without preconditions, and that dominion status like that of South Africa or Canada would be acceptable to many. In an interview with American journalist Carl Ackerman, Collins was critical of the Irish political leaders' failure to seize the opportunity for a truce at the end of 1920:

> A truce would have been obtained after the burning of Cork by the forces of the Crown in December 1920, had our own leaders acted with discretion. There is every reason to believe the British Government was minded to respond favourably to the endeavours of Archbishop Clune. But the English attitude hardened through the too precipitate action of certain of our public men and public bodies.
>
> ...

Several of our most important men gave evidence of an over-keen desire to peace, while proposals were being made and considered. So it was that, although terms of the truce had been virtually agreed upon, the British statesmen abruptly terminated the negotiations when they discovered what they took to be signs of weakness in our councils. They conditioned the truce, then, on surrender of our arms; and the struggle went on.[131]

Later, Collins was to lament:

In my opinion, Mr Lloyd George intended the Act [the Government of Ireland Act, passed in December 1920] to allay world criticism. As propaganda, it might do to draw attention away from British violence for a month or two longer. At the end of the period, most of the English Ministers mistakenly believed Ireland would have been terrorised into submission.[132]

There are others who feel that the July 1921 Truce could have been agreed at this earlier time but that it was abandoned because some British leaders thought that the Irish were too keen on a truce, which was perceived as evidence of Irish weakness. Mulcahy thought that that was the case and echoed that the opportunity was lost 'through the too precipitate action of certain of our public men and public bodies'.[133] Reports poured into London that the IRA was demoralised and that public opinion was turning against them because of their own programme of reprisals. The British thought that the Irish 'needed' a truce, and Lloyd George insisted at the last minute on the surrender of arms—and that was the end of these discussions.[134] Scotland Yard's investigators erroneously reported that de Valera wanted a truce but that Collins had a veto and exercised it.[135] The reports could not have been more wrong. Collins was flexible about the terms of any truce, short of a surrender of arms, but the British Cabinet insisted on the turning in of arms, and this was a non-starter in any Irish circle. As a result, the decision of the British government to keep the emphasis on a military solution persisted into the spring of 1921.

Further attempts at negotiation continued after these failures, and Andy Cope and Collins met several times in complete secrecy. Collins remained sceptical, but he knew that the IRA's military position was beginning to unravel. British military intelligence still expressed confidence that the military could crush the revolt. David Boyle of British intelligence wrote a report predicting military victory in six weeks. This greatly influenced the British Cabinet to shut down peace initiatives.[136] Nevertheless, the Clune negotiations indicated a willingness to continue to negotiate and the recognition that Collins was a 'major player', and the British from this time forward began to accept that a negotiated settlement was possible. As with the military actions, however, negotiations had to proceed at a pace that could be acceptable to both sides; ideologues and militarists on both sides had to be cajoled to the table. Georges Clemenceau was right: 'War is much too important to be left to soldiers'.

Cope's letters to Fisher illustrated the problems he faced: 'taking his career in his hands', he had 'abandoned the traditional methods of the Castle peace parleyings and got into direct and personal contact with the leaders of the Irish people'. He 'had to first convince the powers of Sinn Féin that he meant to play straight with them, and then persuade the powers residing in Dublin Castle and elsewhere that the leaders of the "murder gang" desired an honourable settlement'. Finally, he informed Fisher that 'I have met quite a number of prominent Sinn Féiners—two were sentenced to death in the rebellion and reprieved—and I feel that I have the temper of the present situation'.[137] Cope had contacts at the highest levels of the IRA. When he asked an intermediary to put him in touch with de Valera, she asked, 'Do you not want to meet Michael Collins?' Cope replied, 'No, I meet Michael every night'.[138] Some deemed Cope a traitor. When the Truce was announced, the conservative newspaper *The Morning Post* editorialised: 'While they were still fighting in the illusion that the Government was behind them, Mr Cope was establishing friendly relations with their would-be murderers'.[139]

Beginning in January 1921 and continuing until the Truce in July, both sides suffered the highest casualties of the war. Attacks escalated to new levels of violence in the south-western counties as well as in Dublin, and this led to a number of mid- to large-scale engagements between the IRA and the regular British army. From that point the IRA was fighting with dwindling resources, and the sides moved closer to a political solution. Collins knew how few Volunteers were actually available for service. By the time of the Truce there were scarcely 2,500 Volunteers under arms, and all units were almost out of ammunition. When Tom Barry came to Dublin in May 1921 to report on the progress in Cork, his one request was for more ammunition—and de Valera replied, 'We'll let Mick take care of that'.[140] The British had made it almost impossible to smuggle arms and ammunition, and every bullet had to be made to count.

The British government was also under pressure of time owing to the provisions of the implementation schedule of the Government of Ireland Act. The Bill took two forms: appeasement and coercion. The carrot and the stick were being offered to Ireland concurrently, which Chesterton derided in his pamphlet *The Delusion of the Double Plan*.[141] Throughout the war the British wavered between repression and conciliation, but repression fuelled Irish anger while concession signalled weakness and encouraged people to believe that the IRA were winning. British policy seemed to lurch from one response to another. As General Macready put it, 'Whatever we do, we are sure to be wrong'. The required elections that were included in the conditions of the Act took place in the North and South on 13 and 14 May 1921, and the two devolved parliaments were to take effect immediately afterwards. Just as on the Irish side, the British were split on how to proceed with the war. Chief Secretary Hamar Greenwood argued for more military action and 'not to hesitate at the last gate'.[142] Even Lloyd George was still making bellicose public pronouncements in the spring:

> So long as Sinn Féin demands a Republic, the present evils must go on. So long as the leaders of Sinn Féin stand in this position, and receive the support of their countrymen, settlement is in my opinion impossible.[143]

With time running out, Anderson, Cope and Sturgis increased their efforts to entice Sinn Féin to the bargaining table, and pushed the more militant British to accept that a negotiated settlement was best for them as well. The key intermediary was Cope, who had been working towards this position since his arrival in Dublin Castle. He made contacts with any of the Irish side whom he deemed amenable to negotiation, particularly making overtures to Collins; in Sturgis's words, Cope was talking to all, like 'an octopus grasping everything with its tentacles'.[144] Cope met everyone he could, and astounded some of the Castle authorities. Hervey de

Montmorency said that he could

> not understand how anyone could have been induced to
> undertake such an unpleasant task. Cope must have had
> tremendous courage, patience and a strong stomach to boot, to
> hold interviews with the savage, unsavoury human butchers,
> gloating over their murders of constables and soldiers.[145]

Moves towards negotiation continued, and in April 1921 Edward Stanley, Lord Derby, was sent secretly to Ireland for another series of talks with the Irish, and with de Valera in particular. He stayed at the Gresham Hotel, ineffectively disguised by horn-rimmed glasses and under the name 'Edwards'. His overcoat with his name embroidered into it was found by a chambermaid in his room. He met with de Valera to begin negotiations for a truce, but little progress was made.

The fact that de Valera spent from May 1919 to December 1920 in the US took him out of the mainstream of the Irish military and political efforts. When he returned, he told members of the Dáil that the newspapers in the US were calling the Irish 'murderers' for the way in which they were conducting their guerrilla war. De Valera was determined to bring Collins and the IRA under control and to exert his personal authority over the Irish military effort. He blamed much of his failure to gain American recognition of Ireland on the absence of a conventional IRA military presence. Somewhat inexplicably, de Valera and Brugha were both advocates of larger military actions, with de Valera saying that 'what we want is one good battle a month with about 500 men on each side'.[146] Both de Valera and Brugha had experienced the folly of the Rising and of placing the Irish in areas that could be surrounded by the British (and was to be repeated in the Custom House attack on which de Valera insisted), so they should have known better. De Valera's return signalled a temporary but disastrous change in IRA military tactics in Dublin, but also renewed efforts to seek a political settlement.[147]

Following the Custom House fire on 25 May 1921, the Irish ammunition situation moved from acute to desperate. The British seized a considerable amount of arms and ammunition on that day, and the Dublin Brigade could not withstand the loss of men to death or capture. Dan

McDonnell said that 'things were so bad with all the units that it was a question of how long they could last. We had no ammunition; we had few guns.'[148] Overall, the IRA 'was effectively beaten in Dublin by June 1921'.[149] As so often happened during the war, however, events moved somewhat in parallel, and by spring 1921 the British government was also considering some sort of political settlement. This represented a major change from Walter Long's statement of summer 1920 that 'the British would not bargain with murderers. The thing is unthinkable.'[150] Fisher's appointment of Anderson, Cope and Sturgis to their positions in Dublin Castle some months before looked prescient and was beginning to bear fruit.

Sturgis's views of de Valera and Collins, and their status and roles in any negotiations, were reflected in an intelligence report from June 1920:[151]

> My private opinion is that things are in a very bad way and de Valera knows it. The Volunteers are out of hand and robberies are being carried out without orders. De Valera is of the opinion that he will be able to arrange a scheme with the Northern Parliament and then present it to the British Government for their acceptance. I am sure he has no power over Collins, if he had, and if sincere would he not have ordered the murders to stop at once?[152]

By early spring 1921, the calls for negotiation were increasing to the degree that British intelligence did its best to keep de Valera from being harmed or arrested:

> ... the Intelligence Service has been ordered not to employ their information to secure the arrest of certain individuals, amongst whom was Mr de Valera. It was considered better that he should remain at large, in order that the authorities might have the head of Sinn Féin organisation with whom to treat should the occasion arise. This order was loyally obeyed despite the difficulty of trying not to see him.[153]

By late May 1921 Cope's efforts were bringing the two sides closer, though the process proceeded in fits and starts, as one can imagine. At a London conference the British Cabinet met with General Macready, who outlined the draconian measures that he felt would be necessary if a military option were to go forward, and he indicated that he was prepared to implement such measures. These included provisions that any member of the Dáil, the IRA, the IRB or Sinn Féin was liable to be executed for treason, and that anyone caught with arms would suffer the same fate.[154] Macready emphasised that such a plan could only be effective if implemented 'with utmost thoroughness' and that only by doing so could the morale of the soldiers and police be maintained.[155] He was blunt with the Cabinet: either 'go all out or get out'.[156] It is unclear whether he really thought that such a plan would work or was merely pressuring the Cabinet to make a decision. How the Irish would have reacted to the increased British troops is, of course, unknown, but it is hard to visualise their being able to put up the necessary resistance to such British reinforcements.

Cope and the 'peace faction' of Dublin Castle disagreed with prolonging the military action, feeling that a military solution would require strict martial law, more house searches, more customs inspectors to stop all IRA arms importation, identity passes to be carried by all persons at all times, and the reassignment of every available British soldier from around the world to Ireland. Colonel Sir Hugh Elles, Commandant of the Tank Corps Centre, was asked to submit a report to the Cabinet; he estimated that if such measures were put into effect it might take two years to complete, but there could be no absolute assurance that the measures, as strict as they would have to be, would result in a favourable end to the war.[157] The British had to make a choice: would their military attempt to subjugate Ireland by threats, terror and more violence, or would they attempt to make peace?

Anderson knew that the time for a decision was imminent. He warned that 'military action to be effective must be vigorous and ruthless. Many innocent people will suffer and the element of human error cannot be eliminated.'[158] Sir Basil Thomson believed that the Irish were split and that Collins was leading a more militarist faction against the more moderate de Valera. On 13 May he reported that the IRA was prepared to fight on and repudiate any settlement made by Sinn Féin. (In retrospect, his report may have been premature but also prescient, as shown by events after the Treaty, but his estimation of Collins's militarism versus de Valera's moderation at this time was misinformed.[159])

151

In July 1921 there was still a widely shared belief among most British army officers that the IRA was on the verge of total defeat. Many of the officers believed that the IRA could have been completely crushed within 'weeks', or at most 'six months'. For these men, the government's willingness to negotiate a settlement at this point was almost incomprehensible.[160] This narrative came to dominate the post-conflict official reports compiled by the military.[161] In *The Record of the Rebellion*, compiled in 1922, the British army argued that the IRA was in a desperate position at the time of the Truce:

> The rebel organisation throughout the country was in a precarious position ... The flying columns and active service units ... were being harried and chased from pillar to post, and were constantly being defeated and broken up by the Crown forces; individuals were being hunted down and arrested; the internment camps were filling up ...[162]

A September 1921 report complained further:

> It is small wonder that the rebel leaders grasped at the straw that was offered, and agreed to negotiation ...[163]

At the same time, some Irish commanders in the field scoffed at Cope's efforts, thinking that the Irish were 'winning' the war and that it was the British military who had their backs to the wall. Some reported discussions among the Irish that it was the British who seemed desperate for a truce.[164] For all that was said or thought on both sides, in May 1921 the Irish killed more members of the British security forces than in any of the preceding months of the war, and the Irish losses were commensurate. (As should have become apparent in World War I, and as the US learned in the guerrilla war of Vietnam sixty years later, an attrition-based 'body count' approach is an extremely poor way of determining the course of a war.) But the war depended on the political momentum that had been generated and that could not be moderated by that stage.

Reaction to the 11 July 1921 Truce leading to the Treaty negotiations was mixed. On the British side, Alison Phillips wrote that 'where all the science and all the massed battalions of the Central Powers had failed, the methods of Sinn Féin succeeded. They did so because they reduced, not the British Army, but the British Government and the British people, to that mood of surrender which is the essence of defeat.'[165] Katharine Chorley went further:'the treaty terms, even though they embodied a compromise, were in reality little less than a surrender'.[166] Lord Edward Carson told the House of Commons that 'they [the Treaty terms] were passed with a revolver pointed at your head and you know it … You know it and you know you passed them because you were beaten, because you failed, and the Sinn Féin army in Ireland had beaten you.'[167]

On the Irish side, many felt that the British had been defeated, that since the British had 'agreed to' a truce they had been fairly beaten, and that the treaty negotiations to follow would involve a victorious Irish and a supplicant British delegation. Those same people felt that the British had been humiliated when their officers were compelled to confer with Irish politicians and IRA officers.

However much the British commanders and politicians dismissed the Truce, or however some of the Irish viewed their position as victors, the essential truth of the situation was that the IRA fought the conflict until British politicians were ready to negotiate with them. By the middle of 1921 it had become clear that the British could only win the war militarily and that this would require the use of methods that the British politicians (and their voters) could not accept. The British public would no longer 'tolerate' their politicians' pursuit of, and acceptance of, the casualties, and the opinion of Britain throughout the world was unpalatable to them. Nevertheless, it is by no means clear that the Irish 'won' the war—it would be more accurate to say that they incurred successes rather than victory.[168]

Even so, right to the end, Greenwood and some of the British military leaders remained sceptical of the need for negotiation or the ability to negotiate a political end to the war.[169] Some of them continued to think and assert that 'victory could be in sight' if they deployed more troops, increased executions and imprisoned more Irish. Macready disagreed:

> There are of course one or two wild people about who still hold the absurd idea that if you go on killing long enough, peace will ensue. I do not believe it for one moment but I do believe that

the more people are killed, the more difficult a final solution becomes.[170]

In the May 1919 election Sinn Féin had scored an almost unanimous victory that convinced even General Macready that the British position in Ireland was untenable:

In all constituents [sic] in Southern Ireland, except Dublin University, Sinn Féin has had a complete 'walk-over', not one single Unionist, nationalist or Labour Candidate being even nominated for any of the remaining 124 seats. There are only two conclusions to be drawn from these results. Either the people of Southern Ireland are solidly republican and support and approve of the Dáil Éireann's policy of murder, outrage and boycott, or the gunmen have so terrorized their fellow countrymen that no one dare nominate or support an individual whose views are other than republican. Sinn Féin would have the world believe that the former is the correct conclusion, and that Southern Ireland is unanimously republican. This is not the case, though it is probable that Sinn Féin would have obtained a substantial majority had the Elections been contested.[171]

It was becoming clear, to Macready at least, that a truce was necessary.

As many military men seem to do, both sides would later argue that they had been 'sold out' and betrayed by their politicians, but British and Irish politicians could be forgiven for having lost faith in any positive assessments offered by the military men.[172] Moreover, the British political leaders realised that their support had collapsed and that they were fighting an enemy that would never give up. Macready ultimately supported Cope's efforts to secure a Truce and, on the same day that he acquiesced, South African Prime Minister Jan Smuts arrived in Dublin to throw his weight behind the proposal. Smuts primarily wrote King George V's speech given at Belfast City Hall on 22 June 1921, appealing for Anglo-Irish and North–South reconciliation, and was intimately aware of the internal views of the British Cabinet and government.[173]

The war had developed in phases, and the balance of effectiveness had swung from side to side. Both the Irish and the British responded to political as well as military advances and pressures. There was no simple 'triumph' for either side. Just as the British had difficulty recognising that they could not give the military or police a free hand and that that would hurt their war effort, it took some time for the British politicians to realise that they were going to have to negotiate with those with whom they had said they never would. Neither side could bring the conflict to an end, as both lacked either the military or the coercive capacity. The political will on the part of the British to effect the necessary military escalation was simply not there.[174] By forcing the British to resort to heavy-handed, politically damaging reprisals and by merely surviving, the Irish emerged with an ultimate 'success'. At the Truce, the Irish side had won 'acceptance' by the British as the valid spokespersons for Irish legitimate interests.[175] The British military disdain for the Truce, or for its need, continued after July, however, and was most succinctly expressed in the notes to the Truce document written by General Sir H.S. Jeudwine, GOC of the 5th Division. Considering it inappropriate because he never recognised the IRA as legitimate opponents representing the Irish people, he proscribed the use of the word 'truce' in all correspondence regarding it:

> The word 'truce' has been applied to this Agreement and the situation which follows from it. This word is generally understood as applicable to an armistice between recognised belligerents. It is preferable, therefore, that it should not be used by us in this instance, but that the statement of terms should be referred to as the 'Agreement' and its effects as a 'suspension of activities'.[176]

Collins's views of the need for a truce and a treaty were published in his book *The Path to Freedom*:

> The National instinct was sound—that the essence of our struggle was to secure freedom to order our own life, without attaching undue importance to the formulas under which that freedom would be expressed. The people knew that our government could and would be moulded by the nation itself to its needs. The nation would make the government, not the government the nation.[177]

155

By spring 1921 Collins recognised that the Irish military efforts could not continue, and he endorsed more aggressive political efforts.[178] A political result demanded of British and Irish politicians patience, intelligence, planning, compromise, creativity and the acceptance of personal moral responsibility for the consequences of what was done and not done, as well as what could be done or not done. The military on both sides were nudged into the political solution. With the provisions of a truce made in principal, a political end to the war was in sight. On 11 July the Truce came into effect.

From 1919 the British had deployed over 50,000 troops (including regular army, Black and Tans, Auxiliaries and RIC)[179] against an Irish rebel force that never reached 5,000 active combatants at any one time.[180] However many men the IRA could call upon by the middle of 1921, they were extremely short of equipment, and Tom Barry described a desperate situation:

> They were practically unarmed. Even in the middle of 1920, the whole Brigade armament was only 35 serviceable rifles, 20 automatics or revolvers, about 30 rounds of ammunition per rifle, and 10 rounds for each revolver or automatic. The Volunteers had no transport, signalling equipment or engineering material, machine-guns or any other weapon whatsoever, except a small supply of explosives and some shot-guns. They had no money and were an unpaid Volunteer force.[181]

Collins knew the great advantages that the British military had, as well as the resources that they could call on to increase their military presence in Ireland. He knew that the Irish could not compete in that battle:

> If this citing of our ability to outwit our enemies seems to place me in the category of those who imagine that in time we could have routed them out of the country, let me dissipate that idea quickly. I hold no such opinion. English power rests on military might and economic control. Such military resistance as we were able to offer was unimportant, had England chosen to go at the task of conquering us in real earnestness. There were good reasons for her not doing so.[182]

While the IRA were not winning the war in May and June 1921, neither were they losing outright. They had not been defeated by midsummer 1921, but it is hard to see how they could have withstood the planned British infusion of additional forces. The British would have been able to counter almost every Irish action, but it is also unclear whether Macready's plans could ever have received the full support that would have been necessary. In summer 1921 Collins and the other realists were seriously deterred from continuing the military campaign.

By the time of the Truce in July 1921, the British had imprisoned or interned almost 5,000 leaders and other Volunteers in Ballykinlar, Spike Island, Bere Island, the Curragh and other camps.[183] The British military effort was not enough, although some army personnel estimated that if they had tens of thousands more troops for an extended period of time they *might* be able to pacify Ireland.[184] That was more than a country 'tired to death of war' could bear.[185] The British public would not support the level of military involvement that some military—and *militant*—leaders (as well as some politicians) would have preferred.[186] Nor would it tolerate the terrorist violence that resulted when the British military committed atrocities and reprisals.[187] There was a gradual change in British political and military attitudes, leading to the realisation that coercion, alone, was impossible and that they would now have to revert to a political solution. The military and political realities of 1921 compelled the British government to make concessions that would have been unthinkable in 1916.

The Irish War of Independence shows that the most successful terrorist campaigns are waged for causes, usually nationalist, that are accepted broadly by the public and supported by a major political effort. Fringe groups seeking radical social change have little chance of success. Everything in life boils down to incentives. Unless the people in charge are properly motivated to change, they will happily maintain the *status quo* forever.

One of the finest summations of the sea-change in Irish politics comes from a historian who opposed the period of revolution, W. Alison Phillips, who was strongly against Irish Home Rule and once declared that 'Ireland is not a nation, but two peoples separated by a deeper gulf than that dividing Ireland from Great Britain'. His book *The Revolution in Ireland* was criticised for leaning towards the Unionist point of view, yet he wrote:

The Sinn Féin organisation of which [Griffith] was the founder and inspirer, consisted [in 1904] of a handful of young teachers, poets and journalists, scarcely known outside their own circle, and utterly without political influence; and so they remained for 12 years longer. In 1921 these same men had made themselves the *de facto* rulers of the greater part of Ireland, had worn down the resistance of the British Government and people, and were in a position to dictate terms to the ministers of a power which had just been victorious in a great war. History records no more amazing overturn.[188]

The press was overwhelmingly in favour of the Truce, as were most of the people of both Ireland and Britain. Ireland celebrated the first signs of peace—but not all of Ireland. Many of the IRA rank and file were desperately opposed, and the stage was set for the censorious Treaty debates and the terrible Irish Civil War that followed. Politics, of course, is the art of the possible, balancing competing interests and accepting that sometimes political expediency is necessary. But if it wasn't for idealists and visionaries, nothing would ever change.

Collins, too, celebrated at his old 'hang-out', Vaughan's Hotel. Following the Truce in July 1921 there was a celebratory gathering:

Shortly after the Truce there was a great gathering in Vaughan's Hotel of all the men who were 'round Mick Collins. It was a farewell party given to Harry Boland before proceeding to America. Apart from Mick Collins and Harry Boland there were also present, Gearóid O'Sullivan, Diarmuid O'Hegarty, Liam Mellows, Liam Tobin, Rory O'Connor, Frank Thornton, Colonel Broy, the late Detective-Sergeant McNamara who was working for Mick Collins, Seán Etchingham of Wexford and many others. It was a joyous occasion and Mick Collins recited, 'Kelly, Burke and Shea', and Liam Mellows sang 'McDonnell of the Glens'—an old Scottish song.

Little did we think that night of the events that were in store before another year had passed.

It is well for mortal man that he cannot see into the future.[189]

Notes

[1] Charles Townshend, 'The Irish Republican Army and the development of guerrilla warfare, 1916–1921', *English Historical Review*, vol. 94, no. 371 (1979).

[2] Robert B. Asprey, 'The challenge of guerrilla tactics', *New York Times*, 13 July 1975.

[3] US Field Manual (interim) 3-07.22, *Counterinsurgency Operations* (1 October 2004).

[4] Charles Townshend, *Britain's Civil Wars: Counterinsurgency in the Twentieth Century* (London, 1986), p. 59.

[5] 'Record of the Rebellion in Ireland in 1920–1921 and the Part Played by the Army in Dealing with it', Imperial War Museum, Box 78/82/2.

[6] Keith Jeffery, *The British Army and the Crisis of Empire, 1918–1922* (Manchester, 1984), p. 86.

[7] W.H. Kautt, *Ground Truths: British Army Operations in the Irish War of Independence* (Sallins, 2014), p. 25.

[8] See James Willbanks, *The Tet Offensive: A Concise History* (New York, 2008).

[9] See 'Bloody Sunday' in Chapter 5, which preceded the Clune negotiations outlined below by just a few days.

[10] Major-General Sir S. Hare, KCMG, CB, 'Martial law from the soldier's point of view', *Army Quarterly*, vol. 7 (October 1923 and January 1924); Charles Townshend, 'Martial law: legal and administrative problems of civil emergency in Britain and the Empire, 1800–1940', *Historical Journal*, vol. 25 (1979).

[11] Charles Townshend, 'Military force and civil authority in the United Kingdom 1914–1921', *Journal of British Studies*, vol. 28, no. 3 (1989).

[12] Joost Augusteijn, *From Public Defiance to Guerrilla Warfare* (Dublin, 1996), p. 279.

[13] Ronald Hoffman, Thad W. Tate and Peter J. Albert (eds), *An Uncivil War: The Southern Backcountry during the American Revolution* (Charlottesville, VA, 1985); Carl Berger, *Broadsides and Bayonets: The Propaganda War of the American Revolution* (San Rafael, CA, 1976); 'Guerrilla Warfare in the American Revolutionary War', https://youtu.be/Q87QfuqpOck.

[14] G. Counahan, 'The people backed the movement, 1920', *Capuchin Annual* (1970).

[15] Asprey, 'The challenge of guerrilla tactics'.

[16] Augusteijn, *From Public Defiance to Guerrilla Warfare*, p. 220.

[17] P.B. Leonard, 'The necessity of de-Anglicising the Irish nation: boycotting and the Irish War of Independence', unpublished Ph.D thesis, University of Melbourne (2000).

[18] CI, MCR, Clare, October 1917, CO 904/103.

[19] Jen Ch'I Shan (Qishan) was a Chinese official of the late Qing dynasty (approx. 1830–50). On 20 January 1841, without seeking approval from the Qing imperial court, Qishan agreed to the Convention of Chubai with the British. Among other things, the convention ceded Hong Kong Island to the British. He wrote: 'In olden days guerrilla warfare was part of regular strategy, but there is almost no chance that it can be applied today'.

[20] Mao Zedong, *On Guerrilla Warfare* (Westport, CT, 1961), pp 86–90.

[21] Russell Rees, *Ireland 1905–25, Volume I. Text and Historiography* (Newtownards, 1998), p. 214 *et seq.*

[22] Hansard, 11 May 1916.

[23] See R.B. McDowell, *The Irish Convention of 1917–1918* (London, 1970).

[24] William O'Brien, Witness Statement 1766.

[25] Rees, *Ireland, 1905–1925, Volume I*, p. 231.

[26] See Michael Laffan, 'The unification of Sinn Féin in 1917', *Irish Historical Studies*, vol. 17 (1971).

[27] Frank Gallagher [David Hogan], *The Four Glorious Years* (Dublin, 1953), pp 22–3.

[28] *Hansard*, 24 October 1917. Henry Edward Duke, Chief Secretary for Ireland 1916–18, estimated that Sinn Féin's membership numbered about 200,000 in October 1917. Richard Dawson, *Red Terror and Green* (London, 1920; 1972), p. 118. Just before the December 1918 election a British Cabinet report reckoned Sinn Féin membership at over 100,000—an extraordinary figure by any reckoning, and even more so considering that it was a 'proscribed' organisation, with activists likely to face arrest, imprisonment and worse.

[29] Margaret Ward, 'The League of Women Delegates and Sinn Féin, 1917', *History Ireland*, vol. 4, no. 3 (1996).

[30] Helena Molony, Witness Statement 391.

[31] Ernest Blythe, Witness Statement 939.

[32] Charles Townshend, *The British Campaign in Ireland, 1919–1921* (Oxford, 1975), pp 3–6.

[33] Sinn Féin Party papers, University College Dublin Library.

[34] Dorothy Macardle, *The Irish Republic* (New York, 1937; 1965), pp 915, 232–3.

[35] Diarmuid Lynch, Witness Statement 4.

[36] Michael Staines, Witness Statements 284, 984.

[37] Diarmuid Lynch, Witness Statement 4.

[38] Risteard Mulcahy, 'The development of the Irish Volunteers, 1916–1922', *An Cosantóir*, vol. 40 (Part 1: February 1980).

[39] Padraic Colum, *Arthur Griffith* (Dublin, 1959), p. 343.

[40] Alan Ward, 'Lloyd George and the 1918 Irish conscription crisis', *Historical Journal*, vol. 17 (1974).

[41] General Richard Mulcahy, 'Conscription and the General Headquarters staff', *Capuchin Annual* (1968).

[42] Macardle, *The Irish Republic*, p. 260 *et seq.*

[43] *Manchester Guardian*, 13 May 1918.

[44] Robert Kee, *The Green Flag* (3 vols, London, 1972), p. 619.

[45] See Jerome aan de Wiel, *The Catholic Church in Ireland 1914–1918* (Dublin, 2003).

[46] See Padraig Yeates, 'Was the War of Independence necessary: Labour's 1918 anti-conscription "Plan of Action"—an alternative strategy for independence?', *History Ireland*, vol. 27, no. 1 (2019). Yeates argues that 'the measures proposed by the [Irish Labour Party and Industrial Trades Conference] provide a glimpse of alternative strategies to those adopted during the War of Independence. A struggle for independence based on mass passive resistance would have left us with a more broadly based democracy and a more benign historical legacy than the one we ultimately inherited.'

[47] R.J.Q. Adams and Sidney Poirier, *The Conscription Controversy in Great Britain, 1900–1918* (Basingstoke, 1978).

[48] Francis Costello, 'The role of propaganda in the Anglo-Irish War, 1919–1921', *Canadian Journal of Irish Studies*, vol. 14 (January 1989).

[49] Lionel Curtis, 'Ireland', *The Round Table*, vol. 20 (June 1921).

[50] Seán O'Luing, 'The "German Plot" 1918', *Capuchin Annual* (1969).

[51] Darrell Figgis, *Recollections of the Irish War* (London, 1924), pp 195–221; Gallagher

[Hogan], *The Four Glorious Years*, pp 29–33.

52 Mulcahy, 'Conscription and the General Headquarters staff'.

53 *Ibid.*

54 *Ibid.*

55 Joe Good, *Enchanted by Dreams: The Journal of a Revolutionary* (Dingle, 1946; 1996), p. 130 *et seq.*

56 William Whelan, Witness Statement 369.

57 Frank O'Connor, *The Big Fellow* (London, 1969; 1979), p. 56 *et seq.*

58 For accounts of these plans see Pax Murray; Billy Aherne; Denis Brennan; Seán McGrath; Frank Thornton; Denis Kelleher; Liam Tobin: O'Malley Papers, P17b188, 100, 107. See also Seán McGrath (O'Malley Papers, P17b/100), Leo Henderson (P17b/105) and Fintan Murphy (P17b/107). See also a letter from Florence O'Donoghue to the *Sunday Press*, 25 January 1959. For the best account, by one of the men who went with Brugha from the Dublin IRA, see Good, *Enchanted by Dreams*, pp 130–44.

59 W. Alison Phillips, *The Revolution in Ireland, 1906–1923* (London, 1923), p. 181.

60 Patrick O'Keefe, who was chosen as a candidate and was elected from Cork North, maintained that part of the vote against the 1921 Treaty was an anti-Collins vote, and that Collins first caused the antagonism because he, Boland and O'Hegarty, all IRB men, had hand-picked the candidates for the 1918 election, which was resented particularly by those who had aspirations to enter the Dáil in 1919 but who failed to be nominated. Risteard Mulcahy, *My Father the General: Richard Mulcahy and the Military History of the Revolution* (Dublin, 2009), p. 109.

61 Peter Hart, *Mick: The Real Michael Collins* (London, 2006), p. 183.

62 John Dorney, 'Women, the right to vote and the struggle for Irish independence', *The Irish Story*, 9 February 2018.

63 *Freeman's Journal*, 28 November 1918.

64 *Irish Independent*, 28 November 1918.

65 *Cork Examiner*, 14 December 1918.

66 *The Times*, 15 December 1918.

67 T. Ryle Dwyer, 'The 1918 election that marked a turning point in history', *Irish Examiner*, 5 December 2018.

68 *Irish Times*, 26 November 1918.

69 P.S. O'Hegarty, *The Victory of Sinn Féin* (Dublin, 1924; 1998), pp 23, 25.

70 Hart, *Mick*, p. 197.

71 Fintan O'Toole, 'The 1918 election was an amazing moment for Ireland', *Irish Times*, 8 December 2018.

72 C.S. Andrews, *Dublin Made Me* (Cork, 1979), p. 152.

73 Vincent Byrne, Witness Statement 423.

74 Margaret Ward, 'Women as candidates for election—Kathleen Clarke', in M. Ward (ed.), *In Their Own Voice* (Dublin, 1995; 2001), p. 89.

75 *Ibid.*

76 Letter from Richard Haldane to Edward Saunderson, private secretary to Lord French, 6 January 1919: JDPF 8/1D, French Papers. See Richard Burton Haldane, *An Autobiography* (London, 1929).

77 Florence O'Donoghue, 'Guerilla warfare in Ireland', *An Cosantóir*, vol. 23 (1963).

78 Though the Volunteers were the army of the Irish Republic, the term IRA was never officially adopted. The Volunteers continued to use that term, although the British

ordinarily used 'IRA' or 'Sinn Féiners'. Piaras Béaslaí, 'The Anglo-Irish War', in Gabriel Doherty (ed.), *With the IRA in the Fight for Freedom* (1970 edition), p. 15.

79 *An t-Óglách*, 31 January 1919.

80 T. Ryle Dwyer, 'A momentous day as Dáil meets and first shots of War of Independence occur', *Irish Examiner*, 20 January 2019.

81 Aengus Ó Snodaigh, 'The Declaration of Independence', *An Phoblacht*, 13 January 2000; 'An Chead Dáil Éireann opens', *An Phoblacht*, 20 January 2000; 'Ireland's Independence declared', *An Phoblacht*, 27 January 2000; 'An Address to Free Nations', *An Phoblacht*, 3 February 2000; 'The Democratic Programme', *An Phoblacht*, 9 March 2000.

82 Thomas Johnson, Witness Statement 1755.

83 William O'Brien, Witness Statement 1766.

84 Macardle, *The Irish Republic*, pp 275–7.

85 Eoin Neeson, *The Life and Death of Michael Collins* (Cork, 1968), p. 68.

86 Arthur Mitchell, *Labour in Irish Politics* (Dublin, 1974), pp 107–10. Even after it was amended, the Programme was considered 'communistic' by some TDs, including Piaras Béaslaí, Cathal Brugha and Kevin O'Higgins. See Padraig Yeates, *A City in Wartime, 1914–1918* (Dublin, 2012), pp 298–9.

87 Rees, *Ireland 1905–25, Volume I*, p. 254 *et seq.*

88 *An Phoblacht*, 20 January 2000. Holt claims that there were twenty-seven: Edgar Holt, *Protest in Arms* (New York, 1960), p. 171.

89 See Máire Comerford, *The First Dáil, January 21ˢᵗ 1919* (Dublin, 1969).

90 Some historians have argued that it is a mistake to view the Soloheadbeg ambush in January 1919 as the starting point of the conflict, and that later stages represent a more realistic beginning. See, for example, Joost Augusteijn, 'Review of M. Hopkinson: *War of Independence*', *American Historical Review*, vol. 108, no. 4 (2003). See also Peter Hart, *The IRA at War, 1916–1923* (Oxford, 2003), pp 201–2; John Dorney, 'Did the ambush at Soloheadbeg start the War of Independence?', http://www.theirishstory.com/2019/01/21/opinion-did-the-ambush-at-soloheadbeg-begin-the-irish-war-of-independence/#.XEyCQFVKjcs.

91 Martin Mansergh, 'Physical force or passive resistance: Soloheadbeg—vindicating a democratic mandate for independence', *History Ireland*, vol. 27, no. 2 (2019).

92 Andrew Silke, 'Ferocious times: the IRA, the RIC, and Britain's failure in 1919–1921', *Terrorism and Political Violence*, vol. 27, no. 3 (19 April 2016).

93 *An t-Óglách*, 1 February 1919.

94 *Irish Times*, 22 January 1919.

95 *The Belfast Newsletter*, 22 January 1919. Aengus Ó Snodaigh, 'Press coverage for First Dáil', *An Phoblacht*, 30 March 2000.

96 General Richard Mulcahy, 'Chief of Staff, 1919', *Capuchin Annual* (1970).

97 Fr Séamus Murphy, 'War of Independence seen as Catholic war on Protestants', *Irish Times*, 15 January 2019.

98 Gordon Pattison, *The British Army's Effectiveness in the Irish Campaign 1919–1921, and the Lessons for Modern Counterinsurgency Operations, with Special Reference to C3I Aspects* (UK Ministry of Defence, 1999).

99 *The Times*, 24 March 1919.

100 Figgis, *Recollections of the Irish War*, p. 243.

101 *Ibid.*, p. 244.

102 *Ibid.*

[103] Francis Costello (ed.), *Michael Collins: In His Own Words* (Dublin, 1997), pp 16–17.

[104] Collins papers, National Library of Ireland, MS 5848.

[105] *Dáil Éireann*, vol. 1, 20 August 1919.

[106] *Ibid.*

[107] Carl von Clausewitz, *On War* (Princeton, 1984), p. 406.

[108] Andrews, *Dublin Made Me*, p. 120.

[109] These courts were variously known as 'Dáil Courts', 'Republican Courts' and 'Sinn Féin/Republican Courts' in different sources. For consistency they are referred to here as 'Dáil/Republican Courts'.

[110] See J. Casey, 'Republican Courts in Ireland, 1919–1922', *Irish Jurist*, vol. 5 (1970); Francis Costello, 'The Republican Courts and the decline of British rule in Ireland', *Éire-Ireland*, vol. 25, no. 3 (1990); C.A. Maguire, 'The Republican Courts', *Capuchin Annual* (1984); Mary Kotsonouris, 'Revolutionary justice: the Dáil Éireann Courts', *History Ireland*, vol. 2, no. 3 (1994); Seán M. O'Duffy, Witness Statements 313, 618, 619.

[111] *Irish Times*, 5 July 1920.

[112] Tom Bowden, 'The Irish underground and the War of Independence 1919–1921', *Journal of Contemporary History*, vol. 8, no. 2 (1973).

[113] Arthur Mitchell, *Revolutionary Government in Ireland: Dáil Éireann 1919–1922* (Dublin, 1995), p. 154.

[114] Report of Sir Warren Fisher to the British government, 3 May 1920, HLRO Lloyd George papers, F/33/1.

[115] Charles Townsend, 'The Irish railway strike of 1920—industrial action and civil resistance in the struggle for independence', *Irish Historical Studies*, vol. 21 (1978–9).

[116] General Sir Nevil Macready, *Annals of an Active Life* (2 vols) (London, 1925; 1942), p. 472.

[117] David Fitzpatrick, *Politics and Irish Life, 1913–1921: Provincial Experience of War and Revolution* (Dublin, 1977), p. 143.

[118] Charles Townshend, *Political Violence in Ireland. Government and Resistance since 1848* (Oxford, 1983), p. 361.

[119] Report of Warren Fisher to Lloyd George, Lloyd George papers, F/31/1/32/32-2. Michael T. Foy, *Michael Collins' Intelligence War* (Stroud, 2006; Dublin, 2007), p. 86. See Eunan O'Halpin, *Head of the Civil Service: A Study of Sir Warren Fisher* (London, 1989).

[120] Sir John Anderson papers, CO 904/188.

[121] Sir Alfred Cope, Witness Statement 469.

[122] Mark Sturgis Diaries, UK PRO 30.59, 1–5.

[123] Joseph M. Curran, *The Birth of the Irish Free State, 1921–1923* (University of Alabama, 1980), p. 424.

[124] Msgr John T. McMahon, *The Cream of their Race: Irish Truce Negotiations, December 1920–January 1921* (pamphlet) (Ennis, 1970).

[125] Calton Younger, *Ireland's Civil War* (New York, 1969), p. 128 *et seq.*

[126] Revd J.T. McMahon, Witness Statement 362. See also Most Revd Dr Michael Fogarty, Witness Statement 271.

[127] Cabinet conclusion 77 (20) 6, of App. III, Conference of Ministers, 24 December 1920.

[128] Cope was involved in many discussions of the time, and was often in contact with Collins. He was asked to submit a witness statement of his role and how the negotiations

evolved. He refused to outline his role or the negotiations but submitted the following letter as his statement: 'It is not possible for this history to be truthful ... The IRA must be shown as national heroes, and the British Forces as brutal oppressors. Accordingly the Truce and Treaty will have been brought about by the defeat of the British by the valour of small and ill-equipped groups of irregulars. And so on. What a travesty it will and must be. Read by future generations of Irish children, it will simply perpetuate the long standing hatred of England and continue the miserable work of self-seeking politicians, who, for their own aggrandizement, have not permitted the Christian virtues of forgiveness and brotherhood to take its place. ... Ireland has too many histories; she deserves a rest' (Sir Alfred Cope, Witness Statement 469).

[129] Michael Hopkinson, *The Irish War of Independence* (Dublin, 2004), pp 177–85.
[130] Hart, *Mick*, p. 267.
[131] Hayden Talbot, *Michael Collins' Own Story* (London, 1923), p. 123.
[132] *Ibid.*, p. 135.
[133] Risteard Mulcahy, *My Father the General*, p. 142.
[134] Richard Mulcahy, Béaslaí Notes, vol. II, p. 239.
[135] Report on Revolutionary Organisations, 23 June, 7 July 1921, PRO, CAM 24/125, 126. Irish Intelligence Summary, Special Supplementary Report 259, 1 July 1921. Lloyd George papers, HLRO, F/46/9/25.
[136] Letter from David Boyle to Cabinet, 11 December 1920.
[137] Michael Smith, *The Spying Game* (London, 1996), p. 371.
[138] *Ibid.*, p. 374.
[139] *The Morning Post*, 15 July 1921.
[140] Tom Barry, *Guerilla Days in Ireland: A Personal Account of the Anglo-Irish War* (Dublin, 1981), p. 175 *et seq.*
[141] G.K. Chesterton, *The Delusion of the Double Plan* (undated pamphlet, no place of publication); Holt, *Protest in Arms*, p. 193.
[142] Letter from Hamar Greenwood to Lloyd George on 10 May 1921, Lloyd George papers F/19/4/10.
[143] David Lloyd George, 19 April 1921.
[144] Mark Sturgis Diaries, 4 October 1920, p. 51.
[145] Hervey de Montmorency, *Sword and Stirrup: Memories of an Adventurous Life* (London, 1936), p. 356.
[146] T. Ryle Dwyer, *Michael Collins: The Man Who Won the War* (Cork, 1990), pp 121–2.
[147] J.B.E. Hittle, *Michael Collins and the Anglo-Irish War: Britain's Counter-insurgency Failure* (Chicago, 2011), p. 185.
[148] Daniel McDonnell, Witness Statement 486.
[149] Foy, *Michael Collins' Intelligence War*, p. 220.
[150] Walter Long papers, PRO 947/308.
[151] Mark Sturgis Diaries, UK PRO 30.59, 1–5.
[152] Irish Intelligence Summary, Report No. 259, 1 July 1921, Lloyd George papers, HGLO, F/46/9/25.
[153] T.P. Coogan, *De Valera: Long Fellow, Long Shadow* (London, 1995), p. 216.
[154] Tom Jones Diary, 15 June 1921.
[155] *Ibid.*
[156] Macready, *Annals of an Active Life*, pp 470–90.
[157] Memorandum by Colonel Sir Hugh Elles to the Cabinet. Submitted to the Secretary of State for War, 24 June 1921: PRO CAB/24/185 CP 3075.

[158] Letter from Sir John Anderson to Hamar Greenwood, 15 June 1921, PRO CO 904/232.

[159] Sir Basil Thomson to the Cabinet, 23 June 1921: PRO CAB 24/125 CO 3074.

[160] Silke, 'Ferocious times: the IRA, the RIC, and Britain's failure in 1919–1921'.

[161] Report by the General Officer Commanding-in-Chief on the situation in Ireland for the week ending 9th July, 1921.

[162] The Record of the Rebellion in Ireland in 1919–1921 and the Part Played by the Army in Dealing with It (WO 141/93).

[163] Report on the Military Situation in Ireland at the end of September 1920.

[164] Michael Foy claims that a spy close to the very heart of the Irish leadership passed this information to the British. He speculates that this spy was Erskine Childers's wife, Molly. Foy, *Michael Collins' Intelligence War*, pp 230–6.

[165] Phillips, *The Revolution in Ireland*, p. 245.

[166] Katharine Chorley, *Armies and the Art of Revolution* (London, 1943), p. 52.

[167] Phillips, *The Revolution in Ireland*, p. 244.

[168] Kautt, *Ground Truths*, p. 184.

[169] Letter from Hamar Greenwood to Lloyd George, 5 July 1921. Lloyd George papers F/4/5/21.

[170] Hopkinson, *The Irish War of Independence*, p. 183.

[171] Report by the General Officer Commanding in Chief, The Situation in Ireland for the Week Ending 14th May, 1921 (PRO CAB 24/123).

[172] Silke, 'Ferocious times: the IRA, the RIC, and Britain's failure in 1919–1921'.

[173] See F.S. Crafford, *Jan Smuts: A Biography* (London, 1943).

[174] HLRO F 36/2/19.

[175] William Gamson, *The Strategy of Social Protest* (Belmont, CA, 1990), pp 28–9.

[176] Appendix XXI, 'Interpretation of the Agreement, of 11th July 1921, by GOC 5th Division', p. 120, Record of the Rebellion in Ireland in 1920–1921 and the Part Played by the Army in Dealing with it, Imperial War Museum, Box 78/82/2.

[177] Michael Collins, *The Path to Freedom* (1922; Cork, 1996), p. 133.

[178] T. Ryle Dwyer, *The Squad and the Intelligence Operations of Michael Collins* (Cork, 2005), p. 250.

[179] The cost to the British was over £20 million per year, a cost that Parliament and the government could not justify. 'Expenditure on Imperial Services in Ireland (Circulated for information, by the Chancellor of the Exchequer)', 3 June 1921 (PRO CAB 24/125). Francis Costello, *The Irish Revolution and its Aftermath, 1916–1923* (Dublin, 2003), p. 69; Hopkinson, *The Irish War of Independence*, p. 21.

[180] The number of Volunteers on 'active service' during the War of Independence has always been a subject for debate. When the Pension files were released in 2014, there were 300,000 files accessed; 85,000 applied and over 18,000 individuals received a pension of some amount, but the actual number of men and women who were on 'active service' in the war at any one time seems far fewer. Some have calculated a nominal membership in the IRA during the war at 50,000. Francis Costello (*The Irish Revolution*, p. 88) quotes numbers in excess of that in other sources: 17,470 in Cork, 5,350 in Kerry, 2,270 in Waterford and 2,100 in West Limerick. Later Costello (*op. cit.*, p. 222) indicates that by 'mid-July 1921, the IRA's manpower stood at approximately 3,000 men, with 4,500 interned, and 1,000 under prison sentence'. However, Dorothy Macardle (*The Irish Republic*, pp 358, 448), a republican advocate, indicated that 'the number of Volunteers in action over the greater part of the campaign was about 10,000'. Others

claim that the number of Volunteers 'was estimated at 15,000 active soldiers, although they could keep only about three thousand operating at any one time'; M.R. Fierro, 'British counterinsurgency operations in Ireland 1916–1921: a case study', unpublished MA dissertation, US Naval War College, Newport RI, 1997. Kostic concurs, holding that 'the IRA numbered between 14,000 and 15,000 Volunteers; however, due to a shortage of equipment and ammunition only about 5,000 were active. Collins later said "in the whole of Ireland there were not more than three thousand fighting men"'; Conor Kostick, *Revolution in Ireland: Popular Militancy, 1917 to 1923* (London, 1996), p. 95. Piaras Béaslaí, however, asserted that there were never 'as many as 200 acting together in any single action'; Piaras Béaslaí, *Michael Collins and the Making of the New Ireland* (London, 1926), vol. 2, p. 48. Joost Augusteijn (*From Public Defiance to Guerrilla Warfare*, pp 180–5, 353 *et seq.*) devotes an Appendix to the 'Social Composition of the IRA', and the numbers reveal that active members of the IRA were far fewer than some have claimed. 'By summer of 1921, the IRA was increasingly hard-pressed. It had an estimated 3,000 men on active service' (Rees, *Ireland 1905–25, Volume I*, p. 269); '… the IRA were unlikely to have had more than 3,000 men actually under arms within their brigade structure at any one time' (Costello, 'The role of propaganda in the Anglo-Irish War, 1919–1921').

[181] Barry, *Guerilla Days in Ireland*, p. 9.

[182] Talbot, *Michael Collins' Own Story*, p. 90.

[183] Internees included nineteen brigade commanders, fifty-three brigade staff officers, seventy-seven battalion commanders, 182 battalion staff officers, 1,407 company officers and 1,596 other ranks. E. McCall, *The Auxiliaries: Tudor's Toughs. A Study of the Auxiliary Division of the Royal Irish Constabulary 1920–1922* (London, 2010), p. 165. See Louis J. Walsh, *On 'My Keeping' and in Theirs: A Record of Experiences 'On the Run', in Derry Gaol, and in Ballykinlar Internment Camp* (Dublin, 1921); Liam Ó Duibhir, *Prisoners of War: The Ballykinlar Internment Camp, 1920–1921* (Cork, 2013).

[184] Max Boot, *Invisible Armies: An Epic History of Guerrilla Warfare from Ancient Times to Present* (New York, 2013), p. 255.

[185] Macready, *Annals of an Active Life*, vol. 2, p. 435.

[186] Tim Pat Coogan, *Michael Collins, the Man Who Made Ireland* (London, 1992), p. xii.

[187] William Manchester, *Winston Churchill: The Last Lion* (Boston, 1983), pp 719–20.

[188] Phillips, *The Revolution in Ireland*, p. 1.

[189] Michael Noyk, Witness Statement 707.

4. Propaganda—a war of words

Words are loaded pistols—so aim carefully and make each of them count.
—Jean-Paul Sartre

Guerrilla warfare is greatly reliant on legitimacy. If the British forces and government could make the Irish uprising appear illegitimate, it would be very difficult for the Irish to maintain their campaign. The converse worked for the Irish, of course. With the establishment of the Dáil and Republican Courts, and other aspects of local government falling to the Irish, their legitimacy increased in the eyes of the Irish people and of international opinion. All guerrilla forces need to have an extensive propaganda network, and the IRA/Volunteers had one. T.E. Lawrence wrote that 'the press is the greatest weapon in the armament of the modern commander'.[1] Later, during the Civil War, Éamon de Valera said that 'the newspapers are as usual more deadly to our cause than the machine guns'. Since 1900 the most important development in guerrilla warfare has been the rise of public opinion, enabled by the most modern means of communication of the time.

Only the most zealous advocates of the 'physical-force' campaign believed an ultimate Irish victory to be likely to occur solely as the result of a guerrilla campaign against the vastly superior British military forces.[2] Consequently, almost from the outset the Irish politicians and strategists sought to portray the effort as one involving a small nation seeking merely to secure its democratic national rights against one of the world's most powerful empires. For example, when the IRA campaign to close RIC barracks intensified in the first six months of 1920, as much to hinder RIC intelligence-gathering as to minimise the battlefield, the propaganda effects were maximised: 'Here the psychological element was well to the fore. These evacuated buildings were no longer of use to the Government, but as scorched shells they became a chilling advertisement of its retreat.'[3] The

Irish propaganda effort quickly noted what little effective administrative control the British exercised in much of Ireland.

In a similar vein, throughout the conflict the British were sensitive to the feelings of the Dominions and the United States. They tried to influence public feeling in two separate ways: firstly by portraying the nationalists as intransigent and in collusion with outside opponents, specifically the Germans during the First World War and the Bolsheviks in the period 1919–21, and secondly by attempting to mollify the émigré Irish and their overseas friends through efforts to reach a compromise. Neither approach was very successful. The intransigence of the Irish side was difficult to portray, since the nationalists claimed that they were simply trying to secure rights that the British Parliament had already granted in 1914 with the Home Rule Act and which were later confirmed by the Irish electorate in the election of 1918. Attempts to paint the Irish nationalists as a danger to British society and democratic society in general failed to convince the British public, much less the publics of the Dominions and the United States. The Irish connections with Germany were moot by 1920, and the alleged connections with the Soviet Union were tenuous at best.[4]

Michael Collins was particularly aware of the value of propaganda. In spring 1919 he used the grounds of Patrick Pearse's school, St Enda's, to make a short film advertising the Dáil Loan.[5] He knew that advertisements in newspapers would be censored and so he decided to use the 'new' medium of film. John MacDonagh, brother of the executed Thomas, produced the film at a cost of £600. Collins invited many notables to the school to buy bonds, including Kathleen Clarke, Mrs Margaret Pearse, Grace Gifford Plunkett and Arthur Griffith. Collins and Diarmuid O'Hegarty sat in front of the steps of St Enda's, and the purchasers' bond certificates were signed on the block on which Robert Emmet had been beheaded. Collins had two copies of the film made, and then his men took the film out to theatres and forced the cinema operators to show it—carefully taking it away with them again before it could be confiscated. The film was also shown very effectively in the US;[6] Harry Boland wrote to Collins: 'That film brought tears to me eyes. Gee, Boy! You are some movie actor. Nobody could resist buying a bond and us having such a handsome Minister for Finance.' The film brought Collins's name and image before the public as never before. His appearance in the film is even more remarkable given that as late as the Treaty negotiations in London in 1921 he would deliberately look away from a camera in order to blur his image.

Collins was always conscious of a camera: all photographs show him as well groomed and in most cases posing for the photo.[7] He also established himself in the popular imagination by astutely manipulating Irish newspapers such as the *Irish Independent* and the *Freeman's Journal*. Collins was, in effect, his own 'PR director', using friendly Irish and international journalists to stimulate dramatic headlines and foster his image as a glamorous revolutionary leader, cycling around Dublin dressed as a successful businessman, with documents secreted in his hat or socks.[8] He liked being portrayed as the 'Irish Pimpernel' whom the British could never catch. On 4 April 1919 the second public session of the First Dáil was held, and on that day an Irish-American fact-finding mission was invited to attend—Frank P. Walsh, Edward F. Dunne and Michael J. Ryan, the first Americans to address an Irish parliament since Benjamin Franklin in 1782. The British decided on a raid primarily to capture Collins, but he slipped out the back and watched the raid from the roof next door. When the raid was over, Collins returned—dressed in full Volunteer uniform—to attend the formal social gathering hosted by the lord mayor. That was the first time that Collins had appeared in uniform since Thomas Ashe's funeral in September 1917. As the only man in the room dressed in uniform he stuck out to all, especially to the American delegation. He enjoyed showing off. He was aware of the value of propaganda and used the media of the day to great effect in Ireland, Britain and especially America by always making time for an interview with a visiting journalist. Moreover, he knew just what would capture the attention of foreign press.

During the course of the war, controlling its 'pace' ('prudence', as Mulcahy always called it) was at the forefront of many GHQ policies and decisions.[9] That control of pace had its basis in propaganda as well as in the prosecution of military actions. Collins and the other leaders were concerned about the protection of civilians and civilian property, and they realised that minority interests were as important as the majority interests. The policy and the standards of the IRA played a major part in gathering widespread support for the Irish cause. In contrast, the British policy of reprisals against civilians and civilian property (much of which was owned by loyalists) harmed the British, both at home and abroad.[10]

Collins understood that the Irish could not obtain their own governance by military means alone. The strategic function of their warfare was to defeat the British psychologically and politically. Every IRA 'outrage' was used to provoke British reaction and was a blow to the British will to persist. Collins was playing politics with violence.[11] Those British reprisals would serve two purposes: first, they would mobilise Irish opinion; second, any British brutality in Ireland, freely reported in the British press, would be judged morally intolerable by Britain's liberal-minded political leaders. The British would contribute to their defeat by their own actions, and that was a part of Collins's plan.

Each day over 500,000 newspapers were sold to an Irish public eager to keep abreast of the latest developments.[12] The papers and their reporters were under constant pressure, and violent intimidation was common from both the British and the IRA. The British, primarily the RIC and the Auxiliaries, were especially ruthless in their attempts to silence newspapers. In the middle of the war, when their attempts to close down the *Irish Bulletin* failed, they decided to issue fake editions under a counterfeit *Irish Bulletin* masthead. Nevertheless, there were also examples of republican violence against the press, the most famous of which is the IRA's attack on the *Irish Independent* in December 1919.

Throughout that year, the *Irish Independent* had given extensive coverage to the workings of the newly established Dáil Éireann and the activities of Sinn Féin. By autumn it was the mainstream newspaper that provided Sinn Féin with its most sympathetic coverage. Nevertheless, it consistently denounced the IRA, and its use of violence, as 'the extreme wing of the popular movement'. On 19 December 1919, the IRA ambushed the convoy of the Lord Lieutenant, Sir John French, as it travelled into the city from the train stop at Ashtown. French was returning from his home in County Roscommon, and the IRA had intelligence that he would be travelling in the second car in the group. The attack failed, with French escaping and the IRA suffering one fatality, Martin Savage. The next day's *Independent* editorial called the attack 'a deplorable outrage' and 'a dreadful plan of assassination', while one correspondent compared the ambush to the Phoenix Park murders of 37 years earlier. The editorial enraged the IRA and their anger turned to action the next day, when an IRA group led by Peadar Clancy entered the paper's offices. The *Independent* reported that

Clancy informed the editor, Timothy Harrington, that his paper was to be suppressed for having 'endeavoured to misrepresent the sympathies and opinions of the Irish people' through its coverage of the ambush. The group, some of whom wanted to shoot Harrington, caused 'enormous destruction' to the printing machinery.[13] Despite the damage, the *Irish Independent* was able to restart publication quickly, and throughout 1920 it regularly pushed two aims in its editorials: its support for Irish self-government and its implacable opposition to partition. Further, the paper continued to condemn IRA violence, although it blamed the British government for causing the conflict.

The first 'in-house' publication that was utilised by the Irish after the Rising was *An t-Óglách*, which is often described as a successor to the *Irish Volunteer* that was published before the Rising. The *Irish Volunteer*, known as the official organ of the Irish Volunteers, aimed to provide guidance and to develop the Volunteer movement. It was published from February 1914 and ceased publication on the eve of the Rising.

After two years without an official organ, the concept of resurrecting a secret publication was considered by the Sinn Féin Executive in July 1918. Intended for circulation among its members, *An t-Óglách* renewed the tagline 'The Official Organ of the Irish Volunteer' and its first issue was published on 31 August 1918. Michael Collins, while he was the Volunteer Adjutant General and Director of Organisation, was a regular contributor to the magazine (which was required to reflect the policy of GHQ at the time). *An t-Óglách* played a significant role in GHQ meetings, with the editor required to submit articles and notes to the Volunteers' meetings for consideration. As such, it was something of a 'physical-force' counterbalance to Arthur Griffith's more 'constitutionalist' writings. It was published twice a month initially and successfully managed to remain in circulation despite numerous raids and having to operate in secret to avoid complete closure.[14] Collins played an important editorial role and found many of its writers.

Through their meetings with international reporters in Dublin the Irish gained credibility, and their announcements became far more accepted than those of the British Cabinet. The British government constantly found itself on the defensive, answering charges and accusations appearing in *The Irish Bulletin* and the international press, as well as on the floor of the House of Commons.[15] Lloyd George and Chief Secretary Hamar Greenwood so detested *The Irish Bulletin* that they tried to suppress it several times. Greenwood's bumbling efforts in the Commons were so full of half-truths and dissembling that he continually undermined the government's positions.[16] Later, 'telling a Hamar' became Irish slang for lying.

Complementing the effectiveness of their intelligence work, the Irish held the advantage in the dissemination of propaganda internationally. They continuously pre-empted the British in getting their side of the story told, with far-reaching political impact. This ability to stunt virtually every British attempt to paint the war as they desired kept public and world opinion either pro-Irish or, at least, suspicious of the British position. The importance of propaganda was highlighted by de Valera's decision to spend most of the War of Independence in the United States. In raising international awareness, de Valera made sure that the world was watching Ireland.[17] Shortly after his arrival, de Valera was quoted in the *New York Times*:

> I am in America as the official head of the Republic established by the will of the Irish people in accordance with the principle of self-determination.
>
> We shall fight for a real democratic League of Nations, not the present unholy alliance which does not fulfil the purposes for which the democracies of the world went to war. I am going to ask the people of America to give us a real League of Nations, one that will include Ireland.
>
> That is the reason I am eager to spread propaganda in official circles in America. My appeal is to the people. I know if they can be aroused government action will follow. That is why I intend visiting your large cities and talking directly to the people.[18]

Not to be underestimated, de Valera's trip to the US from June 1919 to December 1920 kept the Irish issue on the pages of American newspapers, and the bulk of US opinion was on the side of the Irish.[19]

Collins also used Dave Neligan, his 'spy in the Castle', to file false reports and to engage in a 'disinformation' campaign inside Dublin Castle.[20] Neligan would file reports indicating a robust, well-armed IRA that was continually recruiting more members, and his reports deceived the Castle authorities into a completely false impression of the abilities of the Irish.

Despite its claim to constitute a sovereign Irish parliament, the role of Dáil Éireann was largely symbolic. Its principal purpose was to assert the existence of a democratically elected Irish Republic. For this reason it was concerned as much with propaganda as with administration. Through the Dáil's Department of Foreign Affairs, republicans proved highly successful in promoting the separatist case. The Dáil's propaganda efforts were initially geared towards asserting Ireland's right to self-determination at the Paris Peace Conference of 1919, which was redrawing international borders. Irish republicans sought to capitalise on US President Woodrow Wilson's rhetoric underlying Anglo-American involvement in a war supposedly fought on behalf of self-determination for small nations.[21] This was an unpromising strategy, given the unlikelihood of the victors redrawing Europe's boundaries against their own interests to reward a movement that had identified itself with their enemy, but the Irish assertion that it 'deserved' to be invited to the conference garnered much international publicity.[22] In March 1919 Edward Dunne (ex-governor of Illinois), Frank Walsh (labour lawyer from Kansas City) and Michael Ryan (from Philadelphia) went to Versailles representing the Irish Race Convention. On 11 June President Wilson saw Walsh and Dunne for 30 minutes and issued a statement that he would do what he could 'unofficially … in the interest of Ireland'. Wilson said: 'You have touched on the great metaphysical tragedy of the day. When I said those words [fighting World War I for the rights of small nations] I said them without knowledge that nationalities existed that are coming to us day after day. Of course, Ireland's case, from the point of view of population, from the point of view of the struggle it has made, from the point of view of interest it has excited in the world, and especially among our own people, whom I am anxious to serve, is the outstanding case of a small nationality.' Wilson concluded that the Paris Peace Conference was only concerned with the territory of defeated nations.[23]

The manipulation of public opinion would become one of the most successful aspects of the Dáil's activities. Propaganda was critical to the outcome of the War of Independence owing to the importance that both sides in the conflict attached to public opinion in Ireland, Britain and throughout the international community. The republican movement's weapons would include not only ambushes and assassinations but also hunger strikes, civil disobedience and the demonstration of its authority through its establishment of local government, policing and courts.

Why did both sides attach so much importance to propaganda? One reason was that Britain was unlikely to be defeated by Irish separatists in any conventional military sense. Pressure on Britain to disengage from Ireland was more effectively exerted by convincing British and international public and political opinion that the use of force against a popular national movement was morally wrong. By drawing attention to the atrocities of the Black and Tans and Auxiliaries, and to the fact that the British government sanctioned their reprisals, republicans called into question the legitimacy of Britain's ability to govern.

As early as the conscription crisis in spring 1918, it became apparent to the Irish (and to the British) leadership that propaganda would play a major role in subsequent events. Arthur Griffith was a career journalist, and Desmond FitzGerald waged a clever propaganda effort from 1918 on. (FitzGerald was appointed Minister for Propaganda by the Dáil and was editor of the *Irish Bulletin* until he was arrested in February 1921.)

Early in the war the republicans took steps to establish their own daily newspaper. There were many weeklies dedicated to the Sinn Féin cause and, even though they had limited circulation, *The Times* described them as carrying out 'a sort of guerilla warfare on the Irish government' months before using that title to describe the republican military campaign.[24] As soon as a paper would arise, the British would suppress it. Arthur Griffith finally established a newspaper that just reprinted stories that had already been published—he called it *Cut and Paste*. Further rumours that Sinn Féin intended to take on professional journalism began as early as January 1919. At the Dáil session on 2 April, Terence MacSwiney of mid-Cork moved to start a daily paper but the matter was referred to the propaganda department. On 12 July a newsletter entitled 'Acts of Aggression Committed in Ireland by the Military and Police of the Usurping English Government' found its way to the mailboxes of select foreign correspondents and British legislators.[25] It was a simple recitation of raids, arrests and alleged assaults by Crown forces taken from full-circulation newspapers. This forerunner of the Dáil's *Irish Bulletin* initially attracted little attention, but as the propaganda department stepped up its efforts the British administration repeatedly took action against the outspoken republican press. The 'Acts of Aggression' newsletter issue of 13 September, following the events in Fermoy, carried its first editorial comment, declaring that 'during the foregoing six days English military terrorism in Ireland reached its high water mark'. It called the arrests and British reprisals 'a wholesale onslaught on the Republican movement' and added that 'not a county in Ireland escaped from this molestation'. Like all propaganda, it was one-sided and made no mention of the IRA attack that had spurred the entire series of events.[26]

While republican propagandists launched rhetorical attacks on the British government, IRA members took the Dáil's suppression in September 1919 as a mandate for further violence. Writing from New York, Patrick McCartan said, 'England has now openly declared war on Ireland'.[27]

At the outset of their campaign, the Irish propagandists relied on three principles:

- to get as much publicity as possible,
- to whip up dislike of Britain by exploiting her clumsy errors of government, and
- to discredit the Irish Parliamentary Party, so that Sinn Féin would ascend to the sole position of representing the Irish people.[28]

In 1919 Collins purchased the building at 76 Harcourt Street for the Dáil for £1,130, and Batt O'Connor immediately set about constructing secret compartments. The Irish met here to formulate their propaganda efforts and the Dáil had an office here from June 1919 until it was raided on 11 November 1919. On that occasion Collins escaped through the skylight to the Standard Hotel:

> Mick Collins was in his own office upstairs and Diarmuid O'Hegarty on hearing the raiders coming, had rushed up the stairs to warn him. What happened up there I don't know except that he got out through the roof by a pre-arranged method while we delayed them as long as possible downstairs. We afterwards heard he had succeeded in getting into the Standard Hotel over the roofs of the intervening houses. It did not seem as if the raid was directed against Mick Collins on this occasion, but rather for the purpose of enforcing the proclamation declaring the Dáil

illegal. Hence the staff came in for attention and arrest as well as the TDs. There was nobody now left but Jenny Mason and myself. Mick returned about 5 o'clock and immediately set to work to reorganise the offices. He transferred the bulk of the work to No. 5 Mespil Road, where he already had an office. Miss Mason went with him and I stayed on in 76, working directly under the instructions which reached me daily through Joe O'Reilly. Mick used to write out in his methodical way a list of instructions regarding the correspondence or any other work he required to be done, as he did not come in regularly during working hours.[29]

In that raid Ernest Blythe, Seán Hayes, Frank Lawless, Michael Lynch, Dick McKee, Fintan Murphy, Dan O'Donovan, Diarmuid O'Hegarty, Paddy O'Keefe, Seán O'Mahony and Patrick Sheehan were arrested and then spent two months in jail.[30] Collins's agent Dave Neligan was one of the men designated to search the offices. Neligan said that he had no intention of finding anything: 'I went upstairs and counted the roses on the wallpaper until the raid was over!' Batt O'Connor had built secret hiding places in the offices, and many papers were hidden before the police could find them.

… [T]he British soldiers raided No. 6 Harcourt Street [earlier in 1919]. Collins escaped to the roof, but I was arrested along with Paddy O'Keefe, the Secretary of Sinn Féin. After a day or two in the Bridewell, we were taken to Mountjoy where we were kept for a month or two before being tried. At that time the policy was that untried prisoners did not go on hunger-strike but that men went on hunger-strike when sentenced. A warder, who was very friendly and was in charge of prison repairs, came to me and said that Collins was prepared to make arrangements for my rescue. As, however, I knew that I had been arrested because of a letter for Dick Mulcahy which had been handed to me by James Kennedy of Nenagh, and which had been found on me in a police search half-an-hour afterwards, and as I did not know what was in the letter or what propagandist use might be made of it, I said that I preferred to be court-martialled. When I was brought up for preliminary hearing I learned the contents of the letter for the first time. It advocated a system of attacks on the parents and relatives of R.I.C. men, which was something of which I completely disapproved. I said at the court-martial that I had no . knowledge of the contents of the letter until it was read for me at the preliminary hearing and that I disagreed with everything in it. As the policeman who first searched me had put the letter back in my pocket without re-inserting it in the envelope and as the District Inspector who followed him did not notice the empty envelope, Dick Mulcahy's name did not come into the case. The sentence of the Court was one year's imprisonment, and, as others were doing, I immediately went on hunger-strike. I was not more than four or five days on hunger-strike when I was released and transferred to the Mater Hospital, where I remained for a few days.

After I was released I was about to visit the Dáil hÉireann offices which were in 76 Harcourt St., a house recently purchased, No. 6 having been left to Sinn Féin. As I arrived near the house I saw lorries around and realised that a raid was in progress. If I had been half an hour earlier I should have walked into a fresh arrest. Collins this time also escaped by the roof. As a matter of fact he owed his escape to the circumstance that a member of the staff, a Miss Lawless, looked out the window and saw the soldiers coming, rushed to the front door and slipped the Yale lock. The result was that the soldiers were sufficiently delayed in getting in to enable Collins to get on the roof and finally get down by a rather dangerous jump into the Standard Hotel. After that, 76 Harcourt St. was not used by any members of the Government.[31]

The British did take boxes of papers in the raid on 76 Harcourt Street and among the most important were reams of Dáil Éireann stationery. Nothing was heard of the cache until March and April 1920, when a number of leading Republicans were murdered in their homes. Before their murder, each had received a death notice on that stolen Dáil stationery. On 14–16 May 1920 every member of the Dáil who was not in prison received a threatening letter. Typed in capitals on the stationery was the threat:

AN EYE FOR AN EYE, A TOOTH FOR A TOOTH.
THEREFORE A LIFE FOR A LIFE.

Arthur Griffith summoned the press on 18 May and told them that the letters were typed on the stationery stolen in the raid. He pointed out that all the death notices had been posted in Dublin, and he accused the British government of being a party to the assassinations of the elected representatives of the Irish people. W.E. Johnstone, Chief Commissioner of the DMP, issued a statement on 27 May denying any involvement in the theft or the death notices. Neither the Irish nor the government made any further comment until September, when the *Irish Bulletin* dropped a bombshell and published copies of the official government correspondence indicating complete knowledge of the plans for assassination on the part of the British, as described below.

All propagandists use partial facts, and both sides used propaganda skilfully. Both British and Irish propagandists were the 'spin doctors' of the day. In all papers—Irish and international—the Irish used selective stories that appeared wide-ranging and objective, even though they were cleverly disguised bias. The *Irish Bulletin* was specifically aimed at the international press and policy-makers. Its intent was to publicise what was being done in Ireland, and why it was done: the world must be made to understand. An 'underground newspaper', it became a useful and trusted source of information for the Irish, British and international daily press, and the bane of the British. It disputed Britain's own propaganda and provided the public with Irish data on the scale of actions by the Dáil and the IRA. Desmond FitzGerald was the first editor, succeeded by Erskine Childers; Piaras Béaslaí, a Dublin journalist, acted as Collins's liaison with IRA/Volunteer HQ.[32] The paper's office, disguised as an Insurance Society, shared a building with the 'Church of Ireland Widows and Orphans Society'. Its journalists included Robert Brennan, Erskine Childers, Desmond FitzGerald and Frank Gallagher (Gallagher wrote *The Four Glorious Years* under the pseudonym of David Hogan, and often inserted themes of religion and morality into his articles[33]). Anna Fitzsimmons ('Miss Fitz') Kelly was the secretary, and the staff included Séamus Heaney, Séamus Hynes (messenger),

Kathleen McGilligan, Kathleen McKenna, Honor Murphy, Sheila Murphy and Michael Nunan. It was published daily (except on Sundays and Bank Holidays) from 11 November 1919 until the Truce.

The official status of the *Bulletin* was made evident in the financial statements submitted to Dáil Éireann by Collins in his capacity as Minister for Finance. These official statements are important also for illustrating the increasing weight attached to propaganda by Collins during the peak of hostilities during 1920–1. In Collins's report of 19 January 1921, in which he summarised the position of propaganda in government finances, he stated that the 1920 allocation to the Publicity Bureau amounted to £407.[34] This was a minuscule sum compared to the allocations granted to the Departments of Foreign Affairs and Home Affairs during the same period, which came to £12,082 and £9,313 respectively. Yet in the same report Collins projected that 'the allowance for propaganda should be increased by a thousand fold [*sic*] for the first six months of 1921, to an estimated £4,000'.[35]

As noted above, the *Irish Bulletin* became a useful source of information for both the Irish and the British daily press, particularly as 'it contradicted statements of British spokesmen, quoting leading British critics of their Government's Irish policy, and supplied facts and figures about the civil and military activities of the Republican Government'.[36] The British government felt the *Bulletin*'s impact to such an extent that its Dublin Castle intelligence network decided to issue fake editions of the paper. Although this action caused some initial confusion between Sinn Féin and the Irish, ultimately the forgeries were a source of embarrassment to the British government. In exposing the bogus issues of the *Irish Bulletin* before the House of Lords in April 1921, Lord Henry Cavendish-Bentinck requested the British Lord Secretary for Ireland to 'ask the benevolent politicians not to waste their money in sending me any more of their forgeries'.[37]

Despite its small staff and its having to be moved constantly in order to avoid detection, the *Bulletin* was read avidly by foreign journalists for its leaked Dublin Castle documents, mail intercepts and eyewitness accounts. After many attempts, the British finally located its offices and confiscated typewriters and duplicating machines. The Castle intelligence department under Ormonde Winter then organised that aforementioned disinformation campaign involving a counterfeit *Bulletin* published from Dublin Castle, whose skilfully slanted articles confused readers for a short time about the

Irish policies and actions. When the genuine *Bulletin* exposed the initial forgery, Winter came up with another well-disguised forgery and the propaganda game continued.[38]

Kathleen McKenna, a member of the staff from the beginning, described the *Irish Bulletin*'s reporting and propaganda efforts:

> The Bulletin was edited from its inception in November 1919 until his arrest on 11th February 1921 by Desmond FitzGerald, whose idea it was, and the information it contained was compiled by him and by Robert Brennan and Frank Gallagher. After Desmond FitzGerald's arrest Erskine Childers who had been appointed Substitute Director of Propaganda by the Dáil edited it for some months till after the Truce.
>
> ....
>
> All the statements made in the Bulletin were substantiated by proofs, and were of such a nature that, were it not for the Bulletin organisation, they would never have received Press publicity. The unmasking of British terrorist methods, the clear, truthful exposition of otherwise unknown aspects of the national struggle, the elaborate, but futile attempts made by the British Intelligence service to suppress it, the publicity given in it to secret orders even prior to their being known in British Headquarters themselves, made of the Irish Bulletin a weapon which had a very considerable part in the breaking down of British morale in Ireland. After the Truce this fact was confirmed by statements made both from Dublin Castle and from Michael Collins.
>
> ...
>
> Each evening I crossed the city to a place known as 'The Dump' over Mansfield's Boot Shop in O'Connell Street and to the offices of Michael Collins first in Mary Street later in Maurice Collins's shop Parnell Street and Devlin's, Parnell Square, to collect documents to be used in the compilation of the Bulletin.[39]

On 19 June 1920 the *Bulletin* reported the words of Lieutenant-Colonel Gerald Brice Ferguson Smyth DSO, King's Own Scottish Borderers, and Divisional Commander for Munster, who addressed RIC members at their barracks in Listowel:

> Well, Men, I have something to tell you. Something I am sure you would not want your wives to hear. Sinn Féin has had all the sport up to the present, and we are going to have the sport now. The police have done splendid work, considering the odds against them. The police are not in sufficient strength to do anything but hold their barracks. This is not enough, for as long as we remain on the defensive, so long will Sinn Féin have the whip hand. We must take the offensive and beat Sinn Féin with its own tactics. Martial law, applying to all Ireland, is coming into operation shortly, and our scheme of amalgamation must be complete by June 21st. If a police barracks is burned or if the barracks already occupied is not suitable, then the best house in the locality is to be commandeered, the occupants thrown into the gutter. Let them die there, the more the better. Police and military will patrol the country at least five nights a week. They are not to confine themselves to the main roads, but make across the country, lie in ambush and, when civilians are seen approaching, shout 'Hands up!' Should the order not be immediately obeyed, shoot and shoot with effect. If the persons approaching carry their hands in their pockets, or are in any way suspicious looking, shoot them down. You may make mistakes occasionally and innocent persons may be shot, but that cannot be helped, and you are bound to get the right parties sometime. The more you shoot, the better I will like you, and I assure you that no policeman will get into trouble for shooting any man. In the past, policemen have got into trouble for giving evidence at coroners' inquests. As a matter of fact coroners' inquests are to be made illegal so that in future no policeman will be asked to give evidence at inquests. We want your assistance in carrying out this scheme and wiping out Sinn Féin. Are you men prepared to cooperate?[40]

There must have been some authorisation for the speech, since General Henry H. Tudor, chief of the police, was present, although Smyth denied giving this speech in this form.

A member of his audience, Constable Jeremiah Mee, replied: 'By your accent, I take it you are an Englishman, and in your ignorance you forget you are addressing Irishmen. These, too, are English [taking off his cap, belt, and arms]. Take them, too.'[41] Collins introduced Mee to the editor of the *Freeman's Journal*, who questioned him at length. Thereafter, both the *Freeman's Journal* and the *Irish Bulletin* covered the story comprehensively. Mee later worked for Countess Markievicz in the Ministry for Labour.[42] In its 21 June 1920 issue the *Bulletin* published lists of RIC men who had resigned. On 17 July 1920 it reported that Lieutenant-Colonel Gerald Smyth had been killed in the Cork City and County Club.

Also in June 1920 the IRA scored one of their most notable propaganda coups with the capture of a British general. Throughout the war the IRA captured numerous British military personnel but, having nowhere to hold such prisoners, the majority of them, with the exception of spies and agents, were released. In the three months from May to July 1920 some 140 prisoners were captured by the IRA in all parts of Ireland, all of whom, with the exception of one man, were disarmed and released. The exception was Brigadier General Cuthbert Lucas.[43]

Lucas had been appointed Commander of the 17th Infantry Brigade in Ireland on 30 October 1919, and in late June 1920, along with two colonels, he was arrested by IRA Volunteers led by Liam Lynch, O/C Cork No. 2 Brigade, while fishing on the River Blackwater near Fermoy, Co. Cork. One of the British officers was wounded while attempting to escape and the Volunteers left his colleague behind to attend to him. Lucas, the commander of the British garrison at Fermoy, was taken to a safe house some distance away, where he could be interrogated. A huge nationwide search by the British military, even using aircraft to scour the countryside, failed to locate him.[44]

Because the area was saturated with British troops Lynch and his men were forced to go on the run almost daily, taking their prisoner with them as they moved from one safe place to another. As they moved, Lucas was 'passed' from one IRA unit to the next. Joe Good was one of the men who guarded Lucas for a while and gave the following account:

> Lucas was the traditional British officer. ... During our first
> conversation, Lucas was looking down the hill at

Templegelantine, and it was a very beautiful view, from where we stood we could see a number of counties. He remarked to me 'This is a country worth fighting for'. 'That's a peculiar comment', I said. 'It reminds me that another general—your predecessor, Cromwell—once made a similar remark'. Lucas smiled slowly and said 'Yes, I believe I remember reading something about that somewhere'.[45]

Good recounted that after being replaced as Lucas's bodyguard he intercepted a telegraph in Limerick that was addressed to 'General Lucas, C/O The Sinn Féiners, Irish Republican Army, Cork'. The British were not too certain of the location or the mode of address, but the message was passed on to Lucas: 'BORN THIS MORNING A SON. BOTH DOING WELL'. The message, telling Lucas of the birth of his first child, was passed on to him in captivity.[46]

In reprisal for Lucas's capture by the IRA, British troops from his brigade attacked and burned houses and shops in Fermoy. Here, too, the local Sinn Féin Hall was wrecked, and the damage done to the town was estimated at several thousand pounds. During the following days and weeks, with still no trace of Lucas, the reprisals were extended to the surrounding villages and into County Limerick.

After five weeks in IRA custody, Lucas managed to loosen the bars on the window of a house where he was being held and made his escape. (It is accepted that the Irish 'allowed' Lucas to escape in that his custody, whilst very casual, was nevertheless a drain on limited IRA resources.) While in custody, despite the huge search for him and having to move about constantly with his captors, Lucas was regularly able to fish and play tennis. In stark contrast to republicans captured by the British, Lucas was treated exceptionally well by his captors, who were relieved in many ways to see the back of him when he made his escape.

In interviews to the press after his escape Lucas told how he was treated as 'a gentleman by gentlemen', and in a sardonic address to his troops he said that the outrages and atrocities carried out by them during his captivity represented 'an over-zealous display of loyalty'. He also returned the clothes that he had been lent during his captivity, and never divulged the names of his captors nor where he was kept. The value of the propaganda that resulted from daily reports in the British press about Lucas's capture and the search for him cannot be overstated. What was a great embarrassment to the British was a propaganda coup and morale boost for the Irish.[47]

The second strand of Republican propaganda was the cultivation of particular journalists and causes. *The Times*, the *Manchester Guardian* and the *Daily News* frequently published stories from Ireland that focused on British atrocities and lacked a sense of balance by failing to report IRA atrocities. Propagandising in the United States by de Valera helped with the flow of funds, and in some cases weapons, as well as creating constraints on the British government's freedom of action. Significantly, it was an American reporter, Carl Ackerman, who mediated between the two sides in the run-up to the Truce in July 1921. Moreover, Lloyd George recognised early on the effect that propaganda was having in the US; while he held little regard for Irish national rights, he believed that a satisfactory 'settlement of the Irish Question is important from the standpoint of world opinion and also for our relations with the Dominions and the United States'.[48]

Through the *Irish Bulletin* and other media outlets, the Irish leaders exploited Britain's own recent propaganda. The British government claimed that it had fought World War I 'to protect defenceless Belgium from German depredations'. The Irish substituted Ireland for Belgium and assigned the role of savages to the British. As they continued to expose British actions worldwide, the Irish accounts of burnings, destruction of libraries and execution of municipal officials drew the simple but effective comparison to the German actions in Liège, Belgium. International opinion and pressure from the British public began to mount against the British military actions and reprisals, and contributed to the British change in attitude towards negotiation.

The Irish were able to utilise another form of propaganda when Terence MacSwiney went on hunger strike in London's Brixton Prison. After the murder of his friend Tomás MacCurtáin, the lord mayor of Cork, on 20 March 1920, MacSwiney was elected as lord mayor. On 12 August 1920 he was arrested for possession of seditious articles and documents, as well as a cipher key to the British codes. Tried by summary court martial and sentenced to two years' imprisonment on 16 August, he was sent to Brixton Prison, where he died on 25 October after 74 days on hunger strike.[49] Significantly, although recognising this as suicide, Roman Catholic authorities failed to give a clear message on the morality of hunger strikes,[50] and many Irish questioned whether it was better to 'fight for Ireland than to die for Ireland'.[51] The long-term effects and the apparent moral advantage that hunger strikers appeared to have in some sections of Irish society created a certain cult surrounding them.[52] On 26 August the British Cabinet stated that 'the release of the Lord Mayor would have disastrous results in Ireland and would probably lead to a mutiny of both military and police in south of Ireland'. The hunger strike was a particularly effective propaganda weapon and MacSwiney gained world attention: Americans threatened the British government with a boycott of British goods, while four countries in South America appealed to the pope to intervene. Protests were held in Germany and France. An Australian member of parliament, Hugh Mahon, was expelled from the Australian parliament for 'seditious and disloyal utterances at a public meeting' after protesting against the actions of the British government.[53]

As MacSwiney's ordeal sparked riots in Brixton, it also spurred the GHQ staff in Dublin into action—or at least into considering action. Their first idea was to take hostages, to be exchanged for MacSwiney's release. In early September Collins told Art O'Brien to 'go ahead with finding that place for a hostage'. A week later O'Brien wrote back about the 'apartments'. As MacSwiney's condition worsened, this became an assassination plot: Lloyd George's death in exchange for MacSwiney's. The rest of the Cabinet were soon included as well. Gunmen were sent from Dublin and Cork to prepare several elaborate plans; some stayed for months. MacSwiney died on 25 October. When Seán McGrath went to Ireland for his funeral, for 'the first time I saw Michael Collins really upset. He talked then about shooting in England.'[54]

On the propaganda front, the British government belatedly launched its response to the *Irish Bulletin*. Dublin Castle's *Weekly Summary*, a four-sheet newsletter, debuted on 13 August 1920. In form and substance it greatly resembled the *Irish Bulletin*: it quoted excerpts from daily publications, captured republican documents and British leaders' speeches, as well as publishing its own editorials. As time progressed, in a memorandum to Hamar Greenwood on 21 April 1921 Lloyd George himself emphasised the need for a heightened propaganda effort.[55] As far as the editing and production of the paper were concerned, Greenwood said that 'this publication is produced by the heads of the police for the benefit of the members of that force who, if no such periodical existed, would have no means of knowing the truth regarding current events in Ireland.'[56] The *Weekly Summary* continually attacked the IRA as a 'murder gang': the Irish complain about reprisals 'while [Irish] gunmen terrorized ordinary, law-abiding Irish people into accepting their illusory republic, republican propaganda subverting the truth about the violence'.[57] It published headlines like 'Reprisals the result of police murder', 'A policy of hitting back', 'Sinn Féiners shouldn't complain', 'Reprisals explained' and 'Sinn Féiners reap the whirlwind'. Throughout the war, the *Weekly Summary* insisted that the rebels were on the verge of defeat.[58]

Unlike the *Irish Bulletin* in its early days, the *Weekly Summary* did not ignore the more offensive actions of the British. In a period when British generals and politicians were debating the necessity or morality of uniformed police or soldiers destroying citizens' property, it stated flatly that Crown forces were responsible for reprisals carried out after republican attacks, but it insisted that murders of policemen or soldiers caused a reaction against people and property only where and when IRA attacks occurred and that such retaliation was natural rather than deliberate.[59] The paper's mandate was to 'give publicity to the facts of the Irish political situation and its incidents which at that time were seriously misrepresented to the public as a result of Sinn Féin and anti-British propaganda'.[60] British leaders were united in both their condemnation of reprisals and their inability or unwillingness to do anything about them. Hamar Greenwood assured the press that reprisals were not government policy and that steps had been taken to prevent them.[61] Macready was much more tolerant of such breaches of discipline, saying that

> the machinery of the law having been broken down they [the police] feel there is no certain means of redress or punishment, and it is only human that they should act on their own initiative.[62]

The *Weekly Summary* regularly reported statements of the so-called 'Anti-Sinn Féin Society', allegedly a group undertaking vigilante actions against violent republicans in the south of Ireland. Historian John Borgonovo persuasively argues that this title was a façade behind which off-duty policemen carried out reprisals against republican suspects.[63] According to Field Marshal Henry Wilson, Prime Minister David Lloyd George was aware of the activities of the Auxiliaries and approved of the reprisals and the murder of republicans.

> He [Lloyd George] reverted to his amazing theory that someone was murdering 2 Sinn Féiners to every loyalist the Sinn Féiners murdered. I told him that, of course, this was absolutely not so, but he seemed to be satisfied that a counter-murder association was the best answer to Sinn Féin murders. A crude idea of statesmanship, and he will have a rude awakening.[64]

On 10 September 1920 the *Irish Bulletin* published its most memorable issue, in which it traced the story of the Dáil stationery stolen from 76 Harcourt Street in that November 1919 raid, the death notices sent to slain Dáil members and other leading Republicans, and the British government's knowledge of and involvement in their deaths. Between 14 and 16 May 1920 each member of the Dáil received a threatening letter on Dáil stationery, reading 'An eye for an eye, a tooth for a tooth, therefore a life for a life'. Further, the *Bulletin* repeated DMP Commissioner W.E. Johnstone's denial on 27 May of any knowledge of the theft or the death notices. Then the story went on: 'Certain official correspondence of high-placed British Government officials in Ireland is now in the hands of the Irish Republican Authorities'. That correspondence was copied and sent to American and British newspapers. It consisted of four reports and letters.

- A report dated 16 January [1920] from Inspector Neil McFeely, who had been on the raid. The report was transmitted to W.C.F. Redmond, Assistant Commissioner, and initialled by him, indicating receipt.
- A letter from the North Dublin Union on 8 April 1920 indicating the arrival of a 'Mr Hyam' and reporting about him to 'P. Atwood'.

These first two documents were important to the story: one was written by an Inspector of 'G' Division, McFeely, and initialled by Assistant

187

Commissioner Johnstone, and the other was significant because both 'Mr Hyam' and 'P. Atwood' were officers on the British General Staff, assigned to the North Dublin Union. And *both documents* were on Dáil Éireann stationery stolen from 76 Harcourt Street in the 11 November 1919 raid. Clearly, the heads of the police and the British General Staff knew, before the denial was issued, that the British had the notepaper and were using it.

- A letter from Captain F. Harper-Shove of the British General Staff regarding a hunger strike in Mountjoy Jail that had just ended. The letter, of itself, had nothing to do with the notepaper, but *it was typed on the very same typewriter on which the death notices had been typed*.
- A letter from 'St Andrew's Hotel, Exchequer Street, Dublin', dated 22 March 1920, written from Captain Harper-Shove to a 'Dear Hardy'. In this letter Harper-Shove indicated that he had been given 'a free hand to carry on … Re our little stunt, I see no prospects until I have got things on a firmer basis, but still hope and believe there are possibilities'.

The 'little stunt' was the assassinations, and they began on 22 March with the assassination of Lord Mayor Tomás MacCurtáin in Cork. Two days before his death he had received one of the death notices. Shortly thereafter James McCarthy of Thurles and Thomas O'Dwyer of Bouladuff were also killed in County Cork; they, too, had received death notices. The method, even the hour, of killing was exactly the same for all three, and all had received a death notice on Dáil Éireann stationery.[65]

On 18 May 1920 Arthur Griffith met with the international press in Dublin and outlined the whole story. The British continued to deny the theft and indicated that a 'complete refutation would follow', but that refutation never came.[66]

On the night of 26–7 March 1921 (Holy Saturday) C Company of the Auxiliaries raided the paper, but all the office personnel escaped. From then on the paper went 'underground' and was published from various offices and homes throughout Dublin—but it never missed an issue until it was closed down after the Truce. On Tuesday 29 March, an issue dated 'Volume IV, No. 56' was published from Maureen Power's front room in Harold's Cross; on the following day there were two issues, one of which was an 'official' forgery put out by Dublin Castle. This forgery collapsed after a month—it was often quoted by the 'real' *Bulletin*—but Collins was extremely concerned about this fake paper; he worried that it would be taken as authentic and might be a great propaganda tool for the British. While the forgeries caused some consternation for a time, however, overall they were a source of embarrassment for the British.

The 'war by words' was not limited to newspapers. The British government's effort to undermine Sinn Féin, particularly in the US, was exemplified by the 1921 publication at its expense of two separate volumes authored by Dublin Castle propagandist C.J.C. Street under the pseudonym 'I.O.'[67] First published in New York by Dutton, the two books sought to defend British policy in Ireland while linking Sinn Féin to subversive forces.[68] They drew largely for their details on the Command Series documents relative to Sinn Féin.[69] According to Street in *The Administration of Ireland, 1920*, Command Series Document 1108 was sufficient in and of itself for revealing 'the whole story of the negotiations between Sinn Féin and Germany, and it is therefore unnecessary to pursue the matter further …'.[70] Street cited a 28 November **1914** letter of Sir Roger Casement to Eoin MacNeill in relation to the publication of an official German declaration of that country's goodwill towards Irish national aspirations, as well as a Republican notice from **1915** to the people of Wexford, urging them to disobey orders published under the Defence of the Realm Act. To Street these *dated* examples

> were typical of the evidence contained in the White Paper which should be perceived by all who wish to understand that Irish point of view.
>
> …
>
> For all history, both recent and remote, shows that the Irish appeal to America is based upon self-seeking and not at all upon racial affinity.[71]

He went on to make what was perhaps one of the most ironic characterisations of the Irish Republican movement ever to come from a publicist seeking to defend Britain's performance in Ireland:

The Irish Republican movement is and always has been the child of an almost incomprehensible selfishness, as the very title of its later advocates, Sinn Féin—'ourselves alone'—indicates.

At Street's time of writing Germany had been vanquished in Europe, and as a result it became necessary to develop a new technique for denigrating the Irish cause in the United States. Thus Street sought to question the loyalty of those Irish activists then operating in the US:

> Finding Germany a broken reed, the Irish malcontents have turned once more to America, as being the country whose population might be expected to be most in sympathy with Irish ideals. The so-called President of the Republic himself made the United States his headquarters for over a year ... and for the last few years there has been a fog of misunderstanding between two great cousin nations, America and England, it should be the earnest endeavour of every true citizen of either to dissipate.[72]

He continued by belittling US politicians and questioning their devotion to the Irish cause, and finally indicated his disdain for American citizens:

> It cannot be too widely realized that a very great part of the Irish Question in America is nothing but the conventional cry of politicians, that the great bulk of the reasoning multitude are no more interested in Ireland than they are in the South Pole.
>
> ...
>
> Owing to the fact that there are some twenty million of Irish descent, the Irish vote is something to be angled for. Politicians of every shade of opinion always have and always will dangle the bait of speeches in the Irish Republican interest before the noses of the electorate, whenever such tactics seem likely to procure them votes.

Street was even less kind to Irish-Americans concerned with Irish independence:

We have one guarantee which will never fail us: that the only type of man who can influence American policy is the man who is first a citizen of the United States and an Irishman incidentally … The converse, the man who places his abandoned nationality first and his American citizenship second, is a man who gains nothing but mistrust in the State in which he dwells.[73]

It must be noted that Street's books were published under the auspices of the British government and reflected the view of at least some of its members. The British continued to characterise those active in support of the Irish cause in America as being less than loyal to the US, while 'painting those interested elected officials as self-centered vote seekers solely interested in exploiting the Irish issue for their own ends'.[74]

Street's books were not the only surreptitious British efforts at propaganda. In the summer of 1921, a series of articles entitled 'Ireland under the New Terror, Living Under Martial Law' appeared in a London magazine. While purporting to be an impartial account of the situation in Ireland, it portrayed the IRA in a very unfavourable light when compared with the British forces. In reality the author, Ernest Dowdall, was an Auxiliary and the series was one of many articles planted by the Dublin Castle Propaganda Department to influence public opinion in a Britain increasingly dismayed at the behaviour of its security forces in Ireland.[75]

In the US Congress there were fourteen days of public hearings conducted by the American Commission on the Conditions in Ireland, between 19 November 1920 and 21 January 1921, in which testimony was heard from thirty-seven witnesses, eighteen of whom came from Ireland. Included among these were Muriel and Mary MacSwiney, the wife and sister of Terence Mac Swiney, the late Mayor of Cork, who had died three weeks earlier after a 74-day hunger strike in Brixton Prison. MacSwiney's death received worldwide attention and nowhere (with the exception of Ireland and Britain itself) more than in the US. Every effort was made by Irish-American organisations to hold him up as a martyr to British oppression. The appearance of the two MacSwiney women before the Commission, both dressed in black, coupled with the lengthy and moving testimony of MacSwiney's sister, was greatly damaging to Britain's own propaganda effort.[76] The Commission's final report was damning for the British:

> We would extend our sympathy to the British people. The army, which is the instrument of their government in Ireland, would also seem to be the instrument of that moral heritage which was their glory ... . The sun of that glory seems finally to have set on Ireland. British 'justice' has become a discredited thing. The official Black and Tans compete for dishonor of Anglo-Saxon civilization with our official lynch mobs.[77]

Just before the Truce in July 1921, the burning of the Custom House in Dublin illustrated the results of the unravelling of control of the military/political/propaganda pace. The attack on the Custom House on 25 May was a resounding propaganda success for the Irish Volunteers, but it contravened the tenets of guerrilla warfare.[78] A guerrilla war is largely one of evasion, and the Irish War of Independence was characterised by the Irish waging a ceaseless and relentless offensive against the weak points of the British—in Dublin and in the countryside—and then withdrawing to attack somewhere else. T.E. Lawrence said that 'most wars are wars of contact, our war [a guerrilla war] is one of detachment'.[79] A fundamental principle of guerrilla warfare is that no battle or skirmish is to be fought unless it will be won. Collins was aware of von Clausewitz's principle that 'War is the continuation of politics by other means', and by this time he was carefully favouring the political view as the object.

Von Clausewitz's dictum had as its central tenets:

- Military action without a clear political objective is useless, and vice versa.
- A guerrilla war event must include propaganda and politics alongside military action.
- All events must recognise a military purpose.

As the War of Independence progressed, especially in County Cork, the Irish perfected their guerrilla tactics. In their ambushes they showed a fine knowledge of site choice and deployment. The Irish quickly learned and adopted the classic ambush tactics:

- Attack with surprise and fury.

- Do the most damage possible.
- Fighting only lasts a few minutes, followed by immediate withdrawal.

They became sophisticated enough to attack a barracks as a feint to draw out a relief force and to funnel that force into an ambush, while *others* simultaneously attacked the empty barracks. Alternatively, the Irish would channel British relief forces into ambush sites chosen by the rebels. They became adept at blocking every road in an area except the one leading to their chosen ambush site, and they knew that the planning of the withdrawal was just as important as the planning of the ambush and assault.

In her excellent book *May 25: Burning of the Custom House 1921*, Liz Gillis provides the most detailed record of the operation and its participants.[80] While there had been plans to attack or burn the building previously, it was Éamon de Valera's return which provided the impetus for this attack. Gillis's research indicates that there were far more men involved in the attack than had been known previously. The operation was carried out by some 280 Volunteers, five of whom were killed: Tommy Dorrins, Seán Doyle, Dan Head, Captain Paddy O'Reilly and his sixteen-year-old brother, Lieutenant Stephen O'Reilly.

When he returned from the US in December 1920, de Valera told members of the Dáil that the American newspapers were calling the Irish 'murderers' for the way they were conducting their war. He declared that 'the odd shooting of a policeman here and there is having a very bad effect, from a propaganda point of view, on us in America. What we want is one good battle about once a month with almost 500 men on each side.'[81] Early in 1921 a meeting was held to finalise plans for the taking of the Custom House. De Valera's first choice was to capture Beggar's Bush Barracks, but Oscar Traynor, O/C of the Dublin Brigade, deemed that impractical.

> The meeting proceeded in a very normal way for some time, and then the President [de Valera] spoke, and he made it clear that something in the nature of a big action in Dublin was necessary in order to bring public opinion abroad to bear on the question of Ireland's case. He felt that such an action in the capital city, which was as well known abroad as London or Paris, would be certain to succeed. He suggested that the capture of the

headquarters of the Black and Tans, which was situated in Beggar's Bush Barracks, would capture the imagination of those he had in mind, apart from the serious blow it would constitute to the enemy.[82]

In the plans for this Custom House operation the military purpose was ignored, and as a result the affair was a débâcle for the Dublin IRA. Five of their number were killed and three wounded. Worse, over 100 were captured—losses they could scarcely afford. The attack sacrificed many experienced Volunteers, and immediate future operations would be degraded by additional and/or prolonged duty for the remaining Volunteers in Dublin. Oscar Traynor noted:

> Following the action at the Custom House and the capture of a large number of highly trained officers, NCOs and men, it was found necessary to carry out an almost complete re-organisation of the various units of the Dublin Battalion. This, of course, necessitated the appointment of a considerable number of new officers, and naturally while this re-organisation was taking place, actions as we had known them before almost ceased, with the exception of those carried out by the remaining members of the Active Service Unit. As time went on the Brigade units gradually assumed their old aggressiveness, and by the time the Truce was approaching a number of reasonably important operations were being planned.[83]

In combat, the consequences of degraded performance owing to physical or mental exhaustion can be much greater than those in the civil arena. Military members not only have to cope with a hostile environment but must also apply lethal force against a dangerous enemy, maintaining vigilance and exercising good judgment, while ensuring that they protect those in their own unit.[84]

In the meeting discussing the operation de Valera countered objections to the plan, saying that 'if 120 men were lost and the job accomplished, the sacrifice would be well justified',[85] but the loss of approximately 40% of the attacking force was a devastating blow to the Dublin Volunteers.[86] One of

Che Guevara's tenets for any guerrilla action is that 'the man must survive the plan'. Part of the original plan called for the Volunteers to set up barricades around the various British garrisons in Dublin, as well as barricades around the Custom House. Michael Collins and others thought the idea impractical. If they had learned nothing else from the Rising, they learned that the Irish should never place themselves in the middle of a battlefield and let the British surround them.[87]

Harry Colley, one of the men who had taken part in the attack, remembered that that night 'in Brigade headquarters there was a great silence. We were thinking our success in burning the Custom House had been too dearly bought by the large number of our best fighters who had been captured.'[88] Paddy Daly thought it necessary to 'conceal our crippled state from the enemy who might otherwise have taken advantage of it to deal us a decisive blow'.[89]

Charles Townshend summed up:

The burning of the Custom House on 25 May proved to be as disastrous as anything that might have been anticipated from bearding the 'Auxies' in their den. The Dublin Brigade lost 100 men in one day—a figure unheard-of since the Rising—and though Republican propaganda made a brilliant job of portraying the operation as a body blow against the government, this did not alter the unfortunate reality of the situation.[90]

The burning of the Custom House increased the confusion in which the British government found itself in the early summer of 1921. On a much smaller scale, the Custom House attack was as significant as Vietnam's Tet Offensive: a propaganda catastrophe that drained the British commitment to an apparently endless war.[91] Along with the reaction to Bloody Sunday and the Kilmichael ambush the previous November, it intensified the mood of the British public and parliament to turn to negotiation to settle 'the Irish question'.

Throughout the war the international press, especially the 'sensational' or 'illustrated press', covered the fighting in Ireland. Some were more even-handed than others, but the uses of artists' renditions were more demonstrative than written accounts.[92] The French periodical *Le Petit*

Journal was one of the more objective newspapers, but on 20 September 1920 it depicted Cork Lord Mayor Terence MacSwiney in the middle of his hunger strike, lying on a bed and being administered to by a Capuchin priest, Fr Dominic O'Connor. MacSwiney looked like a martyr, with his hands seemingly clasped around a cross, and the picture was strikingly emotional. Another French publication, *Le Pelegrin*, a Catholic weekly, ran several pictures of the burning of the Custom House on 25 May 1921; they were highly fanciful illustrations, many of a sort indicating women almost being burned to death inside the Custom House, as well as indicating the whole Custom House Quay in flames.[93] In Italy the Catholic weekly *La Tribuna Illustrata* printed extremely dramatic, and actually fanciful, illustrations of the burning of Cork on 11/12 December 1920. One picture showed a 'looter in plain clothes' standing on a pile of rubble and being shot by law-enforcing British troops, the caption indicating that the British 'had to disperse numerous bands of looters who plundered the corpses between the ruins and flames'.[94] The journals were rarely objective but they kept the Irish struggle in front of the public in their respective countries, especially after the end of World War I in November 1918.

By mid-1920 international pressure, especially from the US, was building on Britain, and the British public, finally realising the progress of the war, was outraged. Sir John Simon wrote to *The Times*:

> The policy of reprisals is both politically disastrous and morally wrong ... it is exposing us to the scorn of the world ... It is turning Mr Lloyd George's heroics about the rights of small nations into nauseating cant. It is undermining the character and self-control of hundreds of young Englishmen by permitting them to indulge in deplorable excesses of every kind.
>
> ...
>
> Surely it has become plain that the policy and method of reprisals must be entirely abandoned and these new forces must be wholly withdrawn and disbanded, and that a truce must be offered in which a new solution may be sought by mutual conciliation and understanding.[95]

The official and unofficial reprisals, and the general behaviour of the Black and Tans and Auxiliaries, provided wonderful 'propaganda of the *mis*deed' for Collins and the Irish propaganda machine.

The British military and police authorities were unable to control the RIC, Black and Tans and Auxiliaries, and at the end of 1920 many of the British politicians and Cabinet realised that there must be a change. Terror had been tried and failed, and the Irish gave no indication that they would accede. *The Nation and Athenaeum* wrote at the end of the year:

> The Government still clings to the belief that they can crush the Irish spirit, destroy some of the bravest and most promising of Ireland's young men and win by these an outward victory. Men of noble spirit and unfaltering courage are dying but their race does not perish. We can spread ruin: that's what we are doing. We can do to Ireland just as much as Austria did to us, or Germany did to Belgium. The end is as certain in this case as in those, for the Irish people, supported as they are by their own spiritual vitality and the sympathy of the world, can keep this struggle alive 'till it ceases to be merely a struggle between Government and the Nation. The Government which refuses to give peace to Ireland may find sooner or later that it has broken the peace of the world.[96]

Propaganda was turning the war against the British, and much of the war's condemnation came from the British themselves. On 1 November *The Times* editorialised that it was 'now generally admitted that a deliberate policy of violence had been conceived and sanctioned by an influential section of the Cabinet'.[97] Reports of atrocities in Ireland blackened Britain's reputation at home and abroad. Following the demolition of several houses in Midleton, Co. Cork, the *Daily Mail* reported that 'this is of course martial law. It is legal and disciplined. It is, we believe, necessary. But it is horrible.'[98] Others were not so sanguine about the 'necessity' of such actions. Former Prime Minister H.H. Asquith wrote: 'I say deliberately that never in the lifetime of the oldest amongst us has Britain sunk so low in the moral scale of nations. Things are being done in Ireland which would disgrace the blackest annals of the lowest despotism in Europe.'[99] *The Times* itself editorialised that 'Deeds have unquestionably been done in Ireland which have lastingly disgraced the name of Britain'. It harshly criticised 'the army's "lynch law"', and wrote that 'an Army already perilously undisciplined, and a police force avowedly beyond control have defiled, by heinous acts, the reputation of England'.[100] General Hubert Gough wrote in the *Manchester Guardian* that

> law and order have given place to a bloody and brutal anarchy in which the armed agents of the Crown violate every law in aimless and vindictive and insolent savagery. England has departed further from her own standards, and further from the standards even of any nation in the world ... than has ever been known in history before.[101]

Archbishop of Canterbury Randall Davidson addressed the House of Commons and asked that 'the government arrange, if possible, a genuine truce, with a view to a deliberate effort after an agreed solution to the Irish difficulty ... The present policy is exposing us to ... hostile criticism even of the most friendly nations of the world.'[102] The British Labour Party repeatedly advocated a British withdrawal from Ireland and self-government for all of Ireland under one assembly. The British, and Lloyd George, were coming under increasing pressure to stop the atrocities that were being reported around the world and to find some solution to the 'Irish problem'.[103]

In April Lloyd George attempted to ameliorate some of the criticism. Writing to the Protestant bishops of Britain, he stressed that his response was necessary

> on account of the responsibility and public influence of the signatories [the bishops].

He then proceeded to tacitly condone the record of the controversial Black and Tans on the basis that

> individuals working under conditions of extraordinary personal danger and strain, where they are in uniform and their adversaries mingle unrecognisable among the ordinary civilian population, have undoubtedly been guilty of deplorable acts.[104]

To the extent that, despite the best efforts of the British government to the contrary, such leading British publications as *The Times*, *The Manchester Guardian*, *The London Daily Herald* and *The New Statesman* continued to strongly criticise the British policy of coercion and reprisals in Ireland, it seems that the propaganda war yielded only limited results from the British standpoint. Indeed, the apparent reversal undergone by British policy in June 1921 by virtue of Lloyd George's decision to attempt a negotiated settlement with the same Sinn Féin Party which for the better part of three years he had sought to eradicate, and which the British propagandists sought to label as terrorists and subversives, suggests that the Irish fared better in the war of words.[105] It must also be stated, however, that the use of official propaganda and the attempt to manipulate events continued to play a central role in the British government's effort to gain a more favourable opinion of its policies in Ireland. The staging, for example, by the Cabinet of King George V's address in opening the Northern Ireland Parliament on 22 June 1921, along with the subsequent effort to maximise the publicity for the king's call for a peaceful resolution of the conflict, helped to provide the climate as well as the *raison d'être* from which the British Cabinet could change its course in Ireland.[106]

Propaganda was one of the most potent weapons of the Irish, but the lack of support for the British army in the British general press was almost as important in influencing British public and international opinion. General Macready railed against the 'blackguard press' and at the 'perfectly futile' way that 'Press Propaganda' was run by the 'frocks' at Dublin Castle. His protests made no difference. He was 'losing the battle of the narrative', and that made it impossible for the British forces to prevail against a 'paltry number of combatants'.[107]

Roy Foster expressed the end result of the propaganda war:

The real point was: when to start negotiations. And in the end, public and political opinion broke the [British] government's nerve while the IRA was still in the field. This was their victory.[108]

Charles Townshend wrote of Collins:

The IRA ... showed a natural grasp of the political and

psychological bearing of guerrilla warfare applied in conjunction with modern publicity techniques. Collins knew the GUN to be but a propaganda weapon, its power of destruction a headline, its detonation a slogan.[109]

The Irish pistols, 'loaded with words', had achieved their aim and won the propaganda war.

Notes

1   T.E. Lawrence, 'The evolution of a revolt', *Army Quarterly and Defence Journal* (October 1920), p. 11.
2   Francis Costello, 'The role of propaganda in the Anglo-Irish War, 1919–1921', *Canadian Journal of Irish Studies*, vol. 14, no. 2 (1989).
3   Charles Townshend, *The British Campaign in Ireland, 1919–1921* (Oxford, 1975), p. 65.
4   G. Dangerfield, *The Damnable Question: A Study in Anglo-Irish Relations* (Boston, 1976), pp 283–90.
5   Gary Evans, 'The raising of the First Dáil Éireann Loan and the British responses to it, 1919–1921', unpublished Ph.D thesis, Department of History, National University of Ireland, Maynooth (February 2012).
6   *Evening Herald*, 6 November 1965.
7   Peter Young, 'Michael Collins—a military leader', in Gabriel Doherty and Dermot Keogh (eds), *Michael Collins and the Making of the Irish State* (Cork, 1998), p. 90.
8   Michael Foy, *Michael Collins' Intelligence War* (Stroud, 2006; Dublin, 2007), p. 120.
9   Mao Zedong's theory of guerrilla warfare indicated that military operations are an important component of revolutionary war but that the underlying principle and fundamental objective is political. It was towards that goal that Mao directed his 'phased strategy' of guerrilla war. The broad strategy underlying all successful guerrilla warfare is that of protracted harassment accomplished by extremely subtle, flexible tactics designed to wear down the enemy. The time gained is necessary either to develop sufficient military strength to defeat the enemy forces in orthodox battle (as Mao did in China) or to subject the enemy to internal and external military and political pressures sufficient to cause him to seek peace favourable to the guerrillas (as Collins and the Irish did). This strategy embodies political, social, economic and psychological factors to which the military element is often subordinated—without, however, lessening the ultimate importance of the military role. Whether called a 'phased,' 'paced' or 'prudent' type of warfare, it is the strategy needed to succeed.
10 Risteard Mulcahy, 'The development of the Irish Volunteers, 1916–1922', *An Cosantóir*, vol. 40 (Part 3: April 1980).
11 Colin S. Gray, 'The Anglo-Irish War 1919–1921: lessons from an irregular conflict', *Comparative Strategy*, vol. 26, issue 5 (8 January 2008).
12 See Ian Kenneally, *The Paper Wall: Newspapers and Propaganda in Ireland, 1919–1921* (Cork, 2008).
13 Ian Kenneally, 'Press played pivotal role in the War of Independence', *Irish Times*, 15 November 2014.

14   See http://www.militaryarchives.ie/ie/bailiuchain/bailiuchain-idirlin/an-toglach-magazine-1918-1933.

15   J.B.E. Hittle, *Michael Collins and the Anglo-Irish War: Britain's Counter-insurgency Failure* (Chicago, 2011), p. 208.

16   Kenneally, *The Paper Wall*, pp 46–75.

17   James P. Walsh, 'De Valera in the United States, 1919', *Records of the American Catholic Historical Society of Philadelphia*, vol. 73, no. 3/4 (1962).

18   *New York Times*, 23 June 1919.

19   Not all publicity generated by de Valera was favourable, however. In Philadelphia, on 1 October, de Valera said: 'As far as England is concerned, the Irish people wished and hoped that Germany might win the war'. Immediately thereafter the American Legion came out against de Valera for not fighting in World War I. Later, when de Valera was in Los Angeles, Harry Chandler, publisher of the *Los Angeles Times*, wrote of him in an editorial that 'his American tour is being staged not to secure real freedom for Ireland, but: First, to stir opposition in this country to Great Britain. Second, to defeat, if possible, the League of Nations. Third to raise funds for the Sinn Féiners of Ireland who slay soldiers and peace officers and who assaulted American soldiers during the war' (*Los Angeles Times*, 16 November 1919). Dave Hannigan, *De Valera in America: the Rebel President's 1919 Campaign* (Dublin, 2008), p. 122.

20   David Neligan, *The Spy in the Castle* (London, 1999).

21   It should be noted that Wilson's statements regarding self-determination were contested even within his own government. His anxious Secretary of State, Robert Lansing, sensed at once that self-determination was a phrase 'simply loaded with dynamite'. As he presciently remarked in a confidential memorandum sent to Wilson on 13 December 1918, 'The more I think about the President's declaration as to the right of "self-determination", the more convinced I am of the danger of putting such ideas into the minds of certain races. It is bound to be the basis of impossible demands on the Peace Congress, and create trouble in many lands … The phrase is simply loaded with dynamite. It will raise hopes which can never be realized. It will, I fear, cost thousands of lives. In the end it is bound to be discredited, to be called the dream of an idealist who failed to realize the danger until too late to check those who attempt to put the principle into force. What a calamity that the phrase was ever uttered! What misery it will cause! Think of the feelings of the author when he counts the dead who dies because he coined a phrase! A man, who is a leader of public thought, should beware of intemperate or undigested declarations. He is responsible for the consequences … What effect will it have on the Irish, the Indians, the Egyptians, and the nationalists among the Boers? Will it not breed discontent, disorder, and rebellion? Will not the Mohammadans of Syria and Palestine and possibly of Morocco and Tripoli rely on it? How can it be harmonized with Zionism, to which the President is practically committed?' Editorial Notebook; Woodrow Wilson's Dynamite, *New York Times*, 14 April 1991.

22   Fearghal McGarry, 'The War of Independence', https://www.qub.ac.uk/sites/irishhistorylive/IrishHistoryResources/Articlesandlecturesbyourteachingstaff/TheWaroffIndependence/.

23   Bernadette Whelan, 'Wilson was urged to support presence of Irish voice at Paris Peace Conference', *Irish Times*, 21 January 2019.

24   *The Times*, 22 September 1919.

[25] *The Irish Bulletin (Acts of Aggression newsletter)*, 12 July 1919. Mike Rast, 'Tactics, politics and propaganda in the Irish War of Independence, 1917–1921', unpublished Master's thesis, Georgia State University (2011).

[26] *The Irish Bulletin (Acts of Aggression newsletter)*, 13 September 1919.

[27] *New York Times*, 14 September 1919. See Patrick McCartan, *With de Valera in America* (Dublin, 1932); Hannigan, *De Valera in America*, p. 100.

[28] David Fitzpatrick, *Politics and Irish Life, 1913–1921: Provincial Experience of War and Revolution* (Dublin, 1977), p. 123.

[29] Sr Eithne Lawless, Witness Statement 414.

[30] Bridie O'Reilly, Witness Statement 454.

[31] Ernest Blythe, Witness Statement 939.

[32] Ian McKeane, 'Michael Collins and the media: then and now', *History Ireland*, vol. 3, no. 3 (1995); K. McKenna, 'The Irish Bulletin', *Capuchin Annual* (1970).

[33] Graham Walker, 'The Irish Dr Goebbels: Frank Gallagher and Irish republican propaganda', *Journal of Contemporary History*, vol. 27, no. 1 (1992).

[34] Mulcahy papers, File 7a, No. 56.

[35] *Ibid.* PRO, CO 904/162/1, Sinn Féin Propaganda, and DE 2/10, Correspondence with Publicity Department 14 February 1920, with a report on the department dated April 1922. Dáil Éireann Reports, National Library, Dublin.

[36] D. George Boyce, *Englishmen and Irish Troubles: British Public Opinion and the Making of Irish Policy, 1918–1922* (London, 1972; Aldershot, 1994), p. 85.

[37] House of Lords Debates, No. 58, V. 2038.

[38] Sir Ormonde Winter, *Winter's Tale* (London, 1955), p. 307.

[38] Kathleen McKenna (née Napoli), Witness Statement 643; McKenna, 'The Irish Bulletin'.

[40] *The Irish Bulletin*, 19 June 1920.

[41] RIC Constable Jeremiah Mee, Witness Statement 379; Dorothy Macardle, *The Irish Republic* (New York, 1937; 1965), p. 360. See J. Anthony Gaughan (ed.), *Memoirs of Constable J. Mee, RIC* (Dublin, 1975).

[42] Anne Marreco, *The Rebel Countess: The Life and Times of Constance Markievicz* (London, 1967), p. 250.

[43] 'General played tennis in IRA custody—remembering the past', *An Phoblacht*, 29 June 1995.

[44] G. Power, 'The capture of General Lucas', in The Kerryman, *Rebel Cork's Fighting Story, 1916–1921* (Tralee, 1961); A Volunteer, 'The IRA campaign in West Limerick—captivity of General Lucas', in The Kerryman, *Limerick's Fighting Story, 1916–1921* (Tralee, 1948); 'Whether Officers in Ireland are on Active Service', NAUK, WO 32/4309.

[45] Joe Good, *Enchanted by Dreams: The Journal of a Revolutionary* (ed. Maurice Good) (Dingle, 1996), p. 166.

[46] *Ibid.*, p. 168.

[47] Francis Costello, *The Irish Revolution and its Aftermath, 1916–1923* (Dublin, 2003), pp 50–3.

[48] Cabinet Records, 15 August 1919.

[49] See Francis Costello, *Enduring the Most: The Life and Death of Terence MacSwiney* (Dublin, 1995); Seán O'Mahony, *The First Hunger Strike—Thomas Ashe, 1917* (Dublin, 2001).

[50] Joseph E.A. Connell Jnr, *Rebels' Priests: Ministering to Republicans, 1916–1924* (Dublin,

2014), pp 38–46.

[51] While in Frongoch Collins approved of hunger strikes, but soon changed his opinion of their usefulness.

[52] George Sweeney, 'Self-immolation in Ireland: hunger strikes and political confrontation', *Anthropology Today*, vol. 9, no. 5 (1993); 'Irish hunger strikes and the cult of self-sacrifice', *Journal of Contemporary History*, vol. 28, no. 3 (1993); D.J. O'Neill, 'The cult of self-sacrifice: the Irish experience', *Éire-Ireland*, vol. 24, no. 4 (1981); Barry Flynn, *Pawns in the Game: Irish Hunger Strikes 1912–1991* (Cork, 2002).

[53] Jason Perlman, 'Terence MacSwiney, the triumph and tragedy of the hunger strike', *New York State Historical Association*, vol. 88, no. 3 (2007).

[54] Peter Hart, 'Operations abroad: the IRA in Britain, 1919–1923', *English Historical Review*, vol. 115, no. 460 (2000).

[55] Cabinet Records, 21 April 1921.

[56] Hamar Greenwood in the *Weekly Summary*, 22 November 1920.

[57] *Weekly Summary*, 8 October 1920.

[58] *Weekly Summary*, 25 February 1921.

[59] *Weekly Summary*, 11 February 1921.

[60] PRO CO 904/168.

[61] *Weekly Summary*, 29 September 1920.

[62] *The Times*, 27 September 1920.

[63] John Borgonovo, *Spies, Informers and the Anti-Sinn Féin Society* (Dublin, 2006), p. 16. See Chapter 6 for a fuller account of the controversy over the Anti-Sinn Féin Society.

[64] C.E. Callwell, *Field Marshal Sir Henry Wilson: His Life and Diaries* (London, 1927), p. 251.

[65] *The Irish Bulletin*, 10 September 1920.

[66] Frank Gallagher [writing as 'David Hogan'], *The Four Glorious Years* (Dublin, 1953), pp 90–4.

[67] Major C.J.C. Street [writing as 'I.O.'], *The Administration of Ireland, 1920* (New York, 1921; London, 1922); *Ireland in 1921* (New York, 1921; London, 1922).

[68] See Brian P. Murphy, *The Origin and Organisation of British Propaganda in Ireland, 1920* (Dublin, 2006).

[69] Costello, *The Irish Revolution*, pp 57–9.

[70] Street ['I.O.'], *The Administration of Ireland, 1920*, p. 361.

[71] *Ibid.*, p. 362.

[72] *Ibid.*

[73] *Ibid.*

[74] Costello, 'The role of propaganda in the Anglo-Irish War, 1919–1921'.

[75] See http://theauxiliaries.com/men-alphabetical/men-d/dowdall/dowdall.html.

[76] *Ibid.*

[77] *Evidence on Conditions in Ireland* (ed. Albert Coyle), American Commission on Conditions in Ireland, Interim Report (Washington DC, 1921), pp 99–101.

[78] John McCann, 'Burning of the Custom House', *The Kerryman*, 17 March 1938.

[79] Lawrence, 'The evolution of a revolt', p. 10.

[80] Liz Gillis, *May 25: Burning of the Custom House 1921* (Dublin, 2017).

[81] T. Ryle Dwyer, *The Squad and the Intelligence Operations of Michael Collins* (Cork, 2005), p. 200.

[82] Oscar Traynor, Witness Statement 340; 'The burning of the Custom House—Dublin's

fighting story', *The Kerryman*, 1939; McCann, 'Burning of the Custom House'.

[83] Oscar Traynor, Witness Statement 340.

[84] N.L. Miller, P. Matsangas and L.G. Shattuck, 'Fatigue and its effect on performance in military environments', *Performance Under Stress* (26 September 2007), pp 231–48.

[85] *An Cosantóir*, vol. 2, no. 1 (1942), pp 3–4.

[86] Gillis (*May 25: Burning of the Custom House 1921*, pp 127–32) underscores that, apart from the considerable destruction caused on the first day, a significant amount of additional damage was also done to the building and to material inside (including files) over subsequent days. It turned out that the Dublin Fire Brigade were less than enthusiastic about tackling the blaze (many were members of the IRA themselves) and, after fires repeatedly broke out again over the following days, soldiers had to take over fire-fighting duties. As much as anything else, the Fire Brigade's apathy was yet another indication of the lack of support for the British authorities in most of Ireland outside Ulster at this stage. See 'Report by the General Officer Commanding in Chief, The Situation in Ireland for the Week Ending 28 May, 1921' (PRO CAB 24/123); Las Fallon, 'Forgotten allies: the Dublin Fire Brigade, 1919–1921', *An Cosantóir* (March, 2019).

[87] T. Ryle Dwyer, *Michael Collins: The Man Who Won the War* (Cork, 1990), p. 120.

[88] Harry Colley, Witness Statement 1617.

[89] General Patrick Daly, Witness Statement 387.

[90] Charles Townshend, 'The Irish Republican Army and the development of guerrilla warfare, 1916–1921', *English Historical Review*, vol. 94, no. 371 (1979).

[91] Foy, *Michael Collins' Intelligence War*, p. 218.

[92] Michael B. Barry, 'The Irish War of Independence as seen by the international press', *The Irish Times*, 3 January 2019.

[93] Gillis, *May 25: Burning of the Custom House*, p. 114.

[94] *La Tribuna Illustrata*, 15 December 1920.

[95] Bureau of Military History, CD/227/16/06.

[96] *The Nation and Athenaeum*, December 1920.

[97] *The Times*, 1 November 1920.

[98] *The Daily Mail*, 1 January 1921.

[99] H.H. Asquith, quoted in *The London Times*, 15 January 1921.

[100] *The Times*, 21 January 1921.

[101] Gen. Hubert Gough, quoted in W. Alison Phillips, *The Revolution in Ireland, 1906–1923* (London, 1923), pp 186–91. See Gen. Hubert Gough, 'The situation in Ireland', *Review of Reviews*, vol. 63 (1921).

[102] Hansard, 6 April 1921.

[103] See Boyce, *Englishmen and Irish Troubles*.

[104] Lloyd George Papers, File F/19.

[105] Costello, 'The role of propaganda in the Anglo-Irish War, 1919–1921'.

[106] Francis Costello, 'King George V's speech at Belfast, 1921: prelude to the Anglo-Irish Truce', *Éire-Ireland*, vol. 22, no. 3 (1987).

[107] General Sir Nevil Macready, *Annals of an Active Life* (2 vols) (London, 1925; 1942), vol. 2, p. 471.

[108] Roy F. Foster, *Modern Ireland, 1600–1972* (London, 1988), p. 502.

[109] Townshend, 'The Irish Republican Army and the development of guerrilla warfare, 1919-1921'.

5. Intelligence—a war of secrets

*To paralyse the British machine it was necessary to strike at individuals.
Without her spies, England was helpless. It was only by means of their
accumulated and accumulating knowledge that the British machine could
operate. Without their police throughout the country, how could they find
the man they 'wanted'?*

—Michael Collins

Intelligence is an absolute requirement for any government. In this case,
intelligence can be defined very broadly as the gathering and processing of
all information, whether open or secret, pertaining to the security of the
state.[1] Von Clausewitz noted that 'by "intelligence" we mean every sort of
information about the enemy and his country—the basis, in short, of our
own plans and operations'.[2] He went on to write: 'A great part of the
information obtained in war is contradictory, a still greater part is false, and
by far the greatest part is doubtful'. Intelligence and tactics were one to
Michael Collins. He determined to push and provoke the British to the
ends of their will, and the key to that was intelligence—and counter-
intelligence: protecting the Irish secrets from British intelligence. As Sun
Tsu saw clearly in the fifth century BC, 'All warfare is based on deception'.

Early in the war the need for an organised Irish intelligence operation,
in the cities as well as in the country, became apparent. The Irish had to
perfect their own intelligence systems, and to frustrate and disorganise
British intelligence services. Even small actions required the gathering of
some information in advance, which is the *raison d'être* of all intelligence
activity. Irish intelligence was divided into two areas: the gathering of
information on British forces and the gathering of information on British
agents. Each company of IRA/Volunteers had its own intelligence officer
(IO), each of whom was encouraged to recruit people in all walks of life
who boasted of their British connections.

Both Michael Collins and Florence O'Donoghue built up their intelligence organisations with two branches. One branch was composed of army personnel, comprising a representative from GHQ under the Director of Intelligence (Collins), a Brigade Intelligence Officer in each brigade, sometimes with some staff, a Battalion Intelligence Officer in each battalion, and a few men in each company detailed for such work.[3] The other branch included a wide variety of men and women, individually selected, who were engaged in duties or employed in positions where they could acquire valuable information about the enemy.[4] The main intelligence effort was directed towards penetrating and undermining all aspects of British government institutions, both civilian and military, including selective 'assassinations'.[5] Through the efficient combination of the work of both branches the Irish were able to partially counterbalance any weaknesses they had on the military side.[6] In recounting the factors that contributed to the success of the IRA in its operations, the admitted superiority of the Irish intelligence services, particularly in the first years of the war, must be taken into account.

Inexperienced personnel who had no rigid ideas about the kind of design needed but who were entirely clear about the results that they wanted from any scheme built up the Irish intelligence organisation from nothing. As the war progressed, Collins in Dublin and O'Donoghue in Cork continued to organise and develop more Irish intelligence. Those living outside the capital often feel that, no matter what the arena (politics, industry, history), Dublin exerts a magnetic pull in terms of resources and exposure; that feeling can become stronger the further one gets from the Liffey, and in a time of crisis it's easy to understand the grip that it exerts. O'Donoghue does not get the credit that he deserves and his operations were equally important to the Irish war effort, especially in south-east Ireland. In a humble yet correct assessment, O'Donoghue wrote:

> For most of the formative period, and continuing up to the Truce, the Director was Michael Collins, and to his initiative, energy and resourcefulness, much of the success of the service is due. Nevertheless, he would have been largely powerless outside Dublin, were it not for the work done in the local brigades.[7]

Though Collins and O'Donoghue did not begin to collaborate formally until March 1920—after the arrival of the Black and Tans—they routinely shared information after that. O'Donoghue said:

> Collins and I, each without the knowledge of each other, were trying to build up something similar but with this difference. I put down the basic organisation in the Companies and Battalions, but had made no progress in the intelligence aspect at that stage, where he had practically no organisation, but had made very considerable progress on the more valuable espionage aspect. Working in Dublin, and with his contacts in London, his opportunities in this regard were much more extensive than mine. Out of the Quinlisk case [see below] there arose a comparing of notes and close contact that proved valuable.[8]

One of Collins's most important services was to pass on to O'Donoghue the RIC police cipher keys for Cork. O'Donoghue organised a team to intercept RIC messages, to decode them and transmit the information back to his Brigade Headquarters. Collins eventually provided O'Donoghue with funds to support local intelligence operations in Cork.[9]

In Dublin, the 'G' Division of the Dublin Metropolitan Police (DMP) was neutralised: after the killing of its most aggressive detectives, other detectives stopped helping the British. The British report after the war noted the effect of Collins's attacks on the DMP:

> Up to the summer of 1919, the military relied for their intelligence almost entirely on the DMP in the city and the RIC in the country, but these sources were practically closed by the end of 1919 by the murder campaign.[10]

By 1920 the DMP was no longer a threat to the Irish and the IRA adopted a hands-off approach.[11] In the country, the RIC and their families were first ostracised and then the RIC were forced back into barracks in larger towns. This left the British intelligence network in tatters. Collins passed information to the country units for their use, and intelligence gleaned in the country was passed back to Dublin and was essential. In Cork,

O'Donoghue ran an intelligence system that rivalled the Dublin operation for efficiency in acquiring intelligence from both military and civilian sources, and in utilising that information for IRA operations.[12]

At the start, their inexperience led the Irish to make some amateurish mistakes. O'Donoghue ran afoul of his own intelligence service and almost ordered his own killing! When a new Irish intelligence officer in Cork, who did not know what O'Donoghue looked like, learned about a resident leaving his house early and returning late and with no apparent employment, he shadowed him to the main police barracks and determined that the suspect must be a detective. He also noted other strangers coming to the house after dark; their late-night business was suspicious and could not be determined. A few weeks later, O'Donoghue was asked to ratify the unknown spy's execution. Fortunately, the procedures that he had laid down to guard against just such a mistake were followed, or he would have ordered his own execution.[13]

Collins, too, experienced a learning curve. He was appointed Director of Intelligence in March 1918, replacing Éamonn Duggan. Very shortly thereafter, on 15 May Éamon Broy secured a list of prominent Sinn Féin members who were to be arrested in the so-called 'German Plot'. Broy passed the list to Patrick Tracy at Kingsbridge railway station, and Tracy passed the list to Harry O'Hanrahan (brother of Michael O'Hanrahan, who was executed after the Rising).

> In the case of the German Plot arrests in May, 1918, a large list of names and addresses of those to be arrested in Dublin came to my hands. There were continual additions to the list but, finally, in May, 1918, the list was complete, and several copies were made. Indirectly, it became obvious to me that the arrests would soon start. I gave Tracy a copy of the complete list on the Wednesday forty-eight hours before the arrests took place. ... On the day of the proposed arrests as far as I recollect it was a Friday I met Tracy and told him: 'To-night's the night. Tell O'Hanrahan to tell the wanted men not to stay in their usual place of abode and to keep their heads'. Meanwhile, preparations were made for the raid. All the detectives, no matter what their usual duties were, several uniformed men and a military party with a lorry were ordered

to stand-to. I had a talk with McNamara [another detective officer and one of Collins's men], and we deliberated on the question of refusing to carry out the arrests and calling on the others not to do so, but we finally decided that such a course of action would do no good whatever, and would probably lead to our dismissal from the service.[14]

Joe Kavanagh, who also worked for Collins in Dublin Castle, gave the list of those to be arrested to another Collins man, Thomas Gay, who passed the list to Collins. In an indication of Collins's inexperience at the time, he gave Gay £5 to pay Kavanagh for the information. Gay knew that Kavanagh would be insulted that Collins would think that he would spy for money, so he never offered it to him. Collins had yet to learn that there were patriotic Irishmen even in the police and the Castle. Collins notified de Valera and the other leaders of the forthcoming arrests, but de Valera chose to ignore the warnings. It was an example of the efficiency of Collins's network and how he seemed to have information even before the Castle had told the police. That series of raids on 17–18 May rounded up many, and these arrests were what brought Collins fully into the intelligence effort.

The efficiency of Irish intelligence was due not only to Collins and O'Donoghue and the operatives working for them but also to three other things:

• An appreciation of the value of intelligence.
• Efficient organisation and exploitation of sources.
• Every member of the Irish forces regarded it as a duty—and many of those who weren't actively on patrol regarded it as such, too.

Even today, military intelligence has four parts: acquisition, analysis, execution and counter-intelligence. One secret to effective intelligence is the sharing of ideas; although there were some problems of communication between Collins, O'Donoghue, GHQ and the country units, for the most part the Irish understood what intelligence was needed and utilised it better than the British.[15] What the British needed in 1917–18 was not so much tactical intelligence on the Irish Volunteers—who were acting mostly in the open—as political intelligence on the shifts in Irish opinion. This they did not have, or ignored.

Any examination of intelligence in the period must also review the performance of the British.[16] In its record prepared after the war, the British War Department identified a combination of three problems that it blamed for its 'failures':

- A vacillating and negligent government.
- A hostile population.
- A jury-rigged intelligence system lacking unity, direction or leadership.[17]

One RIC Divisional Inspector complained: 'Before the war we knew everybody and what he was doing. Now we know nothing. The people are dumb!'[18]

Collins's Department of Intelligence office was on the second floor of a building at 3 Crow Street, above J.F. Fowler, printers and binders, just 500 yards from the entrance to Dublin Castle. Along with his office at 32 Bachelor's Walk, this was technically Collins's main Department of Intelligence office but he came here only infrequently. Sometimes his operatives called this 'the Brain Centre'.

> It was, as I say, early in 1919 that Collins began to create a regular Intelligence Department. He was fortunate in getting the services of Liam Tobin as Chief Intelligence Officer. Tobin had been previously doing Intelligence work for the Dublin Brigade. Later the Assistant Quartermaster General, the late Tom Cullen, was drafted into Intelligence. Next in command came Frank Thornton. The Intelligence Staff was built up slowly, as suitable men were not easily found. A good Intelligence Officer is born, not made, but even the man with a great deal of natural instinct for detective work requires to be taught a great deal of the technique of the business.[19]

Immediately upon taking the position Collins began assembling a staff, and he promoted Liam Tobin to lead it. The trio of Tobin, Cullen and Thornton acted as an equal triumvirate: Collins was the boss, but the success enjoyed by IRA intelligence is attributable at least as much to their canniness as to his direction.[20] Collins is often described as directing every minute detail of the intelligence department, but part of his success in managing as many projects as he did was his ability to delegate. His own interviews refer to 'the trustworthiness of my chief aides'.[21] In contrast, Tony Woods, a veteran of the Dublin Brigade, went so far as to say, 'Tobin, of course, was the real Intelligence man in Dublin in the Tan struggle, not Collins'.[22] This critique likely goes too far in attempting to shift credit for the intelligence war away from Collins, but it is important in that it emphasises the role of his subordinates, and there were differing views of Collins even in those years. Collins's personality often enabled him to attract people who were willing to turn over intelligence to him. His ability to make connections with people and to forge personal bonds was one of his greatest assets. It could also lead him astray, however, as it did with the spies Jameson and Quinlisk, and Collins was very fortunate to have Tobin, Cullen and Thornton turn their more sceptical eyes on some of his 'conquests'.

Under the name of the Irish Products Company, Tobin, Cullen and Thornton operated and carried on the daily activities of intelligence analysis.[23]

I was very happy about this transfer to Intelligence as I liked Michael Collins. I was a great admirer of him. I recognised at an early stage, even as far back as my first contact with him in Liverpool, that he was a dynamic type of individual and, although at that period he was not in any directive position, still he was an outstanding individual on that famous day in Liverpool in 1915. Later on, working with him on organisation, I had a very quiet admiration for him which developed as the years went on. Michael Collins was a man with a determination to make a complete success of everything he put his hands to. He had a marvellous memory, and as I saw repeatedly happen in later years, he would deal with men from all parts of the country at night in our headquarters in Devlin's of Parnell Square, he would make a very casual note about the things which would have to be attended to on the following day or, as often as not, take no note of them at all, but never to my knowledge was anything left unattended to the next day. He was full of the exuberance of life and full of vitality. He had no time for half measures and expected from those who were serving under him the same amount of enthusiasm and constructive energy that he himself was putting into the job.

Michael Collins took a lively interest in the private affairs of each and every individual with whom he came in contact and was always ready to lend a helping hand to assist them to meet their private responsibilities. During the height of the War he travelled from post to post and office on his old Raleigh bicycle and, as often as not, did not leave Devlin's in Parnell Square until just on curfew. I think it is only right to say here, in view of the many and varied accounts given by various writers, who claim to have known Collins and his activities, that he never carried a gun during these journeys, neither was he accompanied by a bodyguard.

In the various activities carried out by the Dublin Squads, ASU and members of the Dublin Brigade, naturally from time to time men got either killed or wounded, but invariably Mick Collins was the first man to visit the relatives of these particular men, to either console them in their adversity or to see in what way he could help them to carry on their home affairs during the absence of their loved ones.

Mick Collins was the ideal soldier to lead men during a revolution such as we were going through and I think all and sundry, whether they subsequently fought against him in the Civil War or not, who had close contact with him, must admit that he was: the one bright star that all the fighting men looked to for guidance and advice during those great days, particularly during 1920 and 1921.

In some of the criticisms that have appeared from time to time about Mick Collins it has been suggested that he drank to excess. These statements are lies. As one who was very closely associated with him during those strenuous days, I can say that Collins rarely took anything and when he did it was a small sherry. Drinking was naturally discouraged everywhere those days because of the necessity of keeping a cool head under the very strenuous circumstances.

In singling out Collins I am doing so only because of the fact that I had such close association with him and knew what the officers and men of the Volunteers thought of him generally, but in singling him out in this fashion I am in no way taking away from the activities of the other members of the staff, Cathal Brugha, Dick Mulcahy or Gearóid O'Sullivan.[24]

The conduct of Collins's war depended on intelligence and, with all their faulty judgements and inaccuracies, Collins realised that the British secret files still constituted Britain's greatest intelligence on Ireland. After Broy let Collins and Seán Nunan into the file rooms of the Great Brunswick Street police station on the night of 7 April 1919 to look over the 'G' Division files on the Volunteers, Collins determined that in order to defeat the British they would have to eliminate their spies. A natural realist like Collins realised how essential it was to shut off the sources of knowledge and blind Dublin Castle. He said that the British 'could replace the men, but couldn't replace what they knew'. He wrote in the *New York American* in 1922:

England could always reinforce her Army. She could replace every soldier that she lost … But there were others indispensable for her purposes that were not so easily replaced.

To paralyse the British machine it was necessary to strike at individuals. Without her spies, England was helpless. It was only by means of their accumulated and accumulating knowledge that the British machine could operate. Without their police throughout the country, how could they find the man they 'wanted'?

We struck at individuals and by doing so we cut their lines of communication and we shook their morale. Only the armed forces and the spies and criminal agents of the British government were attacked. Prisoners of war were treated honourably and considerately and were released after they had been disarmed.[25]

Collins told Éamon Broy: 'I am a builder, not a destroyer. I get rid of people only when they hinder my work.' Collins warned the detectives to look the other way or suffer the consequences. Those who ignored his warnings paid the price. His grasp of the need for intelligence in order to conduct the guerrilla war was perhaps Collins's greatest contribution to that war.

Collins's main 'military' initiative at the start of the war consisted of an all-out offensive against the few indispensable British officers in Dublin: the detectives of 'G' Division of the Dublin Metropolitan Police, who were responsible for tracking and gathering information on political dissidents. At the end of the 1916 Rising Collins watched as they picked out republican leaders for court martial and execution. When he succeeded Éamonn Duggan as Director of Intelligence in January 1919, there were already three G-men feeding intelligence to republicans—Éamon Broy, Joseph Kavanagh and Eugene Smith—but their efforts were disorganised.[26] Collins undertook a policy of meeting face to face with these double agents and recruited as many more of them as possible.[27]

When Collins took over from Duggan there was really no intelligence department as such. Duggan was a solicitor and kept the intelligence files mixed in with his clients' files—and ultimately the British captured the files anyway. The files consisted of current press cuttings indicating the comings and goings of Castle and military personnel and had more social than intelligence value.

As was always the case, politics intervened in all aspects of the war, including the intelligence effort. Before the IRA's offensive in the intelligence war could progress, politics became important in the pursuit of the British detectives. The Dáil's second session opened on 1 April and during its third meeting, on 10 April, de Valera rose and called for all the police forces to be socially ostracised. In doing so, he revived a tactic that had played a large role in the Land War in rural Ireland during the 1870s and 1880s. He stated:

> The people of Ireland ought not to fraternise, as they often do, with the forces that are the main instruments in keeping them in subjugation ... Given the composition of these forces, boycott meant accentuating divisions among Irish people, including family members and community residents.

De Valera said that he was reluctant to move against the RIC and DMP because they were Irish as well. In the course of the speech he called the constabulary 'England's janissaries', and said that they were

> no ordinary civil force, as police are in other countries … The RIC, unlike any other police force in the world, is a military body … They are given full licence by their superiors to work their will upon an unarmed populace. The more brutal the commands given them by their superiors the more they seem to revel in carrying them out—against their own flesh and blood, be it remembered!

He said that 'a full boycott will give them vividly to understand how utterly the people of Ireland loathe both themselves and their calling'.[28]

At no time did de Valera either explicitly call for or forbid violent action against the police, but his call for social ostracism of the men and their families and the warnings issued by the intelligence department required time to take effect.[29] When it did, the 'eyes and ears' of British intelligence were eliminated. Constable John Regan wrote: 'One day when meeting him [an Irish contact], I asked him if he had anything fresh … "I'm finished" he said. "I tell you I'm finished. These fellows are serious, and if you take my tip you'll go a bit easy, too". That ended my getting information from him, and many others, too.'[30] The British were blind and dumb as far as intelligence in the countryside was concerned from then on. (See Chapter 6 for a discussion of the effect of ostracism on the RIC and their families, as well as on the Irish population.)

In Dublin Collins needed a dedicated band of men to carry out his ordered killings. 'The Squad' was initiated on 19 September 1919 (though by that time it had been in operation for four months and had already carried out two killings). Collins and Mulcahy presided at a meeting at which the unit was officially formed. Its initial meeting was on 1 May 1919.[31]

> We met Michael Collins and Dick Mulcahy at the meeting and they told us that it was proposed to form a squad. This squad would take orders directly from Michael Collins, and, in the

absence of Collins, the orders would be given through either Dick McKee or Dick Mulcahy. Dick [Mulcahy] told that we were not to discuss our movements or actions with Volunteer officers or with anybody else. Collins told us that we were being formed to deal with spies and informers and that he had authority from the Government to have this order carried out. He gave us a short talk, the gist of which was that any of us who had read Irish history would know that no organisation in the past had an intelligence system through which spies and informers could be dealt with, but that now the position was going to be rectified by the formation of an Intelligence Branch, an Active Service Unit or whatever else it is called.[32]

William Stapleton was soon chosen to be a member, and he described the method of working in the Squad:[33]

Bill [Tobin] or Tom [Cullen] [from Collins's intelligence staff] would come down and tell us who we were to get. It might be one of the Igoe Gang or a British spy sent over to shoot Collins. Two or three of us would go out with an intelligence officer in front of us, maybe about 10 or 15 yards. His job was to identify the man we were to shoot. Often we would be walking in the streets all day without meeting our man. It meant going without lunch. But other times the intelligence staff would have their information dead on and we could see our quarry immediately we came to the place we had been told he would be at. The intelligence officer would then signal us in the following way. He would take off his hat and greet the marked man. Of course, he didn't know him. As soon as he did this we would shoot. We knew that very great care was taken that this was so. As a result we didn't feel we had to worry. We were, after all, only soldiers doing our duty. I often went in and said a little prayer for the people we'd shot afterwards.[34]

W.C. Forbes Redmond, Belfast RIC Assistant Commissioner of Police, was transferred to Dublin in December 1919 in an effort to bolster the

In Cork Tom Barry followed classic guerrilla tactics: fighting only when the odds looked particularly good, and focusing his efforts on keeping the column away from the enemy. His men travelled light and chose difficult terrain and weather, exhausting and wearing down the British.

Every day was a working day for Collins—and every night, too. From early morning breakfast until he dragged himself to bed, it was the same hurried schedule, and he always dressed as a successful businessman. Collins said that he 'hid in plain sight'.

Following the passage of the Treaty in January 1922, Collins gave speeches to massive crowds. He said that 'we could not have beaten the British by force, but when we have beaten them out by the Treaty, the republican ideal, which was surrendered in July, is restored'. His view was that the Treaty was a 'stepping-stone' that gave Ireland the 'freedom to achieve freedom'.

Although Arthur Griffith was the top-ranking delegate to the Treaty negotiations in London, Collins was recognised as the *de facto* leader. Collins was extremely uncomfort-able with being chosen as a delegate. It was not his field of expertise but he accepted it grudgingly as his duty.

Immediately on taking up the position of Director of Intelligence, Collins began assembling a staff, and he promoted Liam Tobin to lead it. Tony Woods, a veteran of the Dublin Brigade, went so far as to say that 'Tobin, of course, was the real Intelligence man in Dublin in the Tan struggle, not Collins'.

'G' Division Commissioner W.C. Forbes Redmond was staying in the Standard Hotel in Harcourt Street, and Tom Cullen, a man who was high up in the Intelligence staff and in the confidence of Michael Collins, was sent to stay in the same hotel in order to gather information.

De Valera devised the following formula: 'Sinn Féin aims at securing the international recognition of Ireland as an independent Irish Republic. Having achieved that status the Irish people may by referendum freely choose their own form of government.' He subsequently closed the October 1917 Ard-Fheis by declaring, 'We are not doctrinaire Republicans'.

Like Collins, Gen. Richard Mulcahy always kept an eye on the ultimate goal: the removal of British governance. Mulcahy always deemed it prudent to be especially careful about taking any action that could alienate the local population.

Seán Treacy said of the Flying Columns: 'We wanted full-time soldiers who were prepared to fight by night or by day, ready for any adventure. They would constitute a mobile force capable of striking at a given moment in one district and on the next day springing a surprise thirty miles away.'

Prime Minister David Lloyd George's claim to have 'murder by the throat' just ten days before Bloody Sunday (21 November 1920) rang hollow in the British press and encouraged the British government to seek a negotiated solution, leading to the first feelers for negotiation being extended to the Irish in December 1920.

The fact that revolutionary fervour did not exist at the outset was not an impediment to the revolution, as Che Guevara understood later: 'It is not necessary to wait until all conditions for making revolution exist: the insurrection can create them'.

T.E. Lawrence, a contemporary of Michael Collins and the Irish, knew that the goal of a guerrilla war is to make action a series of single combats. He held that 'irregular war is far more intellectual than a bayonet charge'.

Throughout the war, the British wavered between repression and conciliation. British policy seemed to lurch from one response to the other. As General Macready put it, 'Whatever we do, we are sure to be wrong'.

Nancy O'Brien (third from right, seated), Collins's second cousin, worked in the Post Office and was hired to decode messages in the office of Sir James McMahon, Director of Posts and Telegraphs. When told of her new job, Collins said: 'Well, Christ, I don't know how they've held their empire for so long. What a bloody intelligence service they have.' Later she married Collins's brother Johnny. (Photo courtesy of Pól Ó Murchú.)

Colonel Ormonde de L'Epée Winter, Chief of the British Combined Intelligence Services in Ireland. The Irish knew him as the 'Holy Terror' because he was brutal in his interrogation of prisoners. The British held him in no higher regard, as he was known to Mark Sturgis as 'a wicked little white snake … probably entirely non-moral'.

On 14 July 1921 de Valera went to London to negotiate with Lloyd George. Included in the delegation were Arthur Griffith, Count Plunkett, Austin Stack, Robert Barton and Erskine Childers. Collins wanted to go and forcefully pressed to be included but de Valera chose to leave him in Dublin.

POLICE NOTICE.

£1000 REWARD

WANTED FOR MURDER IN IRELAND.

DANIEL BREEN

(calls himself Commandant of the Third
Tipperary Brigade).

Age 27, 5 feet 7 inches in height, bronzed complexion, dark hair (long in front), grey eyes, short cocked nose, stout build, weight about 12 stone, clean shaven ; sulky bulldog appearance ; looks rather like a blacksmith coming from work ; wears cap pulled well down over face.

The above reward will be paid by the Irish Authorities, to any person not in the Public Service who may give information resulting in his arrest.

Information to be given at any Police Station.

In describing the action at Soloheadbeg, Dan Breen wrote that without any authorisation they set out to fire the shots that 'would begin another phase in the long fight for the freedom of our country'. Breen felt that 'we had to kill and can't leave anyone alive afterward'.

Throughout the war Cathal Brugha was the Minister for Defence. His antipathy towards Collins grew, and their personal differences, often expressed in Cabinet meetings, came to a head in the Treaty debates, when Brugha denigrated Collins as a mere publicity-seeker.

In 1922 the IRB held conferences in Dublin for the express purpose of endeavouring to save the IRB from disruption on the Treaty issue. Collins and Liam Lynch were the principal protagonists of the opposing views. Lynch subsequently led the anti-Treaty IRA until he was killed on 10 April 1923, leading to the end of the Civil War.

Mao Zedong's 'Long March' and his writings contributed much to the concept of guerrilla war. 'Popular support is not only necessary for the success of the struggle, but also determines the nature and location of guerrilla operations … The guerrilla must move among the people as a fish swims in the sea.'

The jury in the inquest on the murdered Sinn Féin Mayor of Cork, Tomás MacCurtáin, laid the blame squarely at the door of the RIC and the British Cabinet. The jury issued a verdict of 'wilful murder' against British Prime Minister Lloyd George and against a number of policemen.

Terence MacSwiney's death on 25 October 1920 seemed the most important event that occurred in the country at that time. Ireland went into mourning when he died on the seventy-fourth day of his hunger strike.

Piaras Béaslaí's cousin, Lily Mernin, was 'identified' as one of Collins's most important sources, 'Lt G'. She was employed by Colonel Hill Dillon in Parkgate Street and also worked for Major Stratford Burton at Ship Street Barracks. Mernin would walk up and down the streets of Dublin on the arm of a Volunteer, pointing out British agents who worked in Dublin Castle.

The IRA GHQ staff in 1921 included Michael Collins, Richard Mulcahy, Gearóid O'Sullivan, Éamon Price, Rory O'Connor, Eoin O'Duffy, Seán Russell, Seán McMahon, J.J. O'Connell, Emmet Dalton, Seán Donovan, Liam Mellows and Piaras Béaslaí.

British intelligence operations in Dublin, and he was appointed as the Deputy Assistant Commissioner of the DMP in charge of the 'G' Division. He was completely unfamiliar with Dublin and so he was assigned a 'minder' by Dublin Castle: as luck would have it, the minder was Collins's operative James McNamara. McNamara was thus able to follow Redmond's movements and report to Collins.

Redmond led a raid on Batt O'Connor's home on 17 January and assured Mrs Bridget O'Connor that he 'wouldn't bother her again'.[35] Collins's men made sure of it. Redmond stayed at the Standard Hotel before being killed on 21 January 1920.[36]

> Redmond was stopping in the Standard Hotel in Harcourt Street, and Tom Cullen … a man who was high up on the Intelligence staff and in the confidence of Michael Collins, was sent to stop in the same hotel in order to get all possible information regarding Redmond, particularly about his times of leaving and returning to the hotel, and what he did in the morning and at night.[37]

> One evening I saw Redmond coming down from the Castle but he turned back and went in again. Paddy Daly, Tom Keogh, Vinny Byrne and myself were waiting and Redmond came out again. Tom Keogh turned to Vinny Byrne and myself and told us to cover them off. Redmond went straight up Dame Street, Grafton Street and Harcourt Street, and we followed him. Just as he came as far as Montague Street Paddy Daly pulled out his revolver and shot him under the ear and Tom Keogh pulled out his revolver and shot him in the back. Daly and Keogh carried out the execution, and Byrne and myself acted as a covering party for them.[38]

The first shot shattered Redmond's jaw and he tried to draw a gun, but the second shot in the forehead killed him. Redmond was the highest-ranking casualty in DMP history. *The Times* wrote days later that 'the murder … is accepted as final proof of the existence in Ireland of a criminal organization of the most desperate kind. The crime must have been planned with much care and skill'.[39] It *was* carefully planned. Daly and Joe Dolan stayed in the hotel for two weeks previously to learn about Redmond's movements, and reported to Mick McDonnell, who was in charge of the Squad.

At the end of 1919 British raiders discovered a chequebook from the Munster and Leinster Bank on Dame Street where some of the Dáil Loan funds might be deposited. The bank itself was raided in February 1920, and about £18,000 was seized.[40] These monies were under the name of Daithi Ó Donnchadha (O'Donoghue), and had been 'transferred from Mícheál Ó Coileáin' (Collins).[41] It was this raid that immediately precipitated the death of the bank auditor, Alan Bell.

Bell was particularly close to Lord French, and was specially assigned to this duty in order to cripple the Dáil Loan. He endeavoured to trace all the banks in which Collins deposited the proceeds of the Dáil Loan, and if he had succeeded the Loan would have been at risk. The final Loan total, subscribed by over 135,000 Irish people, was £378,858 in Ireland alone; $5,123,640 was raised separately in the US.[42] Both were huge sums for the time. Of all the money collected for the Loan, the British were only able to confiscate approximately £20,000 of it. Bell, however, had also been an active police agent since the 1880s and had undertaken numerous spying missions in the west of Ireland, sending back reports on Land Leaguers and IRB members. He also reported directly to Sir Basil Thomson, head of British intelligence at Scotland Yard, and the committee on which Bell sat recommended that Sinn Féin 'be infiltrated with spies and some leaders assassinated'. According to Piaras Béaslaí, Collins regarded Bell as one of the most important British intelligence agents in Ireland.[43] Unfortunately for Bell, his inquiry into the Sinn Féin accounts in March 1920 was much publicised in the newspapers, sealing his fate.

Bell was taken off a tram opposite Nutley Lane and Simonscourt Road and shot on 27 March 1920. ('Come on, Mr Bell, your time has come.') Earlier that month he had signed an order requiring banks to disclose all details of clients' accounts. He had been working with Sir John Taylor, the Undersecretary, and had recently seized about £20,000 from accounts in the banks believed to belong to Sinn Féin depositors.

Alan Bell was a Resident Magistrate who came from the North of Ireland to Dublin to locate the Dáil Funds, which were in the bank, and it was decided that he should be executed. He was carrying out his investigations in the Four Courts, and we often waited to get him when he would be passing between the Castle and the Four Courts. We had no possible means of identifying him until the '*Irish Independent*' published his photograph. We discovered that he was living in Monkstown and that he travelled in to Dublin on the Dalkey tram.[44]

Bill Stapleton, Tom Keogh and Joe Dolan were members of the Squad.[45]

Tom Keogh and myself saw Bell on the tram that morning, and tried to follow it on our bicycles to give our men the word that he was coming. The tram was going very fast and we found it very hard to keep up with it. We saw our group of men at the corner of Anglesea Road and signalled to them that Bell was in the tram. We saw them signal the tram to stop and the whole group got into the tram. The next thing we saw was the tram being stopped and Bell being marched out by the group. Tom Keogh and I were just sightseers.

Coming back we saw a policeman standing in the middle of the road. ... I was cycling along leisurely because I did not want to create any suspicion in the mind of the policeman. He put up his hand and I slowed down. The policeman asked me, 'Was there an accident up there?' I looked back and saw a crowd of people running in different directions. 'It looks like it', I said to the policeman. The policeman then said, 'I heard a shot, but if there is any shooting business there I am not going near it'.[46]

Despite the murder of its 'G' Division chief, Redmond, British intelligence in Dublin Castle succeeded in placing two secret agents close to republican intelligence. The first was John Charles (J.C.) Byrne, alias 'Jameson', who ingratiated himself with Collins by posing as a representative of a British soldiers' and sailors' union while Collins was trying to foment disorder among Crown forces by encouraging strikes. 'Jameson' arrived in Dublin with a letter of introduction from Art O'Brien, head of the IRB in London. In a briefing to his staff, Redmond foolishly ridiculed 'G' Division detectives in front of Collins's agent James McNamara, pointing out that he had an operative who made contact with Collins only a fortnight after arriving from London. Redmond boasted to the detectives that they, who knew Dublin so well, could not get close to Michael Collins, while a man who had only recently arrived from England managed to meet him more than once.[47] When Collins agent Dave Neligan heard this, he realised that the only suspect was Jameson, and Collins ordered the intelligence staff to stay away from him.[48] Neligan informed Collins through Éamon Broy, and Jameson was killed a few days later, on 2 March 1920.[49]

As a final test, Collins's intelligence team had lured Jameson to an office at 56 Bachelor's Walk. Jameson told them that he had brought revolvers and other hand guns from England 'for the cause'. He left the heavy portmanteau with Frank Thornton, and it was transferred out of the 56 Bachelor's Walk premises. When McNamara tipped off Collins that there would be a raid on the building later that day, it was further confirmation that Jameson was a spy.

> This was a very interesting individual. He came to Dublin with the highest recommendations from the late Seán McGrath and Art O'Brien in London.
>
> ...
>
> I am not fully aware of what the proposition was in detail that was put up, but it evidently impressed the London leaders because they contacted Mick Collins, who agreed to meet Jameson in Dublin. He actually met Mick Collins in Dublin. Following the meeting, at any rate, he was handed over to Tobin, Cullen and myself. It would appear that his chief activity as far as we were concerned was to procure arms and ammunition on this side of the water. It is rather a peculiar thing that sometimes the cleverest of men are caught out because somebody on the opposite side takes a dislike to them but that is actually what happened in the case of Jameson. Tom Cullen had forcibly expressed his dislike of the man from the beginning, and possibly this had reactions on myself. In any case there were none of us impressed. It was decided to start laying traps for him. He fell into the first trap laid. He arrived with Liam Tobin outside New

Ireland Assurance Society's building at 56 Bachelor's Walk.

... Jameson handed over a portmanteau full of Webley revolvers to me in the hall of Kapp & Petersons, which he stated he had smuggled into the country. His story was that he got them in through communistic channels. They were handed over to me in the hall door of Kapp & Peterson's, Bachelor's Walk. ... When the coast was clear, I handed the portmanteau of revolvers over to Tom Cullen who was waiting at 32 Bachelor's Walk which was Quartermaster General's stores. Before all these things happened we had contacted Jim McNamara of the Detective Division, who was working for us, to keep his ears open for any unusual occurrence on that day, particularly if he heard of any raids to try and give us the information in advance. About mid-day I got a message from McNamara telling me that the New Ireland Assurance Society's premises at Bachelor's Walk would be raided at about 3 o'clock. I naturally had a good look around the premises to make sure that no papers or any documents or guns of any description were left around.

... following other incidents which happened it was finally decided that Jameson was a spy and as such would have to be shot. He met Paddy Daly and Joe [Leonard] by appointment; making sure that no accomplice was shadowing the party he was brought out by tram to meet Mick Collins at Ballymun Road. Naturally Collins wasn't there but Jameson was told that he was going to be shot. ... I think it is sufficient to say that Sir Basil Thomson clinched the matter when he described Jameson (alias Byrne) as one of the best and cleverest Secret Service men that [they] ever had.[50]

Another British agent was Timothy Quinlisk, a former member of Roger Casement's Irish Brigade, formed from Irish prisoners of war in Germany. This affiliation gave him immediate nationalist credentials on his return to Dublin after the war, and the Irish National Aid Association paid his bills for several months. As a former member of the Casement Brigade in Germany he was denied back pay for his period of imprisonment, and he convinced Collins that he was in dire financial straits. He was well educated and spoke French and German fluently; after the war, when he was discharged from the British army, he lived for a time in Dublin and then in Cork City. Always known by Collins and his men by the one name 'Quinlisk', he was a British double agent. Collins and his men suspected him relatively quickly after his appearance, and once Collins gave him £100 to get out of the country. Quinlisk came back for more, however, and that sealed his fate. He was an inept spy: after his reappearance Volunteer leaders quickly placed him under close surveillance and found more than enough reason to execute him. He was told that Collins was in Cork; when he subsequently gave the Cork RIC this information and said that it would be easy for the Cork RIC to capture him, it was clear to Collins that Quinlisk was a spy. He was killed on 19 February 1920 outside Wren's Hotel in Cork.

The Cork No. 1 Brigade Council agreed that he should be shot. The execution party from the Second Battalion consisted of Michael Murphy (O/C) and two others. Murphy coldly recalled of the not-quite-dead Quinlisk: 'I then turned him over on the flat of his back and put a bullet through his forehead'.

> I might here state that on the same evening that Quinlisk was executed, following a raid on the mails by some of our lads, one of the letters written by 'Quinn' (as he called himself) … addressed to the County Inspector, RIC, was found. The letter said that Quinlisk 'had information about Michael Collins and would report again in a few days when the capture of Collins seemed imminent' … The Cork No 1 Brigade Commandant Seán Hegarty got in touch with GHQ, Dublin, immediately following the identification of 'Quinn' as Quinlisk, and word was received back from Mick Collins that Quinlisk was definitely a spy in the pay of the British.[51]

Quinlisk's family knew nothing of his spying activities, and when his father came from Waterford to claim the body about two weeks later he had a confrontation with Murphy, who had been informed by the clerk of the Cork Poor Law Union of the father's application to the workhouse authorities. At the time of the 1911 census the victim's father, Denis, had been an 'acting sergeant' in the RIC, residing at 10 Cathedral Square in Waterford City.

Yet another British spy who attempted to infiltrate Collins's intelligence organisation was Bryan Fergus Molloy,[52] stationed at British payroll headquarters on Parkgate Street, where he worked for the Chief Intelligence Officer, Colonel Stephen Hill Dillon. Through a Sinn Féin TD, Dr Frank Ferran, Molloy was introduced to Batt O'Connor. He told O'Connor that his superiors wanted him to join the British Secret Service but that he'd do so only if he could pass information to Collins. Thereafter Liam Tobin, Tom Cullen or Frank Thornton would meet Molloy in the Café Cairo or Kidd's, but they never trusted him.[53] His true identity was known almost from the start, having been revealed by Piaras Béaslaí's cousin, Lily Mernin, who was a typist for Colonel Hill Dillon.[54] Molloy was killed on 25 March 1920 outside the Wicklow Hotel by a team led by Mick McDonnell.[55]

Richard Mulcahy's claim that 'none of these people would have been killed if they could have been otherwise effectively disposed of either as direct or indirect murderers, and a danger to our whole organisation', by simply keeping away from them seems highly improbable.[56] Collins justified the killing of those deemed to be informers by saying that 'we had no jails and we therefore had to kill all spies, informers, and double-crossers'.[57] Florence O'Donoghue concurred: 'The absence of any facilities for the detention of prisoners made it impossible to deal with the doubtful cases. In practice, there was no alternative between execution and complete immunity.'

Dave Neligan was one of Collins's most important agents and his ability to place himself at the centre of the British administration is almost unbelievable. He originally joined the DMP 'to get away from a boring country life', but he hated the work and resigned on 11 May 1920, going home to Limerick. Collins sent word for him to return to Dublin. Neligan said that he hated working for the British in the Castle; he 'would join a column, do anything but go back to the Castle'. Nevertheless, at Collins's request he returned to become *The Spy in the Castle*.[58] Collins told him that there were plenty of men to join columns but that his contacts and placement in Dublin Castle were vital for the intelligence operation. Neligan convinced his employers in the Castle that his life was in danger back in Limerick and rejoined the service. In May 1921 he joined the British Secret Service and became Agent No. 68, assigned to the district of Dalkey, Kingstown (Dún Laoghaire) and Blackrock. He was warmly congratulated by the major in charge, who shook his hand and said, 'Try to join the IRA, my boy, try to join the IRA!' Neligan was so successful in convincing the British that he was on their side that he later received pensions from the British government as well as from the Irish government: an old IRA pension, one from the Irish police, another from the Irish civil service, and still others from the RIC and the British Secret Service. On being sworn into the Secret Service he took the following oath:

> I … solemnly swear by Almighty God that I will faithfully perform the duties assigned to me as a member of His Majesty's secret service: that I will obey implicitly those placed over me; that I shall never betray such service or anything connected with it even after I have left it. *If I fail to keep this Oath in every particular I realize that vengeance will pursue me to the ends of the earth, so help me God.*[59] [Emphasis in original]

In later life Neligan revelled in having fooled the British, and indicated that upon his resignation he received a personal note from General Henry Tudor, Chief of Police, thanking him for his service, and was awarded a pension of £65 per annum.

Lily Mernin was 'identified' as one of Collins's most important sources, 'Lt G'.[60] She was able to recommend and recruit other typists in British military offices throughout Dublin, including Sally McAsey, who married Frank Saurin. Mernin was supplying information to Collins on the British military just as Broy was supplying information on the DMP. She was employed by Colonel Stephen Hill Dillon in British offices in Parkgate Street, and also worked for Major Stratford Burton, the garrison adjutant at Ship Street Barracks. She would walk up and down the streets of Dublin on the arm of Cullen or Saurin, pointing out British agents who worked in Dublin Castle. She also went to matches at Lansdowne Road Stadium with Cullen and pointed out agents.

One of the contacts referred to, who was invaluable to us was a girl named Miss Lillie [*sic*] Mernin. She was employed as Typist in Command Headquarters of Dublin District, the intelligence branch of which was under the control of Colonel Hill Dillon, Chief Intelligence Officer. This girl put us in touch with other members of the different staffs working for the British Military in Dublin. This girl worked mainly with Frank Saurin and is one to whom a large amount of the credit for the success of Intelligence must go. She is at present employed at GHQ, Irish Army, Parkgate Street.[61]

Collins used his contacts everywhere to recruit more sources. He even developed an organisation in the prisons through which he discovered everything that happened to republican prisoners. Many of the gaolers were his sources—and those who weren't knew that some of their colleagues were reporting to Collins, and that influenced their actions.

The intelligence war produced some of the most incredible stories of the period, some of which ought to be made into films. Fact is often stranger than fiction, and never more so than in the extraordinary tale of a young mother who agreed to spy for the IRA if they would kidnap her son from her in-laws in Britain. The story begins in Wales in 1916, when Limerick-born Josephine Marchmont Brown's husband, Coleridge, went to fight in the First World War. (Brown had changed his name to Marchmont after declaring bankruptcy.) Josephine, Coleridge and their two young sons, Reggie and Gerald, were at that time living with Coleridge's parents in Wales. After Coleridge went to France, Josephine continued to live with her in-laws, but it was an uneasy arrangement; Josephine was a devout Catholic, while her husband's family were staunch Protestants. Her mother had died some years previously, and when her father became ill she moved to Cork to look after him. As her in-laws requested that Reggie stay with them, she left Wales with Gerald. Soon after she returned to Cork, however, her father died, leaving Josephine very much alone in Ireland.

Josephine had a good job in Cork, working as a secretary in Victoria Barracks—now Collins Barracks but then a British army headquarters. In October 1917, about a year after her return to Ireland, came the news that Coleridge had been killed in action at Ypres. Now completely alone, Josephine requested her Welsh in-laws to return Reggie to her in Cork. To her shock, they refused. She sought the advice of Bishop Daniel Colohan of Cork, who advised her to take a custody case against the Browns in the English courts. She did so, but the case, which began in July 1918, went against Josephine when a letter from her dead husband was read in court. In the document, which he had left with a solicitor, Coleridge requested that, in the event of his death, Reggie should be brought up by his own family and not solely by Josephine. She lost the case and returned to her job in Cork, where she was promoted to head of the barracks' secretarial pool.[62]

In desperation, Josephine went to pray to the Virgin Mary in Cork's Holy Trinity Church. As she knelt in the pew, lost in her troubles, a Capuchin priest, Fr Dominic O'Connor, approached her.[63] A republican sympathiser with close links to the IRA, Fr Dominic was chaplain of the Cork No. 1 Brigade and ministered to Terence MacSwiney during his fatal hunger strike. He asked the distressed young woman what was wrong and promised to do his best to help her. He then asked her to give him a code that could be used as a means of making safe contact with her later, so Josephine wrote the letter 'G' on a piece of paper.

Next, the priest approached Florence O'Donoghue. O'Donoghue was trying to build an army from scratch, establishing networks of safe houses, organising raids and sabotaging the British regime, but he was frequently coming up short on the greatest weapon in a guerrilla war campaign—intelligence. He was immediately interested in Josephine's potential as a spy. Josephine explained her role in the barracks and offered to become a spy in return for her son. She had significant bargaining power: as the widow of a member of the British army and a trusted senior clerk in Cork's Victoria Barracks, she had access to highly sensitive information—information that O'Donoghue and his IRA comrades needed desperately.

As O'Donoghue set about getting approval to go to Cardiff to kidnap Josephine's son, she began smuggling sensitive information out of the barracks. In November 1920 the IRA executed five civilians accused of being British informers. In reprisal, British forces attacked Sinn Féin halls and burned safe houses. By now, they suspected that they had a mole in their midst. Realising the growing danger that Josephine was in, O'Donoghue asked Collins whether he could lead the kidnap mission to Cardiff himself, emphasising that it had to be done quickly. The abduction was a success; Reggie, who was now about seven, was smuggled back to Ireland and mother and child were reunited. Reggie stayed with Josephine's sister, and his mother could only meet him in secret for the duration of the war.

Now that the IRA had kept their side of the bargain, Josephine resumed her espionage with renewed vigour. With the war growing dirtier by the day, Josephine's intelligence was of increasing significance to O'Donoghue and the IRA. She obtained details of troop movements, and was even able to provide the Irish with information on informers in their own ranks. Marchmont Brown eventually rose to become Chief Secretary at British Sixth Division Headquarters with almost unlimited access to sensitive army intelligence information.

This remarkable story has a most happy ending. In 1921 O'Donoghue, who was leading the intelligence effort in Cork, was forced to go on the run. On 27 April 1921 Fr Dominic married Florence and Josephine in the dead of night in St Peter and Paul's Church in Cork, while O'Donoghue was in hiding. In July that year Josephine resigned her post at Victoria Barracks, and the couple later settled down in Cork. They went on to have four children of their own, and O'Donoghue later adopted Gerald and Reggie.[64]

Intelligence depends upon quick and dependable communications. Collins claimed that

> almost fifty percent of the telegraphists in Ireland were either active members of the IRA or employed as operatives in our intelligence department. From the telegraphists we got the code which was changed twice a day by Dublin Castle—immensely simplifying the work of our censor in his handling of Government messages. According to admissions made at Dublin Castle at the time, not one telephone message was sent or received that was not tapped by the IRA.[65]

Every available means was employed to acquire intelligence and keep in touch throughout Ireland: railway workers, clerks, waiters, hotel porters and telephone operators, policemen, sailors and dockers were exploited as sources or messengers. Collins particularly used women in all their occupations, as they aroused far less suspicion than men, and the women were not only used as secretaries or office workers but also as couriers for dispatches and weapons.[66] Collins came from a family in which women were in the majority; his mother, Marianne, had been in charge since the death of his father when Michael was seven. He was accustomed to strong, resourceful women and respected them. He found it natural that women should care for him, and he, in turn, appreciated and admired them. He was usually more comfortable in the company of slightly older women—Moya Llewelyn Davies and Lady Hazel Lavery, for example.[67]

Collins simply wouldn't have been able to operate without the aid of his female spies and couriers. He had a small army of them working for him as secretaries, typists, landladies of safe houses and couriers, and all were devoted to him, though many thought that he was difficult to work with because he always concentrated on his work above all else. Lily Mernin, Nancy O'Brien, Molly O'Reilly, Máire Comerford, Eileen McGrane, 'Dilly' Dicker, Sister Eithne Lawless, Moya Llewelyn Davies, Anna Fitzsimmons, Susan Mason and so many others were invaluable to him.[68]

The women working in clubs, post offices, railway stations, British military and civilian offices, boarding houses, hotels, Dublin Castle and elsewhere were in positions to monitor the activities of British agents. All reported to Collins directly or through intermediaries, and he co-ordinated this disparate information. Collins, like the others in his intelligence department, often used the ploy of walking down a street arm in arm with a woman who would squeeze his arm to identify a British officer. His detailed and methodical handling of the information meant that no piece of it, no matter how small or seemingly tangential, did not fill in a piece of the puzzle for him.

Molly O'Reilly began working undercover in the United Service Club in 1918 and became a priceless intelligence source for Collins.[69] She gathered intelligence on British officers who frequented the club, supplying Peadar Clancy with their names and private addresses. When things slackened off at the club, Molly found out that the officers were now going to a club owned by Countess Markievicz and Charlotte Despard—the Bonne Bouche in Dawson Street—for dancing, so she subsequently transferred there. She gathered information on officers and identified 30–35 Secret Service men, again supplying Clancy with names and addresses.

Officers regularly hung up their guns in the gentlemen's room while dancing, and Molly passed that information to Clancy too.[70]

Sir James McMahon was director of the Posts and Telegraphs Office at Dublin's General Post Office (GPO) in 1918–19. One day he called in Nancy O'Brien, Collins's second cousin, who worked in the Post Office administration offices, and told her that the management, knowing of her dedication and work, wanted to promote her within the department. He explained that they knew that Collins got hold of information even before the officers to whom it was sent, and they had to have someone they could trust to do the work in order to safeguard the information. Because of her abilities he was going to hire her to decode messages in his office.[71] When told of her new job, Collins said, 'Well, Christ, I don't know how they've held their empire for so long. What a bloody intelligence service they have!' Nancy had moved to London at the same time as Collins in 1906 and they were always very close. As a spy she was invaluable to Collins, and she would often spend her lunchtime in the ladies' toilet copying papers to give to him later. Once, when Collins berated her for not finding a message in which he was particularly interested, she turned and gave out to him. Later that night he cycled to her home in Glasnevin and apologised, leaving a present of her favourite 'bulls-eye' candies for her. On another occasion, when she was going to Cork because her father had passed away, Collins asked her to carry in her luggage a load of guns that had just come in from England; a policeman helped her with the very heavy case!

Eileen McGrane, a lecturer in the National University (now UCD), lived at 21 Dawson Street. Collins, Arthur Griffith and others came to her home from time to time for meetings in a small room at the centre of the flat. It served as a part-time office for Collins and Ernie O'Malley during the War of Independence.

> Shortly after I took my flat at 21, Dawson St., which was shared by Mary McCarthy and Margot Trench, the Republican government headquarters seemed to have great difficulty in getting suitable rooms for their work. I offered to Michael Collins the use of a small room in the centre of the flat which he was very glad to accept. Of course there was no question of rent. He put into it some office furniture and files of various kinds were

deposited in the office. No official personnel were located there. Mick Collins, Tom Cullen, Arthur Griffith and others came from time to time for conferences or to collect or deposit papers. The principals had a key to the door of the flat and access to the key to the office which was in my custody. The only servant we employed was a cleaner, Mrs McCluskey, whose husband was caretaker in the National Land Bank. He often did guard on the Street outside when Mick Collins came to the office and on one occasion at least gave warning of a raid in the neighbourhood.[72]

The house was raided on 31 December 1920; McGrane was imprisoned in Mountjoy Prison, then sent to Walton Prison in Liverpool and finally returned to Mountjoy. The raid recovered a large bundle of documents that Collins had foolishly left there, including many taken from Dublin Castle and those of the 'G' Division, as well as the DMP headquarters daybook that he carried from his foray into Great Brunswick Street police station. It demonstrated one of his weaknesses: he hated to part with files, even when they ceased to be useful, and he never took sufficient precautions to ensure that the people referred to in the files could not be identified. Some documents that could be traced to Éamon (Ned) Broy were found here, leading to his arrest. This was the Castle's first intimation of the effectiveness of Collins's recruitment within their own ranks, and they began a long process of elimination that finally led them to Broy. McGrane was taken to Dublin Castle, where she was interrogated by Ormond Winter. He was sure that she would talk to him but she spoke not one word in one and a half hours.[73]

Women in intelligence were not limited to Dublin, as Josephine Brown's story indicates. In 1919–21 Brigid Lyons Thornton was going to medical school in Galway and then worked as a doctor at Mercer's Hospital, but she was also a courier to Longford and Galway, carrying weapons and ammunition as well as documents. Whenever confronted on a train or at a roadblock, she wrote, 'I had recourse to a prayer and a piece of feminine guile'.[74] In 1921 she was sent to Mountjoy Prison several times to relay Collins's messages to Seán MacEoin regarding his escape. As a woman and a doctor, she never aroused any suspicion. It was also thought that she would be the best one to assess MacEoin's physical condition. She recalled that she was summoned to meet Collins. 'I took to the air', she wrote. 'I was never so excited or thrilled in my whole life.' She continued to see MacEoin until July, even though none of the escape plans came to fruition. Just after the Truce, Collins sent her word that he would like to see MacEoin, and she went into Mountjoy with him.[75]

Siobhán Creedon worked in the Mallow Post Office and regularly passed on information to Liam Lynch and local County Cork IRA members. She provided most valuable information regarding conscription in 1918, and continued to supply Lynch with transcripts of documents and dispatches.

The Irish were not the only ones to collect intelligence. Although the British were at a disadvantage in many areas, their intelligence acquisition and analysis improved greatly as the war went on. Colonel Evelyn Lindsay Young served as Intelligence Officer with the Connaught Rangers from 1920 to 1922 and knew how dangerous the 'game' was:

> The collection of intelligence was one of the most interesting and risky games over there. Our intelligence was not too intelligent and methods employed were sometimes unorthodox; the only rule was 'get the information' ... the means was most often left to the individual.[76]

Throughout 1920 there was an intelligence war between Collins and the Castle. While it never developed into 'open warfare' on the streets of Dublin, there were many killings and assassinations of individual operatives from both sides. It was a savage battle of wits between the Irish and British services, fought without mercy in the shadows.

The Castle's efforts were headed by Colonel Ormonde de L'Epee Winter, Chief of the British Combined Intelligence Services in Ireland from the spring of 1920 until the Truce. Despite having no previous full-time experience in intelligence, Winter's brief was to reorganise the shambles that British intelligence in Ireland had become.[77] His biggest contribution was a centralised document archive and the production of meta-data to allow the intelligence to be summarised and disseminated—a very modern concept for the time. Unfortunately, in the pre-computing era, the meta-data were lengthy epitomes produced manually; the procedures for dealing with captured documents were clumsy, and long delays could ensue before the intelligence was shared with the operatives or forces who needed the intelligence in order to function. The biggest problem for Winter was that, with the exception of Dublin, he did not control military intelligence. This reflected the poor command and control between the two parts of the British security forces. Earlier, the GOC in Ireland, General Macready, had been given the opportunity to control both the police and the army but turned it down. Thereafter, the police (including the Black and Tans and the Auxiliary Division) and the army often operated independently, with limited intelligence co-operation until the final months of the campaign.[78] In essence, the British intelligence effort under Winter addressed its shortcomings by deploying many more officers while still failing to co-ordinate efforts with the War Office, and army intelligence continued to act independently of the Castle administration. The net result was more and more British operatives, under separate military and civilian commands, never co-ordinating with each other, and the lack of an efficient organisation was telling. In desperation, the British even solicited informers by placing an advert in Irish papers:

> During the last 12 months innumerable murders and other outrages have been committed by those who call themselves members of the Irish Republican Army. Only by the help of self-respecting Irishmen can these murders be put a stop to.
>
> It is possible to send letters containing information in such a way as to prevent them being stopped in the post.
>
> If you have information to give and you are willing to help the cause of Law and Order act as follows:
>
> Write your information on ordinary notepaper being careful to give neither your name nor your address. Remember also to disguise your handwriting, or else to print the words. Put it into an envelope addressed to:
>
> D.W. Ross
>
> Poste Restante
>
> G.P.O. London
>
> Enclose this envelope in another. (Take care that your outer envelope is not transparent.) Put it with a small piece of paper

asking the recipient to forward the D.W. Ross letter as soon as he receives it. Address the outer envelope to some well disposed friend in England or to any well known business in England.

You will later be given the opportunity, should you wish to do so, of identifying the letter and should the information have proved of value, of claiming a REWARD.

The utmost secrecy will be maintained as to all information received.

The intelligence war continued to escalate on both sides, and on 21 November 1920, in the quiet of a Dublin Sunday, small crews of IRA gunmen began the systematic assassination of a group of specially trained and recruited secret servicemen, mostly MI5 and SIS specialists, in the most noted intelligence coup in Dublin.[79] This British unit had been recruited in London in the summer of 1920 and placed in the charge of Major C.A. Cameron. In all, sixty agents were trained and dispatched to Ireland. It now appears certain that the majority of the men assassinated were members of this group, although the Irish made some mistakes in identification and civilians were killed in error.[80]

Earlier that month, Prime Minister Lloyd George had confidently assured his audience at London's Guildhall that the IRA was defeated and that the British 'had murder on the run'.[81] The attack, coming as it did when the British forces felt that they had the IRA at breaking point, was a momentous act of reassertion. Its timing was also crucial for the Irish, since it became apparent to the police—and certainly to Collins—that the IRA boycott of the police was beginning to falter and that general allegiance to the Republican cause could be weakening. Hence Bloody Sunday not only removed a major threat to the IRA but also simultaneously gave a warning to the Irish people that any weakening of their resolve to continue the struggle and support the guerrillas would not be tolerated.[82]

Intelligence chiefs in London were pragmatic: their goal was to locate Michael Collins, thus severing the head from the body of the IRA. Collins was aware of the intensification and knew that he would have to move soon to meet it. He received information from a contact in Scotland Yard that this group of men was coming to Dublin with the avowed intention of smashing the IRA/Volunteers, and particularly Collins's intelligence operation. He could not defeat the British in pitched battles but he could 'put out the eyes and ears' of the intelligence service upon which the military relied.[83]

In late 1920 that special intelligence unit was organised by the British into one whose ultimate purpose was to break Collins's organisation. Their chosen strategy was simple: to assassinate the political members of Sinn Féin who were moving openly in public or who were involved in the military struggle. Following this, they felt, the IRA would be bound to make some moves that would flush its other leaders to the surface. After September 1920 the number of raids increased and intense searches were carried out nightly in the city. The men implementing this policy became known as the 'Cairo Gang'.[84]

Colonel Ormonde Winter controlled and activated the 'Cairo Gang' in Ireland. The IRA/Volunteers knew him as the 'Holy Terror' because he was always prepared to descend to the most extreme methods to obtain information from prisoners. The British held him in no higher regard, as he was known to Mark Sturgis as 'a wicked little white snake … probably entirely non-moral'.[85] In October Winter organised the Central Raid Bureau to co-ordinate the activities of his agents and the Auxiliaries. They soon began to make their presence felt. The Cairo Gang was ruthless and efficient, and had been primarily responsible for tracking down Dan Breen and Seán Treacy, killing Treacy in Talbot Street on 14 October 1920.

For months Collins watched the British getting closer and closer. From their first appearance in Dublin he began gathering information on them, and found that they were usually living as private citizens in respectable rooming houses. He set his own spies to open their correspondence, had the contents of their wastepaper baskets taken by the housemaids and had duplicate keys made for their rooms. Crucially, the IRA co-opted most of the Irish domestic staff who worked in the rooming houses where the officers lived, and all of their comings and goings were meticulously recorded by servants and reported to Collins's staff. He waited and accumulated evidence before he went to the cabinet to seek authorisation for his operation.[86] Lily Mernin worked at Ship Street Barracks for Major Stratford Burton, the garrison adjutant, who was in charge of court-martial proceedings as well as organisation of the billeting of the various military posts throughout Dublin, and she would always make an extra carbon copy of all reports and documents for Collins. She was instrumental in locating the addresses of the British military officers assigned to Dublin:

> Before the 21st November 1920, it was part of my normal duty to
> type the names and addresses of British agents who were
> accommodated at private addresses and living as ordinary citizens
> of the city. These lists were typed weekly and amended whenever
> an address was changed. I passed them on each week to the address
> at Moynihan's, Clonliffe Rd, or to Piaras Béaslaí. The typing of the
> lists ceased after the 21st November 1920.[87]

Locating and eliminating Collins had become the prime goal of all the
British intelligence organisations, and they were getting close. In an October
meeting in the Cairo Café on Grafton Street, a member of the Gang joined
Tom Cullen, Frank Thornton and Charlie Saurin as they were drinking and
pretending to be British spies. The real British officer said to them: 'Surely
you fellows know Liam Tobin, Tom Cullen and Frank Thornton—these are
Collins's three officers and if you can get them we can locate Collins'.[88] If
they knew the names of his lieutenants—numbers one, two and three of his
intelligence staff—the British were getting uncomfortably close, even if they
did not know what any of them looked like. It boded ill for any of Collins's
men who fell into their hands at that time.

In the first two weeks of November the Gang detained some of Collins's
closest advisers. They held Frank Thornton for ten days but he managed to
convince them that he had nothing to do with Sinn Féin. On 10 November
they just missed capturing Richard Mulcahy. On 13 November they raided
Vaughan's Hotel and questioned Liam Tobin and Tom Cullen, but let them
go. Collins, Cathal Brugha, Mulcahy and the military and intelligence
leadership felt that they had no choice but to attack. Mulcahy commented:
'We were being made to feel that they were very close on the heels of some
of us'. He was quite clear about the responsibility of those against whom the
IRA directed their operations on Bloody Sunday:

> They were members of a spy organisation that was a murder
> organisation. Their murderous intent was directed against the
> effective members of the Government as well as against GHQ
> and staff at the Dublin Brigade.[89]

Collins, Brugha, Mulcahy, Dick McKee, Peadar Clancy and others sentenced over twenty British officers at their 35 Lower Gardiner Street meeting on 20 November. The names of fifteen out of the thirty-five selected for assassination were turned down because of insufficient evidence.[90] Earlier historians accepted that the men killed had passed through a rigorous process of elimination before being placed on the list for execution; more recent research, however, questions whether some of the men killed might not all have been intelligence officers, and some were less experienced than previously thought.[91] The operation was to start at 9.00 a.m. sharp. Collins told them all that 'it's to be done exactly at nine. Neither before nor after. These whores [the British] have got to learn that Irishmen can turn up on time.'[92] Paddy Daly, the leader of Collins's Squad, was not one of the men assigned to carry out the attacks on Bloody Sunday, but he was intimately involved in the organisation and planning. He recalled:

> The four Battalions of the Brigade were engaged, and the OC of each Battalion was responsible for a certain area, not his own area because most of the spies were grouped in certain districts. If the 2nd Battalion Volunteers had been confined to their own area, they would not have done anything but the Gresham Hotel job. All other operations allotted to the 2nd Battalion were outside their Battalion area, in fact they were in the 3rd Battalion area.
>
> Seán Russell picked the men for the various operations, and in every case he appointed a member of the Squad in charge of the various groups.[93]

On the morning of 21 November the operation began at 9 a.m., exactly as planned. Some of the men targeted refused to come out of their rooms and were shot in bed. Others came to the door and were shot as they opened it. Of the IRA/Volunteers who had taken part, some would never recover completely from the nerve-shattering work of that morning.[94] By 9.30 the killings were finished. (See Chapter 6 for a discussion of Bloody Sunday as a terrorist event.)

The British military were slow to realise what had happened. About

9.20 General F.P. Crozier was passing 22 Mount Street with a group of Auxiliaries when they heard some shooting. Crozier and the Auxiliaries jumped out and ran to the house. Tom Keogh, who burst through the soldiers as they surrounded him, shot two Auxiliaries who were in the back of the house. After Crozier saw what had happened upstairs he went to the garden, where he found an Auxiliary about to shoot Frank Teeling, one of the Squad who had been wounded. Crozier prevented the summary execution and saw that Teeling was taken to hospital, and then he headed to Dublin Castle. Throughout the city, panicked British officers and their families packed their belongings and moved into the Castle.

Collins's men went out to kill twenty that morning, but some of them could not be found. The publicised and 'official' figures stated that eleven officers were killed and four escaped. The dead included British intelligence officers, British army courts-martial officers, two Auxiliaries, an RIC officer, a number of soldiers in the wrong place at the wrong time and two civilians. In fact eleven British officers, two Auxiliary cadets and two civilians (T.H. Smith and L.E. Wilde) were killed in eight locations:

- 92 Baggot Street Lower: Captain W.F. Newbury (a courts martial officer).
- 119 Baggot Street Lower: Captain George (Geoffrey) T. Baggallay (a one-legged courts martial officer).
- 28 Earlsfort Terrace: Sergeant John Fitzgerald (he was in the RIC and was probably killed for that alone, as the Squad asked for 'Colonel Fitzpatrick').
- 117–119 Morehampton Road: Captain Donald L. McClean (an intelligence officer at Dublin Castle) and T.H. Smith (a civilian landlord not engaged in intelligence).
- 22 Lower Mount Street: Lieutenant H.R. Angliss (alias Patrick 'Paddy' McMahon, a British intelligence agent) and Auxiliary Cadets Garner and Morris.
- 38 Upper Mount Street: Lieutenant Peter Ashmunt Ames and Captain George Bennett (Ames and Bennett were leaders of the intelligence unit).
- 28–29 Pembroke Street Upper: Major C.M.G. Dowling (a British intelligence officer), Colonel Hugh F. Montgomery (a staff officer 'in

the wrong place' who took three weeks to die from his wounds) and Captain Leonard Price (a British intelligence officer).

- Upper Sackville Street, Gresham Hotel: Captain Patrick MacCormack (almost certainly buying horses for the Alexandria Turf Club and not engaged in intelligence activity at all) and L.E. Wilde (a civilian).

Colonel Wilfred James Woodcock DSO, Lancashire Fusiliers, Lieutenant R.G. Murray, Royal Scots, and Captain B.C.H. Keenlyside, Lancashire Fusiliers, were all wounded at 28 Upper Pembroke Street. Woodcock was not connected with intelligence and had walked into a confrontation on the first floor of the house as he was preparing to leave to command a regimental parade at army headquarters.[95] He was in his military uniform, and when he shouted to warn the five other British officers living in the house he was shot in the shoulder and back, but survived. As Keenlyside was about to be shot, a struggle ensued between his wife and Mick O'Hanlon. The leader of the unit, Mick Flanagan, arrived, pushed Mrs Keenlyside out of the way and shot her husband. John Caldow, McLean's brother-in-law and a former soldier with the Royal Scots Fusiliers, was wounded at 117 Morehampton Road. 'Mr Peel', the alias of an unidentified British agent staying at 22 Lower Mount Street, amongst others, escaped unscathed.

Of those killed by the IRA, Ames, Angliss, Bennett, Dowling, MacLean and Price were intelligence officers. Baggallay and Newberry were courts martial officers not involved with intelligence. McCormack and Wilde appear to have been incorrectly targeted or possibly were innocent ex-officers. Fitzgerald was a policeman who was probably mistaken for someone else. Smith was the landlord of a house where some of the army men were staying and was killed by mistake. Morris and Garner were Auxiliaries on their way to warn the barracks, as was Montgomery, who happened to be in the wrong place at the wrong time.[96]

Some of the targets escaped by virtue of not being home, and Collins's men were able to recover only a few papers of import, but if every spy or agent in Ireland had been killed it could have not had a greater effect on Dublin Castle. Dave Neligan stated that the incident 'caused complete panic in Dublin Castle. ... The attack was so well organized, so unexpected, and so ruthlessly executed that the effect was paralyzing. It can be said that the enemy never recovered from the blow. While some of the worst killers escaped, they were thoroughly frightened.'[97]

In the British records, their review of the day concluded:

> The murders of 21st November 1920 temporarily paralysed the special branch. Several of its most efficient members were murdered and the majority of the other residents of the city were brought into Dublin Castle and Central Hotel for safety. This centralisation in the most inconvenient places possible greatly decreased the opportunities for obtaining information and for re-establishing anything in the nature of a secret service.[98]

Captain Robert D. Jeune, who was on the Irish list but slipped out of 28 Upper Pembroke Street just before the attacks, said that 'those of us who had survived were shut up under guard in a hotel where it was impractical to do any useful work'.[99]

The extent and the cold-blooded nature of the killing of the British officers even stunned some of the Irish. Desmond FitzGerald and William Cosgrave were shocked. Arthur Griffith was horrified: 'In front of their wives on a Sunday in their own homes'.

Later that morning, Collins discovered that two of the IRA's most vital members had been captured. Dick McKee, Brigadier of the Dublin Brigade, and Peadar Clancy, Vice-Brigadier, had been caught the night before in Seán Fitzpatrick's house in Lower Gloucester Street—supposedly a 'safe house'. (John 'Shankers' Ryan, the tout who turned them in, was later killed in Hyne's Pub in Gloucester Place.) McKee and Clancy had planned the operation. When he heard the news, Collins screamed, 'Good God. We're finished now. It's all up.' He then ordered his police agent James McNamara to find out where they were being held; McNamara thought it was at the Bridewell. Collins sent McNamara and Neligan to search for them there, but they found that McKee and Clancy had been taken to Dublin Castle. Also on Saturday night, Conor Clune, a Gaelic Leaguer from County Clare, was arrested in Vaughan's Hotel. Clune had nothing to do with the Volunteers and had only come to Dublin to confer with journalist Piaras Béaslaí, but he was staying in Vaughan's, which was a noted IRA meeting place, and so he was taken to Dublin Castle. McKee, Clancy and Clune were killed in the Castle at 11.00 a.m. on that Sunday morning and were dead before their capture became known. Mulcahy realised what their deaths meant to Collins in particular, and to their operations:[100]

> In McKee and Clancy he [Collins] had two men who fully understood the inside of Collins's work and who were ready and able to link up the Dublin resources of the Dublin Brigade to any work that Collins had in hand and to do so promptly, effectively and sympathetically.[101]

Prime Minister David Lloyd George said of the British who had been killed: 'They got what they deserved—beaten by counter-jumpers!' 'Ask Griffith for God's sake to keep his head and not to break off the slender link that has been established. Tragic as the events in Dublin were, they were of no importance. These men were soldiers, and took a soldier's risk.'[102]
Collins said:

> My one intention was the destruction of the undesirables who continued to make miserable the lives of ordinary decent citizens. I have proof enough to assure myself of the atrocities which this gang of spies and informers have committed. Perjury and torture are words too easily known to them. If I had a second motive it was no more than a feeling I would have for a dangerous reptile. By their destruction the very air is made sweeter. For myself, my conscience is clear. There is no crime in detecting and destroying, in wartime, the spy and the informer. They have destroyed without trial. I have paid them back in their own coin.[103]

It was this incident, more than any other, that gained Collins his reputation as a gunman and a 'murderer'. The British press made much of the fact that the men were British spies in civilian clothes, and under assumed names, playing a game of 'kill or be killed'. That same press, for the most part, ignored the activities of the Black and Tans and Auxiliaries later that day at Croke Park.

Following the morning raids, a combined group of British soldiers, Black and Tans and Auxiliaries raided Croke Park.[104] According to the police, the 'official plan' was that fifteen minutes before the final whistle there would be an announcement by megaphone. Instead of the usual 'stewards to end-of-match positions', the crowd would hear someone telling them to leave by official exits and that all men would be searched for weapons. In the event, however, no sooner had the police, Black and Tans and Auxiliaries arrived at the Park than they started shooting. The exact incidents that led to the shooting have never been proven, with each side contradicting the other. The only public and official statement was one by Dublin Castle blaming the IRA for starting the shooting.[105]

Central to all inquiries with regard to Croke Park and still in dispute is the question of who fired first. All that is agreed on is that the firing started at the south-west corner of the pitch, where Jones's Road crosses the Royal Canal. Some witnesses at the subsequent inquiries said that the firing started within the Park, presumably by armed spectators, before the British troops had entered the grounds. Fourteen innocent people attending the match were killed, sixty-two people were injured inside Croke Park during the raid and another twelve were injured in the stampede to escape. Whoever fired first, 'of all the bloody days of the War of Independence, this was the bloodiest of them all—at least in terms of its impact on the public psyche'.[106]

Oscar Traynor claimed that the effect of the IRA killings was 'to paralyse completely the British Military Intelligence system in Dublin'.[107] Frank Thornton elaborated: 'The British Secret Service was wiped out on Bloody Sunday'.[108] Both statements are exaggerations, but Bloody Sunday demonstrated not only the horrific logic of reprisal tactics but also the importance of the intelligence network. In fact, Bloody Sunday did not decisively affect the intelligence war for either side, and many British agents were more effectively on their guard, making a repeat of the attacks impossible. The collection and analysis of intelligence were crucial to the IRA's activities, and it was the productive efficiency of Collins's department in collecting accurate intelligence on the British that ultimately allowed them to launch effective attacks while themselves avoiding detection.[109]

Bloody Sunday was designed to be as spectacular as possible and was intended to coincide with attacks on property in Britain, as much to demonstrate Irish resolve as to tackle the specific problem of dedicated British agents in Ireland. In sum, Collins's 21 November attack was intended as a temporary measure to eliminate some agents, scare off some others, achieve maximum propaganda impact with simultaneous killings, buy time and pre-empt his capture by British intelligence. All these goals had been achieved, but the cost, especially considering the attacks at Croke Park, had been terribly high. Charles Townshend comments that 'though Republican propaganda made a brilliant job of portraying the operation as a body blow against the government, this did not alter the reality of the situation'.[110]

At least in the short term, the IRA's action had the intended effect on British intelligence. Its political effect was also dramatic. And when the news of the Kilmichael ambush in County Cork broke one week later, the British press made Lloyd George's boast of having 'murder by the throat' seem like a fantasy statement. Until Bloody Sunday the British held to their opinion that the Irish were incapable of conducting co-ordinated attacks. After that, their assessment of Irish capabilities changed, as did their outlook and approach.

Since the Bloody Sunday raids, historians have debated whether the results had a greater effect on Irish and British intelligence operations or on politics and propaganda. The executions of the British agents had a shattering effect on the morale of the British in Ireland, as well as in Britain. The British public and government were shocked and could not believe that with all their mighty resources they could be so humiliated. Though Lloyd George fumed about 'murderers' in public, it was this event as much as any other that led him to begin sending emissaries to Ireland in search of peace.

In January 1921 there was another group of British intelligence officers headquartered in the Castle who were assigned to get Collins: the 'Igoe Gang', another 'freelance' group. Named after their leader, Head Constable Eugene Igoe from Galway, they gradually began to play a very significant role. Following Bloody Sunday, the greatest threat to Collins was this 'Gang', who arrived in Dublin early in 1921.

Dublin at this time was anything but a peaceful city. The Dublin Brigade were carrying out ambushes practically every day, despite the fact that the British military were patrolling the streets in armoured cars, Lancia cars and also a foot patrol extended across the roads. To add to this concentration of forces a new menace appeared on the scene. These were grange [sic] of RIC drawn

from different parts of the country under the leadership of Chief
Constable Igoe. They wore civilian clothes, were heavily armed
and moved along the footpaths on both sides of the road looking
out for either city men whom they might know or Volunteers
up from the country. They were not easy to deal with because
they suddenly appeared at most unexpected places and, despite
several attempts our men never got really into action against the
gang proper.[111]

The 'Gang' walked around the city heavily armed, often tailing
IRA/Volunteers, unexpectedly dropping into pubs and shops and generally
making a nuisance of themselves.

Igoe was an RIC man who hailed from the west of Ireland.
Around him, the Castle authorities formed a group of RIC men
who were selected from different parts of the country—especially
those who had a good knowledge of the active officers of the
IRA wanted by the British. Their routine was to visit different
railway termini as trains were arriving or departing, and to see if
any wanted men were travelling. If they happened to capture any
such men, well, it was a gamble whether they ever lived to tell
what had happened to them. The usual report would appear—
'shot while trying to escape'.

This gang adopted the same procedure as did the squad.
They moved along in pairs, on each side of the street or road,
with a distance of a yard or two between each pair. So you will
understand that it was going to be a very heavy operation to get
the lot of them. Igoe and his gang had been moving around for
a little while, when one day they picked up a Volunteer, named
Newell, who was from the west, and who, before being picked
up, was in touch with the Intelligence staff and hoped to be able
to point out Igoe. Up to this time, we had no description of what
he looked like.

... Igoe, himself, or the remainder of the gang, were never
got.[112]

Despite some assertions to the contrary, the Squad never did 'get' Igoe or any of his men. Following the Truce, Igoe seems to have left Ireland and never returned for fear of reprisal.

The British intelligence war is often thought of as being disastrous, with Collins and his men and women consistently out-spying His Majesty's Secret Services. In the immediate post-war period the British made a detailed analysis of their intelligence failures in Ireland; in a flurry of activity, papers were published, conferences held, reports commissioned and lectures given in which the failures were fully acknowledged. It is known that as late as May 1920 the British chief of police in Dublin had an intelligence staff consisting of solely one officer.[113] Its primary source of information, from the political detectives of 'G' Division of the DMP, all but dried up, as Collins ordered the assassination of many of those detectives. Then, by late 1920, intelligence officers were appointed to each divisional commissioner of the RIC to co-ordinate military and police intelligence. The military, present throughout Ireland in force, together with Auxiliaries, had their own intelligence services with young officers, many of them noted for their zeal in intelligence matters.[114]

In partial explanation of the British lack of intelligence, it must be said that prior to and even at the height of the IRA's campaign the 'G' Division in Dublin employed fewer than two dozen men exclusively dedicated to political work, while the RIC's Special Branch consisted not of a nationwide detective force along the lines of Scotland Yard but of a confidential records office based in Dublin Castle, staffed by several clerks, a detective inspector and a chief inspector. The vast bulk of intelligence gathered by Special Branch was collected by ordinary RIC men throughout the country and forwarded to Crimes Special Branch's small office in Dublin Castle for analysis. Until the final year of Dublin Castle's rule there was no 'secret service' in Ireland: Special Branch did not run undercover agents, rarely recruited informers and made little effort to penetrate the organisations of its enemies. The documents gathered there demonstrated the old-fashioned methods employed by the police: republican premises were kept under observation, train stations and other public places were watched, suspects were shadowed from town to town and their speeches were recorded by policemen.

Although some individuals in British service were dismissed on dubious or malicious grounds of spying for the Irish, the files indicate that the quality of evidence demanded for prosecution, or even dismissal, was generally high: little action was taken in many of these cases despite the RIC's efforts to gather incriminating evidence. Consequently, the British administration in Ireland remained penetrated by republican sympathisers despite its periodic attempts to purge potentially subversive employees.

Collins's policies brought success not only in the intelligence wars but also in the eyes of the Irish people. One Volunteer said: 'For the first time in the history of separatism we Irish had a better intelligence service than the British ... This was Michael Collins's great achievement and it is one for which every Irishman should honour his memory.'[115]

There are, however, contrary views of the successes of Collins's intelligence operation. For example, Peter Hart, one of Collins's greatest critics in this regard, asks:

> What did Collins's remarkable achievements actually enable him to do? His sources rarely gave him useful operational intelligence other than warning of some raids and spies. He did not acquire any particular insight into British planning or intentions. The result was a particularly negative and partial one, largely confined to Dublin's inner circles: security from G-Men and spies, not from British intelligence as a whole.[116]

IRA intelligence results mostly exceeded the British counter-intelligence effort, but the IRA's own counter-intelligence was less omnipotent than is popularly represented. The Bloody Sunday shootings killed not only intelligence officers but also legal officers who were required when the army became immersed in law enforcement. According to Peter Hart, the IRA killings of informers in Cork frequently missed the real targets as well.[117]

Further to that, Charles Townshend wrote:

> Alongside organisation and armament, as the foundation of a guerrilla campaign, modern theory would place the creation of a comprehensive intelligence system.[118] The IRA's achievement in this sphere is legendary—in both senses of the word, it now seems.

...

In the first place, the organisation and functioning of the intelligence service within the IRA was far from faultless.

...

Even the most celebrated achievements of IRA intelligence were not without flaw. The apogee of the organisation was Michael Collins's own network in Dublin, which was responsible for the assassination of twelve British officers on 'Bloody Sunday'. According to the IRA, these were members of a secret service group, which was about to put Collins's organisation 'on the spot'; while the Government, displaying the characteristic mentality, denied that any were connected with secret service work, which was not going on anyway. More detached verdicts have usually fallen somewhere between the two ... [119]

Townshend is correct: a 'detached verdict' is necessary. In reviewing Irish (and British) actions in the war, historians have too often viewed policies and results in terms of black and white, right and wrong, heroes and villains, and friends or foes. Such binary constructs are usually wrong. Moreover, results often do not reflect intentions.

A more objective review of the Irish intelligence effort reveals successes but also many failures. Likewise, there were many British intelligence failures but also successes. Collins did not recruit a single policy-making member of the British military, police or government. Furthermore, he knew little of the goings-on in the British Cabinet, and never attempted to penetrate it. Collins's best insights into British government policy came from Andy Cope, who passed along information intentionally. Perhaps the best lesson learned by both sides was that, in the words of Ormonde Winter, intelligence 'alone cannot win a war. It is merely an aid to force, and it is only by action that the desired end can result.'[120] Winter was also right when he concluded that 'one of the outstanding difficulties in the suppression of political crime in Ireland was the fact that the British nation was not at war with Ireland, whilst Ireland was at war with the British nation'.[121] Britain was always one step behind the evolving Irish political situation.

In the narrative of the Irish War of Independence, credit/blame is usually apportioned according to one's viewpoint. The first option is to hail

Collins (in particular, but the other Irish as well) as fighting a one-sided intelligence/military war and winning all the intelligence battles in Dublin and throughout the country.[122] In the second version, the British (and particularly Lloyd George and the hard-liners in the Cabinet and military) 'lost' Ireland by their incompetence and betrayed those who wished to remain part of the 'Empire' for their own selfish ends.[123] Like all absolutes, neither is strictly true. In fact, both the Irish and the British had successes and failures, and both the Irish and British evolved as the war went on.[124]

Collins should be given credit for possessing an evident appreciation of the necessity of the acquisition of information from disparate sources and its analysis as the primary elements of intelligence; for his penetration of the British intelligence service; for his understanding of the need for ruthlessness when required; and for maintaining the security of his own service.[125] His intelligence service did not contribute a great deal directly to the operations of units outside of Dublin, but that was mostly due to the existing circumstances in 1919–21. Most operations were on a local level, and each was planned and conducted in conjunction with local conditions and intelligence.

Collins was bold but not reckless. It should be understood that he was not a superman, that the IRA was vulnerable to British spying insertions, and that by the time of the Truce in 1921 Collins's Irish intelligence operation was almost equalled by the upgrade in British intelligence. Such an objective review also suggests that had the Truce not gone into effect in July 1921 the British efforts to find and capture Collins within a short period could have been successful. Hart suggests that 'time simply ran out' on the British. In terms of a horse race, the British were in the lead at the start, the Irish caught up and actually pulled ahead in the middle, and at the end of the race the British recovered to almost a dead heat.

Nevertheless, even Hart conceded that 'Collins was brilliant, and we must be aware of the limits of his reach. His secret service may well have bested his vaunted rivals, but theirs was one battle not the whole war.'[126] Credit is due to many of the Irish, but 'it's doubtful the revolt would have succeeded without the genius of one man: the Irish Republican Army's *de facto* military commander, Michael Collins, described by one of his foes as a man "full of fascination and charm—but also of dangerous fire".'[127]

If one were keeping score, it could be said that the British lost the intelligence war in tactical terms but that they were more successful strategically in determining just how far Collins and the Irish would go in Treaty negotiations. Collins's goal was to get to those negotiations.

Notes

[1] Paul McMahon, *British Spies and Irish Rebels: British Intelligence in Ireland, 1916–45* (Suffolk, 2008), p. 2.

[2] Carl von Clausewicz, *On War* (Princeton, 1984), p. 117.

[3] Seán Sharkey, 'My role as an Intelligence Officer with the Third Tipperary Brigade (1919–1921)', *Tipperary Historical Journal*, vol. 11 (1998).

[4] Florence O'Donoghue, 'Guerilla warfare in Ireland', *An Cosantóir*, vol. 23 (1963).

[5] Samuel Issacharoff and Richard H. Pildes, 'Targeted warfare: individuating enemy responsibility', *New York University Law Review*, vol. 1521 (2013).

[6] John F. Murphy Jr, 'Michael Collins and the craft of intelligence', *International Journal of Intelligence and Counterintelligence*, vol. 17, issue 2 (17 August 2010).

[7] Florence O'Donoghue, *No Other Law* (Dublin, 1954; 1986), p. 116.

[8] John Borgonovo, *Spies, Informers and the Anti-Sinn Féin Society* (Dublin, 2006), pp 135–6.

[9] *Ibid.*, p. 139.

[10] 'Record of the Rebellion in Ireland in 1920–1921 and the Part Played by the Army in Dealing with it,' Imperial War Museum, Box 78/82/2.

[11] Cabinet Memorandum: 'The Present Military Situation in Ireland and the Proposed Military Policy During the Coming Winter, General Macready, 6th August, 1920', CAB/24/110 Image Reference: 0050.

[12] Piaras Béaslaí, 'How it was done: IRA intelligence', in *Dublin's Fighting Story 1916–21* (Tralee, 1949).

[13] Florence O'Donoghue, 'Lecture on intelligence in the Black and Tan day', National Library of Ireland, MS 31443.

[14] Éamon Broy, Witness Statement 1280.

[15] Murphy, 'Michael Collins and the craft of intelligence'.

[16] Richard Popplewell, 'Lacking intelligence: some reflections on recent approaches to British counter-insurgence 1900–1960', *Intelligence and National Security*, vol. 10, no. 2 (1995).

[17] 'Record of the Rebellion in Ireland in 1920–1921 and the Part Played by the Army in Dealing with it', Imperial War Museum, Box 78/82/2. Sir Hugh Jeudwine papers.

[18] *Ibid.*

[19] Piaras Béaslaí, *Dublin's Fighting Story*, quoted in Frank Thornton's Witness Statement 615.

[20] Peter Hart, *Mick: The Real Michael Collins* (London, 2006), p. 205.

[21] Francis Costello (ed.), *Michael Collins: In His Own Words* (Dublin, 1997), pp 80–1.

[22] Tony Woods, in Uinseonn MacEoin (ed.), *Survivors: The Story of Ireland's Struggle as Told Through Some of Her Outstanding Living People. Notes 1913–1916* (Dublin, 1966), p. 322.

[23] Liam Tobin, Witness Statement 1753.

[24] Frank Thornton, Witness Statement 615.

[25] Piaras Béaslaí, *Michael Collins and the Making of the New Ireland* (London, 1926), p. 319.

[26] Smith, also known as 'Smyth', was the one who smuggled out the information on the 'Castle Document' from Dublin Castle prior to the Rising. See Des White, 'The Castle Document', *History Ireland*, vol. 24, no. 4 (2016). He was also the brother of DMP 'G' Division detective 'Dog' Smith, the first G-man that Collins had executed. Eugene Smyth, Witness Statement 334.

[27] Éamon Broy and Eugene Smyth, in MacEoin (ed.), *Survivors*, pp 52–4.

[28] Éamon de Valera, Minutes of Dáil Éireann, vol. 1 (10 April 1919).

[29] Richard Mulcahy, 'Chief of Staff, 1919', *Capuchin Annual* (1970).

[30] John M. Regan, *The Memoirs of John M. Regan, a Catholic Officer in the RIC and RUC: 1909–1948* (ed. Joost Augusteijn) (Dublin, 2007).

[31] Joseph Leonard, Witness Statement 547.

[32] General Paddy Daly, Witness Statement 387.

[33] William J. (Bill) Stapleton, 'A Volunteer's story', *Irish Independent*, 1916 Golden Jubilee Supplement (April 1966).

[34] Ulick O'Connor, *Michael Collins and the Troubles: The Struggle for Irish Freedom 1912–1922* (New York, 1996), p. 143; William J. (Bill) Stapleton, 'Michael Collins's Squad', *Capuchin Annual* (1969); William Stapleton, Witness Statement 822.

[35] Bridget (Mrs Batt) O'Connor, Witness Statement 330.

[36] Calton Younger, *Ireland's Civil War* (New York, 1969), p. 99.

[37] General Patrick Daly, Witness Statement 387.

[38] Joe Dolan, Witness Statement 663.

[39] *The Times*, 23 January 1920.

[40] Peter Hart (*Mick*, p. 196) has the amount at £4,000.

[41] Daithi O'Donoghue, private statement, 26 March 1951.

[42] Dorothy Macardle, *The Irish Republic* (New York, 1937; 1965), p. 986; Hart, *Mick*, p. 194.

[43] O'Connor, *Michael Collins and the Troubles*, p. 145.

[44] Joe Dolan, Witness Statement 663.

[45] William Stapleton, Witness Statement 822.

[46] General Patrick Daly, Witness Statement 387.

[47] Dave Neligan, quoted in Kenneth Griffith and Timothy O'Grady, *Ireland's Unfinished Revolution: An Oral History* (Boulder, CO, 2002), pp 164–5.

[48] *Ibid.*

[49] David Neligan, Witness Statement 380; General Patrick Daly, Witness Statement 387.

[50] Frank Thornton, Witness Statement 615.

[51] Michael Murphy, Witness Statement 1547.

[52] David Neligan, *The Spy in the Castle* (London, 1999), p. 72, named him Bernard Hugh Mulloy; Hart (*Mick*, p. 238 *et seq.*) named him 'Patrick' Molloy.

[53] Liam Tobin, Witness Statement 1753; Frank Thornton, Witness Statement 615.

[54] Lily Mernin, Witness Statement 441.

[55] Michael McDonnell, Witness Statement 225.

[56] Richard Mulcahy, Béaslaí Notes, vol. 2, p. 46.

[57] Hart, *Mick*, pp 212–14.

[58] Neligan, *The Spy in the Castle*, p. 68 *et seq.*

[59] David Neligan, Witness Statement 380.

[60] Meda Ryan, *Michael Collins and the Women in His Life* (Dublin, 1996), p. 70; Lily Mernin, Witness Statement 441. Rex Taylor did not determine the identity of 'Lt

G.'; however, he wrote that, 'so far as the present writer could ascertain, Lieutenant 'G' was a member of the British Military Intelligence in Ireland. He [sic] was also one of Collins' chief agents as well as being a particular confidant of his'. Rex Taylor, *Michael Collins* (London, 1970), pp 126–9.

61 Frank Thornton, Witness Statement 615.

62 John Borgonovo (ed.), *Florence and Josephine O'Donoghue's War of Independence: A Destiny that Shapes our Ends* (Cork, 2006), pp 110–25.

63 Joseph E.A. Connell Jnr, *Rebels' Priests: Ministering to Republicans, 1916–1924* (Dublin, 2014), pp 38–46.

64 Ailin Quinlan, 'The mother who turned IRA spy to save her son', *Irish Independent*, 25 November 2012.

65 Hayden Talbot, *Michael Collins' Own Story* (London, 1923), p. 85.

66 See Joseph E.A. Connell Jnr, *Unequal Patriots* (Dublin, 2015).

67 See Sinéad McCoole, *Hazel: A Life of Lady Lavery* (Dublin, 1996); *Guns and Chiffon* (Dublin, 1997); *No Ordinary Women: Irish Female Activists in the Revolutionary Years* (Dublin, 2003).

68 See Ryan, *Michael Collins and the Women in His Life*.

69 'Remembering the past: Molly O'Reilly', *An Phoblacht*, 7 October 1999.

70 Author's correspondence and documents from Clare Cowley, granddaughter of Molly O'Reilly; http://mspcsearch.militaryarchives.ie/docs/files//PDF_Pensions/R2/MSP34REF20325MaryTCorcoran/W34E4055MaryTCorcoran.pdf. See Molly O'Reilly in Terry Fagan (ed.), *Rebels and Heroes: Hidden Stories from Dublin's Northside* (Dublin, 2016), p. 54 *et seq.*

71 J.B.E. Hittle, *Michael Collins and the Anglo-Irish War: Britain's Counter-insurgency Failure* (Chicago, 2011), pp 78, 131–2, 152.

72 Eileen McCarville (McGrane), Witness Statement 1752.

73 Michael T. Foy, *Michael Collins' Intelligence War* (Stroud, 2006; Dublin, 2007), p. 198.

74 Dr Brigid Thornton (née Lyons), Witness Statement 259.

75 Florence O'Donoghue (ed.), *IRA Jailbreaks, 1918–1921* (Cork, 1971), pp 146–53.

76 T. Ryle Dwyer, *Big Fellow, Long Fellow: A Joint Biography of Collins and de Valera* (Cork, 2006), pp 137–8.

77 Christopher Andrew, *Her Majesty's Secret Service: The Making of the British Intelligence Community* (New York, 1986), p. 255.

78 Gordon Pattison, 'The British Army's Effectiveness in the Irish Campaign 1919–1921, and the Lessons for Modern Counterinsurgency Operations, with Special Reference to C3I Aspects', UK Ministry of Defence (1999).

79 Tim Carey and Marcus de Burca, 'Bloody Sunday 1920: new evidence', *History Ireland*, vol. 11, no. 2 (2003).

80 Martin C. Hartline and M.M. Kaulbach, 'Michael Collins and Bloody Sunday: the intelligence war between the British and Irish intelligence services', *CIA Historical Review Program* (2 July 1996; approved for release 1994).

81 David Lloyd George, *The Times*, 10 November 1920.

82 See Tom Bowden, 'Bloody Sunday, a reappraisal', *European Studies Review*, vol. 2, no. 1 (1972); 'The Irish underground and the War of Independence 1919–1921', *Journal of Contemporary History*, vol. 8, no. 2 (1973); Anne Dolan, 'Killing and Bloody Sunday, November 1920', *Historical Journal*, vol. 49, issue 3 (2006); Gen. F.P. Crozier, *The Men I Killed* (London, 1937), part 3; *Ireland Forever* (London and Toronto, 1932), p. 95 *et*

seq.; Miceal O'Meara, *Bloody Sunday, 1920–1995: A Commemorative Booklet* (Dublin, 1995); Charles Townshend, 'Bloody Sunday: Michael Collins speaks', *European Studies Review*, vol. 9 (1979).

[83] Carey and de Burca, 'Bloody Sunday 1920: new evidence'.

[84] There is no mention of a 'Cairo Gang' in the reports and records of 1919–22. The first appearance of the term is in Rex Taylor's *Michael Collins* (1958), pp 125–34: 'In Cairo sixteen officers were chosen for a special task ... The Cairo group travelled under assumed names and arrived in Dublin singly on different dates. They were in plain clothes and posing as commercial travellers ... rented flats in Pembroke Street and Mount Street.' The agents frequented the Cairo Café (59 Grafton Street, five doors from the corner of South King Street) and Kidd's Buffet (Kidd's was where the Berni Inn was until the 1980s in Nassau Street; later it was where Lillie's Bordello is now at the bottom of Grafton Street) or the Porterhouse pub at 46 Nassau Street. The Squad called them the 'Cairo Gang', but the origin of the name is unclear.

[85] Mark Sturgis Diary, 1 September 1920, PRO 30/59.

[86] James Gleeson, *Bloody Sunday* (London, 1962), pp 101–23.

[87] Lily Mernin, Witness Statement 441.

[88] Béaslaí, *Michael Collins*, vol. 1, p. 448.

[89] Richard Mulcahy, Béaslaí Notes, vol. 2, p. 51.

[90] Dolan, 'Killing and Bloody Sunday, November 1920'.

[91] Jane Leonard, '"English dogs" or "Poor devils"? The dead of Bloody Sunday morning', in David Fitzpatrick (ed.), *Terror in Ireland* (Dublin, 2012). Leonard gives pen-pictures of the British killed on Bloody Sunday and indicates that 'most of them appeared to be officially employed in other posts, both military and non-military. It is unclear if those were just "aliases" and "cover" jobs or if the men were not actually intelligence agents.' In contrast, see Hittle, *Michael Collins and the Anglo-Irish War*, pp 162–89, in which he argues that all but two of the men were connected with British intelligence.

[92] Taylor, *Michael Collins*, p. 104.

[93] General Paddy Daly, Witness Statement 387.

[94] Margery Forester, *Michael Collins: The Lost Leader* (Dublin, 1989), p. 170.

[95] Caroline Woodcock, the wife of Col. Woodcock, wrote prolifically about her period as a British army wife in Dublin. Her diaries were published as *Experiences of an Officer's Wife in Ireland* (London, 1921; 1994). [Originally published in *Blackwood's Magazine*, no. 1267, vol. 209 (May 1921).]

[96] Wayne Sugg, 'British Intelligence wiped out', *An Phoblacht*, 20 November 1997; 'Bloody Sunday', *An Phoblacht*, 27 November 1997.

[97] David Neligan, Witness Statement 380.

[98] ' Record of the Rebellion in Ireland in 1920–1921 and the Part Played by the Army in Dealing with it', Imperial War Museum, Box 78/82/2, Vol. 2, Intelligence; Brian P. Murphy, *The Origin and Organisation of British Propaganda in Ireland, 1920* (Dublin, 2006), p. 54; Hittle, *Michael Collins and the Anglo-Irish War*, pp 160–77.

[99] Foy, *Michael Collins' Intelligence War*, p. 153.

[100] Seán MacAodh, 'Murder in the Castle', *An Phoblacht*, 22 November 2001; Seán O'Mahony, *Three Murders in Dublin Castle* (pamphlet, Dublin, 2000).

[101] Richard Mulcahy, Béaslaí Notes, vol. 2, p. 51.

[102] Gleeson, *Bloody Sunday*, p. 181.

103 *Ibid.*, p. 191.

104 Michael Foley, *The Bloodied Field* (Dublin, 2014), is the best and most comprehensive account of all the events at Croke Park that afternoon. See also D. Leeson, 'Death in the afternoon: the Croke Park massacre, 21 November 1920', *Canadian Journal of History* (April 2003).

105 Carey and de Burca, 'Bloody Sunday 1920: new evidence'.

106 Mark Duncan, Mike Cronin and Paul Rouse, *The GAA: A People's History* (Cork, 2009), p. 154.

107 Oscar Traynor, Witness Statement 340.

108 Frank Thornton, Witness Statement 510.

109 Maura R. Cremin, 'Fighting on their own terms: the tactics of the Irish Republican Army, 1919–1921', *Small Wars and Insurgencies*, vol. 26, no. 6 (2015).

110 Charles Townshend, 'The Irish Republican Army and the development of guerrilla warfare, 1916–1921', *English Historical Review*, vol. 94, no. 371 (1979).

111 Frank Thornton, Witness Statement 615.

112 Vincent Byrne, Witness Statement 423.

113 See Peter Hart (ed.), *British Intelligence in Ireland, 1920–21: The Final Reports* (Cork, 2002); D. Kostal, 'British Intelligence in Ireland 1919–1921: integration of law enforcement and military intelligence to support force protection', unpublished MS dissertation, US Joint Military Intelligence College, Bethesda, MD (2004).

114 John McGuigan, 'Michael Collins on file?', *History Ireland*, vol. 19, no. 4 (2011).

115 Eunan O'Halpin, 'Collins and intelligence, 1919–1923', in Gabriel Doherty and Dermot Keogh (eds), *Michael Collins and the Making of the Irish State* (Cork, 1998), p. 71.

116 Hart, *British Intelligence in Ireland, 1920–1921*, p. 11.

117 Peter Hart, *The IRA and its Enemies: Violence and Community in Cork, 1916–1923* (Oxford, 1998), pp 293–315. See Chapter 6, notes 38 and 130.

118 B.H. Liddell Hart, 'Foreword', in Mao Tse-Tung and Che Guevara, *Guerrilla Warfare* (London, 1969), p. xv.

119 Townshend, 'The Irish Republican Army and the development of guerrilla warfare'.

120 'Report on the Intelligence Branch of the Chief of Police from May 1920 to July 1921', Col. Ormonde de l'Epee Winter, PRO WO 35/214, p. 13.

121 *Ibid.*

122 Tim Pat Coogan, *Michael Collins, the Man Who Made Ireland* (London, 1992), pp xi–xii.

123 Peter Gudgin, *Military Intelligence: The British Story* (London, 1989), p. 52.

124 Townshend, 'The Irish Republican Army and the development of guerrilla warfare'.

125 O'Halpin, 'Collins and intelligence 1919–1923'.

126 Hart, *British Intelligence in Ireland, 1920–1921*, p. 13.

127 Max Boot, 'Kick the bully: Michael Collins launches the War of Independence', http://www.historynet.com/kick-the-bully-michael-collins-launches-the-1921-irish-rebellion.htm.

6. Terror—propaganda by the deed

Careful application of terrorism is also an excellent form of total communication.

—Michael Collins

This chapter concerns a controversial topic in all guerrilla wars: the utilisation of terror as a weapon. 'One man's terrorist is another man's freedom fighter.'[1] The mere term 'terrorism' is one that is imbued with fear, outrage, panic and political fervour. In few other insurrections was terror as important to the result as it was in the Anglo-Irish War—on both sides.

Terrorism is as old as insurgency, and questions regarding it abound. What is terrorism? How should it be defined? Could it ever be justified? Some have argued that terrorism is not necessarily morally wrong and not morally worse than war, and that if war can be justified then so can terrorism.[2]

It is often hard to distinguish between terrorism and guerrilla warfare.[3] Methods of insurgency and counter-insurgency are brutal, involving fear, torture, executions, extortion and a forcible conversion of the civil population to the goals of the insurgent organisation. While terrorism and guerrilla tactics are two distinct phenomena, there is nonetheless an overlap between them, and in the Irish War of Independence both the British and the Irish used both.[4] Insurgency breeds its own escalatory dynamics: excesses on one side produce excesses on the other side. The British forces used terrorism to continue the subjugation of Ireland, and the Irish used terror to achieve independence.[5] Each side blamed the other for what has been called the turn to terrorism. Indeed, it is in such contexts that the distinction between 'terrorist' and 'freedom fighter' becomes increasingly blurred.[6] Although initially such actions shocked the civilian population, the harsh responses from the British government resulted in a heightened public sympathy towards the

Irish, though some of the Irish actions caused just as much terror.

Terrorism is often used to conduct armed conflict against a militarily stronger enemy when the insurgents are not yet at a stage where guerrilla warfare is viable. Terrorism can also be used to supplement guerrilla warfare. In such cases it is employed to keep the enemy off balance and distracted, principally by conducting strikes against vulnerable targets at the enemy's rear. The mode of struggle adopted by insurgents is dictated by circumstances rather than by choice and, whenever possible, insurgents concurrently use a variety of strategies. Terrorism, which is the easiest form of insurgency, is practically always one of these modes. In the War of Independence, the Irish were the ones using terrorism to keep the British off balance and to intimidate the local population,[7] and it was one of the modes of warfare that they required to achieve their political objectives.[8]

The 'central goal of an insurgency is not to defeat the armed forces, but to subvert or destroy the government's legitimacy, its ability and moral right to govern'.[9] The Irish, like most insurgents, had a natural advantage in this regard because their actions were not constrained by codified law. States, however, must avoid not only wrongdoing but also any *appearance* of wrongdoing that might undermine their legitimacy in the community and international political opinion. As historian Thomas Mockaitis points out, 'In counterinsurgency an atrocity is not necessarily what one actually does but what one is successfully blamed for doing'.[10] During an insurgency there are three ways to conserve State legitimacy: the use of proportionate force, the use of precisely applied force and the provision of security for the civilian population. The British failed in the application of all of these, not only in fact but also in international opinion.

For example, the core tenet of British military strategy was that overwhelming force deployed against the Irish would result in military victory. In a counter-insurgency, however, 'winning' through overwhelming force is often inapplicable as a concept, if not problematic as a goal. In practice, the application of overwhelming force has a negative, unintended effect of strengthening the insurgency by creating martyrs, increasing recruitment and demonstrating the brutality of State forces. Nothing could define the Irish reaction to the terrorist actions of the Black and Tans or Auxiliaries more clearly than that. The use of excessive force may not only legitimise the insurgent group but also cause the State to lose legitimacy in the eyes of the civilian population and internationally. Repression breeds radicals.

A definition of terrorism should meet three criteria. First, it should cover certain paradigmatic instances of what we consider terrorism. Second, the definition should not yet include any moral assessment of the act in question; defining an action and evaluating it are distinct tasks. Third, the definition should single out a certain group of actions, enabling one to clearly distinguish these actions from other kinds of actions—that is, to clearly identify which acts are terrorist by their nature and which are not.[11] Nevertheless, while one cannot initially conflate the evaluation and the classification of acts, one must ultimately consider the morality of such acts.

Some have defined 'terror' as 'apart from a state of mind, a conscious attempt to create an acute fear of violence against the person or property, which may affect individuals, groups or the population at large'.[12] Any definition of terrorism returns to the concept of fear. There is an ancient Chinese proverb of war: victory is gained not by the number killed but by the number frightened. The US State Department and NATO define terrorism as 'premeditated, motivated violence perpetrated against non-combatant groups by sub-national or clandestine agents, acting as individuals or in groups, intended to influence an audience wider than the immediate victim or victims'.[13] That definition seems to eliminate actions by or against State agents, and any definition of terror must include actions by and against State as well as non-State agents. A more inclusive definition is that terrorism is an indirect strategy of using fear or terror induced by violent attacks or force (or the threat of its use) against one group of people (direct target) or their property as a means to intimidate and coerce another group of people (indirect target) and influence their actions in order to reach further political objectives. The violent acts that form part of such a strategy should be called terrorist acts.[14] One of the goals of terrorism is to disturb the normal lives and liberties that people have, which is against human rights. The UN stresses that this is one of the most important ways in which terrorism should be defined. However expressed, almost any definition of terrorism will include the following essential elements:

- the use of violence (or fear of future violence),
- directed at combatants or non-combatants (or civilians),
- intended to induce extreme fear in a population or government

• in order to achieve a political, religious or ideological end.

In the War of Independence, the Irish in particular directed many acts of what must be considered terror at government individuals and forces. The killings of the 'G' Division detectives in Dublin by Collins's 'Squad' provide just one example, as they must be considered 'combatants'. Some of the Irish recognised that at the time and were revolted by such killings in the street. Later, Frank Gallagher wrote about the members of the Squad who became leaders of the Dublin Guard in the Civil War that followed and their easy 'acceptance' of the killings:

> I know there are different views of how to best further the establishment of an Irish Republic. Those who came to worship the gun before 1921 were the first to surrender to Britain at the Treaty time. And they afterwards became those who committed the most terrible outrages on captured Republicans [in the Irish Civil War].[15]

One of the bloodiest days in the war was Bloody Sunday, 21 November 1920, when fourteen men were killed in Dublin on that morning and another fourteen men and women were killed at Croke Park that afternoon. (See Chapter 5 for a full discussion of Bloody Sunday.) Terror lives long after its initial application, and one must consider the nature of the terror used and what it does to those individuals who commit it, as well as its effects on those (or their families) against whom it is committed.[16] For weeks afterwards, the wife of one of the British officers killed claimed that she was haunted by the sounds of gunfire and the laughing of the gunmen, and by the image of one of the killers washing her husband's blood from his hands in her sink. Three weeks after the events she gave birth to a stillborn child.[17] On the Irish side, Charles Dalton was only seventeen when he took part in the Bloody Sunday raid at 38 Pembroke Street. That night he was distraught and couldn't sleep because he 'kept hearing the gurgling of the blood of the man he shot'. His friends tried to comfort him by saying that it was just a faucet running in the upstairs flat.[18] Dalton was later involved in the killings of innocents in the Civil War. What effect did his actions on Bloody Sunday, and throughout the War of Independence, have on him as an intelligence officer in the Civil War?

In the 1940s he was judged to be 'permanently and completely insane'. He had taken to hiding under his bed, convinced that his enemies were coming to take their revenge.[19] He died in hospital as a paranoid schizophrenic. Some others in Collins's Squad seemed to revel in killing. Vinnie Byrne, who gave newspaper and TV interviews until he was an old man, said that 'It was the joy of my life when I was handed a .45 revolver and six rounds …', and that he 'Liked pluggin' British soldiers'.[20]

Some of those who took part in the Bloody Sunday raids were even rebuked immediately by members of their family, but didn't understand their concern:

> I was told that the British had raided the Tipperary Football team where they were staying in Gardiner's Row. We, therefore, decided that there would be no football match for us that day; that we would not attend it, as we thought there would possibly be trouble there. I returned home about 2 o'clock and lunched. After lunch I had been in the habit of going to football matches on a Sunday, and my family asked me was I not going to the match. I said no, that I was feeling tired and would lie down and have a rest. I lay on the couch in the room and fell asleep. I was awakened that evening about 4 o'clock. My wife came into the room crying, with a 'Stop Press' in her hand. I woke up and asked her what was the matter. Before speaking she handed me the 'Stop Press' and wanted to know was this the fishing expedition I had been on [he had told her that he was fishing that morning]. Seeing that there was no use in concealing things any longer from her, I said: 'Yes, and don't you see we had a good catch', or words to that effect. She then said: 'I don't care what you think about it, I think it is murder'. I said: 'No, that is nonsense; I'd feel like going to the altar after that job this morning', and thus I tried to calm her. I don't think she put out any lights in the house during the following winter. I did not stay at home then for about a week. That Sunday night I slept in a grove in the demesne known as St Anne's, which was nearby.[21]

One of those killed on Bloody Sunday was Thomas Herbert Smith, the owner of the house at 117 Morehampton Road in Dublin. At 9.00 a.m.

ten-year-old Percival William Smith opened the door at his home. Ten minutes later, Thomas Smith, Percy's father and an innocent man (one of these 'mistakes'), lay dead. We must wonder about little Percy—and we should grieve for everyone lost to violence. We can't forget that all those killed and those injured physically or emotionally were human beings, and we should recognise the trauma that haunted them for the rest of their lives. Terror does not end with the event.

Terror and violence can be one and the same, and fear and forcible actions often are not classified as 'terror' when they should be. Physical and sexual violence was waged against both men and women during the War of Independence, and historians are just now addressing that perpetrated against women. Rape and sexual assault can certainly be considered forms of terror, and in wartime they are used to punish women as well as to intimidate a population. While serious sexual assaults and the targeted killing of females were apparently rare, actions do not have to descend to that degree to terrorise the female population. Moreover, rape is always under-reported, and even more so during that period. Women were not going to come forward for fear of rejection by their husbands, their families and their communities. Physical abuse was also known to occur during raids, and women in their nightdresses were especially vulnerable to dehumanising actions when their homes were raided and they were forcibly thrown out of their beds. Both the British and the Irish used hair-cutting and other forms of humiliation, and the effects would last far longer than it took the hair to grow out. While much of the terrorising of women by the British occurred during raids, most of the violence against women perpetrated by the IRA consisted of the 'victimisation of policemen's wives and barrack servants'. This included eviction from and destruction of their homes, verbal and written threats, enforced resignation from employment in police barracks, ostracism and exile. The overall absence of reported sexual violence by both sides might indicate a relatively high level of discipline among the Crown forces and the IRA, but research must continue in that vein. Some British reports argued that, far from being a lawless mob, the violence of the Tans and Auxiliaries was somewhat orchestrated: a certain level of venting of frustration and retaliation was permitted but this was controlled and curtailed. Any such argument should not minimise the degrading treatment nor excuse it in any way. Purely and simply, they were criminal acts of the most abhorrent kind.[22]

Terror in Ireland was exacerbated because the actions were so close—most lives were taken at close range, many by a shot from a handgun. That proximity to the violence caused a 'wounding of the mind' that affects one more, and longer, than falling bombs or artillery. Many of those who took part in the violence remained haunted by the blood and fear that they saw on the faces of those killed or wounded right in front of them.

> Terrorism necessarily involves spectacle. This is what grants it the power to terrorize, to assault relations between someone and the world. Terror's damage is contagious: it is not simply the victims of a bomb blast who suffer, but those touched by its rippling consequences and mediatized representations. While terrorism's traumas can be local and specific to the event, its distinctiveness as terror is contained in the excess of effect its violence produces.[23]

To understand the use of terror in the Irish war, we must try to understand its context and meaning. Tactically, its initial and primary purpose was to intimidate the military/police opposition—for example, throwing a grenade into an RIC barracks to make all the RIC men afraid that every time a door or window was opened a grenade could come through it. At a slightly higher level it was used to eliminate political and military leaders and officials in order to destabilise the government.[24] Che Guevara addressed killing by insurgents: 'Terrorism should be considered a valuable tactic when it is used to put to death some noted leader of the oppressing forces well known for his cruelty, his efficiency in repression, or other quality that makes his elimination useful. But the killing of persons of small importance is never advisable, since it brings on an increase of reprisals, including deaths.'[25] So-called 'leadership targeting' is a most effective guerrilla tool, and was utilised in Dublin as well as throughout the country. Todd Andrews wrote in *Dublin Made Me*:

> Assassination, correctly applied by Michael Collins, was the real basis of our relative success.[26]

Such 'selective assassination', refined by Collins, has been deemed the 'pivot of the war effort'.[27] Lord Londonderry, a Northern Ireland minister in 1922, reached much the same conclusion:

> Mr Collins ... achieved his position ... by being one of the leaders of a campaign which Sinn Féin called war, and which I call assassination. He has maintained his position by challenging the British government and by succeeding in compelling the British government to make terms and terms of a character far exceeding the wildest hopes of Mr Collins or any of his supporters.[28]

To view terrorist acts in the War of Independence, it is necessary to distinguish as far as possible between the use of sabotage, which is an effective method of warfare, and terrorism, which is questionably effective and indiscriminate in its results.

> TERRORISM is seen as a law enforcement or military problem.
> INSURGENCY spawning guerrillas is a social problem.
> TERRORISM is a particular tactic.
> INSURGENCY is the rejection of a political order.
> TERRORISM is concerned with means.
> GUERRILLAS are concerned with political change.
> TERRORISTS are seen as unrepresentative and outliers in society.
> GUERRILLAS are the manifestation of deeper, widespread issues in society.
> TERRORISTS resist negotiation.
> GUERRILLAS try to win over the population, leading to a political settlement.
> COUNTER-TERRORISM is tactical, focusing on catching individual terrorists.
> COUNTER-INSURGENCY is strategic, seeking to undermine the insurgent's strategy; capture is a secondary consideration.[29]

Guevara also addressed the effect of terror and sabotage on the civilian population:

> Conduct toward the civil population ought to be regulated by a large respect for all the rules and traditions of the people of the zone, in order to demonstrate effectively, with deeds, the moral superiority of the guerrilla fighter over the oppressing soldier. Except in special situations, there ought to be no execution of justice without giving the criminal an opportunity to clear himself.[30]

Terror, including murder, reprisals and burnings, was used by both the British and the Irish.[31] Charles Townshend wrote that 'The IRA could win an arson competition easily'. Further, Seán Lemass, who was on the Bloody Sunday raids, said: 'On both sides they did terrible things—and they knew it'. Collins's Squad, the IRA Intelligence Unit, began the assassination of detectives and informers in 1919, but by 1920 the State forces had also resorted to a policy of lethal reprisals. British forces employed terrorism in order to maintain the conquest of Ireland and subdue the Irish nationalist movement during the war.[32] Once the War of Independence began, however, the IRA embarked upon its own campaign of terrorism. In time, IRA terror was so effective that many of the British representatives in the courts, police, magistrates and local authorities eventually ceded the authority of their positions to their Irish counterparts, who, with the support of Dáil Éireann, were already running large portions of Ireland.[33] The commission of British reprisals was exacerbated when the Irish propaganda machine successfully capitalised on them, despite the fact that the Irish themselves were carrying out their own reprisals.[34]

In order for terror to be effective, intimidation is key. Guerrillas must balance persuasion and coercion. Coercion is often necessary in any insurgency, as the revolutionaries vie with the government for the loyalty of the people, and so it was for the Irish.[35] All revolutionaries—and certainly the Irish—need assistance, whether it is given willingly or *un*willingly.[36] Those who do not wish to help the cause must be intimidated so that they do not hinder it.[37] Further, the Irish often had to settle for merely preventing assistance to the British through coercion. While most discussions of terror in the period concentrate on the actions of the Black and Tans and Auxiliaries, who certainly committed many acts of gross terror, it cannot be denied that Collins and the Irish engaged in their own campaign of terror in order to intimidate and control the Irish population, as well as committing acts of terror against loyalists and cities and individuals on the British mainland in order to affect the British political position. The British soldiers were told to keep practising shooting when they went home on leave because they might need to use their gun at any time, and the Irish population feared what would happen to their village when they heard of terrorism against another town. Terror can be imagined as well as experienced.

The traditional view that there uniformly existed a symbiotic relationship between the IRA and the community at large has been successfully challenged since the mid-1990s.[38] It is acknowledged that there was widespread support for Irish nationalism, but it must be stressed that the IRA often had to resort to intimidation in order to enforce allegiance to their cause and to its alternative government. It is apparent that important differences existed between parts of the country, and often the level of acceptance for the republican cause was in proportion to the success of the IRA, as well as to the numbers of Protestants and loyalists in the area.[39] Attempts by Sinn Féin supporters to garner support were enforced by intimidation as early as the winter of 1916. In Wexford, people received letters accusing them of sneering at Sinn Féin and threatening that they 'would be made to pay at the next rising'. In Dublin, the 'separation women' (so called because they were given a 'separation allowance' as the wives of British soldiers serving in World War I) were targets of abuse, and threats were made against employers to urge them to reinstate the male Irish prisoners taken after the Rising and to terminate the women's employment.[40]

All revolutionaries must strike a balance between controlling a population and harming it in the process. To do too much damage to the local infrastructure would harm the local economy, which would backfire on the Irish. Controlling too much of a community's affairs would make the IRA appear overbearing and not too different from the British. Intimidation came in many forms, and one that aroused terror in many men—and especially in their families—was the ostracising of the RIC.

Beginning in 1917, and then officially in April 1919, the Irish were told to avoid RIC members and their families throughout Ireland. In January 1919 the Dublin County Inspector wrote:

> There is no boycotting but intimidation in a great way exists owing to the malign influences of Sinn Féin. People are afraid to offend the extremists and comply with their wishes [avoiding contact with the RIC or their families] fearing injury if they did not do so. Also there is no doubt a general scheme on the part of Sinn Féin to intimidate and cow the police to prevent them from doing their duty and to deter young men from joining the police.[41]

'Fearing injury by extremists' is a not-so-subtle form of terrorism. Rumours of terror generate further terror.[42]

The policy of ostracism is more complex than it appears at first glance, and the effects were felt not just by the RIC men and their families but also by many Irish people in the community. The majority of the constables in rural areas were drawn from the same social class, religion and general background as their neighbours. While measures were taken, not always successfully, to maintain an arms-length relationship between police and public, most of the constables and their families became an integral part of their communities. Constables in charge of police stations were required to make regular reports to their superiors, and would from time to time be moved around the district to prevent acquaintanceships from developing too closely, but this policy was not followed assiduously. A constable was not permitted to marry until he had been in the force for some years and was not supposed to serve in his home county, nor in that of his wife, but after marriage their families mingled in schools, churches and community life. Despite their status as an armed force, constables seldom carried guns— only a waist belt, handcuffs and baton. Enforcement of eviction orders in rural Ireland caused the RIC to be widely distrusted by the poor Catholic population as the mid-nineteenth century approached, but later policing generally became a routine of controlling petty misdemeanours such as moonshine-distilling, public drunkenness, minor theft and wilful property crimes.[43] And when violence was involved, it was usually fuelled by passion, alcohol or a combination of the two. Often, along with the priest, the constables would have an informal leadership role in the community and, being literate, would be appealed to by people needing help with forms and letters. Of the RIC's senior officers in 1919, 60% were Irish Protestants and the rest Catholic, while 70% of the rank and file were Roman Catholic and the rest Protestant. RIC men generally conducted themselves with forbearance and dignity in the face of a ruthless terror campaign directed at them. It was their unwillingness to respond in kind that prompted the British government to import the Black and Tans and Auxiliaries to wage a counter-terror campaign. A majority of RIC men were Catholics like their fellow countrymen, and they probably had the same range of political opinions. Their primary loyalty was to their job of keeping the peace and serving the community rather than to any political party or ideology. The RIC were trained for police work, not war, and were woefully ill prepared to take on the counter-insurgency duties that were required in 1919.

On 10 April 1919 Éamon de Valera called for all the police forces to be socially ostracised. He stated:

> The people of Ireland ought not to fraternise, as they often do, with the forces that are the main instruments in keeping them in subjugation … Given the composition of these forces, boycott meant accentuating divisions among Irish people, including family members and community residents.

Even though friendships developed between the RIC and their families and the Irish, by 1919 the RIC as an organisation were reviled as the most obvious instrument of British rule in Ireland.[44] In October the County Inspector for Clare reported:

> The people appear to regard the police as their enemies and have ceased all friendly intercourse with them. Shops continue to supply provisions, but they would rather that the police did not come to them.[45]

It is clear that there was a 'double-edged' intimidation in the ostracism of the RIC and their families. When the Irish were admonished not to have any social or economic congress with them—not to share a pew in church, nor to meet and talk with the families, nor to drink a pint in the pub with the men, nor to sell goods or provisions to them in shops—there was an expressed or implied 'or else', as well. Those Irish who ignored the warnings not to have any dealings with the men and their families ran the risk of being ostracised themselves—or worse.

By mid-1920 those RIC men who were going to be intimidated out of their jobs had left. Those who remained were men who decided to 'stick it out' in the RIC for the duration, or recruits who joined in 1919 or 1920.[46] Later in 1920, however, ostracism of the RIC began to lose its effect. It must be understood that most constables were Irish and that they and their families had been essential and welcome members of their communities before the war. Many Irish people found that they could not 'cut off' connections with men and their families with whom they had had neighbourly relations for many years. Reports noted that boycotts were collapsing around the country, as most of those who could be intimidated had already left the force. The Roscommon County Inspector reported that many of the traders in the area continued to supply the RIC and their families under the pretence that the goods were commandeered.

> The majority of the people are not in favour of the criminal campaign and realise it is not good for them to boycott or display hostility to the Crown forces.[47]

It was said that, 'like the burning of vacant police barracks, by 1921 the work of intimidation [of the RIC] had been largely accomplished'.[48]

Intimidation was bilateral when the policy of ostracism was instituted, and that was another form of terror for the entire community. As always, the simple thought of 'them' versus 'us' is incorrect when recounting the times. When Voltaire wrote *pour encourager les autres*, he could have been thinking of the Irish War of Independence 130 years in the future, and one must continually ask: who were the 'others' the terror was to 'encourage'? In so many cases, the Irish intimidation was directly or indirectly aimed at the Irish people themselves, and was much more complex and nuanced than is often thought. It is impossible to understand what must have been an inescapable part of life—the uncertainty of living in a community where no one was immune from the daily possibility of violence.

> Just as the military phase of the guerrilla war changed as it went on, over the revolutionary period, the practice of terrorism was radically altered, as all protagonists discarded their initial inhibitions, devised new tactics to cope with increasingly difficult opposition, and expressed their growing frustration in ever more ruthless brutality.[49]

As the war continued, intimidation on both sides progressed into actual violence, murders and burnings, and the British began with unofficial and then moved into official reprisals—'authorised punishments'. Lord Hugh Cecil summed up the British position cynically: 'There is no such thing as reprisals, but they have done a great deal of good!' The British used what they called 'extra-legal' means: torture, murder, the burning of homes, businesses and creameries in an attempt to restore order.[50] (Late in the war, in May 1921, Richard Mulcahy wrote to Cathal Brugha giving formal sanction for Irish 'counter-reprisals'.[51]) British military and police discipline mostly held firm throughout 1919, but by January 1920 RIC men began to retaliate in a manner that terrorised the local populations. The British did not understand the will of the Irish and often overreacted. Mao Zedong later had as one of his principles of guerrilla warfare to let the State 'overreact with human rights abuses'.[52] In fact, it was clear that the Irish provoked British reprisals in order to generate propaganda. Michael Hopkinson wrote that

> ... a central, if unstated, aim of the IRA was to provoke a harsh response and hence to court publicity and international sympathy.[53]

British 'reprisals and counter-reprisals' proved to be counter-productive time and time again. Collins needed the British to overreact, and when they did he was able to manipulate that overreaction to mobilise Irish and international opinion to win the all-important political and psychological war. Collins and the Irish continually attacked the British in ways calculated to provoke their blind reactions. This handed the propaganda initiative to the Irish internationally and extended the movement's control over the population, although that was at least partially due to the fact that the Irish were also engaging in terrorism, to intimidate the population.

A further indication of the fact that the Irish also utilised terrorism— and of the confusion that was apparent throughout Ireland as to which side was the 'terrorist' and which the 'counter-terrorist'—is demonstrated in Chapter XVIII, 'Terror and Counter-Terror', of Edgar Holt's book *Protest in Arms*.[54] While it is commonly thought, and written, that the first terror came from the British, and especially from the Black and Tans and Auxiliaries, Holt presents the Irish as being the first to use terror and the Black and Tans as the 'counter-terror' forces. He lists various Irish actions which he deems to be terrorist in nature: the events that followed 20 May 1920, when Irish dockers embargoed British 'war materials' and railway workers followed suit; the killing of Colonel Gerald Smyth in the Cork County Club for his speech to RIC members at their barracks in Listowel on 19 June ('Sinn Féin has had all the sport up to the present, and we are going to have the sport now'); and the killing of policemen in Cork in July. Holt indicates that these led to *counter*-reprisals by the British. As a further example there is Frank Brooke, the chairman of the Dublin and Southeastern Railway. On 30 July Collins intervened in the embargo by making 'non-combatant' supporters of the British war effort in Ireland legitimate targets, and Brooke knew that he was in danger. That day Brooke chaired a meeting at Westland Row Railway Station, and Collins sent Jim Slattery to lead Squad members to kill him.[55] Holt points out that the witnesses and observers at these events raised no outcry because the IRA and its terror had so intimidated them, and that it was clear that the British administration and law were no longer respected. Confusion reigned in Ireland—and in the historiography ever since.

In reality, the British policy of 'unofficial' reprisals (i.e. officially carried out but unacknowledged as such) had been sanctioned at the highest level. In June 1920, British Prime Minister Lloyd George met privately with General Hugh Tudor, the top police 'adviser' at Dublin Castle, appointed by Winston Churchill, and affirmed his full support for the reprisals policy. Tudor was appointed head of the RIC the following November and thereafter the number of reprisals was expanded and more publicly justified.

In August 1920, the month before the burning of Balbriggan, Tudor endorsed the publication by Dublin Castle's propagandists of their newspaper, the *Weekly Summary*. This was a propaganda sheet designed not for the press and public but for the Crown forces themselves, in order to boost morale and 'psyche them up' to carry out the terror policy.

By mid-/late 1920, British reprisals had become accepted British government policy.[56] Lloyd George was willing to place several counties under martial law and allowed the trial of Irish suspects by court martial. He was even willing to turn a blind eye to Black and Tan and Auxiliary rampages and the forcible interrogation and occasional killing of suspects 'while trying to escape'. He said that the activities of the Irish 'could only be met by reprisals',[57] but there were limits beyond which he would not go. He was not willing to bomb cities, as Lord Herbert Kitchener, British Chief of Staff, had done in the Boer War. He was not willing to execute Irish *en masse*, as had been done in the Boer War, nor was he prepared to place them in concentration camps. Actions in war that create fear and terror can become so widespread that historians have questioned whether some situations of atrocity were not so much a consequence of a defect of character as of a misguided sense of judgement of the value of intimidating and coercing the local populations. Of these there are many examples, many involving senior military British leaders in times of stress within a counter-insurgency. Perhaps most notable, or most notorious, was that which took place in South Africa between 1900 and 1902, when Kitchener was in command of British troops. Besides the 1,000 deaths from typhoid as a consequence of inadequate sanitation and hygiene in the field, the internment of civilians was to lead to 3,854 deaths after 155,399 of them had been interned. The burning of 30,000 farms and forty towns in the Orange Free State by May 1901, plus the overall detention without trial of 320,000 internees, of whom 51,000 died, may have been carried out with the best of intentions—to bring the Boer War to a speedy close—but by atrocious means. It took two humanitarian investigations, initially by Emily Hobhouse[58] and then by Dame Millicent Fawcett,[59] to bring matters to public attention. How prescient was Kitchener in his remark that 'I fear it will be many a generation before the Boers forget or forgive this war'!

Lloyd George was not, in short, prepared to treat Ireland as the

British had treated the Boers, or as they treated the Iraqis in 1920, when a much larger revolt was ruthlessly suppressed at a cost of approximately 9,000 lives.[60] These political limitations imposed by British public and parliamentary opinion frustrated many soldiers in Ireland; in the words of Field Marshal Henry Wilson, 'the Shinners are at war with our men, whilst our men are at peace with the Sinn Féin'.[61] General Nevil Macready wrote back: 'If this country was Mesopotamia or Egypt, I should have the greatest pleasure in the world in putting on the most extreme Martial Law, and have done with the thing once and for all'.[62] Earlier in his career Macready, who was known to be a 'hard-liner', had been promoted for his actions in the 1910 miners' strike in Tonypandy, Wales, where he threatened to shoot strikers and earned himself the nickname 'strike breaker'.[63] (At that incident in the south Wales town riots erupted after police attempted to break the miners' picket line. The then Home Secretary, Churchill, sent 200 officers of the Metropolitan police and a detachment of Lancashire Fusiliers to stop the riots. One miner was killed and almost 600 people were injured.) As O/C in Ireland, Macready did not seem to fully comprehend that the Irish would not give up and that such measures as he could take in 'Mesopotamia or Egypt' would not work in Ireland. He was to write that 'no Englishman can fully grasp the psychology of the Irish rebel character'.[64]

As with so much of the war, the British reports afterwards never recognised the effect that their actions truly had on the Irish, or on Irish and international opinion. Regarding reprisals, the official report noted:

> It is not proposed to touch on the question of unofficial reprisals which occurred about this time [late 1920] beyond saying that, thanks to effective Sinn Féin propaganda, they were greatly exaggerated.[65]

Just as that propaganda was a boon for the Irish, it was a bane for the British home audience; there were limits that the British public would not allow to be crossed. Terror was to be restrained by the *realpolitik* of politics and propaganda. Lloyd George and the other Cabinet ministers knew that Churchill's 'iron repression'—a policy of 'murder and counter-murder, terror and counter-terror'—would not be acceptable to the British public.[66] Having just waged a war to liberate Belgium, the British people were not willing to fight indefinitely to subjugate Ireland, especially when the Irish people had expressed their preference for independence.[67]

The brutal reprisal operations carried out by the British from the spring of 1920 brought uniform international condemnation of the policy. While they were often in response to IRA actions, they were more aggressive, long-drawn-out and indiscriminate than the actions to which they were responding. In Britain, the war-weary public were sickened and disgusted by the actions of the Black and Tans and Auxiliaries, whom they viewed as immoral mercenaries. David Fitzpatrick has correctly written that 'the reprisal [was] always more vicious than the incident provoking it'.[68] In fact, their first O/C, General F.P. Crozier, resigned in February 1921 and later described the Auxiliaries as 'soldiers in disguise, under no army and no RIC code'.[69] He claimed that they were being employed to 'murder, rob, loot and burn up the innocent because they could not catch the few guilty on-the-run'.[70] When he resigned, he said, 'I resigned because the combat was being carried out on foul lines, by selected and foul men, for a grossly foul purpose, based on the most Satanic of all rules that "the end justifies the means"'. Crozier summarised the dark stain on the reputation of British Forces:

Had I been told, in 1918, after four and a half years of blood-letting, that in our own British Isles I should be witnessing acts of atrocity, by men in the King's uniform, which far exceeded in violence and brutality those acts I lived to condemn in the seething Baltic, I—well, I would have laughed out loud. I am concerned here with the conduct of Englishmen in the uniform of the Crown, because I greatly respect the Crown and have no wish to see it dragged in the mud.[71]

Within the British military establishment, two of the most vocal critics of the British policy of reprisals were Field Marshal Henry Wilson and General Nevil Macready. Both were concerned that the undisciplined paramilitaries would have an adverse effect on the morale of regular British Army troops.[72] Wilson had a conversation with Lloyd George and Bonar Law on 29 September 1920:

> ... I told them what I thought of reprisals by the Black and
> Tans, and how this must lead to chaos and ruin. Lloyd George
> danced about and was angry, but I never budged. I pointed
> out that these reprisals were being carried out without anyone
> being responsible; men were being murdered, houses burnt,
> villages wrecked ... It was the business of the Government to
> govern. *If these men ought to be murdered, then the Government
> ought to murder them.* I got some sense into their heads and
> Lloyd George went for Hamar Greenwood, Macready, Tudor,
> and others to come over tomorrow night ...[73] [Emphasis
> added]

Clearly, Wilson did not object to the reprisals *per se*, but he wanted them
taken out of the hands of the Black and Tans and directly overseen by
the British military and government.

Macready wrote to Sir John Anderson in February 1921 that the
Auxiliaries 'treat the Martial Law areas as a special game preserve for
their amusement'.[74] (Some Auxiliaries were arrested and tried for
crimes, including three murders, but few were imprisoned for any
period and most were granted probation and returned to their units.[75])
While noting that reprisals were not officially sanctioned, he wrote in
his memoirs:

> Although these unauthorised reprisals at that time had a
> marked effect in curbing the activities of the IRA in the
> immediate localities, and on these grounds were justified, or
> at all events winked at, by those in control of the police, I saw
> that they could only result in the police taking the law into
> their own hands. And lost no time in protesting to the Chief
> Secretary [Hamar Greenwood] on the subject, urging him to
> carry out reprisals as authorised and controlled operations, or
> to stop them at all costs. Unfortunately at that time certain
> persons in London were convinced that terrorism in any
> description was the best method with which to oppose the

gunmen, not realising that apart from all other reasons the gunmen could always 'go one better'.[76]

British General Sir Hubert Gough went even further in condemning their actions:

Law and order have given way to a bloody and brutal anarchy ... England has departed further from the standards even of any nation in the world, not excepting the Turk and the Zulu, than has ever been known in history before![77]

Further, *The Times* editorialised:

Methods, inexcusable even under the loose code of revolutionaries, are certainly not fit methods which the Government of Great Britain can tolerate on the part of its servants.[78]

Collins viewed the Black and Tans, the Auxiliaries and the terror that followed them as a sort of mixed blessing. Clearly the terror instilled by the Black and Tans and the Auxiliaries drove any doubting nationalists into the arms of Sinn Féin, and Collins took full advantage of that. 'Apart from the loss which these attacks entail, good is done as it makes clear and clearer to people what both sides stand for.'[79] Nevertheless, Collins and the Irish did not hesitate to use terror when they felt it necessary for their aims.

Some of the British in Ireland had a different view of the Auxiliaries. Caroline Woodcock, wife of the Colonel Wilfred James Woodcock who was wounded in a raid on Bloody Sunday, spent most of 1920–1 in Dublin and her diaries were later published as a book. She described the Auxiliaries on the streets of Dublin and the street scene:

Soldiers piqueted every corner, and a house-to-house search was made and usually numerous streets affected. Throughout tanks waddled slowly up and down the street ...

During these raids ever the most awe-inspiring sight for me was the car loads of Auxiliaries: eight or ten splendid-looking men in a Crossley Tender, armed to the teeth …

I know little of what the Auxiliaries have done or left undone but I do know that they have put the fear of God into the Irish rebels. When criticising them, it should be never forgotten that these men are the survivors of the glorious company of those who fought and died for England.[80]

The Auxiliaries and the Black and Tans were always on their best behaviour with their compatriots and very careful to hide their excesses from the British people.

The Black and Tans, fearful of the fact that any civilian could be a guerrilla fighter, unleashed their campaign of terror against the entire civilian population as well as the IRA. Simply put, they attempted to use terrorism to crush nationalist sentiment. The sole purpose of their terrorist actions was to 'make an appropriate hell for rebels' in an effort to reduce support for Sinn Féin and the IRA.[81] Major Bernard Montgomery, serving in Cork, dismissed the actions of the Black and Tans and Auxiliaries, saying that 'it never bothered me how many houses were burned. I regarded all civilians as "Shinners" and I never had any dealings with them.'[82] Officially, the Black and Tans were sent in to reinforce the RIC, but they had no intention to 'police' Ireland.[83] While their acts of terrorism were due in part to their lack of discipline, it is clear that many of the methods they employed were a result of British policy rather than the passion of the soldiers.[84] If there was anything that distinguished the terrorist actions of the sides, and the propaganda reactions to them, it would be that the British actions seemed part of a policy whereas the Irish actions seemed more *ad hoc* and employed locally by individuals or individual leaders.

As the war progressed, the British army increasingly burned and looted key economic locations in an effort to impoverish the Irish people, illustrating what the cost of fighting Britain would be.[85] Starting in April 1919, creameries became a prime target. The destruction of creameries caused severe food shortages in the winter, leaving many Irish families starving in the cold.[86] Later in the war, the Black and Tans burned down creameries because they viewed them as recruiting agencies for the IRA.[87] In total, over a hundred were burned to the ground by the war's end.[88] Moreover, as reprisals increased, in June 1920 an RIC report indicated that the force was feeling the effects of Irish actions and that the public shouldn't be surprised that they engaged in reprisals:

> There is a feeling among the police which is becoming prevalent in places where murders of police have been committed that the only way to stop these murders is by way of reprisals or retaliation … It is becoming difficult to restrain men's passions aroused at the sight of their murdered comrades and when they have the means of executing vengeance it is likely that they will use them when driven to desperation.[89]

On 9 August 1920 Parliament passed the Restoration of Order in Ireland Act. In practice it suspended most civil rights, including trial by jury, and allowed trial by courts martial without access to legal representation. The British hard-liners declared victory, but it proved to be a pyrrhic victory at best. Broadening their activities, throughout the summer of 1920 the British systematically destroyed co-operative creameries, mills and bacon factories, effectively destroying much of Ireland's agricultural economy. As reprisals against innocent citizens increased throughout south-western Ireland later that year, the international press reflected almost universal condemnation of the British policy, thus handing another propaganda victory to the Irish.

September 1920 saw an intensification of the war in Ireland, with the British army, the RIC, the Black and Tans and Auxiliaries targeting the civilian population in 'reprisals' that had the sanction of the British government.[90] On 3 September the British regime abolished coroners' inquests in ten Irish counties and replaced them with military inquiries, shielding the Crown forces from the consequences of the reprisals. The previous March, the jury in the inquest on the murdered Sinn Féin mayor of Cork, Tomás MacCurtáin, had laid the blame squarely at the door of the RIC and the British Cabinet: the jury at the inquest had no doubt who killed MacCurtáin. The coroner, James J. McCabe, examined ninety-seven witnesses in all, sixty-four of them being members of the RIC. The inquest took nearly a month before the jury, unimpressed by conflicts of evidence among senior RIC officers in the city, issued a verdict of 'wilful murder' against British Prime Minister Lloyd George and against a number of policemen, some named but with the actual killers described as 'unknown members of the RIC'. Collins's intelligence determined that the killer had been transferred for his own safety to Lisburn, Co. Antrim, and Detective Inspector Oswald Ross Swanzy was shot outside a church there on 22 August 1920. Swanzy was one who had been indicted for 'wilful murder' by the investigating jury. The IRA man who fired the first shots was Seán Culhane, who used MacCurtáin's own gun in the shooting. Dick Murphy and Roger McCorley were also present.[91] Collins wrote of a 'vicious circle':

> As I was in command I decided to collect all my evidence and play them at their own game. This was the start of the vicious circle—the murder race. I intercepted all the correspondence. Inspector Swanzy put Lord Mayor MacCurtáin away so I got Swanzy and all his associates wiped out, one by one, in all parts of Ireland to which the murderers had been secretly dispersed. What else could I do?[92]

The Unionists' reaction to his killing was beyond Collins's worst expectations. Catholic homes (including the parish priest's house) and businesses were burnt in retaliation, and after three days of looting and destruction the entire Catholic population of 1,000 could take no more and fled the town *en masse*. This pattern was soon to establish itself. IRA attacks were followed by the inevitable reprisals. Many of these were the work of Orange mobs and UVF gunmen, but there is clear evidence of an official policy of reprisal at senior level.[93]

Throughout Ireland that pattern emerged whereby attacks by the IRA on Crown forces were followed by British reprisals in which civilians were killed and injured and buildings destroyed or looted. Many such reprisals took place around the country, but the burning of the small town of Balbriggan in north County Dublin in particular received worldwide attention because of its proximity to the capital, where national newspapers and foreign correspondents were based.[94] In addition to the death of two suspected IRA men, the local hosiery factory was burned down, and forty-nine houses and four pubs were destroyed.[95] Further, in December 1920 the Black and Tans sacked County Cork and its capital, Cork City, in a 'wild orgy of looting, wrecking, burning, and drinking'.[96] They set fire to the whole of Patrick Street (the main business district in Cork City), and when the fire brigade came to put it out the Black and Tans cut the hoses with bayonets and turned off the hydrants in order to ensure its complete destruction.[97] In total, the Black and Tans caused damage costing £2.5 million in Cork alone, an amount equal to approximately £90 million today.[98] These examples demonstrate how the British forces used terrorism to crush Irish nationalism by showing the Irish population the debilitating economic consequences of fighting Britain. Florence O'Donoghue wrote that the burning and looting of Cork was not an isolated incident but the application of a policy initiated and approved, implicitly or explicitly, by the British government, and that the British actions were

> a policy of subjugation by terror, murder and rapine, of government by force of arms, of the deliberate destruction of those industries and resources whose absence would inflict the greatest hardship and loss upon the nation; of ruthless hunting down and extermination of those who stood for national freedom.[99]

The British scorched-earth policy began with the burning of the town of Balbriggan by a Black and Tan detachment.[100] On 20 September two Black and Tans were shot in a public house. No evidence was submitted to a court as to who fired the shots and one account said that the shooting was the result of a quarrel, but one of the IRA men later described what happened in his witness statement:

> I ordered them [Black and Tan Head Constable Peter Burke and his brother Sergeant William Burke] to clear out, instead of doing so, they made a rush at me and I had no option but to fire. I shot one of the Head Constables [sic] in the head and wounded the other, who later recovered [Sergeant Burke died on the spot and Head Constable Burke died later], and then my pal and I cleared out the back door and got safely away.[101]

Black and Tans and Auxiliaries were based at the nearby Gormanstown Camp and up to 150 of them descended on Balbriggan that night, intent on revenge. Two young local men, Séamus Lawless and Seán Gibbons, were bayoneted to death on the street by the 'Tans', and a memorial today marks the spot where they were murdered.[102] The British forces proceeded to smash the windows of shops and houses in the small town and then set fire to a hosiery factory, which was completely destroyed. They burned down forty-nine houses, forcing families to flee. Some had to take refuge in the fields.

The foreign press covered the destruction of Balbriggan, the *Manchester Guardian* editorialising about an 'Irish Louvain' and continuing:

To realise the full horrors of that night, one has to think of bands of men inflamed with drink, raging about the streets, firing rifles wildly, burning houses here and there loudly threatening to come again tonight and complete their work.[103]

The Irish and foreign press were united in their condemnation of the Black and Tan reprisals. The *Freeman's Journal* compared it to 'one of the Belgian towns that had been sacked by the invaders'[104] and the *London Daily News* editorialised on 'the barbarous "reprisals" now being systematically and openly carried out by the Black and Tans',[105] while the *Birmingham Post* commented in its editorial that 'it is not by means of reprisals that order can be restored'.[106]

Hamar Greenwood stated in the House of Commons that the Balbriggan episode was regrettable but he proposed no punishments for those involved. He believed instead that 'the best and the surest way to stop reprisals is to stop the murder of policemen',[107] a sentiment he had expressed almost word for word twelve days earlier in the *Weekly Summary*.[108] Mark Sturgis wrote in his diary that if the Auxiliaries had simply 'confined themselves to the dignified shooting of the two prominent Shinners, notorious bad men, the reprisals would have been not so bad ... worse things can happen than the firing up of a sink like Balbriggan'.[109] At the same time that individuals at various levels of the British administration were permitting and encouraging both reprisals and the killings of alleged Sinn Féiners, the press was beginning to recognise that these things were taking place and to criticise the government for allowing them. While the *Irish Bulletin*, which reported such acts throughout the conflict, gained greater credibility among the mainstream press, the *Weekly Summary's* defence of reprisals made the newspaper increasingly infamous and unbelievable.

In fairness, not all descriptions of the Balbriggan 'incident' are Irish-oriented. In his *Protest in Arms* Holt describes the attack as 'the somewhat exaggerated account of the raid on Balbriggan'.[110] He relates that

> Irish propaganda described the affair as 'the sack of Balbriggan', but in fact the damage, wanton though it was, was confined to one part of the town, and only one out of several factories was destroyed. Balbriggan was certainly not burnt to the ground. When Macready went there a few days later he thought that a person who did not know what had happened might have motored through the town without realising there had been an incident.

In his essay 'The price of Balbriggan', David Fitzpatrick gives an indication of the damage to the town. The compensation for the damage paid out by the British government could never fully recompense the victims for their material losses—nor, obviously, for the human costs of the war—but the amount noted by Fitzpatrick would indicate that there was a great deal of damage to the town.[111] However much the Irish propagandists embellished the story, it was certainly effective in creating a worldwide view of the brutality and wanton actions of the Black and Tans and Auxiliaries. The *New York Times* reported the story as 'two attacks' in 'a special cable to the *New York Times*':

> The first onslaught early this morning lasted for two hours, and the second began in the afternoon.
>
>   ...
>
> These reprisals followed quickly on the murder of Head Constable Burke and his brother Sergeant Burke.
>
> When news of the outrage reached Gormanstown, where the RIC are stationed, a large body started off in motor lorries ... and the town was given over to ruthless reprisals.
>
> Scenes of the wildest disorder reigned. Some of the

inhabitants assert that they were driven from their homes at the point of a bayonet. One woman only just succeeded in rescuing her baby from its cot before the house was burned.

This morning the roads leading from the town were crowded with fleeing women and children, some wheeling perambulators

...

In many cases they were bleeding as a result of being hit by flying glass and debris. The Dublin hospitals are dealing with casualties.[112]

Six weeks later, British reprisals took place in Granard, Co. Longford, where the IRA assassinated District Inspector Philip Kelleher on 31 October. On the night of 3 November uniformed men entered the town and burned down a number of buildings. The same night, a convoy of military and police was ambushed in the nearby town of Ballinalee and forced to retreat.[113] *The Times* correspondent visited both towns the following day and described Granard as a scene 'that can scarcely be imagined in a town which is not in the throes of actual war. Most of the businesses and the market hall were smoking ruins.'[114] Despite official denials, the writer concluded that 'No reasonable man ... could come to any other conclusion than that this terrible punishment had been inflicted on the town by the R.I.C.'.

By late 1920 some Irish newspapers were risking official censorship by their editorials. The *Irish Independent* declared that 'Nobody in Ireland accepts as truthful any statement made by the British Government'.[115] Even the *Irish Times*, usually a loyalist paper, editorialised about the reprisals:

If only the people in Britain knew. Everywhere in Ireland today you hear that cry 'why do these things happen?' Why are servants of the Crown not charged with pillage and arson and what amounts to lynch law even with drunkenness and murder! How can the reign of terror be stopped?[116]

Despite the wave of attacks, in November 1920 Lloyd George assured a Guildhall audience in the City of London that British forces were winning the conflict. According to the prime minister, 'We have murder by the throat in Ireland'. He described the rebel campaign as 'a spectacle of organized assassination, of the most cowardly character'. He then insisted that 'There will be no peace in Ireland, there will be no conciliation, until this murder conspiracy is scattered'. After the reorganisation of the police, 'we struck the terror, and the terrorists are now complaining of terror'.[117] An editorial in *The Times* argued that the prime minister 'committed himself to war upon large sections of the Irish people and his government was engaged in an effort to scourge Ireland into obedience'.[118]

Tom Barry put the Irish strategy of retaliation for British burnings into effect in County Cork:

> … what I did was to stop the destruction of our property by the British. It was [British Major A.E.] Percival started it: they started burning up houses in the martial law area, small farmers' houses, labourers' cottages. Well, the only way you can fight terror is with terror, that's the only thing that an imperialist nation will understand. We sent a message to them that for every house of ours they burned, we'd burn two of the big houses, the Loyalist mansions. That wasn't a policy from Dublin. If you had a GHQ at the time of seven Napoleons it wouldn't have done any good because of the lack of communications. But the British went on with their burning campaign, and they found out that we meant what we said because we kept raising the ante … When they burned four, we burned eight. And we didn't let them just sell up their lands and run back to England. We put a ban on all sales of this property because we weren't going to have them leave Ireland with money in their pockets from land they'd stolen from the people.[119]

At times the IRA turned to terror against those of the Irish population whom they thought were helping the British, as well as against British or loyalist targets. In January 1921, Cork Brigade No. 2 reported that they were experiencing a great deal of hostility from local farmers and that they were finding it hard to billet in their area. 'What is to be done with such people?'[120] The IRA resorted to terrorism to keep the people 'in line', and Tom Barry admitted that executions were necessary in 1921. In May 1921 his column reported that an ambush had had to be abandoned and Barry blamed an informer whom 'he was unable to trace'.[121] As another example of local units acting without GHQ authorisation (or 'claimed knowledge'), Richard Mulcahy insisted that no civilian should be liable for IRA punishment 'unless they were active enemies of the national cause'. On 14 May 1921 he wrote to Cathal Brugha (Minister for Defence) that 'no-one shall be regarded as an enemy of the state, whether they be described locally as a Unionist, Orangeman, except that they are actively anti-Irish in their outlook and in their actions'.[122] Yet Barry admitted that he never sought sanction for any execution.[123] He went further in his dismissive opinion of GHQ: 'right through to the end our General Headquarters didn't know what a flying column was doing until they read about it in the paper'.[124]

Barry identified the three groups liable to be executed as 'spies and informers':

- Irishmen who 'sold out for gold',
- ex-servicemen who still owed allegiance to Britain, and
- wealthy landowners with a vested interest in maintaining the British government.[125]

Michael Hopkinson has expressed another view, in that the increased British effectiveness in Cork in 1921 'emphasised the need to root out informers and led to a big rise in the execution of so-called spies leading to something of a "vendetta"'.[126] The British report after the war indicated that there were many in the area who were giving information to the British, and the IRA killed those whom they suspected of doing so. The report noted that Protestant loyalists in west Cork had actively assisted the British

> ... in the Bandon area where there were many Protestant farmers who gave information. Although the Intelligence Officer of the area was exceptionally experienced and although the troops were most active it proved almost impossible to protect those brave men, many of whom were murdered while almost all the remainder suffered grave material harm ...[127]

In recent years, Peter Hart has written that 'many suspects were guilty only by association. Almost all victims were officially described as "spies or informers", but in practice this could mean anything.' Hart found that, though some were genuine 'spies and informers', many were just those who did not assist the IRA.[128] 'They were killed not for what they did but for who they were: Protestants, ex-soldiers, tramps and so on down the communal blacklist.'[129] Hart contended: 'It might be suggested that Protestants and ex-soldiers were naturally hostile to the IRA, and more likely to be working with the police and military, and to be shot. This was not so. The authorities obtained little information from either group and in fact by far the greatest damage was done by people within the organisation, or their relatives.'[130]

While there were certainly some killed to settle personal scores or in a 'vendetta', there were clearly those in Cork who were assisting the British.[131] The West Cork County Inspector reported in January 1921 that 'information is being freely given and I believe it will still be given'.[132] Further, the records of Major A.E. Percival, compiled after the war, give evidence that information was forthcoming from loyalists in Cork. His post-war lectures given to the British Staff College were definitive on the point:

> The most profitable methods [of obtaining information] were as follows:
>
> (i) Most important of all, an I.O. must move about the country and hunt for information. It will not come to him if he sits in his office all day.
>
> (ii) He must keep in close touch with the Loyalists—especially those who are not afraid to tell them what they know.
>
> This is not always an easy thing to do, as if the IRA suspected a Loyalist of giving information or being too friendly with the Crown Forces, it meant certain death for him. It was our usual practice therefore to approach their houses after dark and very long night journeys had to be made in order to do this.[133]

The British records after the war indicate that information was forthcoming from loyalists in the area, and that many suffered the consequences of talking to the British forces. British intelligence officers were constantly on the lookout for such information; while it proved invaluable, it also dried up as the war progressed. The officers had

> been considerably developed and better able to deal with any information which came to hand and that at the same time the proclamation of Martial Law had undoubtedly frightened a large number of civilians and made them more willing to give information to the Crown forces. This fact, apparently, was realised by the rebel leaders as, commencing in February, a regular murder campaign was instituted against Protestant Loyalists and anybody who might be suspected of being an 'informer', quite irrespective of whether he really was or not. This campaign was intensified as time went on, and it had the result of making information very hard to obtain.[134]

General Macready also indicated that information on the IRA was being given to British forces, and he reported to the Cabinet that the IRA was brutal in its attempts to halt the flow:

> Information continues to come in more freely and the murder lately of several men believed by the IRA to be informants points to the feeling of insecurity existing amongst them.[135]

Tom Barry noted instances in which he put on an Auxiliary uniform and talked to individuals in Cork, leading them to give information regarding IRA activities that would be of interest to the British. He did this in February 1921 with Thomas Bradfield, who had been accused of arranging 'to give further information [to the Auxiliaries] later on through his local clergyman and pressed very hard for the immediate capture and execution of certain local boys who were members of the IRA'.[136] Barry met with Bradfield in uniform, and when Bradfield was deceived into giving information leading to Barry's column Barry had him killed that night.[137] Barry and the other Irish leaders determined that they would make it 'unhealthy' for Irishmen to betray their fellows, and to make it deadly for the British to exploit them.

Those who were deemed 'spies and informers' were not just executed in County Cork or the south-west and Munster.[138] Moreover, some of the witness statements taken by the Bureau of Military History in the 1940s–50s demonstrate that the Irish also committed barbarous acts throughout Ireland, but these are seldom glamorised in more romantic accounts. One of the most grisly executions happened in County Kilkenny, for example. William Kenny, an ex-British soldier who had reported the IRA's activities to the RIC, was executed in August 1920. When John Walsh, the O/C in Kilkenny, determined that the British might hear the gunfire if Kenny was shot, the IRA chose another method for his execution.

> We gagged and blindfolded him, and having bound his arms and legs, we dropped him into the River Barrow just a few yards from [Blanchfield's] eel house. The water at this point would be 8 or 10 feet deep and, as an additional precaution, we tied a 56 lb weight to his body before dropping him into the river. As far as I can now recollect, the date of Kenny's execution was 31 August 1920. About two months later, his decomposed body was washed ashore about three miles down the river and, with two other volunteers, I had the gruesome task of again tying weights and heavy stones to the body and dropping it into the river for a second time.[139]

Whether or not it was the only way open to them, and whether or not it can be justified, the reality was that the Irish chose terror on this scale in order to discourage the passing of information to the British, as well as to settle local scores and to exact revenge on people considered to be pro-British in retaliation for the sufferings of northern nationalists.

After two years of terror and counter-terror, many in nationalist Ireland had come to accept the idea of a war against the British state. By then, to voice criticism anywhere in Ireland would have been distinctly dangerous. The degree of enthusiasm for political violence is difficult to gauge, but it varied greatly by age, by social class, by locality and even by gender.[140] Leaders of the IRA were quite open about this in later years. In fact, it was a matter of pride to recall what little support they had initially enjoyed and how it was necessary to 'manufacture' that support.

If part of the story of the War of Independence was of a cycle of attack and reprisal, another part was of a tactical game of wits in which the Crown forces attempted to prevent guerrilla attacks and to track down and destroy the guerrillas themselves—and, in reverse, the Irish forces trying to track down British intelligence agents and 'spies and informers'. In recognition of the reluctance of the nationalist population to support an IRA offensive, Richard Mulcahy believed that the people had to be educated and 'led gently into open war'.[141] Collins and the Irish military acted from a position of certainty on the course of action that the people of Ireland ought to pursue, and thus there was an Anglo-Irish war. For many, however, this was a terror-laden strategy that had been imposed on them.

The IRA commanders in the field recognised that they needed popular support to survive. In the first half of 1921, however, some of them were reporting increasing public hostility towards the IRA in a number of regions. This raised questions among the Irish leadership concerning how long they could remain a viable force. As always, politics were important, and with such difficulties in mind the Sinn Féin leadership became more interested in a negotiated settlement.[142] Further, the IRA's continual sniping, ambushing and attacking in Dublin provided a great deal of propaganda value throughout the war. The attacks showed the world, and particularly the members of the international press who visited Dublin, that the British government was not in control of what had to be the most heavily patrolled city of the time. Richard Mulcahy was firmly of the view that Dublin was the most important military objective in the country. He felt that such attacks there as appeared in the international and British press counted for much more than anything else happening in the country.

Actions were not limited to the southern counties of Ireland. Republican activity in Londonderry and Belfast, which were rocked by sectarian riots throughout the conflict, took on an organised nature.[143] Police and military posts were simultaneously attacked in Derry on 1 April, and British propagandist C.J.C. Street pronounced that attacks on Belfast police became routine.[144]

Action in Northern Ireland was alarming, but attacks in Britain itself threatened public panic. In 1920 the IRA extended their attacks to the British mainland. John Pinkman wrote:

The ordinary English people couldn't have cared less about what was happening in Ireland, being unconcerned about these reports of murder and destruction there. IRA headquarters in Dublin wanted to impress upon the English people that a war of terror was being waged in their name against the Irish people, and reluctantly ordered massive reprisals to be carried out in England to show the English the kind of havoc that was being wrought in Ireland.[145]

Rory O'Connor, who was O/C Britain at the time, coordinated the attacks there. GHQ instructed him to confine the attacks to England: there were to be no attacks in Scotland or Wales. He was also told to minimise civilian casualties as much as possible. Finally, he was told to avoid attacks on businesses, factories or farms that employed many Irish so as not to displace them from employment.

The November 1920 burnings of seventeen warehouses in Liverpool were just the first of a series of republican sabotage missions. Cathal Brugha pushed GHQ staff to emphasise operations in Britain; by March 1921 this had evolved into a sustained campaign, and Brugha led squads of Volunteers to London on abortive assassination missions.[146] Nationalism blossomed in all the 'Little Irelands' in British cities, and by 1921 there were more than 2,500 Volunteers in Britain. The IRA terrorism in Britain was motivated at least partly by revenge. When Ernie O'Malley reported to Dublin in July 1920, he told GHQ that the country officers 'pressed hard for a campaign in Britain to counteract the destruction of creameries by the military and RIC'.[147] When Collins sent men to Britain, he told them that their attacks were 'by way of reprisals that were being carried out by Black and Tans'.[148] In his witness statement Paddy O'Donohue said that Collins's aim was 'to bring home to the British people the sufferings and conditions to which the Irish were being subjected'.[149] Liverpool IRA officer Edward M. Brady said that the arson and sabotage efforts were in retaliation for the destruction wrought by police in Ireland.[150]

The first attacks were on warehouses on the Liverpool docks on 27 November 1920. On 9 March 1921, a series of fires began to break out at farms in Cheshire, Lancashire and Liverpool.[151] Three days later, *The Times* reported that republicans had specifically targeted property near Liverpool owned by an Auxiliary section leader serving in Ireland.[152] One of Collins's agents was John Harrington, a young doctor at Richmond Hospital in North Brunswick Street. He had access to the medical records of members of the British forces treated at the hospital and at the North Dublin Union, and he was able to pass along to intelligence their home addresses in Britain. This resulted in the fire-bombing of the homes of many relatives of Auxiliaries or Black and Tans in retaliation for reprisals. On 2 April fires broke out in various hotels in Manchester.[153] In April 1921 armed IRA men raided Lyons' Café in Manchester, firing shots into the air to disperse customers and staff and dousing the premises in paraffin. Before setting the building alight, one Volunteer explained their actions: 'We are doing what you are doing in Ireland'.[154] In May a London timber-yard went up in flames, and republicans raided and burned the homes of Auxiliaries and Black and Tans in the capital, St Albans and Liverpool.[155] During the night of 16 June, armed and masked men raided railway stations all around London. They assaulted railway employees, burned signal huts, cut telegraph and signal wires, and fired on police when they tried to interfere.[156] The campaign had the desired effect of altering the normal course of life in Britain. Between 1 and 3 July, London police searched carts, examined drivers' licences and noted vehicles moving in and out of the city. The *New York Times* correspondent wrote that there 'was practically a complete cordon' around the capital.[157]

One of the most famous attacks in Britain was an assassination that took place after the Treaty and was one of the immediate precipitating factors leading to the start of the Civil War in June 1922. Following Bloody Sunday, Field Marshal Sir Henry Wilson pleaded with Churchill for the imposition of martial law in Ireland, and that was finally done on 10 December 1920. After retiring from the army in December 1921, Wilson served briefly as a Member of Parliament and also as security adviser to the Northern Ireland (Unionist) government. He was an unrepentant imperialist and Unionist, and thought the Truce and Treaty irresponsible. At the time, he was acting as military adviser to the Northern Ireland government and was particularly close to James Craig. The Treaty of 6 December 1921 split the republican movement in Britain as thoroughly as in Ireland, with pro- and anti-Treaty camps rapidly being established on either side of an uncertain middle ground.

Thus was precipitated the assassination of Wilson on 22 June 1922 by Reggie Dunne, O/C of the London IRA, and another London veteran of the British army, Joseph O'Sullivan.[158] Wilson had been trailed on a journey to unveil a war memorial at Liverpool Street Station, London. Following the ceremony, he returned home, where O'Sullivan and Dunne shot him as he was walking between the taxi from which he had just alighted and the door of his residence in Eaton Square.[159]

> Joe went in a straight line while I determined to intercept him [Wilson] from entering the door. Joe deliberately levelled his weapon at four yards range and fired twice. Wilson made for the door as best he could and actually reached the doorway when I encountered him at a range of seven or eight feet. I fired three shots rapidly, the last one from the hip, as I took a step forward. Wilson was now uttering short cries and in a doubled up position staggered towards the edge of the pavement. At this point Joe fired again and the last I saw of him he [Wilson] had collapsed.[160]

In addition to Wilson, two policemen and a civilian were wounded whilst O'Sullivan and Dunne tried to escape; however, they were quickly caught and arrested. O'Sullivan had lost a leg in World War I, so an attempt to escape on foot seems incomprehensible. Moreover, their lack of planning was apparent: they had no escape system arranged and had to find and buy their own weapons only a week before the shooting. O'Sullivan had gone to work that day and the assassination was carried out on his lunch break.[161]

The motives for Wilson's killing are not difficult to find. Seán Moylan recalled that Collins often stated that Wilson was a thorn in his side and repeatedly made the procurement of arms in Britain much more difficult. Dunne, like most Irish nationalists, was growing more and more outraged by the continuing attacks on Catholics in Northern Ireland and he blamed Wilson, in his capacity as military adviser to the Northern Ireland government, for those attacks.[162] Nevertheless, while the motives may be suggested, the question of who was ultimately responsible remains more elusive.

It has become accepted (although it was not publicly known at the time) that Collins ordered Wilson's assassination some months previously.[163] British suspicions regarding Collins's involvement were suggested, as documentation mentioning Collins had allegedly been found on the arrested men.[164] Moreover, Joe Sweeney, the pro-Treaty military leader in County Donegal, recalled that Collins informed him of his decision to order the shooting of Wilson. In addition, Sweeney stated that Collins seemed very pleased upon hearing the news that the order had been carried out.[165] Conversely, Emmet Dalton, one of Collins's closest confidants at the time, indicated that 'Collins was angry that the London IRA had taken an irresponsible attitude "at this time"'.[166] Dorothy Macardle wrote that 'popular belief attributed the assassination to the IRB. It was thought Michael Collins ordered it.'[167] Margery Forester agreed:

> There can be little doubt that such an order [for Wilson's assassination] had been given, most probably by Collins, in pre-Treaty days … But Collins was not a man who absent-mindedly left execution orders unrevoked. It is infinitely more probable that, far from doing so, he renewed the order to Dunne shortly before it was carried out, when the Belfast pogroms were at their height.[168]

There is no clear and convincing evidence that Dunne and O'Sullivan were the tools of a conspiracy or that Collins gave the order in particular. The attack itself did not bear the hallmarks of a well-planned and organised assault, as had those by Collins's Squad throughout the war. Collins briefly met Dunne only two weeks before the assassination, but the results of that meeting are not known. It was one of the most infamous terrorist actions of the war, and no one knows who gave the order.[169]

It must be said that, in a way, the British and Irish terrorist methods worked. The Black and Tans and Auxiliaries so cowed the Irish that many simply ran away and deserted their homes and businesses at the thought that the 'Tans' or 'Auxies' were coming to an area. On the other hand, local populations often asked the IRA/Volunteers to move along. IRA leaders were told that if they ambushed a lorry in the morning, the British would return at night to take their revenge on the local town and population, and the IRA would shift their operations elsewhere. As a result, the British were often able to impose their will on a population just by intimidation, while further intimidation of the population often allowed the Irish forces to remain in an area where they were not welcome. Ronan Fanning, Professor at University College Dublin, in his 1975 lecture 'Transition from revolution to politics' said that 'violence will always hold the key to success'.[170] He stressed that 'all revolutionaries demonstrate ambivalence toward democracy'.[171] In 2013 Fanning and Martin Mansergh[172] reviewed and discussed David Fitzpatrick's book *Terror in Ireland*[173] on an RTÉ radio show.[174] (Both questioned whether 'political violence' should be substituted for 'terror' in the book's essays.) Fanning and Mansergh agreed that the War of Independence did 'not degenerate to a war of ambushes and assassinations' because the war did not 'degenerate'—that was the chosen strategy of the Irish leaders. Those leaders had seen the defeat of the Easter Rising and recognised that a new and different strategy was necessary. They 'believed that a strategy of assassinations and ambushes would work—and it did'. Fanning further noted the question in the introduction of the book, 'Could a mutually acceptable settlement in Ireland be achieved without terror?', and he said that 'My answer, regretfully, is "No"'. Mansergh interjected: 'Or not unless different people acted in very different ways'. Mansergh reiterated: 'Don't imagine for a second that violence doesn't produce results. It may not produce the results one wants—but it works.' Fanning concluded that 'war is hell, and hellish actions result', and Mansergh noted that 'it doesn't have to be guerrilla war—it is in all wars'. War is dehumanising and brutal, and guerrilla war is particularly so. We don't like the thought of terror being effective — but it works. On both sides, military action could only go so far, but military action was necessary in conjunction with political and propaganda pressures.

> There is not a shred of evidence that Lloyd George's Tory-dominated government would have moved from the 1914-style niggardliness of the Government of Ireland Act of 1920 to the larger, if imperfect generosity of the Treaty if they had not been compelled to do so by Michael Collins and his assassins. Indeed, the evidence points the other way.[175]

Overall, the IRA was able to mobilise public support throughout the war—slowly at first, and then the Irish public became more in step with the Irish separatist aspirations. Initially this was an expression of constitutional nationalism that was embodied in the protests against conscription in 1918.[176] The identification of Sinn Féin with popular issues in 1917–18 also led to support for more radical policies, but such support was not universal. Beginning in 1917, intimidation and violence were necessary during arms raids, and after 1918 to enforce the alternative Irish administration and the boycott of British institutions. Direct defiance of British rule, such as non-payment of taxes, required a large measure of enforcement. Moreover, the need for public support meant that the Irish rarely inflicted serious injuries, and the focus on 'hearts and minds' prevented most injuries from being reported to the British.[177] O'Donoghue wrote of 'one thing they [the British] lacked which the IRA had in generous measure—the co-operation of the people and without it they were blind and impotent'.[178]

Indiscriminate violence utilised by the British forces aggravated the population to a much greater extent than similar IRA violence and helped to justify the Irish military campaign, at least in international opinion. The 'emotive' effect of the British violence was far stronger. Combined with the fear and intimidation, it enabled the IRA to operate safely in many areas.[179] In Dublin, the divided loyalty of the population did inspire violence against some anti-republican civilians, but the relatively anonymous environment ensured a relatively safe functioning of the IRA.

The success of the IRA and the level of violence directed at the British depended on two factors: its ability to organise people behind it and the capacity to deal with the opposition it encountered in the community. Those factors, then, were connected with the IRA's integration within the community and the continued support for constitutional or military means of securing Irish independence.[180] Still, one must accept that violence was used by both sides. Sebastian Barry's words are hard to improve upon:

> We may or may not damn all sides of that era equally, but we must be prepared to acknowledge sins committed by those with whom we agree as well as those with whom we disagree.

Basil Thomson, Director of Intelligence for the British Home Office, wrote to Lloyd George in April 1921:

> The country folk who were opposed to the operations of the IRA ... do not now mind, and although they are opposed to murders they are in favour of ambushes. They are beginning to be proud of their Irish heroes, in spite of all the restrictions imposed by martial law.[181]

Ultimately, some writers concluded that the IRA conduct during the war, though often violent, was carefully calculated not to exceed the limits of what the Irish public would allow.[182] Vladimir Lenin was alleged to have said that 'The purpose of terrorism is to terrorise', although the statement has also been attributed to Michael Collins. Whatever its origin, the theory worked well for both. The IRA took great pains to identify itself as the legitimate military arm of a representative Irish government fighting against a foreign invader, but a further examination indicates not only that the Irish used terrorism themselves but also that it was their policy to provoke British terrorism for propaganda and political purposes. 'The IRA was helped not only by its own circumspection but also by British violence that undermined that government's legitimacy.'[183] The response of the Irish, British and international press to terrorism cannot be overemphasised in explaining Lloyd George's agreement to negotiate with the Irish.

Collins and the Irish were astute enough to avoid what they saw as excesses, especially against the common people of Ireland. Collins's restraint, recognition of the need to 'pace' the war and most of all his realism were his strengths. Unlike most guerrilla leaders, he knew when to stop fighting even though he had not achieved all of his goals.

Notes

1   Burton M. Leiser, 'Terrorism, guerrilla warfare, and international morality', *Stanford Journal of International Studies*, vol. 39 (1977); Charles R. King, 'Revolutionary war, guerrilla warfare, and international law', *Case Reserve Journal of International Law*, vol. 91 (1972); G.I.A.D. Draper, 'The status of combatants and the question of guerrilla warfare', *British Year Book of International Law*, vol. 173 (1971).

2   Anne Schwenkenbecher, *Terrorism: A Philosophical Inquiry* (e-book: https://www.palgrave.com/us/book/9780230363984).

3   E.J. Doyle, 'The employment of terror in the forgotten insurgency: Ireland 1919–1922', unpublished MS dissertation, US Defense Intelligence College, Bethesda, MD (1969).

4   Stephen Donovan, 'The multiple functions of terrorism: how the IRA used terrorism to resist British control while the British utilized terror to conquer the Irish people' (https://www.trentu.ca.undergratuate/documents//S.Donovan.doc).

5   Robert W. White, 'From gunmen to politicians: the impact of terrorism and political violence on twentieth-century Ireland', *Journal of Conflict Studies*, vol. 27, no. 2 (2007).

6   Richard Clutterbuck, *Guerrillas and Terrorists* (Athens, OH, 1980), p. 24; *Terrorism and Guerrilla Warfare* (London and New York, 1990).

7   Scott Stewart, 'The difference between terrorism and insurgency', *Strategy* (26 June 2014); Ariel Merari, 'Terrorism as a strategy of insurgency', *Terrorism and Political Violence*,

vol. 5, no. 4 (December 1993).

8 See Brian Hughes, *Defying the IRA: Intimidation, Coercion and Communities during the Irish Revolution* (Liverpool, 2016).

9 Courtney E. Prisk, 'The umbrella of legitimacy', in Max G. Manwaring (ed.), *Uncomfortable Wars:Toward a New Paradigm of Low Intensity Conflict* (Boulder, CO, 1991).

10 Thomas R. Mockaitis, *British Counterinsurgency, 1919–1960* (London, 1990), p. 37; 'The origins of British counterinsurgency', *Small Wars and Insurgencies*, vol. 1, no. 3 (December 1990).

11 Schwenkenbecher, *Terrorism: A Philosophical Inquiry.*

12 David Fitzpatrick (ed.), *Terror in Ireland, 1916–1923* (Dublin, 2013), p. 5.

13 US Government Counterinsurgency Guide (January 2009).

14 Schwenkenbecher, *Terrorism: A Philosophical Inquiry.*

15 Letter from Frank Gallagher to Joseph McGarrity, 25 June 1938.

16 Jane Leonard, '"English dogs" or "poor devils"? The dead of Bloody Sunday morning', in Fitzpatrick (ed.), *Terror in Ireland*. Leonard gives pen-portraits of the British killed on Bloody Sunday and indicates that most of them appeared to be officially employed in other posts, both military and non-military. It is unclear whether those were just 'aliases' and 'cover' jobs or whether the men were genuinely not intelligence agents. In contrast, see J.B.E. Hittle, *Michael Collins and the Anglo-Irish War: Britain's Counterinsurgency Failure* (Chicago, 2011), pp 162–89, in which he argues that all but two of the men were connected with British intelligence.

17 Anne Dolan, 'Killing and Bloody Sunday, November 1920', *Historical Journal*, vol. 49, no. 3 (2006).

18 Charles Dalton, Witness Statement 434; *With the Dublin Brigade* (London, 1929). See the Ernie O'Malley papers, UCD archives, p/17/b/1122/(22).

19 John Dorney, 'How the Civil War "murder gang" tried to take over as judge, jury and executioners', *Irish Independent*, 20 August 2017.

20 Quoted in Calton Younger, *Ireland's Civil War* (New York, 1969), pp 114–15. Vincent Byrne, Witness Statement 423.

21 Pat McCrea, Witness Statement 413.

22 Marie Coleman writes that, 'despite many bitter attacks and reprisals, serious and violent physical or sexual assaults against women were rare … Such violence was physical, psychological, and specific to gender (but falling short of sexual assault), rather than sexual or fatal … There is ample evidence attesting to physical assaults on women by the Black and Tans and Auxiliaries. Frequently this took the form of cutting off their hair … In September 1920 five members of Cumann na mBan in Galway were subjected to this unofficial punishment in reprisal for a similar attack carried out by the IRA on a woman who had given evidence to a military court. This incident indicates that the IRA was equally liable to commit such attacks and there are many instances of women who were friendly with the police or who worked for them being treated similarly. The majority of violence against women perpetrated by the IRA was the "victimisation of policemen's wives and barrack servants" … The first Dáil's efforts, albeit unsuccessful, to achieve foreign recognition for the republic would have been hampered by reports of callous treatment of women. In a similar vein, the British authorities in Ireland would have been well aware of the potential damage to Britain's reputation internationally if stories of rape and sexual assault of Irish women began to emerge. From the British viewpoint the avoidance of sexual violence allowed them to

draw a clear contrast with their recent enemy, the autocratic Germany of the Kaiser, whose army had resorted to widespread rape and sexual assault in Belgium at the start of the First World War … Violence towards women was certainly a feature of the War of Independence, yet the evidence available indicates that it was limited in nature and scope. The targeted killing of females was very rare.' Marie Coleman, 'Women escaped the worst of the brutalities in the War of Independence', *Irish Examiner*, 27 November 2015; 'Violence against women in the Irish War of Independence, 1919–1921', in Diarmuid Ferriter and S. Riordan (eds), *Years of Turbulence: The Irish Revolution and its Aftermath* (Dublin, 2015); Louise Ryan, '"Drunken Tans": representation of sex and violence in the Anglo-Irish War (1919–1921)', *Feminist Review*, no. 66 (Autumn 2000). In contrast, Linda Connolly argues that 'women were in fact the subject of sexual assaults and violent attacks during the period which may have not been reported and therefore the evidence needs to be re-examined'. Linda Connolly, 'Sexual violence a dark secret in the Irish War of Independence and Civil War', *Irish Times*, 10 January 2018; Ailin Quinlan, 'Wartime sexual violence against women "ignored"', *Irish Times*, 9 July 2018); Linda Connolly, 'Did women escape the worst of the brutalities between 1919–1921?' (https://www.maynoothuniversity.ie/research/research-news-events/ latest-news/did-women-escape-worst-brutalities-between-1919-1921); Niall Murray, 'The rarely spoken about violence against women during the Irish revolution', *Irish Examiner*, 12 September 2017. See Gabrielle Machnik-Kékesi, 'Gendering bodies: violence as performance in Ireland's War of Independence (1919–1921)', unpublished MA thesis, Concordia University Montreal (2017).

[23] Michael Richardson, 'Terrorism: trauma in the excess of affect', in R. Kurtz (ed.), *Cambridge Critical Concepts: Trauma and Literature* (Cambridge, 2018).

[24] Giovanni Costigan, 'The Anglo-Irish conflict, 1919–1921: a war of independence or systematized murder?', *University Review*, vol. 5, no. 1 (1968).

[25] Che Guevara, *Principles of Guerrilla Warfare* (http://www3.uakron.edu/worldciv/ pascher/che.html).

[26] C.S. Andrews, *Dublin Made Me* (Cork, 1979), p. 60. See M.C. Havens, Carl Leiden and Karl M. Schmit, *The Politics of Assassination* (Englewood Cliffs, NJ, 1970).

[27] Tom Bowden, *Beyond the Limits of the Law* (London, 1978), p. 159.

[28] Tom Garvin, *1922: The Birth of Irish Democracy* (Dublin, 1996), p. 159.

[29] G. Sitaraman, 'Counterinsurgence, the War on Terror and the laws of war', *Virginia Law Review* (2009).

[30] Guevara, *Principles of Guerrilla Warfare*.

[31] G.K. Chesterton, *What are Reprisals?* (pamphlet, undated, no place of publication).

[32] See Katherine Hughes, *English Atrocities in Ireland: A Compilation of Facts from Court and Press Records* (New York, 1920).

[33] Tom Bowden, 'The Irish underground and the War of Independence 1919–1921', *Journal of Contemporary History*, vol. 8, no. 2 (1973).

[34] Charles Townshend, *The British Campaign in Ireland, 1919–1921* (Oxford, 1975), pp 40–57.

[35] J.L. Hammond, 'A tragedy of errors', *The Nation*, 8 January 1921; 'The terror in action', *The Nation*, 30 April 1921.

[36] See Brian Hughes, *Defying the IRA*.

[37] M. Elliott-Bateman, 'Ireland: the impact of terror', in Michael Elliott-Bateman, John Ellis and Tom Bowden (eds), *Revolt to Revolution—Studies in the 19th and 20th Century*

European Experience (Manchester, 1974).

[38] Joost Augusteijn, *From Public Defiance to Guerrilla Warfare* (Dublin, 1996), pp 251 *et seq.*, 294 *et seq.*, 310 *et seq.*

[39] See Peter Hart, *The IRA and its Enemies: Violence and Community in Cork, 1916–1923* (Oxford, 1998); Charles Townshend, 'The Irish Republican Army and the development of guerrilla warfare, 1916–1921', *English Historical Review*, vol. 94, no. 371 (1979); David Fitzpatrick, *Politics and Irish Life, 1913–1921: Provincial Experience of War and Revolution* (Dublin, 1977); Cormac O'Malley, *The Men will Talk to Me* (Cork, 2010); William Sheehan (ed.), *British Voices from the Irish War of Independence 1918–1921: The Words of British Servicemen Who Were There* (Cork, 2007); Meda Ryan, *Tom Barry: IRA Freedom Fighter* (Cork, 2003); Barry Keane, 'The IRA response to Loyalist co-operation during the Irish War of Independence, 1919–1921' (https:// www.academia.edu/27954537/ The_IRA_response_to_Loyalist_cooperation_in_County_Cork_during_the_Irish_Wa r_of_Independence). Hart's *The IRA and its Enemies* (and the follow-up articles and reviews) has been the subject of a voluminous and rancorous debate in Ireland since its publication in 1998. In academic journals, in the press and in the electronic media Hart has been accused repeatedly of deliberately distorting evidence. The controversy turns on Hart's depiction of Irish revolutionary violence, and in particular on a chapter entitled 'Taking it out on the Protestants', in which the IRA was portrayed as fundamentally sectarian. The articles and books are far too extensive for complete inclusion here, but one should be aware that there are many sides to the debate and seek further information for a balanced view of the claims and counter-claims regarding 'informers' in the War of Independence (particularly in County Cork), and whether the IRA engaged in killings outside the bounds of war which could be termed 'ethnic cleansing'. Andrew Bielenberg, 'Protestant emigration from the south of Ireland, 1911–1926' (lecture given at the 'Understanding our history: Protestants, the War of Independence, and the Civil War in Cork' conference at University College Cork, 13 December 2008). See note 131.

[40] O'Malley papers, P 17 b 88; Andrews, *Dublin Made Me*, p. 90.

[41] CI, MCR, Dublin, January 1919, CO 904/108.

[42] For a discussion of the effects and consequences of terror on individuals see Anne Dolan, 'The shadow of a great fear: terror and revolutionary Ireland', in Fitzpatrick (ed.), *Terror in Ireland*.

[43] John M. Regan, *The Memoirs of John M. Regan, a Catholic Officer in the RIC and RUC: 1909–1948* (ed. Joost Augusteijn) (Dublin, 2007); Samuel Waters, *A Policeman's Ireland: Recollections of Samuel Waters, RIC* (ed. Stephen Ball) (Cork, 1999).

[44] P.B. Leonard, 'The necessity of de-Anglicising the Irish nation: boycotting and the Irish War of Independence', unpublished Ph.D thesis, University of Melbourne (2000).

[45] CI, MCR, Clare, October 1917, CO 904/103.

[46] Brian Hughes, 'Persecuting the Peelers', in Fitzpatrick (ed.), *Terror in Ireland*.

[47] CI, MCR, Roscommon, January 1920, CO 904/114.

[48] W.J. Lowe, 'The war against the RIC, 1919–1921', *Éire-Ireland*, vol. 37, nos 3–4 (2002).

[49] Fitzpatrick (ed.), *Terror in Ireland*, p. 8.

[50] A.G. Gardiner, 'Stop the Terror', *Daily News*, 6 November 1920.

[51] S. Tery, 'Raids and reprisals: Ireland: Eye-witness (1923)' (trans. Marilyn Gaddis Rose), *Éire-Ireland* (Summer 1985).

[52] Mao Zedong, in Edmund Jocelyn and Andrew McEwen, *The Long March* (London,

2006), p. 46.

53   Michael Hopkinson, *The Irish War of Independence* (Dublin, 2004), p. 79.

54   Edgar Holt, *Protest in Arms* (New York, 1960), pp 210–20.

55   James Slattery, Witness Statement 445.

56   Andrew Silke, 'Ferocious times: the IRA, the RIC, and Britain's failure in 1919–1921', *Terrorism and Political Violence*, vol. 27, no. 3 (19 April 2016).

57   Martin Gilbert, *Winston S. Churchill, Vol. 4. 1916–1922: The Stricken World* (Boston, 1974), p. 461.

58   Birgit Susanne Seibold, *Emily Hobhouse and the Reports on the Concentration Camps during the Boer War 1899–1902* (Stuttgart, 2011).

59   Janet Howarth, *Dame Millicent Garrett Fawcett [née Millicent Garrett], 1847–1929* (Oxford, 2004).

60   Max Boot, *Invisible Armies: An Epic History of Guerrilla Warfare from Ancient Times to Present* (New York, 2013), p. 255.

61   Letter from Wilson to Macready, 7 June 1920, IWM/NMC, Vol. A.

62   Letter from Macready to Wilson, 13 July 1920, IWM/NMC, Vol. A.

63   General Sir Nevil Macready, *Annals of an Active Life* (2 vols; London, 1925; 1942), vol. 2, p. 426.

64   *Ibid.*, p. 466.

65   'Record of the Rebellion in Ireland in 1920–1921 and the Part Played by the Army in Dealing with it', Imperial War Museum, Box 78/82/2. James S. Donnelly Jnr,. '"Unofficial" British Reprisals and IRA Provocation, 1919-1920: the cases of three Cork towns', *Eire-Ireland*, Vol. 45 (2010).

66   Winston S. Churchill, *The World Crisis, 1911–1918* (London, 1931), p. 297.

67   Boot, *Invisible Armies*, p. 256.

68   David Fitzpatrick, 'Ireland since 1870', in R.F. Foster (ed.), *The Oxford Illustrated History of Ireland* (Oxford, 1989).

69   General Frank P. Crozier, *Ireland Forever* (London and Toronto, 1932), p. 133.

70   Dorothy Macardle, *The Irish Republic* (New York, 1937; 1965), p. 373.

71   General Frank P. Crozier, *The Men I Killed* (London, 1937), p. 119.

72   John Ainsworth, 'British security policy in Ireland, 1920–1921: a desperate attempt by the Crown to maintain Anglo-Irish unity by force', paper presented at the 11th Irish-Australian Conference, Queensland University of Technology, School of Humanities and Social Science (25–30 April 2000).

73   Diary of Sir Henry Wilson, 29 September 1920.

74   Kenneth Griffith and Timothy O'Grady, *Ireland's Unfinished Revolution: An Oral History* (Boulder, CO, 2002), p. 193.

75   See www.theauxiliaries.com/index.html.

76   Macready, *Annals of an Active Life*, vol. 2, p. 498.

77   General Sir Hubert Gough papers, Imperial War Museum.

78   *The Times*, 28 September 1920.

79   Letter from Collins to Donal Hales, 13 August 1920.

80   Caroline Woodcock, *Experiences of an Officer's Wife in Ireland* (London, 1921; 1994), pp 48–50.

81   Frank Packenham, *Peace by Ordeal* (London, 1935; 1972), p. 50.

82   Sheehan (ed.), *British Voices from the Irish War of Independence*, p. 144.

83   Ulick O'Connor, *A Terrible Beauty is Born: The Irish Troubles, 1912–1922* (London, 1975),

p. 135.

84 Hopkinson, *The Irish War of Independence*, p. 79.
85 Oonagh Walsh, *Ireland's Independence, 1880–1923* (London, 2002), p. 70.
86 Holt, *Protest in Arms*, p. 234.
87 Hopkinson, *The Irish War of Independence*, p. 80.
88 *Ibid.*
89 Cork RIC County Inspector's Report, June 1920.
90 Sir John Allesbrook Simon, 'Irish reprisals: Auxiliary Division's record', *The London Times*, 25 April 1921.
91 Jim McDermott, *Northern Divisions: The Old IRA and the Belfast Pogroms, 1920–1922* (Belfast, 2001), p. 50 *et seq.*
92 Hayden Talbot, *Michael Collins' Own Story* (London, 1923), pp 124–5.
93 The lesson of aggressive action in Belfast would not have been lost on pragmatists like Collins. Logically, he would have to continue to give moral and physical support to the Belfast IRA units if he didn't want them to atrophy, but to demand a high level of proactive operations from them would inflict a high cost on the Catholic community in the North. McDermott, *Northern Divisions*, p. 58.
94 *An Phoblacht*, 27 August 2010.
95 Hopkinson, *The Irish War of Independence*, p. 80.
96 Holt, *Protest in Arms*, p. 232.
97 *Ibid.*
98 Maurice Walsh, *The News from Ireland: Foreign Correspondents and the Irish Revolution* (Dublin, 2008), p. 70.
99 Florence O'Donoghue, 'The sacking of Cork City by the British', in Gabriel Doherty and Dermot Keogh (eds), *Michael Collins and the Making of the Irish State* (Cork, 1998); Martin F. Seedorf, 'The Lloyd George government and the Strickland Report on the burning of Cork 1920', *Albion: A Quarterly Journal Concerned with British Studies*, vol. 4, no. 2 (1972).
100 O'Connor, *A Terrible Beauty is Born*, p. 136.
101 Michael Rock, Witness Statement 1399.
102 Ross O'Mahony, 'The sack of Balbriggan and tit-for-tat killing', in Fitzpatrick (ed.), *Terror in Ireland* (Dublin, 2012).
103 *Manchester Guardian*, 23 September 1920.
104 *Freeman's Journal*, 22 September 1920.
105 *London Daily News*, 23 September 1920.
106 *Birmingham Post*, 23 September 1920.
107 Martin Seedorf, 'Defending reprisals: Sir Hamar Greenwood and the "Troubles", 1920–1921', *Éire-Ireland* (Winter 1990).
108 *Weekly Summary*, 8 October 1920.
109 Mark Sturgis, *The Last Days of Dublin Castle: The Mark Sturgis Diaries* (ed. Michael Hopkinson) (Dublin, 1999), p. 43.
110 Holt, *Protest in Arms*, pp 219–20.
111 David Fitzpatrick, 'The price of Balbriggan', in Fitzpatrick (ed.), *Terror in Ireland.*
112 *New York Times*, 21 September 1920.
113 *The Times*, 5 November 1920.
114 *The Times*, 6 November 1920.
115 *Irish Independent*, 20 October 1920.

[116] *The Irish Times*, 20 November 1920.

[117] *The Times*, 10 November 1920.

[118] *Ibid.*

[119] Tom Barry, quoted in Griffith and O'Grady, *Ireland's Unfinished Revolution: An Oral History*, p. 221.

[120] 2nd Southern Division Orders, UCD Archive, O'Beirne Ranelagh papers, p. 9.

[121] Cork No. 3 Brigade, War Diary, 14 May 1921, Mulcahy papers, MSS P7 A/II/2.

[122] Maryann G.Valiulis, *Portrait of a Revolutionary: General Richard Mulcahy and the Founding of the Irish Free State* (Blackrock, 1992), p. 53.

[123] Tom Barry, *Guerilla Days in Ireland: A Personal Account of the Anglo-Irish War* (Dublin, 1981), p. 106.

[124] Tom Barry, quoted in Griffith and O'Grady, *Ireland's Unfinished Revolution: An Oral History*, p. 143.

[125] *Ibid.*

[126] Hopkinson, *The Irish War of Independence*, p. 111.

[127] 'Record of the Rebellion in Ireland in 1920–1', vol. 2, 1922, Jeudwine papers 72/82/1, Imperial War Museum. See footnotes 39 and 131 for more information on the controversial debate regarding the activities of informers in County Cork.

[128] Hart, *The IRA and its enemies*, pp 298–300.

[129] *Ibid.*, p. 311.

[130] Peter Hart, 'Class, community and the Irish Republican Army in Cork, 1917–1923', in P. O'Flanagan, C.G. Buttimer and G. O'Brien, *Cork History and Society* (Dublin, 1993), pp 963–81, especially p. 979.

[131] In many views and instances of the War of Independence, it is this either/or—a 'binary construct'—that is the difficulty for some commentators. History is seldom 'black or white'; one must understand that in many cases the evidence is not there for a definitive, one-sided view, while in other instances a more nuanced, objective and multi-faceted view is called for. There were some who were killed to settle scores, some who were killed as a result of internal feuds and some who were killed because they were passing information to the British. It is reasonable to assume that former soldiers, loyalists or Protestants would be more likely to give information to the British. The reasons for the killings are not, however, mutually exclusive; there were informers killed, as well as those who were in the 'suspect classifications' as defined by Hart and others but who were not informers. It is important to note that of the 196 civilians killed by the IRA as 'spies or informers' nationwide 75% were Catholic and 25% were Protestant (Anglican, Presbyterian or Methodist), approximately the ratio of Catholics to Protestants as found in the general population of the time. In County Cork, the number of Protestants killed (for whatever reason) was 30% of the total, and this larger proportion can be attributed to the larger loyalist and Protestant communities in Cork, who were staunchly pro-British and consequently were more likely to assist the British forces.

[132] County Inspector, West Cork Riding, January 1921, CO 904/114.

[133] Major A.E. Percival, quoted in Sheehan (ed.), *British Voices from the Irish War of Independence*, p. 134.

[134] 'Record of the Rebellion in Ireland in 1920–1', vol. 1, March 1922; see also a letter to Strickland about this document, 1 March 1922, in the Strickland papers EPS 2/3, Imperial War Museum. A second volume was submitted in April and printed in May

1922: *Record of the Rebellion in Ireland in 1920–1*, vol. 2, Jeudwine papers 72/82/1, Imperial War Museum.

135 National Archives, CAB/24/120/25. 'Report by the General Office Commanding-In-Chief on the situation in Ireland for Week Ending 19th February, 1921', p. 152.

136 Denis Lordan, Witness Statement 470; William Desmond, Witness Statement 832; Willie Foley, Witness Statement 1560; Anna Hurley-O'Mahoney, Witness Statement 540.

137 Barry, *Guerilla Days in Ireland*, p. 127.

138 Pádraig Óg Ó Ruairc, 'Spies and informers beware', *An Cosantóir* (March 2019).

139 John Walsh, Witness Statement 966. One of the most striking features of the Bureau of Military History Witness Statements and Military Service Pensions Collection is the willingness of former IRA members to identify by name the people they killed.

140 For a fuller discussion of the IRA's activities in Cork see Thomas Earls Fitzgerald, 'The execution of "spies and informers" in West Cork, 1921', in Fitzpatrick (ed.), *Terror in Ireland*.

141 Fr Séamus Murphy, 'War of Independence seen as Catholic war on Protestants', *Irish Times*, 15 January 2019.

142 Russell Rees, *Ireland 1905–25, Volume I. Text and Historiography* (Newtownards, 1998), pp 268–70.

143 See McDermott, *Northern Divisions*.

144 Major C.J.C. Street, *Ireland in 1921* (New York, 1921; London, 1922), p. 56.

145 John A. Pinkman, *In the Legion of the Vanguard* (Cork, 1998), pp 32–3.

146 Edward Brady, *Ireland's Secret Service in England* (Dublin, 1924), pp 24–5.

147 Ernie O'Malley, *On Another Man's Wound* (Dublin, 1936; 1979), p. 188.

148 George Fitzgerald, Witness Statement 684.

149 Paddy O'Donoghue, Witness Statement 847.

150 Brady, *Ireland's Secret Service in England*, p. 27.

151 *The Times*, 10 March 1921; Peter Hart, 'Operations abroad: the IRA in Britain, 1919–1923', *English Historical Review*, vol. 115, no. 460 (2000); Mike Rast, 'Tactics, politics and propaganda in the Irish War of Independence, 1917–1921', unpublished Master's thesis, Georgia State University (2011).

152 *The Times*, 12 March 1921.

153 Dean Kirby, 'The IRA and Manchester: how terror unit waged war on the city', *The Manchester Evening News*, 20 January 2013.

154 Gerard Noonan, *The IRA in Britain 1919–1923, 'In the Heart of Enemy Lines'* (Liverpool, 2017), p. 86.

155 *The Times*, 4 April 1921.

156 *The Times*, 11 May 1921.

157 *New York Times*, 4 July 1921.

158 Peter Hart, 'Michael Collins and the assassination of Sir Henry Wilson', *Irish Historical Studies*, vol. 28, no. 110 (November 1992).

159 See http://www.nickelinthemachine.com/2008/10/knightsbridge-michael-collins-and-the-murder-of-field-marshall-sir-henry-wilson/.

160 Dunne's report was smuggled out of prison and was published in the *Sunday Press*, 14 August 1955. Peter Hart, *The IRA at War, 1916–1923* (Oxford, 2003), p. 194.

161 Statements of A.A. Wilson and Ernest John Jordan, Lloyd George papers, F/97/1/30.

162 Dunne's prison letters (NLI MS 2653). Statement of Robert Dunne (Reggie's father), Lloyd George papers, F/97/1/30. Collins was greatly affected by attacks on Catholics in the North, and was engaged in many schemes that he thought would give them

relief. G.B. Kenna, *Facts and Figures of the Belfast Pogroms 1920–1922* (Dublin, 1922; 1997 edn, ed. Thomas Donaldson), p. 130. Others, however, have written that Collins's efforts were counterproductive. See Robert Lynch, 'The Clones affray, 1922: massacre or invasion?', *History Ireland*, vol. 12, no. 3 (2004): 'The Clones affray also illustrates the shadowy and confused role of Michael Collins, who, stuck in his cocoon of conspiracy, continued in his deluded belief that an aggressive IRA policy could achieve similar results to those of the War of Independence. His failure to understand the Northern situation meant that his policy was at best a failure and at worst counterproductive, doing little else but confirming unionist prejudices and highlighting the Northern Catholic minority's vulnerability.'

[163] McDermott, *Northern Divisions*, p. 191.

[164] The papers found on Dunne were determined to be irrelevant to the assassination. The Special Branch's investigation determined that the two men acted on their own. Conclusions of a Conference (CAB 23/30, c. 36 [22], and Appendix 3).

[165] Michael Hopkinson, *Green against Green* (Dublin, 2004), p. 112 *et seq.*; Kenneth Griffith and Timothy O'Grady, *Curious Journey: An Oral History of Ireland's Unfinished Revolution* (London, 1982), p. 281. See notes of conversations with Sweeney held in 1962 and 1964, Mulcahy papers (P7D/43).

[166] Meda Ryan, *The Day Michael Collins Was Shot* (Dublin, 1989), p. 20.

[167] Macardle, *The Irish Republic*, p. 737.

[168] Margery Forester, *Michael Collins: The Lost Leader* (Dublin, 1989), p. 316.

[169] Patrick O'Sullivan and Frank Lee, 'The execution of Field Marshal Sir Henry Wilson: the facts', *Sunday Press*, 10 August 1958.

[170] Ronan Fanning, 'Leadership and transition from the politics of revolution to the politics of party: the example of Ireland, 1914–1939', paper delivered to the International Congress of Historical Societies, San Francisco (27 August 1975).

[171] John Regan, 'Irish public histories as an historiographical problem', *Irish Historical Studies*, vol. 37, no. 146 (November 2010).

[172] Mansergh was a TD for the Tipperary South constituency, a Senator and a Minister of State, and was instrumental in formulating Fianna Fáil policy during the negotiations for the Good Friday Agreement signed in 1998. In the interests of full disclosure, Mansergh launched the author's book, *Dublin Rising*, in 2015.

[173] Fitzpatrick (ed.), *Terror in Ireland*.

[174] RTÉ Radio 1, '*Off the Shelf*', 16 February 2013.

[175] Ronan Fanning, 'Michael Collins—an overview', in Doherty and Keogh (eds), *Michael Collins and the Making of the Irish State*.

[176] Griffith and O'Grady, *Ireland's Unfinished Revolution: An Oral History*, p. 33.

[177] Augusteijn, *From Public Defiance to Guerrilla Warfare*, p. 277.

[178] Florence O'Donoghue, 'Guerilla warfare in Ireland', *An Cosantóir*, vol. 23 (1963).

[179] Bryan Ryan, *A Full Private Remembers the Troubled Times* (Hollyford, 1969), p. 40.

[180] Augusteijn, *From Public Defiance to Guerrilla Warfare*, p. 334.

[181] Letter from Basil Thomson to Lloyd George, 14 April 1921.

[182] Maura R. Cremin, 'Fighting on their own terms: the tactics of the Irish Republican Army, 1919–1921', *Small Wars and Insurgencies*, vol. 26, no. 6 (2015).

[183] *Ibid.*

7. From Truce to Treaty

It was a time for settlement that would secure the British withdrawal and evacuation.

—Michael Collins

On 22 June 1921 King George V opened the Northern Ireland Parliament in Belfast with a speech calling for 'an end of strife amongst her [Ireland's] people, whatever their race or creed'.

Members of the Senate and of the House of Commons.

For all who love Ireland, as I do with all my heart, this is a profoundly moving occasion in Irish history. My memories of the Irish people date back to the time when I spent many happy days in Ireland as a midshipman. My affection for the Irish people has been deepened by the successive visits since that time, and I have watched with constant sympathy the course of their affairs.

I could not have allowed myself to give Ireland by deputy alone my earnest prayers and good wishes in the new era which opens with this ceremony, and I have therefore come in person, as the head of the Empire, to inaugurate this parliament on Irish soil. I inaugurate it with deep felt hope and I feel assured that you will do your utmost to make it an instrument of happiness and good government for all parts of the community which you represent.

This is a great and critical occasion in the history of the Six Counties—but not for the Six Counties alone, for everything which interests them touches Ireland, and everything which touches Ireland finds an echo in the remotest parts of the Empire. Few things are more earnestly desired throughout the English speaking world than a satisfactory solution of the age long Irish problems, which for generations embarrassed our forefathers, as they now weigh heavily upon us ...

I am confident that the important matters entrusted to the control and guidance of the Northern Parliament will be managed with wisdom and with moderation, with fairness and due regard to every faith and interest, and with no abatement of that patriotic devotion to the Empire which you proved so gallantly in the Great War ...

My hope is broader still. The eyes of the whole Empire are on Ireland today, that Empire in which so many nations and races have come together in spite of ancient feuds, and in which new nations have come to birth within the lifetime of the youngest in this Hall.

I am emboldened by that thought to look beyond the sorrow and the anxiety which have clouded of late my vision of Irish affairs.

I speak from a full heart when ... I appeal to all Irishmen to pause, to stretch out the hand of forbearance and conciliation, to forgive and to forget, and to join in making for the land which they love a new era of peace, contentment, and goodwill ...

For this the parliament of the United Kingdom has in the fullest measure provided the powers; for this the parliament of Ulster is pointing the way.

The future lies in the hands of my Irish people themselves.

May this historic gathering be the prelude of a day in which the Irish people, North and South, under one parliament or two, as those parliaments may themselves decide, shall work together in common love for Ireland upon the sure foundations of mutual justice and respect.[1]

Prime Minister Lloyd George had previously submitted a speech to the king, who asked whether it could be rewritten. Lloyd George then asked South African Prime Minister Jan Smuts to draft a new speech, and that was the one the king gave.

Smuts drafted a warm plea for civil peace and pressed it on Lloyd

George. Lloyd George thereafter accepted Smuts's proposal and soon made it his own. George V deserves some of the credit. His initiative was perhaps the greatest service performed by a British monarch in modern times.[2]

Lloyd George and his government took their cue from the king's widely praised speech. As the message stressed several times that Ireland should stay within the British Empire, they could reiterate this as the official policy guiding any settlement proposals.[3] The king's call for a cessation of violence undercut conservative arguments at Westminster that the rebellion should be stamped out before imposing a political solution. Two days after the speech, *The Times* declared that 'now was the moment for a Truce'.[4]

Lloyd George was a minority in a Cabinet composed mostly of hardliners; although he realised the necessity for negotiations and a political accord, he had to overrule the majority to bring that about. As a result, he moved quickly to capitalise on the opening given by the king's speech. On 24 June he wrote to de Valera, asking for a meeting between themselves and Northern Ireland Prime Minister James Craig to 'explore to the utmost the possibility of a settlement'.[5] De Valera initially insisted that no settlement was possible until Lloyd George recognised Ireland's 'essential unity, and right of national self-determination'.[6] Over the next two weeks a series of letters circulated between Dublin, Belfast and London. De Valera met with Craig and other Unionists to discuss the possibilities of co-operation between Unionist and republican Ireland. He also met Prime Minister Smuts, who assured him that the British government earnestly desired a settlement.[7] By 8 July de Valera had dropped his conditions and agreed to a one-on-one meeting with Lloyd George.[8]

The Truce did not come as a surprise, as the negotiations that led to it were well publicised, but republicans disagreed on whether it was necessary. Kerry Volunteer Con Casey later insisted that 'the IRA never felt stronger'.[9] GHQ organiser Seán MacBride said that he was annoyed by the cessation of hostilities, as 'we were on the way to really make things hotter'.[10] Many republicans viewed the Truce itself as a validation of the legitimacy of their military and political campaigns. Liam de Roiste TD called it 'a recognition of our national status as coequal with England'.[11] On the British side, General Macready insisted that the republicans were on the verge of defeat when the Truce was declared, and Conservative and Unionist polemicists dubbed the cessation a surrender to gunmen.[12]

On 8 July 1921 de Valera convened a consultation preparatory to a Truce; Dublin Lord Mayor Laurence (Larry) O'Neill, General Sir Nevil Macready, Lord Midleton (representing Southern Unionists), Arthur Griffith and Robert Barton attended the meeting. James Craig refused to attend. The following day, the terms of the Truce were agreed upon and settled at a 3 p.m. meeting in Dublin's Mansion House between General Macready, Colonel J. Brind and Alfred W. Cope for the British, and Robert C. Barton and Éamonn J. Duggan for the Irish. The terms went into effect at noon on 11 July 1921. From the time of the Truce, Macready described Collins as

> the easiest to deal with ... He had what few of his countrymen possess, a sense of humour and, above all, the gift during conversation of sticking to essentials ... he would complete the discussion with the least possible waste of time.[13]

On behalf of the British, the Truce called for:

> No incoming troops, RIC and auxiliary police and munitions.
> No movements for military purposes of troops and munitions, except for maintenance drafts.
> No provocative display of force, armed or not armed.
> It is understood that all provisions of this Truce shall apply to the Martial Law area equally to the rest of Ireland.
> No pursuits of Irish officers, or men, or war material, or military stores.
> No secret agents, noting descriptions or movements, and no interference with the movements of Irish persons, military or civil, and no attempt to discover the haunts or habits of Irish officers and men.
> Note: there are other details concerning courts, motor transport etc. to be dealt with later.

On the Irish side it was agreed:

Attacks on Crown Forces and civilians to cease.

No provocative display of force, armed or not armed.

No interference with British Government or private property.

To discountenance [sic] and prevent any action likely to cause disturbance of the peace which might necessitate military interference.

Collins was not entirely pleased with the Truce. He wrote to Moya Llewellyn Davies that it was

... only the first step. The days ahead are going to be the truly trying ones and we can only face them with set faces and hearts full of hope and confidence.[14]

He also wrote to Harry Boland, who was in the US:

There's something about [it] which I don't like, and I have the impression that the whole thing is pressing on me. I find myself looking at friends as if they were enemies—looking at them twice just to make sure that they are really friends after all. I mention no names. After all it may be a wrong impression that's got into me. Frankly, though, I don't care for things as they are now.[15]

Collins's fears were well founded, as during the five months of the Truce the frustrations, antagonisms and personality clashes that had festered during the War of Independence contributed to many of the divisions that were to occur during the Treaty debates and after ratification.[16] During the war the IRA/Volunteers mostly showed a strong sense of responsibility and discipline, but the Truce led to many acts of bad public behaviour. Many of those who 'joined' the IRA/Volunteers at that time were deemed 'Trucileers' and had not been involved in any action during the war. Their activities, and the adverse influence of the circumstances created by the Truce that Collins had feared, all had their effects on the genesis of the Civil War.[17]

Upon the establishment of a Truce, everything for the Irish depended on positioning.[18] The key was to position themselves to best advantage whether the Truce lasted or not, and whether they were able to get what they wanted from the upcoming negotiations or not. It was vital that they not be seen as responsible if the Truce failed, or for rejecting what international opinion would deem a reasonable offer from the British. If the British made what was deemed to be such an offer and the Irish turned it down, the British would be politically empowered to declare a true war, embodying many of the measures that Macready had said would be necessary for the British to 'win' the war. Nevertheless, the Irish negotiators were between a rock and a hard place: they could not accept or compromise too quickly or too much or they would lose the most militant members of the IRA, who thought that they were winning anyway.

On 14 July de Valera went to London to negotiate with Lloyd George. Included in the delegation were Arthur Griffith, Count Plunkett, Austin Stack, Robert Barton and Erskine Childers. Collins forcefully pressed to be included but de Valera chose to leave him in Dublin. At first he said that this was because he didn't want Collins to be photographed in case they returned to war, but he later indicated that he wanted to leave at least one senior politician in Dublin. This was an 'all Sinn Féin' delegation, breaking the unwritten rule that a Volunteer should be present at all negotiations. On the night before they left, Collins again argued that he should be included in the delegation, but de Valera refused. It was an acrimonious meeting, and both left upset. Next day, de Valera had the first of four meetings with Lloyd George at 10 Downing Street. Lloyd George told his secretary, Geoffrey Shakespeare, that he 'listened to a very long lecture on the wrongs done to Ireland starting with Cromwell, and when I tried to bring him to the present day, he went back to Cromwell again. It reminded me of a circus round-about when I was a boy.'[19]

From the outset it was de Valera's intent to show as little of his hand as possible. The formal British proposals were delivered to the Irish on 18 July: a twenty-six-county dominion; defence restrictions limiting the size of the Irish army; a prohibition on an Irish navy; insistence on free trade; and 'an allowance for the full recognition of the existing powers and privileges of the Parliament of Northern Ireland'. On the following day de Valera indicated that he would accept being a dominion but that the British offer was not of unfettered dominion status. He also indicated that Northern Ireland must be represented within the all-Ireland parliament, otherwise the only alternative was for the twenty-six counties to be a republic. Lloyd George offered a limited form of dominion, with Northern Ireland remaining as it was, no military or fiscal autonomy for the south and Home Rule government as part of the United Kingdom. The talks quickly stalled when de Valera insisted on prior recognition of Irish sovereignty and Lloyd George refused. 'This means war,' replied Lloyd George. De Valera dismissed the British proposals and called Lloyd George's bluff, as he was not to be seen carrying the British proposals home with him.

After the July meetings de Valera knew that he was not going to get a republic or 'External Association'. The best the Irish could hope for was the status of a self-governing dominion within the British Commonwealth. Several times he told the Cabinet and the Dáil that 'we are not doctrinaire Republicans', and the Irish delegation never looked for a republic in the negotiations; their purpose was to minimise the role of the king. One thing was absolutely clear from the London meetings and the follow-on correspondence between de Valera and Lloyd George: there was no question of a republic. Both the Cabinet in Dublin and the Cabinet in London were aware of that. De Valera clearly grasped what was on offer: an acceptance of partition, an Irish Free State with the same dominion status as Canada or Australia, an oath of some sort to the Crown, and the installation of a governor general.[20] The republic had been shelved before the negotiations began and everyone concerned, particularly de Valera, recognised this.[21]

Upon his return to Dublin de Valera convened a Cabinet meeting to persuade the members to agree to a settlement. He wanted to present a plan to the Irish people that would acknowledge Ireland's freedom and accept the same *de facto* status as the dominions. Two days later he reconvened the meeting and presented his concept of 'External Association' with the British Commonwealth.[22] De Valera knew that the king had to be written into the agreement, but how could Ireland make the king utterly powerless? He said that he came up with the idea of External Association while tying his shoes one morning:

- Independence for Ireland regarding domestic affairs.
- Alignment with the British Empire on foreign affairs.
- The king was to be the head of the association.

In effect, it was what India received in 1948, but it was impractical politics in 1922. The debate on the forthcoming negotiations had already begun even though it had not been agreed to hold negotiations.

De Valera wrote to Prime Minister Smuts: 'I was greatly disappointed with the British government's proposals. They seem quite unable to understand the temper of our people, or appear not to have the will to realise the opportunity that is now presented to them.' On 31 July de Valera asked Smuts to continue to be involved:

My dear General Smuts:
I received your letter of July 29th, and have had two conversations with Mr Lane. He will tell you that the proposals of the British Government will not be accepted here.

Unless the North East comes in on some reasonable basis no further progress can be made. An Ireland in fragments nobody cares about. A unified Ireland alone can be happy or prosperous.

To the British Commonwealth group and to Britain itself Ireland would readily become friendly, but it is only in freedom that friendship could come. To the principle of national self-determination our people are devotedly attached, for they recognise in it a principle vital to the peace of the world. The Republic is the expression of that principle in their own regard. These then they will not readily abandon, but they are prepared to make great sacrifices in other directions.

The question of procedure and form as distinguished from substance are very important, as I pointed out to you. The British do not seem to realise this at all. Your understanding of the situation is particularly necessary at that end therefore.

I am very glad you are able to remain on for a little time longer. I know how your people are clamouring for you, but the cause you are assisting is a truly great and worthy one.

Very sincerely yours,
Éamon de Valera[23]

The First Session of the Second Dáil was held on 16 August 1921 in the Round Room of Dublin's Mansion House. There were 130 Republican

TDs, six Nationalist TDs and forty-four Unionist TDs (who absented themselves as usual). All TDs present took the oath to the Dáil. The Dáil was to consider de Valera's correspondence and negotiations with London, and the British offer of dominion status for Ireland. On 17 August the Dáil's Foreign Representatives were named as follows: John Chartres (Germany), Harry Boland (USA), Seán T. O'Kelly (Paris), George Gavan-Duffy (Rome), Art O'Brien (London), Dr Patrick McCartan (Russia), Éamon Bulfin (Argentina) and Frank W. Egan (Chile).[24] De Valera addressed the Dáil: 'I would be willing to suggest to the Irish people to give up a good deal in order to have an Ireland that could look to the future without anticipating distracting internal problems'. On 22 August he told the Dáil that 'the minority in Ulster had a right to have their sentiments considered to the utmost limit. If the Republic were recognised I would be in favour of giving each county power to vote itself out of the Republic if it so wished.'[25]

In a private session later on 23 August, de Valera told the TDs that if they were determined to make peace only on the basis of recognition of the Republic they were going to be faced with war—only this time it would be a real war of British reconquest, not just a continuation of limited military coercive measures 'in support of the civil police' to force people to obey the law. He clearly indicated his willingness to compromise, even on partition: 'I do not consider myself bound to consider anything, I feel myself open to consider anything'.

On 7 September Lloyd George wrote to de Valera, requesting a 'definite reply as to whether you are prepared to enter a conference to ascertain how the association of Ireland with the community of nations known as the British Empire can best be reconciled with Irish national aspirations'. He proposed that the conference should begin at Inverness, Scotland, on 20 September. De Valera could delay no longer. A reading of the Official Correspondence Relating to the Peace Negotiations June–September 1921 makes it clear that Lloyd George was offering dominion status for the twenty-six counties and nothing else. De Valera was committed to an imaginative and far-sighted scheme of his own creation, that of an external association between Ireland and Britain, but he failed to communicate to his colleagues the strength of his feelings on this subject. What is not in doubt is that de Valera knew before the delegation left Ireland that the offer of an Irish Republic was not on the table for discussion.

De Valera told the Cabinet that he was not going to the negotiations. Reviewing his motives, his decision to stay in Dublin was based on solid grounds. He knew that those who went were likely to become scapegoats—with the radicals if they compromised, and with the moderates if they did not. 'We must have scapegoats', de Valera told the Cabinet.[26] In essence he was following the well-established diplomatic maxim that principals should not engage in negotiations but should remain in reserve as the ultimate arbiters. Where that broke down in this case was that Lloyd George was fully engaged in the negotiations, and de Valera's absence undoubtedly left the Irish delegation at a disadvantage. He also had other motives. By staying away he hoped to protect his status as president of the Irish Republic, and thus the Republic itself, rather than being involved in invidious negotiations about it, in which he might be accused of a conflict of interest. De Valera's other concern, a very natural one for any political leader, was to preserve the unity of the movement. He thought that he could keep the more extreme republican wing on board by staying at home. He may have contemplated joining the delegation at the very end but, if so, he left it much too late. De Valera was a devoted admirer of Machiavelli and especially of his *The Prince*.

> If the Prince's advisors tell him he is not going to get what he
> desires, he shouldn't go to the negotiations.

De Valera had also seen how US President Woodrow Wilson lost touch with the American public while in Versailles and he did not want to follow that example. Collins was determined that de Valera should go. A vote was taken in the Cabinet, with each member being asked whether he should go. Arthur Griffith, W.T. Cosgrave and Collins voted in favour, while Cathal Brugha, Austin Stack and Robert Barton voted against. With the vote tied, de Valera voted not to go. In the final analysis, his decision not to go to London was a mistake, and one that he was to regret and try to justify all his life. Tellingly, whenever there were negotiations during his time as taoiseach, de Valera always led the delegation and took personal control. It was a mistake that he was determined not to make again.

On 14 September 1921 the plenipotentiaries were chosen for the Treaty negotiations: Arthur Griffith, Robert Barton, Collins, George Gavan-

Duffy and Éamonn Duggan. Gavan-Duffy objected to the term 'plenipotentiaries' but de Valera insisted. Collins complained that 'it was an unheard of thing that a soldier who had fought in the field should be elected to carry out negotiations. It was de Valera's job, not his.'[27] Still, Collins was also aware that the IRA was exhausted and that any agreement, even a compromise, was preferable to fighting a ruinous war.

Collins addressed the Dáil after a very heated debate:

To me the task is a loathsome one. If I go, I go in the spirit of a soldier who acts against his judgment at the orders of a superior officer.[28]

Later, he was more explicit to the IRB:

I have been sent to London to do a thing which those who sent me knew had to be done but had not the courage to do it themselves. We had not, when the terms were offered, an average of one round of ammunition for each weapon we had. The fighting area in Cork … was becoming daily more circumcised [*sic*] and they could not have carried on much longer.[29]

On 15 September de Valera proposed that the army (IRA/Volunteers) 'be put on a regular basis'. The Cabinet, in late November, affirmed: 'The supreme body directing the Army is the Cabinet. The immediate executive representative of the Government is the Minister for Defence who is, therefore, Administrative Head of the Army. The Minister for Defence is a civilian. All Army appointments are to be sanctioned by the Minister for Defence, who is to have the power of nomination and veto.'

On 18 September, Lloyd George wrote to de Valera:

From the very outset of our conversation I told you that we looked to Ireland to own allegiance to the Throne, and to make her future as a member of the British Commonwealth. That was the basis of our proposals, and we cannot alter it. The status which you now claim in advance for your delegates is, in effect, a repudiation of that basis.

The basis of the conference in London was the 'Gairloch Formula', according to which the status of a republic, as previously demanded by de Valera, was not acceptable; instead, the negotiations were to ascertain 'how the association of Ireland with the community of nations known as the British Empire may best be reconciled with Irish national aspirations'. Collins later argued that the restrictions of the 'Gairloch Formula' eliminated any pretence of sustaining a request for the Republic:

> If we all stood on the recognition of the Irish Republic as a prelude to any conference we could very easily have said so, and there would have been no conference … it was the acceptance of the invitation that formed the compromise. I was sent there to form that adaption, to bear the brunt of it.[30]

It has often been charged that, as a military man, Collins was too prone to interpret political rhetoric literally. Yet Robert Barton—who, though he signed the Treaty, later disagreed with it and changed his position—also came to the same conclusion:

> The English refused to recognise us as acting on behalf of the Irish Republic and the fact we agreed to negotiate at all on any other basis was possibly the primary cause of our downfall. Certainly [it was] the first milestone on the road to disaster.[31]

When asked to be a member of the delegation, Arthur Griffith agreed but told de Valera: 'You are my chief, and if you tell me to go, I'll go. But I know, and you know, that I can't bring back a Republic.'[32] De Valera explained to the Dáil why he insisted that Collins go to London: 'It was from the personal touch and contact I had with the Minister for Finance that I knew he was vital to the delegation'. Collins disagreed and was to say again that 'It was the acceptance of the invitation that formed the compromise'.[33] The Irish delegation was therefore committed to advancing Irish nationalism rather than establishing a republic.

In September de Valera had further talks with Prime Minister Smuts, who came to Ireland at the behest of Lloyd George to mediate. In their conversations, Smuts indicated that Britain would never give the Irish a 'republic' and that in fact the South Africans had never asked for one. Smuts said, 'Ask what you want, but not a republic'. 'If the status of a dominion is offered', de Valera replied, 'I will use all our machinery to get the Irish people to accept it.'[34] Smuts reported on his Irish visit to the British Cabinet the next day. De Valera authorised members of the government to open negotiations with Britain in October.

On 30 September 1921 de Valera issued a final 'acceptance' of the Treaty Conference 'Terms' in a letter to Lloyd George:

> We have received your letter of invitation to a Conference in London on October 11th 'with a view to ascertaining how the association of Ireland with the community of nations known as the British Empire may best be reconciled with Irish national aspirations'.
>
> Our respective positions have been stated and are understood and we agree that conference, not correspondence, is the most practical and hopeful way to an understanding. We accept the invitation, and our Delegates will meet you in London on the date mentioned 'to explore every possibility of settlement by personal discussion'.[35]

Regarding the wording of the correspondence, J.J. Lee has written:

> So scholastic a scrutineer of texts as de Valera can hardly have overlooked the significance of 'how' rather than 'whether' in this formula, which already contained the seeds of compromise as Collins correctly observed in the Treaty debate.[36]

While de Valera was not prepared to lead the delegation in negotiations, this did not prevent him from attempting to direct events from Dublin. Accordingly, he drew up the following document of *instructions*, which he circulated to the plenipotentiaries on 7 October, one day before they left for London:

> (1) The Plenipotentiaries have full powers as defined in their credentials.

(2) It is understood before decisions are finally reached on a main question, that a dispatch notifying the intention to make these decisions will be sent to members of the Cabinet in Dublin, and that a reply will be awaited by the Plenipotentiaries before final decision is made.

(3) It is also understood that the complete text of the draft treaty about to be signed will be similarly submitted to Dublin and a reply awaited.

(4) In case of a break the text of final proposals from our side will be similarly submitted.

(5) It is understood that the Cabinet in Dublin will be kept regularly informed of the progress of the negotiations. [37]

De Valera clearly intended that these instructions, particularly clauses 2 and 3, would enable him to veto any draft document that he considered unacceptable. It is also accepted that these 'instructions' were formulated in order to placate Cathal Brugha and Austin Stack, who were much more doctrinaire and ideological than the Irish people, who were desperately anxious for a settlement. Griffith and Collins, for their part, were unhappy with the limitations, and they chose to ignore these further instructions, which had not been approved by the Cabinet, considering them only as guiding principles, not mandatory. There are contrasting views of these 'instructions'. A rigid interpretation is not reconcilable with the 'plenipotentiary' credentials, defined as 'one who is invested with the full power of independent action on behalf of the government'. Since the Dáil had already conferred full plenipotentiary powers, the instructions from the Cabinet, an inferior body, were not legally binding in any instance in which they limited the powers of the delegation. Brugha and Stack, however, viewed the 'instructions' as requiring the delegation in London to keep the Cabinet in Dublin duly informed at every step and not to sign the final draft without submitting it to the Cabinet and awaiting a reply.[38]

Thus there was an implicit contradiction hanging over the negotiations: were the delegates plenipotentiaries or acting on instructions to report back to the Cabinet? The plenipotentiary status conferred by the Dáil was superior to instructions from the Cabinet. The delegates in London were not pleased with what they deemed to be interference from de Valera. In October Griffith sent a letter to de Valera emphasising that they were plenipotentiaries and that they were not to be instructed on all the minutiae of the negotiations.

Originally, Harry Boland was to go to London as a secretary to the delegation, along with Childers, Diarmuid O'Hegarty and Fionan Lynch, but de Valera sent him back to the US instead. Boland told Joe McGrath: 'I have a nice job to prepare Irish-America for a compromise'. He was 'going back to America on the President's instructions to prepare the American people for something less than a Republic'.[39]

At the outset of negotiations both sides were ready to compromise. The British were demoralised and under pressure at home and from international opinion. Collins knew that the Irish were out of arms, especially ammunition. Richard Mulcahy agreed that to drive the British from anything more substantial than a police barracks was beyond them. Lloyd George was the head of a coalition government and greatly reliant on the Conservatives to remain in power, as they significantly outnumbered his Liberals both in Cabinet and in Parliament. He lost his position as prime minister in October 1922, and he placed much of the blame for that on the compromises that led to the Treaty.

From the time of the Truce in July and during the weeks leading up to the signing of the Treaty, and even in the Treaty debates that followed, the precise form that a government should take was imagined and debated by different wings in Sinn Féin—from Arthur Griffith's vision of a dual monarchy to acceptance of dominion status, and from de Valera's concept of 'External Association' to those who were adamant that only a republic would be acceptable. All of the women TDs in the Dáil were ready to reject anything less than a republic with full independence from Britain. Tensions mounted as the delegates went back and forth to London and then returned with the Agreement.

There were several meetings of both the Dáil and the Cabinet as the negotiations continued through October and November. De Valera continued to press his plan for external association, but no one really knew what he wanted. 'External Association' was an impossible concept in the minds of the British negotiators. Extremist Republicans, and most TDs, saw no virtue in any kind of association with Britain. Collins simply could not see the point of repeatedly presenting the 'External Association' in the negotiations, and

Griffith, though he argued strenuously for it in London, was unconvinced.[40]

The Irish delegation intended that if there were to be a 'break' it would be on Ulster. Sovereignty, status and the role of the king were most important to the leaders; Ulster and partition were most important to the people.

> The chief mistake the Irish delegation made was to allow the two all-important issues of the Crown and Ulster to become confused. They did not sufficiently single out Ulster as the issue on which to challenge the British. This was largely because, though the unity of Ireland was more important than the issue of allegiance to most Irish citizens, the issue of allegiance was of equal importance to the minority of Republican dogmatists whom the delegates also represented.[41]

It was not the first—nor would it be the last—time that the Irish leaders were out of touch with the wishes of the Irish people.

Griffith's unilateral agreement with Lloyd George in early November prevented that break on Ulster.[42] Griffith was asked in a private meeting to 'help' Lloyd George avoid a Conservative revolt. Griffith said that if Lloyd George would agree to a Boundary Commission the Irish would not break on Ulster. None of the other delegates knew of this meeting or of Griffith's assurance to Lloyd George. Griffith did not sign or initial any agreement, but honoured his word when Lloyd George showed him the minutes of that earlier meeting near the end of the negotiations. From that point, partition ceased to be a main point of contention.

The last Irish Cabinet meeting was held on 3 December, when de Valera rejected the proposed treaty mainly on the grounds that the oath was unacceptable. Brugha said that as Collins and Griffith had been doing 'most of the negotiating' the British had selected 'their men'. Griffith was outraged, but Collins just considered who it was that said it. During a break in the meeting Collins met with Seán Ó Muirthile, who enumerated the IRB's reservations. They were basically the oath (Collins passed along one that he had previously given to the British) and the positions that had been presented on defence and partition. When the Cabinet meeting resumed, Griffith again pointed out that he would never break on the issue of the Crown. He said that he would not sign a treaty but would bring it back to the Dáil. Although the discussion took several hours and many issues were discussed, the oath was the single item that caused the most criticism. Prior to the meeting's adjournment, it was decided that the delegation should return to London with the same powers and instructions. Griffith, Collins and Duggan went back to London on one boat, while Gavan-Duffy, Barton and Childers travelled on another. The intention to negotiate further is implicit in the circumstances and was explicit in the Cabinet minutes, but clearly it was not a delegation in which the Cabinet could have confidence that it would conclude a treaty on the grounds discussed in that last meeting.

Collins said that he was confused because de Valera had proposed an oath that was consistent with dominion status. He said that the proposals had been discussed again and again with the British and had been rejected, and that he was not going to go over the same issues again. The British again flatly rejected 'External Association', as Collins predicted. Thereafter, in meetings with the British, Collins attacked hard on defence and trade issues. Griffith wanted further discussion on the oath and insisted that the law and practice of the Crown as applied in Canada should govern the action of the British in Ireland. All the arguments had been presented before and the British rejected them again.

On 5 December Lloyd George inserted more drama into the negotiations: he held up two envelopes and said that one of them was to be delivered to a destroyer, which would take it to James Craig in Belfast that night. One contained news that there would be a treaty, while the other indicated that there was no treaty. Collins said that Lloyd George threatened the Irish delegates with a renewal of 'terrible and immediate war' if the Treaty were not signed at once. Lloyd George's secretary, Geoffrey Shakespeare, said he knew that Lloyd George was bluffing on the 'war', but he was not bluffing that he had gone as far as he could. Referring the Treaty back to Dublin that night by telephone was not an issue: Collins, Barton and Gavan-Duffy all said that they had not thought of it, and Childers wrote that he had not thought of it either. Griffith reasoned: 'I like what I see; I can accept this Treaty'. He got what he always wanted: a single king over two countries, going back to his famous articles on 'The Resurrection of Hungary'. He had first channelled this idea in a series of twenty-seven articles in his *United Irishman* newspaper in 1904.[43] Collins came around; it was a stepping-stone for him. Collins, Griffith and Barton thought that they had fulfilled their duty and signed around 2.30 a.m. that night. Gavan-Duffy and Duggan signed the next morning. (It should be noted that Collins's celebrated stepping-stone argument—his admission that the Treaty conferred not freedom but the freedom to achieve freedom—also contributed to the corrosion of his revolutionary reputation in the eyes of those who opposed the Treaty because it offered not so much an inducement to recognise how much had already been achieved as a calculus for future progress.)

On 6 December 1921 Articles of Agreement for a Treaty were formally signed in London, and two days later the Irish Cabinet met to debate the provisions.[44] Griffith's decision to sign forced the others to their decisions. Only Griffith was absolutely sure that he was doing the right thing, and he was not a man to be dissuaded from what he deemed to be the right course. It has been written that Barton and Gavan-Duffy signed under pressure from the other three plenipotentiaries. Duggan said that he signed because Collins did. And Collins followed Griffith.[45] Collins was acutely aware of the weakened military position of the IRA/Volunteers. Moreover, he was 'convinced that Ireland could not get substantially better terms and that the alternative to settlement was war and defeat'. He agonised over his decision, but in the taxi that night he announced that he was going to sign.[46] He was under no illusion about what the Treaty meant, but it was really no more or less than he had expected from the start.

The Irish people generally welcomed the Treaty. The 'establishment' was massively in favour:

- The Catholic Church
- The press
- Business interests
- Three hundred and twenty-eight local councils and bodies[47]
- The Supreme Council of the IRB (only Liam Lynch was opposed)
- The majority of the GHQ staff

The IRA rank and file, however, were mostly opposed. Many of those who were the most effective and active commanders in the War of Independence were opposed. The position of the IRA was: 'We are Ireland—not the people. Going back to the Rising, we represent Ireland—the people don't.'

Those in attendance at the Irish Cabinet meeting of 8 December were Barton, Brugha, Collins, Cosgrave, de Valera, Griffith, Stack, Childers and Gavan-Duffy. Collins and, especially, Griffith returned from London thinking that there could be dissatisfaction over the Treaty but that de Valera would believe that the delegation had acted as he would have wanted. They were quickly disillusioned.[48] De Valera was furious, feeling that the delegates had folded under pressure. Moreover, he felt personally betrayed.[49] At the end of an extremely angry six-hour meeting, Brugha, de Valera and Stack voted against the Treaty. Barton (angry, opposed in principle but honour-bound to stand by his signature), Collins, Cosgrave and Griffith voted for it. De Valera denounced the delegates for their breach of faith in failing to consult him before signing, but Barton countered by insisting that the real problem had been caused by de Valera's refusal to attend the conference.[50] De Valera said that he would resign if the Dáil accepted the Treaty, while both Griffith and Collins said that they would do the same if it were rejected. Later, de Valera told the Dáil:

> ... now I would like everybody clearly to understand that the plenipotentiaries went over to negotiate a Treaty, that they could differ from the Cabinet if they wanted to, and that in anything of consequence they could take their decision against the decision of the Cabinet.[51]

That evening de Valera issued a press statement, which he called a 'Proclamation to the Irish People', indicating that he could not recommend acceptance of the Treaty:

> The terms of this agreement are in violent conflict with the wishes of the majority of this nation, as expressed freely in successive elections during the past three years. I feel it my duty to inform you immediately that I cannot recommend the acceptance of this treaty either to Dáil hÉireann or to the country. In this attitude I am supported by the Ministers of Home Affairs [Austin Stack] and Defence [Cathal Brugha] ... The greatest test of our people has come. Let us face it worthily

without bitterness, and above all, without recrimination. There is a definite constitutional way of resolving our political differences—let us not depart from it, and let the conduct of the Cabinet in this matter be an example to the whole nation.[52]

The normal division of opinion that was bound to result from the signing of the Treaty was immensely complicated by the fact that instead of two parties there were really three: republican diehards, moderates and de Valera.[53] The issues of the Treaty might have appeared simple enough— peace or a resumption of the war, a conceptual republic or a positive dominion status—but there were no simple questions for TDs with little political experience who were easily swayed by emotional attachments or other considerations.

The Treaty proposed the establishment of the Irish Free State, consisting of all thirty-two counties. The Unionists of Northern Ireland promptly denounced this as a gross betrayal, despite a provision stipulating that they could withdraw from the Irish Free State within a month of the Treaty's ratification. In that case, however, a Boundary Commission would redraw the border in line with the wishes of the inhabitants. Collins and the other signatories maintained the broad belief that the Boundary Commission would 'deliver' an acceptable resolution for the South. (On 5 March 1922, Collins and Griffith addressed a massive rally in front of the Bank of Ireland building in College Green. Collins said that 'we could not have beaten the British by force, but when we have beaten them out by the Treaty, the republican ideal, which was surrendered in July, is restored'.[54] On 20 April 1922 Collins spoke to another huge crowd there. He gave his view that the Treaty was a 'stepping-stone' that gave the 'freedom to achieve freedom'. He also assured them that the Boundary Commission would give large parts of Northern Ireland to the Free State on the basis of demographics.[55])

Thus the partition issue was not a real factor in the Treaty split, which was primarily over the oath of allegiance to the British Crown to be taken by Irish parliamentarians. The key questions in the Dáil debates and in the Cabinet were the oath, the republic and the Crown, not partition. The lack of importance accorded to discussion of partition can be seen in the records of the debates: only nine pages of the public Dáil debates dealt with partition, and over 300 pages did not. Likewise, in the private debates, only three of 181 pages were devoted to partition.[56]

The next day the Dáil assembled in private session and de Valera proposed his 'External Association', or 'Document Number Two' (Collins gave it that name, and it stuck). It was rejected and de Valera 'withdrew' it, asking that it be held as confidential. With regard to partition, Document Number Two included the six partition clauses of the Treaty verbatim. The only difference was a declaration to the effect that 'the right of any part of Ireland to be excluded from the supreme authority of the national parliament and government' was not being recognised, but for the sake of internal peace and in order to divorce the Ulster question from the overall Anglo-Irish dispute de Valera said that he was prepared to accept the partition clauses of the Treaty, even though they provided 'an explicit recognition of the right on the part of Irishmen to secede from Ireland'.[57] When he read the document, Griffith challenged de Valera regarding 'recognition'. 'Obviously,' Griffith said, 'any form of association necessitates discussion of recognition in some form or another of the head of the association.' Some form of recognition of the Crown was inevitable.

On 19 December the debates continued, and de Valera and Collins stated their positions on the Treaty. Collins said:

> What I want to make clear is that it was the acceptance of the invitation that formed the compromise. I was sent there to form that adaptation, to bear the brunt of it. Now as one of the signatories of the document I naturally recommend its acceptance. I do not recommend it for more than it is. Equally I do not recommend it for less than it is. In my opinion it gives us freedom, not the ultimate freedom that all nations desire and develop to, but the freedom to achieve it.[58]

After the debate on 22 December, Kathleen Clarke came to visit Collins. She had spoken against the agreement and said that if her husband Tom were alive he would not vote for it. Collins responded: 'I wouldn't ask you to vote for it. All I ask is that, if it's passed, you give us a chance to work it.'[59]

On 21 December 1921 the Dáil adjourned on the motion of Collins to reassemble on 3 January 1922. The debates resumed and continued for five days in the Convocation Hall of the National University of Ireland.[60]

Prior to the close of the last Mansion House session, de Valera addressed the Dáil and said:

> I would like my last word here to be this: we have had a glorious record for four years; it has been four years of magnificent discipline in our nation. The world is looking at us now.[61]

The Christmas break was crucial to the debates; the TDs went home and encountered pressure for peace. But tempers worsened after the break.

Though there was disagreement over the lack of a named 'Republic', dominion status versus 'External Association' and Ulster partition, the primary disagreement continued to be over the oath required in the Treaty:

> I ... do solemnly swear true faith and allegiance to the Constitution of the Irish Free State as by law established and that I will be faithful to HM George V, his heirs and successors by law, in virtue of the common citizenship of Ireland and Great Britain and her adherence to and membership of the group of nations forming the British Commonwealth of Nations.[62]

It was noted at the time that there was no oath of 'allegiance' to the king but rather an oath to be 'faithful'. Care was taken to explain that 'allegiance' denoted 'obedience', whereas to be 'faithful' denoted equality between the two countries, but the explanation fell on the deaf ears of the TDs.

On 7 January 1922 the Dáil voted 64–57 to ratify the Treaty. A total of 122 TDs answered the roll for the day, but Eoin MacNeill (who would have voted in favour), as chairman, did not vote. Frank Drohan resigned, as he was unwilling to vote for the Treaty but did not want to flout the will of his constituents and vote against it. Tom Kelly (who would have voted in favour) was too ill to attend. Laurence Ginnell (who would have voted against) did not attend, as he was in Argentina. Five TDs (Collins, de Valera, Griffith, Liam Mellows and Seán Milroy) represented more than one constituency. All such TDs cast only one ballot, however, even though Griffith objected strenuously to such multiple constituencies being 'disenfranchised'. Had their 'second vote' been counted, the Treaty would have passed by one more vote.

It was an afternoon meeting, beginning at 4 p.m. Voting began at 8.35 p.m. with Diarmuid O'Hegarty calling the roll, continuing until 9 p.m. Those who voted for the Treaty were:

Robert Barton, Piaras Béaslaí, Ernest Blythe, Patrick Brennan, Éamon (Frank) Bulfin, Seámus Burke, C.M. Byrne, Thomas Carter, Michael Collins, Richard Corish, Philip B. Cosgrave, William T. Cosgrave, John Crowley, Liam De Roiste, James Derham, James N. Dolan, George Gavan-Duffy, Éamonn J. Duggan, Desmond FitzGerald, Paul Galligan, Arthur Griffith, Seán Hales, Dr Richard Hayes, Michael Hayes, Seán Hayes, William Hayes, P.J. Hogan, Peter Hughes, Andrew Lavin, Frank Lawless, Seán Leddy, Fionan Lynch, Joseph Lynch, Joseph MacBride, Seán MacEoin, Alex McCabe, Dr Patrick McCartan, Daniel McCarthy, Seán McGarry, Dr J.P. McGinley, P.J. McGoldrick, Joseph McGrath, Joseph McGuinness, Justin McKenna, Seán Milroy, Richard Mulcahy, James Murphy, George Nicolls, Thomas O'Donnell, Eoin O'Duffy, John O'Dwyer, Kevin O'Higgins, Padraig O'Keefe, Padraig Ó Maille, Daniel O'Rourke, Gearóid O'Sullivan, Lorcan Robbins, William Sears, Michael Staines, Joseph Sweeney, James J. Walsh, Peter Ward, J.B. Whelehan and Dr Vincent White.

Those who voted against the Treaty were:

E. Aylward, Harry Boland, Cathal Brugha, Daniel Buckley, Frank Carty, Erskine Childers, Kathleen Clarke, M.P. Colivet, Conor Collins, Daniel Corkery, Dr Seán Crowley, Dr Brian Cusack, Éamon Dee, Thomas Derrigg, Éamon de Valera, James Devins, Séamus Doyle, Dr Ada English, Seán Etchingham, Frank Fahy, Dr Frank Ferran, James Fitzgerald Jr, Thomas Hunter, David Kent, James Lennon, Joseph MacDonagh, Seán MacEntee, Mary MacSwiney, Seán MacSwiney, Countess Constance Markievicz, Thomas McGuire, Liam Mellows, P.J. Moloney, Seán Moylan, Charles Murphy, Seán Nolan, Count P.J. O'Byrne, P.S. O'Cahill, Kate O'Callaghan, Daniel O'Callaghan, Art O'Connor, Joseph

O'Doherty, Thomas O'Donoghue, Samuel O'Flaherty, Brian O'Higgins, J.J. O'Kelly ('Sceilg'), Seán T. O'Kelly, Seán O'Mahoney, Margaret Pearse, George Noble Count Plunkett, Séamus Robinson, Éamon Roche, P.J. Rutledge, Dr James Ryan, Philip Shanahan, Austin Stack and W.F.P. Stockley.[63]

There were six women TDs, and the oath was anathema to their socialist and republican beliefs.[64] They felt that, as well as betraying their dead comrades' convictions, it would continue to subject Ireland to the British government and its class-ridden political system. They were opposed to compromise and all voted against the Treaty.[65] Four* of the six (known as the 'Black Widows') had lost male relatives in the Rising or the War of Independence: Kathleen Clarke* (wife of Thomas Clarke and sister of the executed Ned Daly), Dr Ada English, Mary MacSwiney* (elder sister of Terence), Countess Markievicz, Kate O'Callaghan* (wife of Michael O'Callaghan, a former lord mayor of Limerick) and Margaret Pearse* (mother of Patrick and Willie). Expressing the views of all of the women, and many of the male members of the Dáil, Dr Kathleen Lynn wrote:

> Peace Terms, but what a peace! Not what Connolly and Mallin and countless died for. Please God the Country won't agree to what Griffith, Barton, Gavan-Duffy, Duggan, and Mick Collins had put their names to, more shame to them, better war than with such a peace. It is terrible how many who should know better seem quite pleased with the terms.[66]

The HQ staff of the IRA were split on the issue. Those opposed to the Treaty were:

Cathal Brugha, Minister for Defence
Austin Stack, formerly Deputy Chief of Staff
Liam Mellows, Director of Purchases
Rory O'Connor, Director of Engineering
Seán Russell, Director of Munitions
Seámus O'Donovan, Director of Chemicals
Oscar Traynor, O/C of the Dublin Brigade

Those in favour of the Treaty were:

Richard Mulcahy, Chief of Staff
J.J. O'Connell, Assistant Chief of Staff
Eoin O'Duffy, Deputy Chief of Staff
Michael Collins, Director of Intelligence
Diarmuid O'Hegarty, Director of Organisation
Piaras Béaslaí, Director of Publicity[67]

On 9 January de Valera resigned and put himself forward for re-election as president; he was defeated on 10 January (by 60 to 58 votes). Griffith was elected; de Valera did not vote. De Valera's expressed view was that 'The Republic must exist until the people disestablish it'.[68] He also said:

I hope that nobody will talk of fratricidal strife. That is all nonsense. We have a nation that knows how to conduct itself.[69]

Notes

[1] *The Times*, 23 June 1921.
[2] A.J.P. Taylor, *English History 1914–1945* (London, 1965), pp 156–7.
[3] Francis Costello, 'King George V's speech at Belfast, 1921: prelude to the Anglo-Irish Truce', *Éire-Ireland*, vol. 22, no. 3 (1987).
[4] *The Times*, 24 June 1921.
[5] *Documents on Irish Foreign Policy*, vol. I, Doc. No. 135, 24 June 1921.
[6] *Documents on Irish Foreign Policy*, vol. I, Doc. No. 136, 24 June 1921.
[7] *The Times*, 28 June 1921.
[8] *Irish Bulletin*, 9 July 1921.
[9] Con Casey, in Uinseonn MacEoin (ed.), *Survivors: The Story of Ireland's Struggle as Told Through Some of Her Outstanding Living People. Notes 1913–1916* (Dublin, 1966), p. 373.
[10] Seán MacBride, *That Day's Struggle: A Memoir 1904–1951* (ed. Caitriona Lawlor) (Dublin, 2005), p. 39.
[11] Liam DeRoiste, Treaty Debates, Dáil Éireann, vol. 3, 22 December 1921.
[12] General Sir Nevil Macready, *Annals of an Active Life* (2 vols; London, 1925; 1942), vol. 2, p. 596.
[13] *Ibid.*, p. 602.
[14] James Mackay, *Michael Collins: A Life* (Edinburgh, 1996), p. 201.
[15] Rex Taylor, *Michael Collins* (London, 1970), p. 142.
[16] Sheila Lawlor, 'Ireland from Truce to Treaty, war or peace? July to October 1921', *Irish Historical Studies*, vol. 22 (1980).

17 Many of the leaders of the IRA outside Dublin were blindsided by the Truce and most disagreed with it. They thought the IRA was 'winning' and would soon have a military victory. See Liam Deasy, *Brother Against Brother* (Cork, 1998), p. 11 *et seq.*; Ernie O'Malley, *The Singing Flame* (Dublin, 1978), p. 13: 'We were gaining ground, each day strengthened us and weakened our enemy; then why was it necessary to stop hostilities?' The IRA of July 1921 were stronger in number—in spite of several thousands arrested—than they were in July 1920. In addition there were ten times more experienced, tough fighters'—Tom Barry to Raymond Smith, *Irish Independent*, 7 July 1971.

18 Peter Hart, *Mick: The Real Michael Collins* (London, 2006), p. 277.

19 T. Ryle Dwyer, *I Signed my Death Warrant: Michael Collins and the Treaty* (Cork, 2007), p. 32.

20 Tim Pat Coogan and George Morrison, *The Irish Civil War* (London, 1998), p. 20.

21 P.S. O'Hegarty, *The Victory of Sinn Féin* (Dublin, 1924; 1998), pp 46–8.

22 Calton Younger, *Ireland's Civil War* (New York, 1969), p. 166 *et seq.*

23 See http://www.difp.ie/docs/1921/Anglo-Irish-Treaty/145.htm.

24 Seán T. O'Kelly, Witness Statements 611, 1765; George Gavan-Duffy, Witness Statement 381; Patrick McCartan, Witness Statements 99, 100, 766; Éamon Bulfin, Witness Statement 497.

25 Second Dáil, Dáil Éireann, private session, p. 153. Members of the IRA in Northern Ireland were particularly distressed at de Valera's statement that 'For his part, if the Republic were recognized he would be in favour of giving each party the power to vote itself out …'. In his statement, de Valera was confirming what he had told the Dáil on 22 August 1921, before the Treaty was negotiated. Jim McDermott, *Northern Divisions: The Old IRA and the Belfast Pogroms, 1920–1922* (Belfast, 2001), p. 107.

26 Dwyer, *I Signed my Death Warrant*, p. 61.

27 Batt O'Connor, *With Michael Collins in the Fight for Independence* (London, 1929), p. 171.

28 Dwyer, *I Signed my Death Warrant*, p. 46.

29 Manuscript of Seán Ó Muirthile, Richard Mulcahy papers, UCD.

30 Benjamin Kline, 'Churchill and Collins 1919–1922: admirers or adversaries?', *History Ireland*, vol. 1, no. 3 (1993).

31 See http://oireachtasdebates.oireachtas.ie/debates%20authoring/debateswebpack. nsf/ takes/Dáil1921121900003.

32 O'Hegarty, *The Victory of Sinn Féin*, p. 87.

33 Collins, Dáil Éireann Treaty Debates, Dáil Reports, GSO, p. 32.

34 Dwyer, *I Signed my Death Warrant*, p. 24.

35 Frank Gallagher [writing as David Hogan], *The Four Glorious Years* (Dublin, 1953), p. 321.

36 J.J. Lee, *Ireland 1912–1985* (Cambridge, 1989), p. 48; 'De Valera's use of words: three case-studies', *Radharc*, vol. 2 (2001).

37 Gallagher/Hogan, *The Four Glorious Years*, p. 322.

38 Desmond FitzGerald, 'Mr Packenham on the Anglo–Irish Treaty', *Studies: The Irish Jesuit Quarterly Review*, vol. 24 (1935).

39 Jim Maher, *Harry Boland: A Biography* (Cork, 1998), p. 159 *et seq.*

40 Younger, *Ireland's Civil War*, p. 166.

41 Robert Kee, *The Green Flag* (London, 1972), p. 724.

[42] Diary of Thomas Jones, 10 November 1921. He was Lloyd George's personal secretary. (See note 56 for further comment on partition and the Boundary Commission.)

[43] *The Resurrection of Hungary: A Parallel for Ireland* (pamphlet, 1904).

[44] Though all discussion in the Dáil, the newspapers and most books refer to a 'Treaty', the English and Irish delegates did not sign a Treaty. They signed a document entitled 'Articles for Agreement'. The words 'For a Treaty' were added to the English copy, but by that time the Irish copy was being delivered to Ireland. Frank Pakenham, *Peace by Ordeal* (London, 1935; 1972), p. 246. For consistency and to conform to other sources, the discussion here will refer to the 'Treaty'.

[45] Hart, *Mick*, p. 319.

[46] Joseph Curran, *The Birth of the Irish Free State, 1921–1923* (University of Alabama, 1980), p. 130.

[47] Michael Hopkinson, *Green against Green* (Dublin, 2004), p. 35.

[48] See Padraig Colum, *Arthur Griffith* (Dublin, 1959), p. 309. 'Griffith expected objections to [the Treaty], but he was reckoning on the President's support.' Desmond FitzGerald had to tell him, in the words he had heard himself from Austin Stack, 'He's dead against it now, anyway'.

[49] Many of the IRA felt betrayed as well. 'The officers and men I met seemed dazed. Some had been crying, their eyes were swollen. We awaited the arrest of the delegates. They had no authority to sign without first referring the matter to their Cabinet.' O'Malley, *The Singing Flame*, p. 43.

[50] Robert Barton, Witness Statement 979; Russell Rees, *Ireland 1905–25, Volume I. Text and Historiography* (Newtownards, 1998), p. 289.

[51] T. Ryle Dwyer, *De Valera: The Man and the Myths* (Swords, 1992), p. 85.

[52] *Irish Independent*, 9 December 1921.

[53] Frank O'Connor, *The Big Fellow* (London, 1969; 1979), p. 134.

[54] T. Ryle Dwyer, *Michael Collins and the Civil War* (Cork, 2012), p. 82.

[55] McDermott, *Northern Divisions*, p. 156 *et seq.*; G.B. Kenna, *Facts and Figures of the Belfast Pogroms 1920–1922* (Dublin, 1922; 1997, ed. Thomas Donaldson).

[56] When Collins told Kathleen Clarke on 22 December that he was going to 'work the Treaty', he was indicating his future intent. Publicly he said that the Treaty 'gives us the freedom to achieve freedom' or that it was a 'stepping-stone', but his true plan was to 'work the Treaty' and move to a united Ireland. All the evidence indicates that Collins was totally committed to ending partition. In the months after the Treaty was signed, he had not only exerted diplomatic pressure but also taken political risks in giving military support to the IRA divisions in the North and on the border. In the debates, Seán Hales (who was pro-Treaty and was killed by the IRA for voting for the Treaty) said: 'If I thought this Treaty which has been signed was to bar our right to freedom, if it was to be the finality, I wouldn't touch it but I took that it is to be a jumping off point to attain our alternative ends, because if it is one year or in ten years, Ireland will regain that freedom which is her destiny and no man can bar it. The only thing is that at the present moment if there is anything like a split it would be more dangerous than anything else ... Posterity will judge us all yet. There is no getting away from that. When the time comes there is one thing certain. Speaking from the column which I was always with through the battlefields and willing and ready to carry on the fight but still I look upon that Treaty as the best

rock from which to jump off for the final accomplishment of Irish freedom' (http://oireachtasdebates.oireachtas.ie/debates%20authoring/debateswebpack.nsf/ta kes/Dáil1921121900003). Liam Weeks and Michael O'Fathartaigh, *The Treaty: Debating the Irish State* (Sallins, 2019). While Rory O'Connor and the anti-Treaty party held the Four Courts from April to June 1922, Collins was trading the new weapons that the British were providing to the Free State army with O'Connor, who sent those new weapons to the IRA in the North. Moreover, Collins was knowingly involved in the kidnapping of Northern RIC men and holding them as hostages. Collins was the only one of the signatories to the Treaty to mention the word 'partition' in the debates, and it was he, far more than anyone else in the Free State government, who was willing to invade the North in order to achieve unification. He did believe in the Boundary Commission, but his other actions indicate his willingness to use military force in the North if necessary. Collins was greatly affected by attacks on Catholics in the North, and was engaged in many schemes that he thought would give them relief. While he indicated that he was greatly opposed to partition, he said that he would not countenance 'coercing' Ulster. 'If we are not going to coerce the North East corner, the North East corner must not be allowed to coerce.' Thomas Jones, *Whitehall Diary, Volume III, Ireland 1918– 1925* (ed. Keith Middlemas) (London, 1971), p. 77. Collins addressed partition in a speech in Armagh on 4 September 1921, stressing that the Unionists would not be coerced by republicans, but he also emphasised his opposition to partition, promising 'to those who are with us that no matter what the future may bring we will not desert them'. Éamon Phoenix, *Northern Nationalism: Nationalist Politics, Partition and the Catholic Minority in Northern Ireland, 1890–1940* (Belfast, 1994), p. 147.

It is difficult to reconcile some of Collins's statements and writings with his apparent military intentions. Further, others have written that some of Collins's efforts were counterproductive. See Robert Lynch, 'The Clones affray, 1922: massacre or invasion?', *History Ireland*, vol. 12, no. 3 (2004): 'The Clones affray also illustrates the shadowy and confused role of Michael Collins, who, stuck in his cocoon of conspiracy, continued in his deluded belief that an aggressive IRA policy could achieve similar results to those of the War of Independence. His failure to understand the Northern situation meant that his policy was at best a failure and at worst counterproductive, doing little else but confirming unionist prejudices and highlighting the Northern Catholic minority's vulnerability.' Even among those who believed in the Boundary Commission it was thought that there would be a one-sided transfer of land from the North to the Free State; when the Commission met in 1925 and some land in Donegal was to be transferred to the North the Commission fell apart. Enda Staunton, 'The Boundary Commission debacle 1925, aftermath and implications', *History Ireland*, vol. 4, no. 2 (1996).

57 Dáil Éireann, private session, p. 153. Members of the IRA in Northern Ireland were particularly distressed by de Valera's statement that, 'For his part, if the Republic were recognized he would be in favour of giving each party the power to vote itself out …'. De Valera was confirming what he had told the Dáil on 22 August 1921, before the Treaty was negotiated. McDermott, *Northern Divisions*, p. 107. McDermott opines (p. 138) that that is the reason why so many republicans in the North sided with Collins rather than de Valera when the split occurred over the terms of the Treaty.

58 See http://oireachtasdebates.oireachtas.ie/debates%20authoring/debateswebpack.

nsf/ takes/Dáil1921121900003.

59 Kathleen Clarke (ed. Helen Litton), *Revolutionary Woman: My Fight for Ireland's Freedom* (Dublin, 1997), p. 188. Further, Collins, Mulcahy and Eoin O'Duffy all gave assurances to the divisional commanders of the IRA in the north-east that, 'Although the six counties did not benefit as much as the rest of Ireland by it [the Treaty], it was the best that possibly could have been got at the time and it was the intention of the Dáil members and the members of the GHQ staff who supported it, to work to try to overcome the Treaty position with regard to Ulster'. Letter from Séamus Woods to Mulcahy, 29 September 1921, S1801/a, SPO.

60 See http://www.oireachtas.ie/parliament/education/historicaldebatesandspeeches/.

61 Dáil Éireann, Official Report: Debate on the Treaty between Great Britain and Ireland, 21 December 1921, pp. 105–6.

62 Articles of Agreement for a Treaty between Great Britain and Ireland, Article 4.

63 See http://www.oireachtas.ie/parliament/education/historicaldebatesandspeeches/.

64 See Jason Knirck, *Ghosts and Realities: Female TDs and the Treaty Debate* (New Jersey, 1997); *Women of the Dáil* (Dublin, 2006).

65 Mary Cullen and Maria Luddy, *Female Activists, Irish Women and the Change, 1900–1960* (Dublin, 2001), p. 80.

66 Diary of Kathleen Lynn, 7 December 1921.

67 Dáil Éireann, Parliamentary Debates, vol. 3, 7 January 1922.

68 Padraig de Burca and John Boyle, *Free State or Republic?* (Dublin, 1922; 2002), p. 78.

69 Dáil Éireann, Parliamentary Debates, vol. 3, 7 January 1922.

8. Conclusion: Aftermath and influence of the Irish War of Independence

What few remember is that the script followed by groups as diverse as the Vietcong and the Taliban was written in Ireland during its 1919–1921 War of Independence ...

—Max Boot

However spontaneous and idealistic it may appear, guerrilla warfare has become understood as a science, calling for objectivity on the part of its practitioners and giving guerrilla struggles a tendency towards universality. Collins clearly did not underestimate the importance of organisation and administration, even in a guerrilla war. He ultimately controlled the apparatus. As in most guerrilla wars, however, and certainly in the few successful ones, the Irish tactics, techniques and procedures do not appear to have been part of a plan deliberately conceived and constructed in advance. All wars are unique but guerrilla wars have similarities, and the successful warriors learn to use the best strategies and tactics from the 'last' wars to fight the 'next' wars.[1] The Irish learned from the past, and guerrilla warriors who followed learned from the Irish as well. In combating insurgency, the failures often have more to teach than the successes. The odds are always stacked against the insurgents: in terms of resources and manpower their opponents usually vastly outmatch them, so their eventual defeat is hardly surprising. When the insurgents 'succeed', however, it is worth sitting up and paying very close attention indeed.[2]

Colin Gray put it thus: one should not suggest that the judgements drawn from the Irish war can serve as a general paradigm or template for the conduct of all insurgencies that followed, but when those judgements are reviewed and translated into 'lessons' it is tempting to suggest that, if one understands the belligerents in, the course of and the outcome of the Irish war, then one has the lessons to learn for the conduct of future insurgencies or counter-insurgencies.[3] Context is crucial. The 'how-to' requires an examination of what worked and what did not. For example, both sides in the Irish War of Independence used coercion. Both sides resorted to terror: murder, executions or extra-judicial killings. Such actions on the part of the Irish deterred others but more importantly provoked the official and unofficial reprisals of the British—and that is exactly what Collins wanted. It makes no sense to isolate such actions from the record of the war. They were integral to it and its results.

Ireland's war presents an interesting variation of what is now called 'compound war theory', and as a result the Irish War of Independence is timely and relevant far beyond its historical interest. In an age of worldwide communications and a pervasive media, with conflicts often muddied by conflicting moral and ethical claims to the high ground, it is difficult for a democracy to wage a counter-insurgency campaign. Politicians and soldiers would do well to examine the unique circumstances of the Anglo-Irish struggle and attempt to anticipate the traps that ensnared both sides and eventually led to a British withdrawal. Often the military actions required to quell the insurgency will provide the insurgents with the other elements of compound war needed to ensure success, i.e. lack of political will on the part of the larger forces and the effects of propaganda on that political will. In reality, the purpose of the IRA was not so much to defeat the British army as to force Britain to negotiate a settlement based on the Irish claim to independence.

The Irish did not 'have a plan at the outset and stuck to it'. Just as in succeeding insurrections, the Irish adopted previous strategies and tactics, then adapted them, and adapted them again and again. The lessons learned from the Irish war worked for the Special Operations Executive (SOE) in World War II, were of limited value in Malay, inspired the Israelis in their war of independence and then were considerably used by Che Guevara in Cuba. All warriors must improvise and adapt, and guerrilla warriors more so than conventional warriors. Later revolutionaries sought to learn from the Irish experiences (as the Irish did from their predecessors) what to avoid, what to employ, and what is possible, probable and profitable. They learned what to do, what not to do, how to exploit their opponent and, hopefully, to change more than just the name plates on the doors after years of fighting. Historian of guerrilla war Max Boot elaborates:

In the 21st Century we've become used to ragtag rebels beating military superpowers. Armed with little more than the will to carry out shocking acts of terrorism and the savvy to cultivate worldwide sympathy through the media, the little guy has come out on top more often than you'd expect. The paradigms are the 1962 French defeat in Algeria, America's 1975 withdrawal from Vietnam, and Russia's disaster in Afghanistan in the 1980s. The United States was similarly dealt defeats in Beirut in 1983 and in Somalia in 1993. It almost happened in Iraq—and may yet happen in Afghanistan. What few remember is that the script followed by groups as diverse as the Vietcong and the Taliban was written in Ireland during its 1919–1921 War of Independence, the first successful revolt against the British Empire since the creation of the United States of America.[4]

In retrospect, it is clear that Collins and the Irish leaders realised during 1919–21 that the three-cornered approach of military action, politics and propaganda, all augmented by intelligence, was the approach they had to take in order to achieve native Irish governance. It was this realisation, rather than specific theorising about a prolonged guerrilla war in Frongoch or the other British prisons, which led to the pursuit of a guerrilla success that ended in the Truce of July 1921. Any early discussions of the course the war was to take were in recognition of a complete rejection of open regular warfare, but the specifics were unknown. Charles Townshend wrote that 'the means were dictated by circumstance. Slender resources created the style of warfare, rather than a conviction that it held a real hope of success.'[5] Collins was deeply conscious of the sufferings of the Irish, but he realised that these harsh guerrilla tactics must continue. With few men and little ammunition, he knew that he could not beat the British by force, but he could defeat them through their retaliatory conduct and the resulting propaganda pressures brought to bear on them. Collins was not the only one who saw what was happening to the people of Ireland during the war. One of the Black and Tans (who were never known for compassion) wrote that 'as always happens the real sufferer in this fratricidal war was the non combatant—civilians were being targeted by both sides'.[6]

The Irish had the benefit of a natural growth of the historic guerrilla idea of not committing the whole force at the start. A series of favourable circumstances (British mass imprisonments, an attempt at conscription, British over-reactions, British reprisals and international opinion against the British, among others) all contributed to the Irish ability to control the pace of the war and employ larger numbers of Volunteers at critical times. Once the war was under the overall direction of GHQ, the possibilities for the Irish quickly became evident and ensured that the many varieties of guerrilla war could be used to the full. As Florence O'Donoghue summarised:

> The seeds of all subsequent growth and expansion would appear to be contained in the vital decision not to repeat the pattern of earlier risings, not to commit the national destiny in that day to the hazard of a single blow.[7]

The Irish nationalist of 1919–21 took little account of the *history* of British rule. Following the 1916 Rising, nationalism took account only of the *fact* of British rule. In 1920 Richard Dawson wrote:

> Our Nationalism is not founded upon grievances. We are not opposed to English misgovernment, but to English government in Ireland. Here, then, we are face to face with an abiding principle of insurgency. Evil memories may be transient, withered by time or effaced by gratitude, but hatred of a fact persists so long as the fact continues.[8]

Ultimately, the Irish strategy was based on the fundamental principle that superior political will, properly employed, could defeat a greater economic and military power. Collins and the Irish organised to ensure political rather than military success, after understanding that the Irish could not 'win' militarily but neither could the British defeat them by military power alone. The strategic function of the Irish guerrilla war was to defeat the British psychologically and politically. The tactical function of the Irish flying column was to remain alive and in operation. As the ultimate pragmatist, Collins realised that since he could not win a military campaign his prime mission was to keep the IRA vital and active. He had to prevent the restoration of order, and he sought to keep the IRA's military forays going until the British government decided that it had had enough of the violent disorder in Ireland—and the negative publicity that entailed. Collins did not seek an unattainable military victory but a dignified British withdrawal. Learning to adjust is the key to success in any insurgency, and the Irish adjusted and improvised their military—and their political— strategies better than the British. (It must be noted, however, that by the end of the war the British military were catching up; had the war continued, they would have exerted even greater military pressure on the Irish forces.)

A government cannot outfight an insurgency; it must out-govern the rebels. Bernard Fall, one of the most respected writers on guerrilla warfare of the twentieth century, wrote that 'a government which is losing an insurgency is not being outfought—it is being out-governed'.[9] The British did not govern Ireland well. The Irish did not 'win' the war but they 'succeeded' by defeating the British political will. The British never did learn that 'the more force you use in counterinsurgency action, the less effective you are'. Collins recognised that the war would not be won militarily. The IRA would play an important role but it would not be decisive. If guerrillas attempt to win solely by military force they will lose.

The Irish War of Independence demonstrated that, given some favourable circumstances, an insurrection has a fair chance of success. The Irish conditions that contributed to that were:

The opposing army [the British] is for one reason or another prevented from exerting its full strength. Not only were the guerrilla tactics of harassment and hit-and-run preventing the British from taking on the Irish using their full might, but the political climate in Britain prevented it as well.

The general population must be sympathetic to the revolutionary forces, and be prepared to give secret support. In the Irish war, this was magnified because of the general homogeneity of the population throughout the country.

The IRA was at least loosely controlled and there was a general military strategic and political plan.

Operations can be carried on over a long term, and mistakes like being surrounded in buildings in Dublin, as was the case in the Easter Rising, are avoided. The long-term process continues to escalate, and in doing so the Irish wore down both the military and political morale of the British. The actions can be carried on in the countryside, where the geography will give quick cover to the insurgents, and the same principles apply in the city.[10]

It is vital to understand the relationship between the British armed forces and the community of Britain: Parliament, the press, the churches and the general population. These relations developed as the war continued, and finally led to the progress of the war being influenced by the whole social and political scheme of Britain as well as by its military.

The British post-mortem on the Irish War of Independence attributed their 'failure' to strategic intelligence shortcomings as well as military shortcomings.

The Army is only the spear point; it is the shaft of the spear and the force behind it that drives the blow home. During the last two years it would appear that the true state of affairs in Ireland was not realised in Great Britain, at all events, until it was too late. Consequently, the want of a suitable and clear policy was felt and sufficient importance was not, perhaps, attached to convincing the country of the need for putting one into force … The first lesson we learn is the necessity for a good intelligence system so that the Government advisors may be in a position to appreciate the situation justly and to put it squarely, fully and honestly before the Cabinet.[11]

Equally clearly, it was apparent that the British military did not understand the true effect of the Irish effort in politics and propaganda on British and international opinion until it was too late.

One of Michael Collins's critics, Peter Hart, still placed Collins—and the Irish War of Independence—in context for future conflict:

Irish republicans invented modern revolutionary warfare, with all its mass parties, popular fronts, guerrilla warfare, underground governments, and continuous propaganda campaigns. What Michael Collins and company did in post-Great War Ireland, Mao, Tito, and Ho Chi Minh would do during and after the next great war.[12]

The events of the Irish War of Independence are relevant to the conduct of irregular warfare in the twenty-first century.

Scarcely two years after the Truce, Ireland's place in history and contributions to guerrilla war techniques, tactics and procedures were firmly established by two British officers who had fought hard against them. In October 1923 Major A.E. Percival, who had served as Intelligence Officer of the 1st Battalion of the Essex Regiment in Cork, wrote to his friend Major Bernard Montgomery, who had served with the 17th Infantry Brigade in Cork. Percival was preparing two lectures on guerrilla tactics, using Ireland as his model, and asked Montgomery's advice. Montgomery wrote back:

My own view is that to win a war of this sort, you must be ruthless. Oliver Cromwell or the Germans would have settled it in a very short time. Nowadays public opinion precludes such methods, the nation would never allow it, and the politicians would lose their jobs if they sanctioned it. That being so, I consider that Lloyd George was right in what he did, if we had gone on we could probably have squashed the rebellion as a temporary measure, but it would have broken out again like an ulcer the moment we removed the troops. I think the rebels would probably [have] refused battles, and hidden their arms etc. until we had gone. The only way therefore was to give them some sort of self-government and let them quash the rebellion themselves; they are the only people who could really stamp it out, and they are still trying to do so, and as far as one can tell they seem to be having a fair amount of success.[13]

Those who wish to study guerrilla warfare in the Irish War of Independence and to determine its effect on subsequent guerrilla actions need look no further than the British 'irregular' efforts in World War II. The Special Operations Executive (SOE) was established in 1940 to support or create resistance movements in Europe and to organise widespread sabotage and subversion as an extension of the British war effort. It was consciously outside and contrary to the Rules of War and was accompanied by military coups and sabotage raids organised by other branches of the secret services in pursuit of British war aims.[14]

M.R.D. Foot, a British intelligence officer involved in clandestine activities, went on to write numerous books and articles on the subject, including the official history of the SOE. In 1969 he delivered a lecture in Dublin to the Military History Society on 'Michael Collins and Irregular Warfare'. Present at the lecture, he subsequently noted, were

> an alarmingly large number of former participants [in the Anglo-Irish War] ... including Collins's chief of staff in the Troubles [Richard Mulcahy], subsequently commander-in-chief of the Irish Army ... three silent survivors of the Twelve Apostles; his personal bodyguard [Dave Neligan]; and two former members of the detective division in Dublin Castle, who had doubled their official task by acting among his leading intelligence agents [Éamon Broy].

Foot emphatically noted that lessons (or personnel) from the 'goings-on in Ulster in 1913–21' played no role in subversive British activity in the war of 1939, but that

> what Collins did in Dublin had a noticeable impact ... through two of his junior but intelligent opponents, [Major] J.C.F. Holland and [Major] C. McV. Gubbins ... Both were profoundly impressed with the powerlessness of regular troops against the resolute gunmen who could rely on the local population not to give them away ... both saw the advantages, in economy of life and effectiveness of effort, of the Irish guerrilla they could not see. And both were determined that next time, if there had to be a next time, guerrilla tactics should be used by the British instead of against them.

...
Ireland had become a world model of how to conduct a successful insurrection against an occupying colonial power.

Following the removal of British forces from Ireland in 1922–3, J.C.F. Holland undertook a special study of irregular warfare at the War Office and was put in charge of the secret service unit set up to work on it in 1938. When offered the chance to pick an associate, he chose his old colleague Colin Gubbins, whom he had met as a major in Ireland during the War of Independence. In early 1939, and building on their Irish experience, they proposed a comprehensive plan for an army of sabotage and subversion to operate outside the laws of war in taking on the enemy through flying columns, civic disobedience, the execution of traitors and enemy agents, explosions and intelligence. In 1940 they were tasked with establishing the SOE, which General Gubbins later went on to command. Foot concluded:

> The Irish can thus claim that their resistance provided an originating impulse for resistance to tyrannies worse than any they had had to endure themselves.[15]

Gubbins got the hang of guerrilla warfare whilst serving in Ireland, and learned how much mayhem could be caused by a disciplined and shadowy army of operatives fighting on their own territory and employing hit-and-run tactics. He served as an intelligence officer in Kildare in 1921–2 and his introduction to guerrilla warfare consisted of a three-day course organised by the HQ 5th Division. The course was an indication that the British were beginning to understand guerrilla war tactics as applied by the Irish, and all officers arriving in the country after October 1920 were required to attend it. When the IRA's ambush tactics became clear, the British army developed a manual of standard operating procedures to be followed in responding to them, and their records indicate that this tactical doctrine reduced their casualties. Gubbins characterised his service in the conflict as 'being shot at from behind hedges by men in trilbys and mackintoshes and not allowed to shoot back'.[16] His experiences in the Anglo-Irish War stimulated his lifelong interest in irregular warfare, and his personal reflections on the conflict indicate his view that the British responses were lacking in flexibility and individual initiative. When Gubbins was assigned as the training officer for the SOE, he applied the tactics and used the lessons that he had learned in Ireland twenty years earlier.[17] He was an admirer of Collins's tactics and considered him the master of guerrilla warfare.[18]

One of the lessons drawn from the Irish War of Independence was the importance of captured enemy documents, which provided the British forces with a wealth of invaluable intelligence on the IRA—the British in fact made their best intelligence discoveries from captured Irish documents. In his memoirs Ormonde Winter argued that British intelligence gradually improved between Bloody Sunday and the Truce, 'largely because the Irish had an irresistible habit of keeping documents which were likely to be uncovered in raids'.[19] As the war continued and the pace of raids increased, intelligence gleaned from captured documents could lead to two or three further raids. The War Office report after the war stated:

> In Dublin both the military and the police agreed that their most important sources of information were captured documents.
>
> ...
>
> After the first important capture which, to a great extent, was fortuitous, other searches were made from the addresses noted and names obtained, and the snowball process continued, new arrests and the obtaining of a more intimate knowledge of the plans, resources, and methods of the rebel organisation, besides material for valuable propaganda.
>
> ...
>
> These documents were not only the foundations on which the IRA List and Order of Battle were built, but seizure usually led to further raids and the capture of more documents until GHQ, IRA, were entirely demoralised. Up to 1920 Sinn Féin had taken few precautions to safeguard or destroy their papers and the documents taken in Dublin in this period were of the highest importance in that they contained more details and completer [sic] and more accurate lists of names than was the case later. It is possible that, had the importance of documents been realised in

country districts, and had those captured at this time been more carefully scrutinised and analysed, the source might have proved a fruitful one, but, unfortunately, many papers were destroyed, many were not examined, and this side of intelligence was not developed until the IRA had begun to take what steps they could to safeguard themselves.

...

Fortunately, however, IRA officers often did keep documents that they could have destroyed with advantage and without loss of efficiency, and these provided excellent evidence against persons whom it was intended to try or intern.[20]

Some British troops in the country were able to recover documents, and they proved invaluable. In December 1920, Auxiliaries captured Ernie O'Malley in a raid in Kilkenny, where he was breaking his journey on his way back to Dublin. O'Malley customarily carried all his notes and papers with him. He was eating in a safe house when the Auxiliaries broke in, and his notebooks were on the window-sill. When the British examined O'Malley's notes, they found that the Kilkenny area had 'four brigades of eight battalions with 103 rifles, 4,900 rounds of rifle ammunition, 471 shot-guns and 3,490 rounds of shot-gun ammunition'. The notebook also listed all the names of the Kilkenny Brigade. As they left, the Auxiliary O/C announced 'We have the lot!' and they were delighted.

The Auxies were so pleased with what they found in the book that they ran to tell each other and decided to burn the premises. They set fire to hay, straw and outhouses and sent a Crossley tender to Woodstock for petrol to burn the dwelling house.

...

The petrol having arrived, the occupants of the house were compelled to leave, and the Auxies spilled the petrol on the bedding, furniture, floors, etc. They broke windows to ensure a draught and, having set the house on fire, remained for some time watching the flames.[21]

In the days that followed, the Auxiliaries used the notebook to seek out and arrest most of the leaders of the Kilkenny Brigade. While in prison O'Malley met two other prisoners from the area, who told him that the Auxiliaries had arrested 'the whole countryside' and that, mad with rage, they were murdering half the people they took'.[22]

Richard Mulcahy's flat in Cullenwood House was raided on 31 January 1920 and many of his papers were found. They caused a sensation in Dublin Castle, as they 'gave evidence of a really big, determined and fairly well organised conspiracy', along with plans describing Volunteers going abroad to put the electricity plant for Manchester out of action and for the destruction of the Liverpool docks.[23] Mulcahy never seemed to understand the risk of keeping comprehensive records, or the potentially disastrous effects of their capture. Several times the British captured his records and those of Collins. Once Mulcahy wrote to Liam Lynch, 'These things have to be put down in writing', arguing that this outweighed the 'accompanying danger that if any of this material falls into enemy hands it discloses our mind fairly completely to them'.[24] That same night, a raid on Eileen McGrane's home at 21 Dawson Street yielded a bundle of Collins's documents, which he had foolishly left there. This was one of Collins's weaknesses: he hated to part with files, even when they ceased to be useful, and he never took sufficient precautions to ensure that the people referred to in the files could not be identified.[25] This raid gave the Castle the first intimation of the effectiveness of Collins's recruitment within their own ranks, and they began a long process of elimination that led them to Éamon (Ned) Broy. Some documents traced to Broy were found in McGrane's home, leading to his arrest. Mulcahy didn't learn his lesson, and on 21 March 1921 another of his houses was raided; included in the captured documents was a list of all the individuals the IRA had marked for assassination, as well as plans for the demolition of a canal in Manchester. Upon establishing the SOE, one of the key security features that Gubbins introduced was: 'Commit as little as possible to writing. Memorise if you can. If you must carry documents, select what you must carry. Burn all secret waste and carbons.'[26]

Several British officers who served in Ireland during the war as intelligence officers went on to leadership positions in World War II. Five who later achieved fame were Major (later General) Kenneth Strong, Major (later General) Arthur Percival, Major (later Field Marshal) Bernard Montgomery, Lieutenant (later Field Marshal) Gerald Templer and Major (later General) Colin Gubbins.

Gubbins and Holland were not the only officers with Irish experience to formulate intelligence and partisan tactics to be written down and then used in later wars. General Hugh Tudor chose as his Chief of Intelligence an artilleryman, the Anglo-Irish Colonel Ormonde de l'Epée Winter, who had some little previous experience in British intelligence. Winter had risen to command a division in World War I and Tudor himself came from the Royal Artillery, as did Gubbins. In fact, it is surprising just how many British artillery officers serving in Ireland were involved in counter-insurgency/intelligence and propaganda roles and went on to write about their Irish experiences or to play key roles in British intelligence operations in World War II. Col. Hervey de Montmorency, an Anglo-Irish aristocrat, was another World War I artillery officer who returned to Ireland as a bitter opponent of separatists and worked under Winter as the intelligence officer of the Auxiliaries in County Westmeath. Books by or about all of them were written, including their memories of the Irish campaign, and all contained lessons that were used in later wars.[27]

The IRA inspiration for SOE strategy is, however, regularly played down in some British accounts of the SOE (Foot is an exception), and this is hardly surprising. Britain is not in the habit of announcing to the world that it learns anything much from Ireland. After fighting Irish insurgencies for centuries, to be promoting and organising them, as they did in World War II, was a novelty. Moreover, Foot's views on this issue have come under attack. That post-war British military officials might have second thoughts about legitimising the Irish as a source of terrorism and insurgency like the SOE, as Foot argued, is entirely understandable.

Eunan O'Halpin has written extensively about Ireland and British intelligence. He dismisses the notion of an IRA/Sinn Féin inspiration for the SOE—or, indeed, the idea that Britain learned anything from its war in Ireland:

Few British military thinkers sought to draw wider lessons from the Irish War of Independence. A number of officers who were to make their names as intelligence or irregular warfare specialists, such as J.C.F. Holland of the War Office think-tank GS(R), which in 1939 developed into MI(R), Colin Gubbins of the Special

Operations Executive (SOE) and Kenneth Strong, Eisenhower's chief of intelligence in 1944–5, had served in Ireland between 1919 and 1922. (Gubbins commanded the detachment which provided the field gun with which the Provisional Government troops shelled the Four Courts at the commencement of the Civil War, and was also in charge of the handover of the gun-carriage lent to the Irish to bear the remains of Michael Collins.)

Undue emphasis has been placed on the importance for such officers of the experience of Irish rebellion and counter-insurgency. In 1969, M.R.D. Foot, the official historian of the Special Operations Executive (SOE) in France, presented a celebrated lecture in Dublin on 'Michael Collins and Irregular Warfare'. Amongst his audience was the British Ambassador, Andrew Gilchrist, himself an old SOE hand, who thought the lecture brilliant. So too did Gilchrist's closest Irish friends, Colonel David Neligan and Major-General Seán Collins-Powell, respectively Collins's spy in the Castle in 1920 and 1921 and Collins's nephew. Gilchrist bemoaned the absence of a single politician from the ruling Fianna Fáil party at the lecture. But perhaps the Fianna Fáilers were right to doubt the weight of the speaker's argument, because a survey of inter-war British military thought and planning yields very few references to the intelligence, counter-insurgency, or irregular warfare lessons of the Irish campaign of 1919–21.[28]

O'Halpin's colleague, Keith Jeffery of Queen's University Belfast, who also specialised in British intelligence and was appointed to head the team writing the official history of MI6, drew the same conclusions as O'Halpin with regard to the Irish counter-insurgency:

Scarcely any lessons with regard to counter-insurgency campaigning generally were drawn from the Irish experience … M.R.D. Foot has, however, asserted that in the persons of J.C.F. Holland and C. McV. Gubbins, both of whom had served in Ireland, the experience of that campaign was not entirely lost, at least in its contribution to SOE.[29]

Jeffery, however, seems to have changed his opinion of the value of the Irish war, even if the British army did not study it, as he wrote in 2014:

> The Record [of the Rebellion in Ireland 1919–1921 and the Part Played by the Army in Dealing with it, Imperial War Museum, Box 78/82/2] is full of fascinating detail, and explanations advanced by soldiers who had lost the campaign in Ireland. It would have been of tremendous assistance after 1969 when British troops once more were deployed in Ireland against a violent republican challenge, but there is no evidence that in the late 1960s anyone thought to revisit the experience of the early 1920s to ascertain if there might be any 'lessons learned' of use in the new situation.[30]

For over fifty years the Irish War of Independence seemed to be forgotten in some military literature, except in Ireland. In the period between the World Wars, when Britain was formalising its counter-insurgency doctrine, Ireland was 'airbrushed' from official British histories. Nevertheless, Black-and-Tan-style policing policies (and some of the personnel) would reappear in Palestine, a campaign that ended in 1948 with a British exit even more ignominious than in Ireland.[31] Despite a seeming lack of interest on the part of the British military to acknowledge anything learned from Ireland, a number of commentators have summarised the principal lessons. Apart from the obvious ones about having a unified and coherent policy, not seeking quick fixes and not underestimating the enemy, the principal lessons that can be drawn from the Irish campaign are the following:

- The need to have a unified intelligence system, particularly between civil and military authorities.
- The understanding of hit-and-run tactics, escape and evasion.
- The need to target the most radical elements, including the use of less coercive methods against moderates.
- The avoidance, if possible, of tit-for-tat violence and terror measures against civilians.
- The need to consider effects on the wider stage, i.e. propaganda.

- Rapid and secure communications.
- The need to deal promptly with security breaches and to protect sources, i.e. protection of documents.[32]

The current UK Ministry of Defence position is in agreement with Gubbins and Foot as regards the value of studying the Irish War of Independence:

> The 30 months between these killings in January 1919 [Soloheadbeg] and the truce in July 1921 also represent a counter-insurgency campaign by the British military and political establishment. This campaign would become extremely influential for insurgent groups throughout the 20th century as it demonstrated how an ill-trained, ill-equipped but well-motivated movement can combine political and military approaches in an economical and successful way, even against a much larger and technologically powerful enemy. It is also useful and instructive for analysts studying today's counter-insurgency campaigns, as it is reasonably well documented, was fought around modern concepts of guerrilla warfare, including religiously inspired propaganda[33] and martyrdom operations, and showed the effectiveness or otherwise of a range of security policies and insurgent responses.[34]

In addition, the current US Army Field Manual *Information Operations: Doctrine, Tactics, Techniques, and Procedures* notes the performance of the Irish War of Independence and the Volunteers' strengths and structure, including security, efficiency and speed of action, unity of effort, survivability, geography, and the social structures and cultures of the society.[35] This manual also notes that 'the best weapons for counterinsurgency do not shoot bullets'. The Irish political and propaganda efforts were at least as effective as their military weapons.

To win the support of the population, counter-insurgency forces must create incentives for co-operating with the government and disincentives for opposing it. The leaders of both the counter-insurgency and insurgent forces must stress the importance of focusing more on the social, economic and political development of the people than on simple material destruction. In a later Irish war, British General Frank Kitson noted that ideas are a motivating factor in insurgent violence: 'The main characteristic which distinguishes campaigns of insurgency from other forms of war is that they are primarily concerned with the struggle for men's minds'.[36] Insurgencies fight for political power as well as for an idea. According to US Marine General Charles C. Krulak, to fight back 'you need a better idea. Bullets help sanitize an operational area … They don't win a war.'[37]

While the strategy and tactics used in Ireland were not much of a factor in the British counter-insurgency in Malay in the 1950s, winning the 'hearts and minds' of the people has become enshrined as a pivotal component of counter-insurgency warfare ever since General Sir Gerald Templer declared in 1952 that it would be the key to success in fighting the communists.[38] Templer famously remarked that 'The answer [to the uprising] lies not in pouring more troops into the jungle, but in the hearts and minds of the people'.[39] His plan of war was not to *terrorise* the population but to *control* them, offering the Malays independence. His view was that 'the shooting side of this business is only 25% of the trouble'.[40] He realised that it was not a popularity contest but that the counter-insurgents must provide, first, security for the population and then, second, the legitimacy of the government. Insurgency versus counter-insurgency is a struggle to see who can provide better governance for the population; Templer realised this and the population made its choice. The Malayan Emergency is still regarded as the shining paradigm of how to properly wage a counter-insurgency campaign, and Templer's emphasis on hearts and minds established a fixation on these operations in military circles. (It must be understood that the Malay insurgency, and Templer's method of combating it, was characterised by geographical and demographic factors that were peculiar to it and were not often possible to replicate in later insurgencies. Under the Briggs Plan employed by Templer, however, the British administration replaced soldiers with civilian police who gained the trust of the community by building long-term relationships. The British also developed an information campaign to portray the police as civil servants whose job it was to protect civilians. By 1953 these efforts had reduced violence and increased trust in the government and have been used in successful counter-insurgency actions ever since to win 'hearts and minds'.[41]) Certainly the IRA won, and the British lost, the hearts and minds of the Irish population in the War of Independence.

A young Vietnamese expatriate named Nguyen Ai Quoc was working as a cook in London until 1919. He later changed his name to Ho Chi Minh. Clearly, Ho and Võ Nguyên Giáp launched the war against the French and Americans in Vietnam with the classic guerrilla tactics of hit-and-run operations, assassination of government officials and terrorising the local population into submission. In addition, Ho executed an effective international propaganda offensive that undermined American resolve in the same way that Collins and the Irish had turned British and international public opinion against London's Irish policy. While the 'urban legend' that Ho cried when he heard of Terence MacSwiney's death is probably apocryphal (he left London before October 1920), there is no doubt that his guerrilla tactics mirrored those used by the Irish.[42]

In her book *Tom Barry: Freedom Fighter*, Meda Ryan recounts how both Menachem Begin in Israel and Che Guevara in Cuba wrote to Barry for advice.[43] Diverse nationalist guerrilla movements in the decades that followed emulated Collins's pioneering urban warfare tactics and skilful use of propaganda. While governments regularly decry terrorism as ineffective, the terrorists themselves have an abiding faith in their violence, and for good reason. Terrorism's intractability is also due to the capacity of terrorist groups to learn from one another. Those terrorist groups that survive the onslaught directed against them by governments and their police, military, and intelligence and security services do so because they absorb and apply lessons learned from their predecessors. Theirs is a trade and they learn it from one another. For instance, the Jewish terrorist group Irgun, led by Begin, consciously modelled itself on the IRA and studied the Irish War of Independence. Israel's Yitzhak Shamir so revered Collins that he took the code name 'Micail' during Israel's war for independence in the late 1940s.

As a further example of a guerrilla studying the Irish War of Independence, Che Guevara utilised the Irish tactics in developing his own tactics in Cuba. He concluded:

- Popular forces can win a war against the army.
- It is not necessary to wait until all conditions for making revolution exist; the insurrection can create them.

- In underdeveloped Cuba the countryside was the basic area for armed fighting.

Guevara's book on guerrilla warfare could be considered a review of the tactics, procedures and procedures of the Irish War of Independence. Consider the following:

> In these conditions [in Cuba] popular discontent expresses itself in more active forms. An attitude of resistance finally crystallizes in an outbreak of fighting, provoked initially by the conduct of the authorities.
>
> Let us first consider the question: Who are the combatants in guerrilla warfare? On one side we have a group composed of the oppressor and his agents, the professional army, well armed and disciplined, in many cases receiving foreign help as well as the help of the bureaucracy in the employ of the oppressor. On the other side are the people of the nation or region involved. It is important to emphasize that guerrilla warfare is a war of the masses, a war of the people. The guerrilla band is an armed nucleus, the fighting vanguard of the people. It draws its great force from the mass of the people themselves. The guerrilla band is not to be considered inferior to the army against which it fights simply because it is inferior in firepower. Guerrilla warfare is used by the side which is supported by a majority but which possesses a much smaller number of arms for use in defence against oppression.
>
> Why does the guerrilla fighter fight? We must come to the inevitable conclusion that the guerrilla fighter is a social reformer, that he takes up arms responding to the angry protest of the people against their oppressors, and that he fights in order to change the social system that keeps all his unarmed brothers in ignominy and misery. He launches himself against the conditions of the reigning institutions at a particular moment and dedicates himself with all the vigor that circumstances permit to breaking the mold of these institutions.
>
> As blows are dealt the enemy, he also changes his tactics, and

in place of isolated trucks, veritable motorized columns move. However, by choosing the ground well, the same result can be produced by breaking the column and concentrating forces on one vehicle. In these cases the essential elements of guerrilla tactics must always be kept in mind. These are: perfect knowledge of the ground; surveillance and foresight as to the lines of escape; vigilance over all the secondary roads that can bring support to the point of attack; intimacy with people in the zone so as to have sure help from them in respect to supplies, transport, and temporary or permanent hiding places if it becomes necessary to leave wounded companions behind; numerical superiority at a chosen point of action; total mobility; and the possibility of counting on reserves. If all these tactical requisites are fulfilled, surprise attack along the lines of communication of the enemy yields notable dividends.[44]

If one substitutes 'Irish' for the Cuban situation, one can see how remarkably closely the two wars resemble one another. In Ireland the war developed slowly, as more and more Irish came over to the side of the Volunteers. Certainly, Guevara's 'provoked initially by the conduct of the authorities' could refer to the executions and imprisonments following the Rising and the threat of conscription in 1918, in addition to the hundreds of years of the Irish living under British rule. The British in Ireland could certainly be defined as 'a group composed of the oppressor and his agents, the professional army, well armed and disciplined, in many cases receiving foreign help as well as the help of the bureaucracy in the employ of the oppressor'. Why did the IRA fight and why was it successful? Guevara's answer is that the 'guerrilla fighter is a social reformer, that he takes up arms responding to the angry protest of the people against their oppressors, and that he fights in order to change the social system that keeps all his unarmed brothers in ignominy and misery. He launches himself against the conditions of the reigning institutions at a particular moment and dedicates himself with all the vigor that circumstances permit to breaking the mold of these institutions.' While the Irish War of Independence did not lead to a great social revolution, there is no doubt that it was fought to give the Irish their own government. Finally, Guevara could be defining flying columns when he writes: 'the essential elements of guerrilla tactics must always be kept in mind. These are: perfect knowledge of the ground; surveillance and foresight as to the lines of escape; vigilance over all the secondary roads that can bring support to the point of attack; intimacy with people in the zone so as to have sure help from them in respect to supplies, transport, and temporary or permanent hiding places'. To this day, the Irish War of Independence can provide inspiration and direction to insurgents.

Guevara's tenet that it was 'not necessary to wait until all conditions for making revolution exist; the insurrection can create them' was certainly true of the Irish war and mirrored James Connolly's views on revolt. Connolly spent a lifetime studying revolution and he knew that Irish history was filled with men who waited for the right moment and then lost their chance. In Connolly's view, an insurrection must be a 'leap in the dark'.[45]

One of the major problems in all guerrilla wars is what happens after 'regime change'—what is now called 'nation-building'. Order does not arise by chance; someone has to design it and make it happen. The Truce of July 1921 caught the rank and file of both sides by surprise; both thought that they were winning. Neither side 'won', however; both sides went to the bargaining table to make pragmatic compromises. And it must be said that James Connolly and other socialists who pursued goals in the 1916 Rising would have been sorely disappointed. Indeed, Sinn Féin subscribed largely to a doctrine grounded in a conservative nationalism. It was with some accuracy that Kevin O'Higgins stated during the early days of the Free State government: 'I think that we were probably the most conservative-minded revolutionaries that ever put through a successful revolution'.[46] Todd Andrews described the men of his local Sinn Féin Club in Rathfarnham as being

> ... astonishingly conservative. It might be expected that men who were prepared to support a rebellion against the political status quo would have shown some liberality of view but social questions such as housing, public health, education were seldom mentioned.[47]

In any event, the concept of a 'socialist republic revolution' was never in the plans thereafter.[48] It should be emphasised that the active leadership in

1916–21 of such Irish republicans of the left as Peadar O'Donnell and Liam Mellows does little to alter that reality. According to O'Donnell, 'All the [IRA] leadership wanted was a change from British to Irish government: they wanted no change in the basis of society. It was a political not a social revolution.'

Michael Laffan agreed:

> Sinn Féin's interventions in labour, agrarian and other social problems were not designed primarily to help the underpaid or the landless, but to calm them, and its leaders showed little concern with improving the living standards of the poor before the British departed. Here Sinn Féin followed an established tradition. Its predecessor, the Irish Parliamentary Party, had feared the British remedies for Irish grievances might blunt the demand for Home Rule.[49]

The War of Independence, while bringing the British to the bargaining table for the first time, was not a clear military victory and certainly did not produce a social revolution. There were many forces opposing one another in Ireland—liberalism v. conservatism; socialism v. capitalism; dominion (or even monarchy) v. republic—but no new form of government was certain. Florence O'Donoghue wrote:

> I do not think that in 1917, or indeed during the following years of struggle, any of us thought very much about forms of government. I had no clearer definition of national freedom than that envisaged by the ejection of British troops and British machinery of government out of the country. Republicanism was no more than a convenient term of expression, not a faith or a belief in a particular form of government.[50]

During the whole period there were short-term goals for the Irish, military and propaganda victories, but there were no long-term solutions to the political problems facing them, least of all what form any new government was to take. Throughout the war, the term 'republic' was used to indicate a vaguely defined independence. Freedom from Britain, alone, was considered the sole end in itself. The revolutionaries thought that it was enough just to topple the British government in Ireland. Once that had been achieved, the more prosaic business of what comes next could be resolved. Vincent Gookin, a seventeenth-century English colonist in Ireland, wrote ruefully that 'the unsettling of a nation is an easy work; the settling of a nation is not'. Little or no thought—and certainly no preparation—was given to what was to come afterwards. This didn't seem to matter until the Truce came into effect in July 1921. Collins was absolutely explicit about the need for the Treaty negotiations:

> The fighting area in Cork ... could not have carried on much longer.
> If we all stood on the recognition of the Irish Republic as a prelude to any conference we could very easily have said so, and there would have been no conference ...
> It was the acceptance of the invitation that formed the compromise ...

By the time of the election on 16 June 1922 the people wanted peace.

Some of Collins's key contributions to modern guerrilla warfare were:

- The degree to which he understood the connection between intelligence and guerrilla warfare. Intelligence drives operations. In modern military/intelligence parlance, he used 'predictive intelligence and ops-intel fusion'. Collins was ahead of his time.
- The recognition that politics and propaganda are as important as military weapons.
- The bringing of guerrilla warfare to the city.
- The use of IEDs to counter the mechanisation of the British.

Collins preferred strategies of provocation (to undermine support for the British) and exhaustion (to convince the British to leave Ireland). Modern insurgents use the same formula to wear down enemy forces.

There is no doubt that Collins was a natural intelligence officer and a political genius, but he was also a 'physical-force' nationalist who exploited a weak British security policy to wage a ruthless and bloody intelligence and guerrilla war. Collins's great achievement was to manoeuvre the British into an untenable political position and to bring them to negotiations, not to eliminate British military forces. He brought his charismatic leadership, a forceful style and a commanding presence to all the positions he held. What set him apart from other guerrilla fighters was that he was always thinking not just of war but also of peace and how to achieve it as quickly and advantageously as possible.[51] He took revolutionary strategy to a new level. His genius lay in recognising and exploiting the British shortcomings to the fullest. He outworked and outwitted British intelligence. Of the War of Independence, Collins wrote:

> We took as much of the government of Ireland out of the hands of the enemy as we could, but we could not grasp all of it because he used the whole of his forces to prevent us doing so.
>
> We were unable to beat him out of the country by force of arms. But neither had he beaten us ... We had made Ireland ungovernable for him.
>
> The British had not surrendered and had no need to agree to humiliating terms any more than we would have done. It was time for a settlement that would secure for us their withdrawal and evacuation. There was duress, of course. On their side, the pressure of world opinion to conform with the practice of their professions. On our side, the duress the weaker nation suffers against the stronger, the duress to accept really substantial terms.[52]

Churchill, who seemed to be an implacable foe of Collins throughout the war, described him thus:

> Successor to a sinister inheritance, reared among fierce conditions and moving through ferocious times, he supplied those qualities of action and personality without which the foundation of Irish nationhood would not have been re-established.[53]

There were many heroes in the Irish War of Independence and Michael Collins was one of them, but they are uncomfortable heroes to some. In every war—particularly guerrilla wars—both sides commit outrageous acts, and the Irish War of Independence was no different. Collins and the others were not saints. He said that his methods were 'The only way a small nation can fight an empire'.

Collins knew that peace would be achieved eventually; the only question was the price. He knew that the Irish would have to talk to the British sooner or later, and the cleverest men always do it sooner rather than later. It was one thing to know this but quite another to have the ruthlessness to take the necessary steps. Collins was ruthless in an efficient manner and was able to specifically target his intelligence operations for the greatest effect, and he stands out among his contemporaries for never wavering when such ruthlessness was required. He encouraged negotiation when it was clear that no purpose was to be served by prolonging the violence.

The Irish War of Independence shows that the most successful guerrilla campaigns are waged for causes, usually nationalist, that have widespread acceptance among the population and are supported by political parties and by some military forces. Guerrillas do better if they fight a democratic nation—Britain in this case—with a free press that will help to magnify their actions while restraining the official response. Collins recognised the value of propaganda as used by the Irish side, and the dissatisfaction with the way the war was proceeding as reported in the British press, and took advantage of both. Charles Townshend wrote of Collins:

> The IRA ... showed a natural grasp of the political and psychological bearing of guerrilla warfare applied in conjunction with modern publicity techniques.
>
> Collins knew the gun to be but a propaganda weapon—its power of destruction a headline, its detonation a slogan.

Collins described his emotions on the day that Dublin Castle was turned over to the Irish. He wrote that he never

> ... expected ... to see the day ships should sail away to England with the Auxiliaries and Black and Tans, the RIC and the British soldiery ... Nor did we ever expect to see the Auxiliary Division marching out of Beggar's Bush Barracks ... How could I have

ever expected Dublin Castle itself formally surrendered into my hands? We had red carpets laid out for us on that momentous morning and I recalled my only previous visit to those grim precincts as the driver of a coal-cart, with a price on my head! That was the time that we planned our counter-intelligence system in the Holy-of-Holies itself.[54]

Even today, Collins remains a controversial and polarising figure of the War of Independence. It was the supreme irony that his former comrades would kill the man who planned guerrilla warfare in Ireland in a guerrilla ambush in his home county. In British eyes he was just 'a gunman', a terrorist, albeit a romantic terrorist, but Collins saw reality much more clearly than the romantic republicans around him. He has been described as a man of emotions, impulsive and with a violent temper, but he was also a man of patience: his view that the war had to be 'paced' indicates that he knew patience was essential. Time is a weapon. Insurgencies are psychological and political more than military struggles. The IRA needed to remain alive for longer than the nerves of liberal Britain could stand, and it succeeded. Irish governance, not military victory, was always the goal. Collins and the Irish succeeded there, too. Conversely, the British military goal was not to defeat Sinn Féin but to assist in the establishment of stability within the British governing of Ireland. The British failed in their mission.

Collins was a man of imagination, with a vision of the future and an unbreakable will. He was a brilliant administrator, a pragmatist who, though he said that he was a 'soldier, not a politician', was always attempting to make a deal, and to the very end of his life he was making compromises for Ireland. He epitomised Lawrence's famous view:

All men dream, but not equally. Those who dream by night in the dusty recesses of the mind, wake in the day to find it was vanity. But the dreamers of the day are dangerous men for they may act their dreams with open eyes to make it possible.[55]

Immediately after the Treaty was ratified in January 1922, Collins moved his primary office to Dublin's City Hall. On the mantelpiece of his office he had a bronze plaque bearing Theodore Roosevelt's words:

I wish to preach, not the doctrine of ignoble ease, but the doctrine of the strenuous life, the life of toil and effort, of labor and strife; to preach that highest form of success which comes, not to the man who desires mere easy peace, but to the man who does not shrink from danger, from hardship, or from bitter toil, and who out of these wins the splendid ultimate triumph.[56]

If success can be defined as doing more with less, then Collins must be counted among the great guerrilla planners of the twentieth century. His multiplicity of roles—and their centrality—was what distinguished him from the other participants of the time. He was extremely effective as Minister for Finance, as President of the IRB and as Intelligence Director, but he was surprisingly naïve when dealing with British agents posing as friends. He could be rash but could also be calculating and patient. His strength lay in his attention to detail and his readiness to organise anybody willing to help in the struggle. He understood the limits of what could be achieved by violence, and when to forgo violence for negotiation. He divided his time between political, financial, intelligence and military matters, and especially evidenced a capacity for knowing his enemy. While Collins always said that he was 'a soldier, not a politician', to the end of his life he epitomised what we would now recognise as a modern-day multinational CEO—one who was always willing to make a deal, and to 'deal' with the anti-Treaty IRA as willingly as with the British. The remarkable thing is not that he failed but that he almost succeeded.

Collins was a 'daytime dreamer', a man of 'toil and effort' who understood politics and propaganda and wanted more than 'mere easy peace'. He could be quite ruthless and domineering, and to a disturbing degree was a law unto himself. He was a man who needed—and even craved—absolute control. His personality and actions aroused both admiration and enmity.

In his lifetime he was acclaimed as the man who won the war. As a negotiator he won high regard from Churchill and Birkenhead, though he had his share of impetuosity in judgement. Beyond question, he had the courage and ruthlessness that make for achievement in revolutionary times. Nor was there any obvious limitation to his powers; he had all manner of qualities and with experience was deemed likely to acquire all the great ones. Yet of him at the last it has to be written 'He died young'. A man may not be judged by the great things he might have done.[57]

His legacy may be complicated and contradictory yet it requires no embellishment to provide it with potency.

Michael Collins was an enigma, but he shook an empire.

Notes

1   Major B.C. Denning, MC, 'Modern problems of guerilla warfare', *Army Quarterly* (January 1927).
2   Andrew Silke, 'Ferocious times: the IRA, the RIC, and Britain's failure in 1919–1921', *Terrorism and Political Violence*, vol. 27, no. 3 (19 April 2016).
3   Colin S. Gray, 'The Anglo-Irish War 1919–1921: lessons from an irregular conflict', *Comparative Strategy*, vol. 26, no. 5 (8 January 2008).
4   Max Boot, 'Kick the bully: Michael Collins launches the War of Independence' (http://www.historynet.com/kick-the-bully-michael-collins-launches-the-1921-irish-rebellion.htm).
5   Charles Townshend, 'The Irish Republican Army and the development of guerrilla warfare, 1916–1921', *English Historical Review*, vol. 94, no. 371 (1979).
6   Douglas Duff, *Sword for Hire* (London, 1934), p. 64.
7   Florence O'Donoghue, 'Guerilla warfare in Ireland', *An Cosantóir*, vol. 23 (1963).
8   Richard Dawson, *Red Terror and Green* (London, 1920; 1972), p. 151.
9   Bernard Fall, 'The theory and practice of counterinsurgency', *Naval War College Review* (April 1965). See David Kilcullen, 'Counterinsurgency *redux*', opinion paper by the Chief Strategist in the Office of the Coordinator for Counterterrorism, US State Department, Washington DC (undated).
10 W. Alison Phillips, *The Revolution in Ireland: 1906–1923* (London, 1923), p. 191.
11 William Sheehan, *Hearts and Mines: The British 5th Division, Ireland, 1920–1922* (Cork, 2009), pp 138–9.
12 Peter Hart, *The IRA at War, 1916–1923* (Oxford, 2003), pp 3–4.
13 Letter from B.L. Montgomery to A.E. Percival, 14 October 1923, Montgomery papers, Imperial War Museum. Lieutenant General A.E. Percival, two lectures on 'Guerrilla warfare—Ireland 1920–1921', Imperial War Museum, Folder 411, pp 19–23.
14 P.K. Wilkensen and J. Bright Ashley, *Gubbins and the SOE* (London, 1993), p. 94; Sir Colin Gubbins, 'SOE and the coordination of regular and irregular warfare', lecture and discussion in Michael Elliott-Bateman (ed.), *The Fourth Dimension of Warfare*, vol. 1 (Manchester, 1974).
15 M.R.D. Foot, *SOE in France: An Account of the Work of the British Special Operations Executive in France 1940–1945* (London, 1966; 1968), pp 57–69; 'The IRA and the origins of the SOE', in M.R.D. Foot (ed.), *War and Society: Historical Essays in Honour and Memory of J.R. Western 1928–1971* (New York, 1973).

[16] Gubbins Private Papers; Gubbins, 'SOE and the coordination of regular and irregular warfare'.

[17] SOE training and operations, which were directly based on studies of the IRA, became the basis of counter-insurgency doctrine in the post-1945 period and laid the foundation of British Special Forces. Ian Beckett and John Pimlott (eds), *Armed Forces and Modern Counter-Insurgency* (London and Sydney, 1985), p. 17; Timothy Llewellyn Jones, 'The development of British counter-insurgency policies and doctrine, 1945–52', unpublished Ph.D dissertation, King's College, University of London (1991); E.H. Cookridge, *Inside SOE: The Story of Special Operations in Western Europe, 1940–45* (London, 1966); Special Operations Executive: SOE Training Manual (https://ironwolf008.files.wordpress.com/2010/07/the-wwii-soe-training-manual-rigden.pdf).

[18] J.B.E. Hittle, *Michael Collins and the Anglo-Irish War: Britain's Counter-insurgency Failure* (Chicago, 2011), p. 125.

[19] Sir Ormonde Winter, *Winter's Tale* (London, 1955), p. 303.

[20] 'Record of the Rebellion in Ireland in 1920–1921 and the Part Played by the Army in Dealing with it', Imperial War Museum, Box 78/82/2.

[21] *Irish Press*, 17 December 1936.

[22] Ernie O'Malley, *On Another Man's Wound* (Dublin, 1936; 1979), p. 256.

[23] Risteard Mulcahy, 'Michael Collins and the making of a New Ireland', a paper read to the Irish Historical Society, 10 February 1976, *Studies* (Autumn 1976).

[24] Chief of Staff to O/C Southern Command, 25 April 1921, Mulcahy papers, P7 A/LL/18.

[25] Michael Hopkinson, *The Irish War of Independence* (Dublin, 2004), pp 94–5.

[26] The World War II SOE Training Manual, p. 39 (https://ironwolf008.files.wordpress.com/2010/07/the-wwii-soe-training-manual-rigden.pdf).

[27] See Winter, *Winter's Tale*; Hervey de Montmorency, *Sword and Stirrup: Memories of an Adventurous Life* (London, 1936); E. McCall, *The Auxiliaries: Tudor's Toughs. A Study of the Auxiliary Division of the Royal Irish Constabulary 1920–1922* (London, 2010).

[28] Eunan O'Halpin, *Spying on Ireland: British Intelligence and Irish Neutrality during the Second World War* (Oxford, 2008), pp 26–7.

[29] Keith Jeffery, 'Intelligence and counter-insurgency operations: some reflections on the British experience', *Intelligence and National Security*, vol. 1, no. 1 (1987), pp 118–47; 'Some problems and lessons of the Anglo-Irish War in the twentieth century', in Peter Dennis and Jeffrey Grey (eds), *An Art in Itself: The Theory and Conduct of Small Wars and Insurgencies* (London, 2006).

[30] Keith Jeffery, 'Foreword', in W.H. Kautt, *Ground Truths: British Army Operations in the Irish War of Independence* (Sallins, 2014), p. xiv.

[31] Charles Townshend, 'In aid of civil power: Britain, Ireland, and Palestine 1916–1948', in Daniel Marston and Carter Malkasian (eds), *Counterinsurgency in Modern Warfare* (Oxford, 2008), pp 19–36.

[32] Gray, 'The Anglo-Irish War 1919–21: lessons from an irregular conflict', lists 28 lessons. Another study that compares British effectiveness against Irish OOTW (Operations Other Than War) doctrine is Michael R. Fierro, 'British counterinsurgency operations in Ireland 1916–1921: a case study' (unpublished MA dissertation, Naval War College, Newport, RI, 1997).

[33] For a discussion of the role of religion in the events from 1916 to 1921 see John

Newsinger, 'I bring not peace but a sword: the religious motif in the Irish War of Independence', *Journal of Modern History*, vol. 13, no. 3 (1978).

[34] Gordon Pattison, 'The British Army's effectiveness in the Irish campaign 1919–1921, and the lessons for modern counterinsurgency operations, with special reference to C3I aspects', UK Ministry of Defence (1999).

[35] US Army Field Manual FM-3-13, *Information Operations: Doctrine, Tactics, Techniques, and Procedures*, 3-19 (28 September 2003).

[36] General Frank Kitson, *Bunch of Five* (London, 1977), p. 290.

[37] General Charles Krulak, quoted in Evan Thomas, Rod Nordland and Christian Caryl, 'Operation Hearts and Minds', *Newsweek* (29 December1992/5 January 1993).

[38] Brian Lapping, *End of Empire* (London, 1985), p. 224.

[39] Noor R. Ampssler, 'Hearts and minds: Malayan campaign re-evaluated' (https://www.defenceviewpoints.co.uk/articles-and-analysis/hearts-and-minds-malayan-campaign-re-evaluated).

[40] Simon C. Smith, 'General Templer and counter-insurgence in Malaya: hearts and minds, intelligence and propaganda', *Intelligence and National Security*, vol. 16, no. 3 (2001).

[41] Richard Stubbs, *Hearts and Minds in Guerrilla Warfare: The Malayan Emergency, 1948–1960* (Singapore, 1989), pp 155–64.

[42] Hittle, *Michael Collins and the Anglo-Irish War*, p. 226.

[43] Meda Ryan, *Tom Barry: IRA Freedom Fighter* (Cork, 2003), p. 25.

[44] Che Guevara, *Che Lives: General Principles of Guerrilla Warfare* (http://www.che-lives.com/home/modules.php?name=Content&pa=showpage&pid=4).

[45] Seán Cronin, 'Connolly's great leap in the dark', *Capuchin Annual* (1977).

[46] Dáil Reports, vol. 2, pp 1910, 1923.

[47] C.S. (Todd) Andrews, *Dublin Made Me* (Cork, 1979), pp 99–100.

[48] Patrick Lynch, 'The social revolution that never was', in T. Desmond Williams (ed.), *The Irish Struggle 1916–1926* (Toronto, 1966).

[49] Michael Laffan, 'Labour must wait: Ireland's conservative revolution', in Patrick Cornish (ed.), *Radicals, Rebels, and Establishments* (Belfast, 1985).

[50] John Borgonovo (ed.), *Florence and Josephine O'Donoghue's War of Independence: A Destiny that Shapes our Ends* (Cork, 2006), p. 32.

[51] Peter Hart, *Mick: The Real Michael Collins* (London, 2006), p. 242.

[52] M.L.R. Smith, *Fighting for Ireland: The Strategy of the Irish Republican Movement* (New York, 1995), p. 38.

[53] Roy Jenkins, *Churchill: A Biography* (London, 2001), p. 366.

[54] Michael Collins, 'Clearing the road—an essay in practical politics', in William FitzGerald (ed.), *The Voice of Ireland: A Survey of the Race and Nation from All Angles, by the Foremost Leaders at Home and Abroad* (Dublin, 1924), p. 42.

[55] T.E. Lawrence, *The Seven Pillars of Wisdom* (privately published, 1926; Wordsworth edn, 1997), p. 7.

[56] Theodore Roosevelt, 10 April 1899.

[57] Nicholas Mansergh, *The Unresolved Question: the Anglo-Irish Settlement and its Undoing, 1912–72* (New Haven, CT, 1991), p. 214.

Bibliography

MANUSCRIPT, NEWSPAPERS AND PRINTED PRIMARY SOURCES

Sir John Anderson papers, PRO CO 904/188.
Arrangements Governing the Cessation of Active Operations in Ireland, Cmd 1534 XIX (1921).
Blackwood's Magazine.
Ernest Blythe papers, University College Dublin Library.
British Cabinet 'Irish Situation Committee Reports and Minutes, 1920-1921', Cabinet Series Nos 23 and 27.
British Cabinet Weekly Survey of the State of Ireland Memorandum, 29 July 1921, PRO CAB 24/126/72, p. 4.
British Parliamentary Archive Papers, 'The Irish Uprising, 1914–1921'.
British War Office, *Manual of Military Law* (London, 1914).
Cathal Brugha papers, University College Dublin Library.
The Capuchin Annual.
Michael Collins papers, PRO CO 904/196.
Michael Collins papers (MSS 40,420–40,433, 5848), National Library of Ireland.
Archive, Michael Collins Centre, Castleview, Clonakilty, Co. Cork.
Colonial Office papers, reports from RIC County Inspectors, PRO CO 904 109.
The Constabulary Gazette.
The Cork Examiner.
The Cork People.
An Cosantóir.
Dáil Éireann:
      Correspondence Relating to Peace Negotiations, June–September, 1921.
      Minutes of the Proceedings of the First and Second Parliaments of Ireland, 1919–21.
      Minutes of the Treaty Debates, 1921–2.
The Daily Mail.
The Daily News.
The Daily Telegraph.
'Defense of the Realm Act 1914 and Restoration of Order in Ireland Act 1920', WO 35/66.
Department of Foreign Affairs, Documents on Irish Foreign Policy: *The Anglo-Irish Treaty, December 1920–December 1921*, edited by C. Crowe, R. Fanning, M. Kennedy, D. Keogh and E. O'Halpin. National Archives of Ireland.
Éamon de Valera papers, University College Dublin Library.
Dublin Gazette.

Éire-Ireland: A Journal of Irish Studies.

Evidence on Conditions in Ireland, edited by A. Coyle (Washington DC: The American Commission on Conditions in Ireland, 1921).

The Freeman's Journal.

Frank Gallagher papers, National Library of Ireland.

General Sir Hubert Gough papers, Imperial War Museum.

General Sir Colin Gubbins papers, Imperial War Museum.

Arthur Griffith papers, National Library of Ireland.

Hansard Parliamentary Records, House of Commons Debates, House of Lords Debates, 1803–2005 (London: UK Parliament, http://hansard.millbanksystems.com/).

Hicks, W.W., 'Memorandum on British Secret Service Activities in this Country, November 2, 1920'. Doc. 9771-745-45, Declassification no. 740058, 15 April 1987.

History Ireland.

Hue and Cry (Dublin Castle).

Intelligence Notes, 1913–1916: Preserved in the State Paper Office, edited by B. Mac Giolla Choille (Dublin: Oifig an tSoláthair, 1966).

'Ireland and the General Military Situation', Memorandum by the Secretary of State for War, May 1921 (PRO CAB 24/123).

The Irish Bulletin.

Irish Historical Studies.

The Irish Independent/Sunday Independent.

Irish Intelligence Summary, Special Supplementary Report 259, 1 July 1921.

The Irish Jurist.

The Irish Press.

The Irish Race Convention: Souvenir Program (Philadelphia, 1919).

Irish Republican Brotherhood papers, University College Dublin Library.

The Irish Review.

'The Irish Situation', Memorandum by the Secretary of State for War, 3 November 1920 (PRO CAB 23/23/2).

The Irish Sword.

The Irish Times.

The Irish Uprising: 1914–1921 (Her Majesty's Stationery Office, 2000).

The Irish Volunteer.

Irish Volunteers papers, University College Dublin Library.

Lieutenant General Sir Hugh Jeudwine papers, Imperial War Museum, Box 72/82/2.

The Journal of British Studies.

The Journal of Contemporary History.

The Journal of the Irish Military Society.

The Kerryman.

Seán Lemass papers, University College Dublin Library.

The Limerick Echo.

The Limerick Leader.

The London Daily Sketch.

Walter Long papers, PRO 947/308.

Patrick McCartan papers, National Library of Ireland.

Seán MacEntee papers, University College Dublin Library.

General Seán MacEoin papers, University College Dublin Library.

Joseph McGarrity papers, National Library of Ireland.

Eoin MacNeill papers, National Library of Ireland.

Nevil Macready correspondence with Field Marshal Henry Wilson, Imperial War Museum.

Macready Committee Report, Cabinet Paper 1317, 19 May 1919, 'Formation of a special force for service in Ireland', PRO WO 32/9517.

Mary MacSwiney papers, University College Dublin Library.

Terence MacSwiney papers, University College Dublin Library.

Military Archives of Ireland, Cathal Brugha Barracks.

'British Over-sea Commitments, 1919, 1920, 1921', Liaison Papers 1921–1922, Box 4.

Frank Thornton papers.

Bureau of Military History Witness Statements:

Aghlas (Ashe), Nora: Statement 645. Aherne, Maurice: Statement 483. Archer, Liam: Statement 819. Barrington, Gilbert: Statement 773. Barry, Dr Alice: Statement 723. Barrett, Annie: Statement 1133. Barton, Ducibella: Statement 936. Barton, Robert C.: Statement 979. Béaslaí, Piaras: Statements 261, 675. Beaumont, Seán: Statement 709. Begley, Flor: Statements 32, 1771. Berry, Patrick: Statement 942. Blythe, Ernest: Statement 939. Bolger, John: Statement 1745. Booker, Joseph: Statement 776. Bourke, Dr F.S.: Statement 172. Bratton, Eugene: Statement 467. Breen, Dan: Statements 1739, 1763. Brennan, Robert: Statements 125, 779, 790. Brennan, Timothy: Statement 584. Browne, Msgr Patrick: Statement 729. Broy, Éamon: Statements 1280, 1284, 1285. Bulfin, Éamon: Statement 497. Bryan, Annie: Statement 805. Bryan, Dan: Statement 947. Byrne, Bernard C.: Statement 631. Byrne, Christopher: Statements 167, 642. Byrne, James: Statement 828. Byrne, Joseph: Statement 461. Byrne, Tom: Statement 564. Byrne, Vincent: Statement 423. Carragher, Thomas: Statement 681. Carrigan, James: Statement 613. Clancy, Mary: Statement 806. Clarke, James: Statement 1026. Clarke, Dr Josephine: Statement 699. Clifford, Seán: Statement 1279. Coghlan, Francis X.: Statement 1760. Colley, Harry: Statement 1687. Connolly, Cornelius: Statement 602. Cope, Sir Alfred (Andy): Statement 469. Cordial, Michael: Statement 1712. Cosgrave, William T.: Statements 268, 449. Cronin, Cornelius: Statement 1726. Cronin, Jeremiah: Statement 1020. Crowe, Patrick: Statement 775. Crowe, Tadgh: Statement 1658. Crowley, Tadgh: Statement 435. Culhane, Seán: Statement 746. Cullen, James: Statement 1343. Cummins, Michael: Statement 1282. Cunningham, James W.: Statement 922. Curran, Revd M.J.: Statement 687. Dalton, Charles: Statement 434. Dalton, Richard: Statement 1116. Daly, Denis: Statement 110. Daly, Madge: Statements 209, 855. Daly (O'Daly, Ó Dalaigh), Gen. Patrick: Statement 387. Daly, Patrick G.: Statement 814. Daly, Una: Statement 610. Davis, Francis (Frank): Statement 496. De Barra, Leslie Price, Bean: Statement 1754. De Roiste (Roche), Liam: Statement 1698. Deasy, Liam: Statement 562. Desmond, William: Statement 832. Dolan, Joseph: Statements 663, 900. Donnelly, Simon: Statements 113, 433, 481. Dore, Éamon: Statements 153, 392, 515. Doyle, James: Statement 1640. Duffy, John: Statement 580. Duggan, George C.: Statements 1071, 1099. Duggan,

James 'Spud': Statement 1684. Murphy, Jeremiah: Statement 772. Murphy, Michael: Statement 1547. Murray, Séamus: Statement 308. Myles, William: Statement 795. Neligan, David: Statement 380. Ni Bhriain, Máire: Statement 363. Norris, William: Statement 595. Noyk, Michael: Statement 707. Nugent, Lawrence: Statement 907. Nunan, Seán: Statement 1744. O'Brien, Patrick: Statement 812. O'Callaghan, Cait: Statement 6880'Carroll, Michael: Statement 1609. Ó Cathain, Padraig: Statement 1572. O'Connor, Bridget (Mrs Batt): Statement 330. O'Connor, Paddy: Statement 813. O'Donel, Geraldine: Statement 861. O'Donnell, Mrs Bernard (née Eithne Coyle): Statement 750. O'Donoghue, Daithi: Statement 548. O'Donoghue, Florence: Statement 554. O'Donoghue, Humphrey: Statement 1351. O'Donoghue, Patrick: Statement 847. O'Donoghue, Very Revd Thomas: Statement 1666. O'Donovan, James: Statement 1713. O'Donovan, Julia: Statement 475. O'Driscoll, Seán: Statement 1518. O'Duffy, Seán M.: Statements 313, 618, 619. O'Dwyer, Patrick: Statement 1432. O'Flanagan, Michael: Statement 908. O'Flynn, William: Statement 1235. O'Hegarty, P.S.: Statement 26. O'Hegarty, Seán: Statement 54. O'Keefe, John (Jack): Statement 1291. O'Keeffe, Patrick (Paudeen): Statement 1725. O'Keeffe, Seán: Statement 188. O'Keefe, William T.: Statement 1678. O'Kelly, J.J. (Sceilg): Statements 384, 427. O'Kelly, Fergus: Statement 351. O'Kelly, Seán T.: Statements 611, 1765. O'Mahoney, John: Statement 1662. O'Malley, John: Statement 912. O'Neill, Edward: Statement 203. O'Reilly, Brigid: Statement 454. O'Reilly, Michael W.: Statement 886. O'Reilly, Stephen J.: Statement 1761. Ormond, Patrick: Statement 1283. O'Shaughnessy, Daniel: Statement 1956. O'Shea, Seán: Statement 760. O'Sullivan, Diarmuid: Statement 375. O'Sullivan, Mary: Statement 465. O'Sullivan, Patrick: Statements 34, 878. O'Sullivan, Tadgh: Statement 792. O'Toole, James: Statement 1084. Peppard, Thomas: Statement 1399. Pinkman, Charles: Statement 1263. Prendergast, Seán: Statement 1952. Price, General Éamon: Statement 995. Purcell, Robert: Statement 53. Quinlan, Dr Catherine: Statement 1364. Ramsbottom, James: Statement 1512. Reidy, Thomas: Statements 1422, 1477. Reilly, Bernard: Statement 349. Reynolds, Peter: Statement 350. Roberts, George Henry: Statement 1045. Robinson, Séamus: Statements 156, 1721, 1722. Ryan, Desmond: Statements 724, 725. Ryan, Dr James: Statement 70. Saunders, Seán: Statement 817. Saurin, Charles: Statement 288. Saurin, Frank: Statement 715. Sheehan, Patrick: Statement 1088. Slattery, Declan: Statement 1245. Slattery, James (Jim): Statement 445. Smyth, Eugene: Statement 334. Stack, Michael: Statement 525. Stack, Una: Statements 214, 418. Staines, Michael: Statements 284, 943, 944. Stapleton, William James (Bill): Statement 822. Thornton, Dr Brigid (née Lyons): Statement 259. Thornton, Frank: Statements 510, 615. Thunder, Joseph T.: Statement 460. Traynor, Oscar: Statement 340. Walsh, John: Statement 966. Walsh, Richard: Statement 400. Whelan, Patrick: Statement 1449. White, George: Statement 956. Wordsworth, Mrs A.K.: Statement 1242.

'The Military Situation in Ireland', Memorandum by Colonel Sir Hugh Elles, 24 June, 1921 (PRO CAB 24/125/77).
The Morning Post.
General Richard Mulcahy papers, University College Dublin Library.

The Nation and Athenaeum.

New Ireland.

New York Times.

North Dublin Inner City Folklore Project and Museum, Railway Street, Dublin.

Notes on IRA movements in 6th Division Area, Weekly Situation Report, Commander-in-Chief Ireland to Cabinet, 30 April 1921, CAB. 24 CP. 2911.

Michael Noyk papers, National Library of Ireland.

Batt O'Connor papers, University College Dublin Library.

Rory O'Connor papers, University College Dublin Library.

Florence O'Donoghue papers, National Library of Ireland.

Diarmuid O'Hegarty papers, University College Dublin Library.

Seán T. O'Kelly papers, National Library of Ireland.

Ernie O'Malley papers, University College Dublin Library.

An t-Óglách.

Outrages, Ireland. Cmd 63 and 709 (1920).

Outrages, Ireland. Return showing the number of serious outrages. Cmd 1165, (1921).

Gordon Pattison, *The British Army's Effectiveness in the Irish Campaign 1919–1921, and the Lessons for Modern Counterinsurgency Operations, with Special Reference to C3I Aspects* (UK Ministry of Defence, 1999).

Lieutenant General A.E. Percival papers, 'Guerrilla Warfare in Ireland, 1919–1921', Imperial War Museum, Folder 411, pp 19–23.

An Phoblacht.

Count George Noble Plunkett papers, National Library of Ireland.

'The Present Military Situation in Ireland and the Proposed Military Policy During the Coming Winter', Memorandum by General Nevil Macready, 6 August 1920, PRO CAB 24/110/50.

'Record of the Rebellion in Ireland in 1920–1921 and the Part Played by the Army in Dealing with it', Imperial War Museum, Box 78/82/2.

Report on Bloody Sunday, PRO WO 35/38.

'Report by the General Officer Commanding in Chief, The Situation in Ireland for the Week Ending 14th May, 1921', PRO CAB 24/123.

'Report by the General Officer Commanding-in-Chief on the situation in Ireland for the week ending 9th July, 1921'.

'Report on the Intelligence Branch of the Chief of Police from May 1920 to July 1921', Colonel Ormonde de l'Epee Winter, PRO WO 35/214.

Report of the Labour Commission to Ireland (London: Labour Party, 1921).

Report of the Proceedings of the Irish Convention (Dublin: His Majesty's Stationery Office, 1918).

'Report on Revolutionary Organisations', 23 June, 7 July 1921, PRO, CAM 24/125, 126.

Royal Commission on the Rebellion in Ireland, Report (1916), Cmd. 8279, Minutes of Evidence, Cmd. 8311.

Royal Irish Constabulary, Auxiliary Division Register, PRO HO 184/50-1.

Royal Irish Constabulary List and Directory (Dublin: His Majesty's Stationery Office, 1920).

Royal Irish Constabulary Manual; or Guide to the Discharge of Police Duties (Dublin: His Majesty's Stationery Office, 1909).

Desmond Ryan papers, University College Dublin Library.
An Saorstat.
Sinn Féin Rebellion Handbook (Dublin: *The Irish Times*, 1917).
Sinn Féin Party papers, University College Dublin Library.
Sinn Féin and Other Republican Suspects 1899–1921: Dublin Castle Special Branch, Files
    CO 904 (193–216), United Kingdom, Colonial Office Record Series, vol. 1
    (Dublin: Eneclann, 2006).
Austin Stack papers, National Library of Ireland.
General Sir E.P. Strickland papers, 'The Irish Rebellion in the 6th Divisional Area:
    From after the 1916 Rebellion to December 1921', Imperial War Museum.
Studies: The Irish Jesuit Quarterly Review.
Mark Sturgis Diaries, PRO 30.59, 1–5.
The Sunday Express.
The Sunday Tribune.
The Times (London).
Trinity College Dublin Library, Manuscript Department:
    R. Erskine Childers papers.
    Fogarty, M., Letter on the Death of Thomas Ashe from the Bishop of Killaloe,
        30 September 1914.
    Plunkett, G.N., 'Letter to the People of North Roscommon upon Election to
        Office', 17 March 1917 (MS 2074).
US Army Field Manual FM 100-6, *Information Operations* (27 August 1996).
US Army Field Manual FM 3-13, *Information Operations: Doctrine, Tactics, Techniques, and
    Procedures* (28 September 2003).
US Army Field Manual, *Countermobility* (2004).
US Army Field Manual (interim) 3-07.22, *Counterinsurgency Operations* (1 October
    2004).
US Army Field Manual FM 3-25, *Counterinsurgency* (2006).
US Department of Defense, *Counterinsurgency,* Joint Publication 3-24 (22 November
    2013).
US Department of State Files, Division of Western European Affairs, 1921, 841
    d.00/340 and d.00/402.
US Government Counterinsurgency Guide (January 2009).
US Joint Chiefs of Staff, Joint Pub 3-07, *Joint Doctrine for Military Operations Other
    Than War* (Washington, DC, 1995).
US Marine Corps, FMFRP 12-18, *Mao Tse-tung on Guerrilla Warfare* (3 April 1989).
US Marine Corps, FMFRP 12-25, *The Guerrilla and How to Fight Him* (2 January
    1990).
US Marine Corps, Warfighting Publication 3-33-5 (2006).
The Weekly Summary (Dublin Castle).
*Who Burnt Cork City? A Tale of Arson, Loot, and Murder: The Evidence of Over Seventy
    Witnesses* (Dublin: Irish Labour Party & Trade Union Congress, 1921).
Field Marshal Sir Henry Wilson Papers, Imperial War Museum, DS/MISC/80,
    HW/2/2B.
The Wolfe Tone Annual.

BOOKS

Aalen, F.H.A. and Whelan, K., *Dublin City and County from Prehistory to the Present* (Dublin, 1992).

aan de Wiel, J., *The Catholic Church in Ireland 1914–1918* (Dublin, 2003).

Abbott, R., *Police Casualties in Ireland, 1919–1922* (Cork, 2000).

Adams, R.J.Q. and Poirier, S., *The Conscription Controversy in Great Britain, 1900–1918* (Basingstoke, 1978).

Adas, M., *Prophets of Rebellion* (Chapel Hill, NC, 1979).

Aitken, W.M. (Lord Beaverbrook), *The Decline and Fall of Lloyd George* (London and New York, 1963).

Alderman, C.L., *The Wearing of the Green: The Irish Rebellion, 1916–1921* (New York, 1972).

Alexander, Y. and O'Day, A. (eds), *Ireland's Terrorist Dilemma* (Dordrecht, 1986).

Ambrose, J., *Seán Treacy and the Tan War* (Cork, 2005).

Ambrose, J., *Dan Breen and the IRA* (Cork, 2007).

Anderson, J., *Che Guevara: A Revolutionary Life* (New York, 2010).

Andrew, C., *Her Majesty's Secret Service: The Making of the British Intelligence Community* (New York, 1986).

Andrew, C. and Dilks, D. (eds), *The Missing Dimension: Governments and Intelligence Communities in the Twentieth Century* (London, 1984).

Andrews, C.S., *Dublin Made Me* (Cork, 1979).

Anon., *Arthur Griffith: A Study of the Founder of Sinn Féin* (Dublin, 1917).

Arthur, Sir G., *General Sir John Maxwell* (London, 1932).

Ash, B., *The Last Dictator: A Biography of Field Marshal Sir Henry Wilson* (London, 1968).

Asprey, R.B., *War in the Shadows: The Guerrilla in History* (originally published in two volumes, 1975; updated and published in one volume, New York, 1994).

Asquith, H.H. (Earl of Oxford and Asquith), *The Paisley Policy* (London, 1920).

Augusteijn, J., *From Public Defiance to Guerrilla Warfare* (Dublin, 1996).

Augusteijn, J. (ed.), *The Irish Revolution* (Basingstoke, 2002).

Baker, J., *My Stand for Freedom: Autobiography of an Irish Republican Soldier* (Westport, 1988).

Ball, S. (ed.), *A Policeman's Ireland: Recollections of Samuel Waters, RIC* (Cork, 1999).

Ballinger, W.A., *The Men that God Made Mad* (New York, 1969).

Bambury, C., *Ireland's Permanent Revolution* (London, 1986).

Barry, T., *The Reality of the Anglo-Irish War, 1920–21, in West Cork: Refutations, Corrections and Comments on Liam Deasy's 'Towards Ireland Free'* (Dublin, 1974).

Barry, T., *Guerilla Days in Ireland: A Personal Account of the Anglo-Irish War* (Dublin, 1981).

Bartlett, T. and Jeffrey, K. (eds), *A Military History of Ireland* (Cambridge, 1996).

Barton, B., *From Behind a Closed Door: Secret Court Martial Records of the 1916 Easter Rising* (Belfast, 2002).

Béaslaí, P., *With the IRA in the Fight for Freedom: The Red Path of Glory* (*The Kerryman*, undated, c. 1922).

Béaslaí, P., *How It Was Done: IRA Intelligence: Dublin's Fighting Story* (London, 1926).

Béaslaí, P., *Michael Collins and the Making of the New Ireland* (2 vols) (London, 1926).

Béaslaí, P., *Michael Collins* (London, 1937).

Becket, I.W.F., *Modern Insurgencies and Counter-insurgencies: Guerrillas and their Opponents since 1750* (London and New York, 2001).

Beckett, J.C., *The Making of Modern Ireland, 1603–1923* (New York, 1963).

Beckett, J.C., *A Short History of Ireland* (London, 1973).

Beckett, J.C., *The Anglo-Irish Tradition* (Ithaca, NY, 1976).

Begley, D., *The Road to Crossbarry: The Decisive Battle of the War of Independence* (Bandon, 1999).

Bell, J.B., *The Gun in Politics: An Analysis of Irish Political Conflict, 1916–1986* (New Brunswick, NJ, 1991).

Bell, J.B., *The Secret Army: The IRA* (Dublin, 1997).

Beloff, M., *Imperial Sunset* (2 vols) (New York, 1970).

Bennett, D., *The Encyclopaedia of Dublin* (Dublin, 1991).

Bennett, R., *The Black and Tans* (London 1964; 2001).

Berger, C., *Broadsides and Bayonets: The Propaganda War of the American Revolution* (San Rafael, CA, 1976).

Bew, P., *Ireland: The Politics of Enmity, 1789–2006* (Oxford, 2007).

Birrell, A., *Things Past Redress* (London, 1937).

Boland, K., *Up Dev* (Dublin, 1977).

Boot, M., *Invisible Armies: An Epic History of Guerrilla Warfare from Ancient Times to Present* (New York, 2013).

Borgonovo, J. (ed.), *Florence and Josephine O'Donoghue's War of Independence: A Destiny that Shapes our Ends* (Cork, 2006).

Borgonovo, J., *Spies, Informers and the Anti-Sinn Féin Society* (Dublin, 2006).

Bowden, T., *The Breakdown of Public Security: The Case of Ireland 1916–1921 and Palestine 1936–1939* (London, 1977).

Bowden, T., *Beyond the Limits of the Law* (London, 1978).

Bowers, C.G., *Ireland's Orators. A History of Ireland's Fight for Freedom* (New York, 2009).

Bowman, J., *De Valera and the Ulster Question, 1917–1973* (Oxford, 1982).

Boyce, D.G., *Englishmen and Irish Troubles: British Public Opinion and the Making of Irish Policy, 1918–1922* (London, 1972; Aldershot, 1994).

Boyce, D.G. and O'Day, A. (eds), *The Ulster Crisis* (Basingstoke, 2006).

Boyle, A., *The Mystery of Erskine Childers* (London, 1977).

Brady, C. (ed.), *Interpreting Irish History: The Debate on Historical Revisionism* (Dublin, 1994).

Brady, E., *Ireland's Secret Service in England* (Dublin, 1924).

Brasier, A. and Kelly, J., *Harry Boland: A Man Divided* (Dublin, 2000).

Breen, D., *My Fight for Irish Freedom* (Dublin, 1964).

Brennan, M., *The War in Clare, 1911–1921: Personal Memoirs of the Irish War of Independence* (Dublin, 1980).

Brennan, R., *Allegiance* (Dublin, 1950).

Brennan, R., *Ireland Standing Firm: My Wartime Mission in Washington and Éamon de Valera: A Memoir* (Dublin, 2002).

Brennan-Whitmore, W.J., *With the Irish in Frongoch* (Dublin, 1917).

Brewer, J.D., *The Royal Irish Constabulary: An Oral History* (Belfast, 1990).

Brinton, C., *The Anatomy of a Revolution* (London, 1965).

Briollay, S. (writing under the pseudonym of Roger Chauvire), *Ireland in Rebellion*

(Dublin, 1922).

Briscoe, R., *For the Life of Me* (London, 1958).

Broad, R. and Downing, T., *The Troubles* (London, 1980).

Bromage, M.C., *De Valera and the March of a Nation* (New York, 1956).

Bromage, M.C., *Churchill and Ireland* (Notre Dame, IN, 1964).

Browne, C., *The Story of the 7th: A Concise History of the 7th Battalion Cork No. 1 Brigade IRA from 1915–1921* (undated, no place of publication).

Browning, E., *Slaughtered Like Animals: A Detailed Examination of the Killing of 17 Members of the Royal Irish Constabulary by the IRA at Macroom, County Cork, on 28th November 1920, and Similar Notorious Incidents in that Period* (London, 2011).

Brugha, M. MacSwiney, *History's Daughter* (Dublin, 2005).

Buckley, D., *The Battle of Tourmakeady, Fact or Fiction: A Study of the IRA Ambush and its Aftermath* (Dublin, 2008).

Bull, P., *Land, Politics and Nationalism* (Dublin, 1996).

Burleigh, M., *Blood and Rage: A Cultural History of Terrorism* (New York, 2009).

Butler, D. and Freeman, J., *British Political Facts, 1900–1960* (New York, 1961).

Butler, E., *Barry's Flying Column: The Story of the IRA's Cork No. 3 Brigade, 1919–1921* (London, 1971).

Callwell, C.E., *Small Wars: Their Principles and Practice* (London, 1903).

Callwell, C.E., *The Tactics of Home Defence* (Edinburgh, 1908).

Callwell, Major-General Sir C.E., *Field Marshal Sir Henry Wilson: His Life and Diaries* (London, 1927).

Campbell, C., *Emergency Law in Ireland, 1918–1925* (Oxford, 1994).

Campbell, F., *Land and Revolution: Nationalist Politics in the West of Ireland: 1891–1921* (Oxford, 2008).

Carey, T., *Hanged for Ireland* (Dublin, 2001).

Carroll, F.M., *American Opinion and the Irish Question, 1910–1923* (Dublin, 1978).

Carroll, F.M. (ed.), *The American Commission on Irish Independence 1919. The Diary, Correspondence and Report* (Dublin, 1985).

Carty, J., *Ireland—From the Great Famine to the Treaty of 1921* (Dublin, 1951).

Chevasse, M., *Terence MacSwiney* (Dublin and London, 1961).

Childers, R.E., *The Framework of Home Rule* (London, 1911).

Childers, R.E., *Military Rule in Ireland* (Dublin, 1920).

Chorley, K., *Armies and the Art of Revolution* (London, 1943).

Chubb, B., *The Government and Politics of Ireland* (Stanford, 1982).

Churchill, W.S., *The World Crisis, 1911–1918* (London, 1931).

Clarke, G., *Everyday Violence in the Irish Civil War* (Cambridge, 2016).

Clarke, K. (ed. H. Litton), *Revolutionary Woman: My Fight for Ireland's Freedom* (Dublin, 1997).

Clausewitz, C. von (ed. and trans. M. Howard and P. Paret), *On War* (Princeton, 1984).

Clifford, B., *War, Insurrection and Election in Ireland, 1914–21* (Belfast, 1997).

Clutterbuck, R., *Guerrillas and Terrorists* (Athens, OH, 1980).

Clutterbuck, R., *Terrorism and Guerrilla Warfare* (London and New York, 1990).

Coalter, M., *Rebel with a Cause: Dan Breen and the IRA* (Cork, 2006).

Coates, T. (ed.), *The Irish Uprising, 1914–1921: Papers from the British Parliamentary Archive* (London, 2000).

Cockerill, Brigadier General Sir G., *What Fools We Were* (London, 1944).

Coleman, M., *County Longford and the Irish Revolution* (Dublin, 2003).

Coleman, M., *The Irish Revolution, 1916–1923* (Dublin, 2013).

Collier, B., *Brass Hat: A Biography of Field Marshal Sir Henry Wilson* (London, 1961).

Collins, M. (ed. T.P. Coogan), *The Path to Freedom* (1922; Cork, 1996).

Collins, P. (ed.), *Nationalism and Unionism: Conflict in Ireland, 1885–1921* (Belfast, 1994).

Collins, T., *The Irish Hunger Strike* (Dublin, 1986).

Colum, P., *Arthur Griffith* (Dublin, 1959).

Colvin, I.D., *Life of Lord Carson*, vols II and III (London, 1934). [See Marjoribanks, E., for vol. I.]

Comerford, J.J., *My Kilkenny IRA Days: 1916–22* (Kilkenny, 1980).

Comerford, M., *The First Dáil, January 21st 1919* (Dublin, 1969).

Comerford, R.V., *Ireland* (London, 2003).

Conlon, L., *Cumann na mBan and the Women of Ireland, 1913–25* (Kilkenny, 1969).

Connell, J.E.A. Jr, *Rebels' Priests: Ministering to Republicans, 1916–1924* (Dublin, 2014).

Connell, J.E.A. Jr, *Unequal Patriots* (Dublin, 2015).

Connell, J.E.A. Jr, *Dublin Rising 1916* (Dublin, 2015).

Connell, J.E.A. Jr, *Michael Collins: Dublin 1916–1922* (Dublin, 2017).

Connell, J.E.A. Jr, *Who Shot Michael Collins?* (Dublin, 2018).

Connolly, C., *The Illustrated Life of Michael Collins* (Boulder, CO, 1996).

Connolly, J., *Labour in Irish History* (Dublin, 1910; 1983).

Connolly, J., *The Re-conquest of Ireland* (Dublin, 1915).

Connolly, L., *The Irish Women's Movement* (New York, 2002; Dublin, 2003).

Coogan, T.P., *Ireland Since the Rising* (London, 1966).

Coogan, T.P., *Michael Collins, the Man Who Made Ireland* (London, 1992).

Coogan, T.P., *De Valera: Long Fellow, Long Shadow* (London, 1995).

Coogan, T.P., *The Twelve Apostles: Michael Collins, the Squad, and Ireland's Fight for Freedom* (London, 2016).

Coogan, T.P. and Morrison, G., *The Irish Civil War* (London, 1998).

Cooper, D., *Old Men Forget* (London, 1953).

Corkery, D., *The Hounds of Banba* (1920).

Costello, F., *Enduring the Most: The Life and Death of Terence MacSwiney* (Dublin, 1995).

Costello, F. (ed.), *Michael Collins: In His Own Words* (Dublin, 1997).

Costello, F., *The Irish Revolution and its Aftermath, 1916–1923* (Dublin, 2003).

Cottrell, P., *The Anglo-Irish War: The Troubles of 1913–1922* (Oxford, 2006).

Cottrell, P. (ed.), *The War for Ireland* (Oxford, 2009).

Cowell, J., *A Noontide Blazing: Brigid Lyons Thornton, Rebel, Soldier, Doctor* (Dublin, 2005).

Crafford, F.S., *Jan Smuts: A Biography* (London, 1943).

Creel, G., *Ireland's Fight for Freedom* (New York, 1919).

Cronin, S. *The Story of Kevin Barry.* (Cork, 1971).

Cronin, S., *Ideology of the IRA* (Ann Arbor, MI, 1972).

Cronin, S., *Frank Ryan: The Search for the Republic* (Dublin, 1980).

Cronin, S., *Irish Nationalism: Its Roots and Ideology* (Dublin, 1980).

Cronin, S., *Washington's Irish Policy, 1916–1986. Independence, Partition, Neutrality* (Tralee, 1987).

Crowley, T., *In Search of Michael Collins* (Castleview, Clonakilty, 2015).

Crozier, F.P., *Impressions and Recollections* (London, 1930).

Crozier, General F.P., *A Brass Hat in No Man's Land* (London, 1930).

Crozier, General F.P., *A Word to Gandhi: The Lesson of Ireland* (London, 1931).

Crozier, General F.P., *Ireland Forever* (London and Toronto, 1932).

Crozier, General F.P., *The Men I Killed* (London, 1937).

Cullen, M. and Luddy, M., *Female Activists, Irish Women and the Change, 1900–1960* (Dublin, 2001).

Curran, J.M., *The Birth of the Irish Free State, 1921–1923* (University of Alabama, 1980).

Curtin, N., *The Revolution in Ireland, 1879–1923* (Oxford, 1994).

Curtis, E., *A History of Ireland* (London, 1964).

Curtis, L., *The Cause of Ireland: From the United Irishmen to Partition* (Belfast, 1994).

Czira, S.G., *The Years Flew By* (Dublin, 1974).

Dalton, C., *With the Dublin Brigade* (London, 1929).

Dangerfield, G., *The Damnable Question: A Study in Anglo-Irish Relations* (Boston, 1976).

Darling, Sir W., *So it Looks to Me* (London, 1952).

David, E. (ed.), *Inside Asquith's Cabinet. From the Diaries of Charles Hothouse* (London, 1977).

Davis, R.P., *Arthur Griffith and Non-Violent Sinn Féin* (Dublin, 1974).

Dawson, R., *Red Terror and Green* (John Murray, 1920; London, 1972).

De Blacam, A., *Towards the Republic* (Dublin, 1918).

De Blacam, A., *What Sinn Féin Stands For* (Dublin, 1921).

De Burca, P. and Boyle, J., *Free State or Republic?* (Dublin, 1922; 2002).

de Montmorency, H., *Sword and Stirrup: Memories of an Adventurous Life* (London, 1936).

de Wet, C.R., *Three Years' War* (New York, 1902).

Deasy, L., *Towards Ireland Free: The West Cork Brigade in the War of Independence, 1917–1921* (Dublin, 1973).

Deasy, L., *Brother Against Brother* (Cork, 1998).

Desmond, S., *The Drama of Sinn Féin* (London, 1923).

Dillon, G.P., *All in the Blood* (Dublin, 2007).

Diner, H., *Erin's Daughters in America* (Baltimore, 1983).

Dingley, J., *The IRA: The Irish Republican Army* (Santa Barbara, CA, 2012).

Doherty, G. and Keogh, D. (eds), *Michael Collins and the Making of the Irish State* (Cork, 1998).

Doherty, G. and Keogh, D., *De Valera's Ireland* (Cork, 2003).

Dolan, A. and Murphy, W., *Michael Collins: The Man and the Revolution* (Cork, 2018).

Donnelly, M., *The Last Post: Glasnevin Cemetery* (Dublin, 1994).

Doyle, A.C., *The Great Boer War* (New York, 1902).

Doyle, J., Clarke, F., Connaughton, E. and Somerville, O., *An Introduction to the Bureau of Military History, 1913–1921* (Dublin, 2002).

Duff, D., *Sword for Hire* (London, 1934).

Duff, D., *The Rough with the Smooth* (London, 1940).

Duffy, S.M., *The Integrity of Ireland: Home Rule, Nationalism, and Partition, 1912–1922* (Madison, NJ, 2009).

Duncan, M., Cronin, M. and Rouse, P., *The GAA: A People's History* (Cork, 2009).

Dunn, D., *Peter's Key: Peter DeLoughry and the Fight for Irish Independence* (Cork, 2012).

Dwane, D.T., *The Early Life of Éamon de Valera* (Dublin, 1922).

Dwyer, T.R., *Éamon de Valera* (Dublin, 1980).

Dwyer, T.R., *Michael Collins and the Treaty* (Dublin, 1981).

Dwyer, T.R., *De Valera's Darkest Hour, 1919–1932* (Dublin, 1982).

Dwyer, T.R., *Michael Collins: The Man Who Won the War* (Cork, 1990).

Dwyer, T.R., *De Valera: The Man and the Myths* (Swords, 1992).

Dwyer, T.R., *Tans, Terror and Troubles: Kerry's Real Fighting Story, 1913–1923* (Cork, 2001).

Dwyer, T.R., *The Squad and the Intelligence Operations of Michael Collins* (Cork, 2005).

Dwyer, T.R., *Big Fellow, Long Fellow: A Joint Biography of Collins and de Valera* (Cork, 2006).

Dwyer, T.R., *I Signed my Death Warrant: Michael Collins and the Treaty* (Cork, 2007).

Dwyer, T.R., *Michael Collins and the Civil War* (Cork, 2012).

Ebenezer, L., *Fron-Goch and the Birth of the IRA* (Llanrwst, 2006).

Edwards, O.D., *Éamon de Valera* (Cardiff, 1987).

Eichacker, J.M., *Irish Republican Women in America* (Dublin, 2002).

Elliott, M., *Wolfe Tone: Prophet of Irish Independence* (New Haven, CT, 1989).

Elliott-Bateman, M., Ellis, J. and Bowman, J. (eds), *Revolt to Revolution—Studies in the 19th and 20th Century European Experience* (Manchester, 1974).

Ellis, P.B. (ed.), *Eyewitness to Irish History* (Hoboken, NJ, 2004).

English, R., *Ernie O'Malley, IRA Intellectual* (Oxford, 1998).

English, R., *Armed Struggle: a History of the IRA* (London, 2003).

Enright, S., *The Trial of Civilians by Military Courts* (Dublin, 2012).

Fagan, T. (ed.), *Rebels and Heroes: Hidden Stories from Dublin's Northside* (Dublin, 2016).

Fallon, C., *Soul of Fire: A Biography of Mary MacSwiney* (Dublin, 1986).

Fanning, R., *Fatal Path* (London, 2013).

Fanning, R., *Éamon de Valera: A Will to Power* (London, 2015).

Farragher, S.P., *Dev and his Alma Mater* (Dublin, 1984).

Farrell, B., *The Founding of Dáil Éireann* (Dublin, 1971).

Farrell, B., *Chairman or Chief? The Role of the Taoiseach in Irish Government* (Dublin, 1971).

Farrell, B., *Seán Lemass* (Dublin, 1983).

Farrell, B. (ed.), *The Creation of the Dáil* (Dublin, 1994).

Farry, M., *Sligo: 1914–1921* (Trim, 1993).

Farwell, B., *The Great Anglo-Boer War* (New York, 1976).

Feehan, J.M., *The Shooting of Michael Collins: Murder or Accident?* (Cork, 1991).

Feeney, B., *Sinn Féin—A Hundred Turbulent Years* (Dublin, 2002).

Feeney, T., *Seán MacEntee: A Political Life* (Dublin, 2008).

Fennell, T., *The Royal Irish Constabulary: A History and Personal Memoir* (Dublin, 2003).

Ferriter, D., *Judging Dev: A Reassessment of the Life and Legacy of Éamon de Valera* (Dublin, 2007).

Ferriter, D., *A Nation not a Rabble* (Dublin, 2014).

Figgis, D., *A Chronicle of Jails* (Dublin, 1917).

Figgis, D., *The Irish Constitution Explained* (Dublin, 1922).

Figgis, D. [writing as 'Michael Ireland'], *The Return of the Hero* (London, 1923).

Figgis, D., *Recollections of the Irish War* (London, 1924).

FitzGerald, D., *Prelude to Statecraft* (London, 1939).

FitzGerald, G. (ed. F. FitzGerald), *Reflections on the Irish State* (Dublin, 2003).

Fitzgerald, W.G. (ed.), *The Voice of Ireland: A Survey of the Race and Nation from All Angles, by the Foremost Leaders at Home and Abroad* (Dublin, 1924).

Fitzgibbon, C., *The Life and Times of Éamon de Valera* (New York, 1973).

Fitzpatrick, D., *Politics and Irish Life, 1913–1921: Provincial Experience of War and Revolution* (Dublin, 1977).

Fitzpatrick, D. (ed.), *Revolution: Ireland, 1917–1923* (Dublin, 1990).

Fitzpatrick, D., *The Two Irelands* (Oxford, 1998).

Fitzpatrick, D., *Harry Boland's Irish Revolution* (Cork, 2003).

Fitzpatrick, D. (ed.), *Terror in Ireland, 1916–1923* (Dublin, 2013).

Fitzpatrick, S., *Recollections of the Fight for Irish Freedom and of the Part Played by the 3rd (South) Tipperary Brigade Irish Volunteers, More Colloquially 'IRA' as from Spring/Summer of 1920* (privately published, n.d.).

Flynn, B., *Pawns in the Game: Irish Hunger Strikes 1912–1991* (Cork, 2002).

Foley, C., *Legion of the Rearguard: The IRA and the Modern Irish State* (London, 1992).

Foley, M., *The Bloodied Field* (Dublin, 2014).

Follis, B.A., *A State Under Siege: The Establishment of Northern Ireland* (Oxford, 1995).

Foot, M.R.D., *SOE in France: An Account of the Work of the British Special Operations Executive in France 1940–1945* (Government Official History Series) (London, 1966; 1968).

Forester, M., *Michael Collins: The Lost Leader* (Dublin, 1989).

Foster, R.F., *Modern Ireland, 1600–1972* (London, 1988).

Foster, R.F., *The Oxford History of Ireland* (Oxford, 1989; 1992).

Fox, R.M., *Rebel Irishwomen* (Dublin and Cork, 1935).

Fox, R.M., *Green Banners: The Story of the Irish Struggle* (London, 1938).

Foy, M.T., *Michael Collins' Intelligence War* (Stroud, 2006; Dublin, 2007).

Fraser, T.G. and Jeffery, K. (eds), *Men, Women and War* (Dublin, 1993).

French, Hon. E.G.F., *The Life of Field Marshal Sir John French* (London, 1931).

French, Lord J., *The Despatches of Lord John French*, vol. 1 (London, 1917).

Gaucher, R., *The Terrorists* (London, 1968).

Gallagher, F., *Days of Fear: A Diary of A Hunger Strike* (London, 1928).

Gallagher, F. [writing as 'David Hogan'], *The Four Glorious Years* (Dublin, 1953).

Gallagher, F., *The Indivisible Island: The Story of the Partition of Ireland* (London, 1957).

Gallagher, F. (ed. with introduction by T.P. O'Neill), *The Anglo-Irish Treaty* (London, 1965).

Gamson, W., *The Strategy of Social Protest* (Belmont, CA, 1990).

Gardiner, É., *Dublin Castle and the Anglo-Irish War: Counter-Insurgency and Conflict* (Cambridge, 2009).

Garvin, T., *Nationalist Revolutions in Ireland, 1858–1928* (Oxford, 1987).

Garvin, T. (ed.), *The Revolution in Ireland* (Basingstoke, 1988).

Garvin, T., *1922: The Birth of Irish Democracy* (Dublin, 1996).

Gates, D., *The Spanish Ulcer: A History of the Peninsular War* (New York, 1986).

Gaughan, J.A. (ed.), *Memoirs of Constable J. Mee, RIC* (Dublin, 1975).

Gaughan, J.A., *Austin Stack: Portrait of a Separatist* (Dublin, 1977).

Gaynor, E. (ed.), *Memoirs of a Tipperary Family: The Gaynors of Tyone, 1887–2000* (Dublin, 2003).

Geraghty, T., *The Irish War* (London, 1998).

Giáp, Võ Nguyên, *People's War, People's Army: The Military Art of People's War* (New York, 1971).

Gibbon, M., *Inglorious Soldier* (London, 1968).

Gilbert, M., *Winston S. Churchill, Vol. 4. 1916–1922: The Stricken World* (Boston, 1974).

Gillis, L., *The Fall of Dublin* (Cork, 2011).

Gillis, L., *May 25: Burning of the Custom House 1921* (Dublin, 2017).

Girvin, K., *Seán O'Hegarty: Officer Commanding First Cork Brigade, IRA* (Cork, 2007).

Gleeson, J., *Bloody Sunday* (London, 1962).

Golding, G.M., *George Gavan Duffy, 1882–1951* (Dublin, 1982).

Good, J., *Enchanted by Dreams: The Journal of a Revolutionary* (Dingle, 1946; ed. M. Good, 1996).

Gray, T., *The Irish Answer* (London, 1966).

Greaves, C.D., *Liam Mellows and the Irish Revolution* (London, 1971; 1987).

Griffith, K., *Hang Up Your Brightest Colours: The Real Story of the Life and Death of Michael Collins* (documentary film, 1972).

Griffith, K. and O'Grady, T., *Ireland's Unfinished Revolution: An Oral History* (Boulder, CO, 2002). [Originally published as *Curious Journey: An Oral History of Ireland's Unfinished Revolution* (London, 1982).]

Grinnell, L., *DORA at Westminster* (Dublin, 1918).

Grob-Fitzgibbon, B., *Turning Points of the Irish Revolution: The British Government, Intelligence and the Cost of Indifference* (Palgrave, 2007).

Gudgin, P., *Military Intelligence: The British Story* (London, 1989).

Guevara, E. 'Che', *Principles of Guerrilla Warfare* (New York, 1961).

Gwynn, D., *De Valera* (London, 1933).

Gwynn, D., *The History of Partition, 1912–1925* (Dublin, 1950).

Hammes, Col. F.X., *The Sling and the Stone: On War in the 21st Century* (Zenith Military Classics, 2006).

Hammond, B., *Soldier of the Rearguard* (Fermoy, 1977).

Hannigan, D., *De Valera in America: the Rebel President's 1919 Campaign* (Dublin, 2008).

Harkness, D.W., *The Restless Dominion: The Irish Free State and the British Commonwealth of Nations, 1921–1931* (London, 1969; New York, 1970).

Harnett, M., *Victory and Woe: The West Limerick Brigade in the War of Independence* (Dublin, 2002).

Harrison, H., *The Neutrality of Ireland* (London, 1932).

Harrison, H., *Ulster and the British Empire* (London, 1939).

Hart, P., *The IRA and its Enemies: Violence and Community in Cork, 1916–1923* (Oxford, 1998).

Hart, P. (ed.), *British Intelligence in Ireland, 1920–21: The Final Reports* (Cork, 2002).

Hart, P., *The IRA at War, 1916–1923* (Oxford, 2003).

Hart, P., *Mick: The Real Michael Collins* (London, 2006).

Hartley, S., *The Irish Question as a Problem in British Foreign Policy, 1914–1918* (London, 1987).

Havens, M.C., Leiden, C. and Schmit, K.M., *The Politics of Assassination* (Englewood Cliffs, NJ, 1970).

Haverty, A., *Countess Markievicz: An Independent Life* (London, 1988).

Hennessy, T., *Dividing Ireland: World War One and Partition* (Milton Park, 1998).

Henry, R.M., *The Evolution of Sinn Féin* (Dublin, 1920).

Hepburn, A.C., *Ireland, 1905–1925. Volume II* (Newtownards, 1998).

Herlihy, J., *The Royal Irish Constabulary* (Dublin, 1997).

Herlihy, J., *The Royal Irish Constabulary: A Complete Alphabetical List of Officers and Men, 1816–1922* (Dublin, 1999).

Herlihy, J., *The Dublin Metropolitan Police: A Complete Alphabetical List of Officers and Men, 1836–1925* (Dublin, 2001).

Hittle, J.B.E., *Michael Collins and the Anglo-Irish War: Britain's Counter-insurgency Failure* (Chicago, 2011).

Hoffman, R., Tate, T.W. and Albert, P.J. (eds), *An Uncivil War: The Southern Backcountry during the American Revolution* (Charlottesville, VA, 1985).

Hogan, J. (ed. Donncadh Ó Corráin), *James Hogan: Revolutionary, Historian and Political Scientist* (Dublin, 2001).

Holmes, R., *The Little Field Marshal: Sir John French* (London, 2005).

Holt, E., *Protest in Arms* (New York, 1960).

Hood, F., *The Military Impact of Counter-Mobility* (Salisbury, 2002).

Hopkinson, M., *Green against Green* (Dublin, 2004).

Hopkinson, M., *The Irish War of Independence* (Dublin, 2004).

Hoppen, K.T., *Ireland since 1800: Conflict and Nationalism* (London, 1989).

Horgan, J.J., *Lemass* (Dublin, 1997).

Howard, M., *War in European History* (Oxford, 2001).

Howarth, J., *Dame Millicent Garrett Fawcett [née Millicent Garrett], 1847–1929* (Oxford, 2004).

Hughes, B., *Defying the IRA: Intimidation, Coercion and Communities during the Irish Revolution* (Liverpool, 2016).

Hughes, K., *English Atrocities in Ireland: A Compilation of Facts from Court and Press Records* (New York, 1920).

Hyam, R., *Britain's Declining Empire: The Road to Decolonization, 1918–1968* (Cambridge, 2006).

Irish Free State Official Handbook, *Saorstát Éireann* (Dublin, 1932).

Jackson, A., *Ireland: 1798–1998* (Oxford, 1999).

James, R.R., *Churchill: A Study in Failure, 1900–1939* (London, 1972).

Jeffery, K., *The British Army and the Crisis of Empire, 1918–1922* (Manchester, 1984).

Jeffery, K., *The Secret History of MI6, 1909–1949* (London, 2011).

Jenkins, R., *Asquith* (London, 1964).

Jenkins, R., *Churchill: A Biography* (London, 2001).

Johnson, R., Whitby, M. and France, J. (eds), *How to Win on the Battlefield* (London, 2010).

Jones, T., *Lloyd George* (London, 1951).

Jones, T. (ed. K. Middlemas), *Whitehall Diary, Volume I, 1916–1925* (London, 1969).

Jones, T. (ed. K. Middlemas), *Whitehall Diary, Volume III, Ireland 1918–1925* (London, 1971).

Jordan, A.J., *W.T. Cosgrave: Founder of Modern Ireland* (Westport, 2007).

Joy, S., *The IRA in Kerry, 1916–1921* (Cork, 2005).

Kautt, W.H., *The Anglo-Irish War, 1916–1921: A People's War* (Westport, CT, and London, 1999).

Kautt, W.H., *Ambushes and Armour: The Irish Rebellion 1919–1921* (Dublin, 2014).

Kautt, W.H., *Ground Truths: British Army Operations in the Irish War of Independence* (Sallins, 2014).

Kearns, K., *Dublin Tenement Life: An Oral History* (Dublin, 1994).

Kearns, K., *Dublin Street Life and Lore* (Dublin, 1997).

Kearns, L. (ed. A.P. Smithson), *In Times of Peril* (Dublin, 1922).

Keatinge, P., *A Place Among the Nations* (Dublin, 1978).

Kee, R., *The Green Flag* (combining three separate volumes entitled *The Most Distressful Country, The Bold Fenian Men* and *Ourselves Alone*) (London, 1972).

Kee, R., *Ireland: A History* (London, 1981).

Keegan, J., *Intelligence in War: Knowledge of the Enemy from Napoleon to al-Qaeda* (New York, 2003).

Kenna, G.B., *Facts and Figures of the Belfast Pogroms 1920–1922* (Dublin, 1922; ed. Thomas Donaldson, 1997).

Kenneally, I., *The Paper Wall: Newspapers and Propaganda in Ireland, 1919–1921* (Cork, 2008).

Keogh, D., *Twentieth-Century Ireland: Revolution and State Building* (Dublin, 2005).

The Kerryman, *Dublin's Fighting Story, 1916–1921, Told by the Men Who Made it* (Tralee, 1947; ed. D. Ferriter and B. Ó Conchubhair, Cork, 2009).

The Kerryman, *Kerry's Fighting Story, 1916–1921, Told by the Men Who Made it* (Tralee, 1947; ed. J.J. Lee and B. Ó Conchubhair, Cork, 2009).

The Kerryman, *Limerick's Fighting Story, 1916–1921, Told by the Men Who Made it* (Tralee, 1948; ed. R. O'Donnell and B. Ó Conchubhair, Cork, 2009).

The Kerryman, *Rebel Cork's Fighting Story, 1916–1921, Told by the Men Who Made it* (Tralee, 1961; ed. P. Hart and B. Ó Conchubhair, Cork, 2009).

The Kerryman, *Sworn to be Free: The Complete Book of IRA Jailbreaks, 1918–1921* (Tralee, 1971).

Kitson, General F., *Bunch of Five* (London, 1977).

Knirck, J., *Ghosts and Realities: Female TDs and the Treaty Debate* (New Jersey, 1997).

Knirck, J., *Imagining Ireland's Independence: The Debates over the Anglo-Irish Treaty of 1921* (Plymouth, 2006).

Knirck, J., *Women of the Dáil* (Dublin, 2006).

Kostick, C., *Revolution in Ireland: Popular Militancy, 1917 to 1923* (London, 1996).

Kotsonouris, M., *Retreat from Revolution: The Dáil Courts, 1920–1924* (Dublin, 1994).

Laffan, M., *The Partition of Ireland, 1911–1925* (Dundalk, 1983).

Laffan, M., *The Resurrection of Ireland: The Sinn Féin Party, 1916–1923* (Cambridge, 1999).

Lalor, J.F. (ed. L. Fogarty), *James Fintan Lalor, Patriot and Political Essayist (1807–1849)* (Dublin, 1919).

Lankford, S., *The Hope and the Sadness: Personal Recollections of Troubled Times in Ireland* (Cork, 1980).

Lapping, B., *End of Empire* (London, 1985).

Laqueur, W., *Guerilla Warfare: A Historical and Critical Study* (London, 1977).

Lavelle, P., *James O'Mara: A Staunch Sinn Féiner* (Dublin, 1961).

Lawrence, T.E., *Seven Pillars of Wisdom* (privately published, 1926; Wordsworth, 1997).

Lazenby, E., *Ireland—A Catspaw* (London, 1928).

Lee, J.J., *Ireland 1912–1985* (Cambridge, 1989).

Lee, J. and Ó Tuathaigh, G., *The Age of de Valera* (Dublin, 1982).

Leeson, D., *The Black and Tans: British Police and Auxiliaries in the Irish War of Independence, 1920–1921* (Oxford, 2012).

Leiberson, G. (ed.), *The Irish Uprising, 1916–1922* (New York, 1966).

Lenihan, E., *Defiant Irish Women* (Cork, 1991).

Liddell Hart, B.H., 'Foreword', in Mao Tse-tung and Che Guevara, *Guerrilla Warfare* (London, 1962).

Liddell Hart, B.H., *Lawrence of Arabia* (New York, 1991).

Lowe, W.J., *Disbandment and After: The Old RIC in the New Free State* (undated).

Luddy, M. and Murphy, C., *Women Surviving: Studies in Irish Women's History in the 19th and 20th Centuries* (Dublin, 1990).

Lynch, D. (ed. F. O'Donoghue), *The IRB and the 1916 Insurrection* (Cork, 1957).

Lysaght, D.R. O'Connor, *The Republic of Ireland* (Cork, 1970).

Macardle, D., *The Irish Republic* (New York, 1937; 1965).

MacAtasney, G., *Seán MacDiarmada: The Mind of the Revolution* (Dublin, 2005).

MacBride, J. (ed. A.J. Jordan), *Boer War to Easter Rising: The Writings of John MacBride* (Westport, 2006).

MacBride, S. (ed. C. Lawlor), *That Day's Struggle: A Memoir 1904–1951* (Dublin, 2005).

McCall, E., *The Auxiliaries: Tudor's Toughs. A Study of the Auxiliary Division of the Royal Irish Constabulary 1920–1922* (London, 2010).

McCartan, P., *With de Valera in America* (Dublin, 1932).

McCarthy, J.R., *Kevin O'Higgins* (Dublin, 2006).

McCoole, S., *Hazel: A Life of Lady Lavery* (Dublin, 1996).

McCoole, S., *Guns and Chiffon* (Dublin, 1997).

McCoole, S., *No Ordinary Women: Irish Female Activists in the Revolutionary Years* (Dublin, 2003).

McCullagh, D., *De Valera, Vol. 1: Rise* (Dublin, 2017).

MacCurtain, F., *Remember It's for Ireland: A Family Memoir of Tomás MacCurtain* (Cork, 2008).

McDermott, J., *Northern Divisions: The Old IRA and the Belfast Pogroms, 1920–1922* (Belfast, 2001).

McDonnell, K.K., *There is a Bridge at Bandon* (Cork, 1972).

McDonnell, V., *Michael Collins: Most Wanted Man* (Cork, 2008).

McDowell, R.B., *Crisis and Decline: The Fate of the Southern Unionists* (Dublin, 1998).

McDowell, R.B., *The Irish Convention of 1917–1918* (London, 1970).

MacDowell, V., *Michael Collins and the Irish Republican Brotherhood* (Dublin, 1997).

MacEoin, U. (ed.), *Survivors: The Story of Ireland's Struggle as Told Through Some of Her Outstanding Living People. Notes 1913–1916* (Dublin, 1966).

McGarry, F., *The Rising: Ireland: Easter 1916* (Oxford, 2010).

McGee, O., *The IRB: The Irish Republican Brotherhood from the Land League to Sinn Féin* (Dublin, 2005).

McGough, E., *Diarmuid Lynch: A Forgotten Irish Patriot* (Cork, 2013).

McGuinness, C.J., *Sailor of Fortune: Adventures of an Irish Sailor, Soldier, Pirate, Pearl-Fisher, Gun-Runner, Rebel and Antarctic Explorer* (Philadelphia, 1935).

McInnes, C. and Sheffield, G.D., *Warfare in the Twentieth Century: Theory and Practice* (London, 1988).

Mackay, J., *Michael Collins: A Life* (Edinburgh, 1996).

McMahon, P., *British Spies and Irish Rebels: British Intelligence in Ireland, 1916–*

1945 (Suffolk, 2008).

MacManus, M.J., *Éamon de Valera* (Dublin, 1944).

Macready, General Sir N., *Annals of an Active Life* (2 vols) (London, 1925; 1942).

MacSwiney, T., *Principles of Freedom* (Dublin, 1921; 1936).

Maher, J., *The Flying Column: West Kilkenny, 1916–1921* (Dublin, 1988).

Maher, J., *Harry Boland: A Biography* (Cork, 1998).

Malcom, E., *The Irish Policeman: 1822–1922: A Life* (Dublin, 2006).

Malone, J. (trans. P.J. Twohig), *Blood on the Flag: An Autobiography of a Freedom Fighter* (Ballincollig, 1996).

Malone, T., *Alias Seán Forde* (Danesfort, 2000).

Manchester, W., *Winston Churchill: The Last Lion* (Boston, 1983).

Mansergh, N., *The Unresolved Question: the Anglo-Irish Settlement and its Undoing, 1912–1972* (New Haven, CT, 1991).

Mao Zedong (Mao Tse Tung) (trans. Brigadier General Samuel Griffith, USMC), *On Guerrilla Warfare* (Westport, CT, 1961).

Marjoribanks, E., *Life of Lord Carson*, vol. I (London, 1932). [See Colvin, I.D., for vols II and III.]

Markievicz, Countess C., *A Call to the Women of Ireland* (Dublin, 1918).

Markievicz, Countess C., *Prison Letters of Countess Markievicz* (London, 1987).

Marreco, A., *The Rebel Countess: The Life and Times of Constance Markievicz* (London, 1967).

Martin, H., *Insurrection in Ireland* (London, 1921).

Marx, K. and Engels, F. (ed. R. Dixon), *The Irish Question* (Moscow, 1971).

Matthews, K., *Fatal Influences: The Impact of Ireland on British Politics 1920–1925* (Dublin, 2004).

Maye, B., *Arthur Griffith* (Dublin, 1997).

Menzies, C. [writing as 'A Woman of No Importance'], *As Others See Us* (London, 1924).

Midleton, Earl of, *Ireland—Dupe or Heroine* (London, 1932).

Mitchell, A., *Labour in Irish Politics* (Dublin, 1974).

Mitchell, A., *Revolutionary Government in Ireland: Dáil Éireann, 1919–1922* (Dublin, 1995).

Mitchell, A. and Ó Snodaigh, P. (eds), *Irish Political Documents: 1916–1949* (Dublin, 1985).

Mitchell, D., *Women on the Warpath* (London, 1966).

Mockaitis, T.R., *British Counterinsurgency, 1919–1960* (London, 1990).

Moody, T.W. and Martin, F.X., *The Course of Irish History* (Cork, 1967).

Moran, M., *Executed for Ireland: The Patrick Moran Story* (Cork, 2010).

Moylan, S., *Seán Moylan: In His Own Words* (Millstreet, 2003).

Moynihan, M. (ed.), *The Speeches and Statements by Éamon de Valera, 1917–1973* (Dublin, 1980).

Mulcahy, R., *Richard Mulcahy (1886–1971), A Family Memoir* (Dublin, 1999).

Mulcahy, R., *My Father the General: Richard Mulcahy and the Military History of the Revolution* (Dublin, 2009).

Mulholland, M., *The Politics and Relationships of Kathleen Lynn* (Dublin, 2002).

Mullins, B., *Memoirs of Billy Mullins, Veteran of the War of Independence* (with introduction by M. O'Rourke) (Tralee, 1983).

Murphy, B.P., *John Chartres: Mystery Man of the Treaty* (Dublin, 1995).

Murphy, B.P., *The Origin and Organisation of British Propaganda in Ireland, 1920* (Dublin, 2006).

Murphy, G., *The Year of Disappearances* (Cork, 2010).

Murphy, G., *The Great Cover-Up: The Truth about the Death of Michael Collins* (Cork, 2018).

Nankivell, J.M. and Loch, S., *Ireland in Turmoil* (London, 1922).

Neeson, E., *The Life and Death of Michael Collins* (Cork, 1968).

Neeson, E., *Birth of a Republic* (Dublin, 1998).

Neeson, E., *The Battle of Crossbarry* (Cork, 2008).

Neilson, K. (ed.), *Go Spy the Land: Military Intelligence in History* (Westport, CT, 1992).

Neligan, D., *The Spy in the Castle* (London, 1999).

Nelson, J., *Michael Collins: The Final Days* (Dublin, 1997).

Ni Dheirg, I., *The Story of Michael Collins* (Cork, 1978).

Nic Shiubhlaigh, M. (as told to E. Kenny), *The Splendid Years* (Dublin, 1955).

Nicholson, Sir H., *King George V* (London, 1952).

Noonan, G., *The IRA in Britain 1919–1923, 'In the Heart of Enemy Lines'* (Liverpool, 2017).

Norman, D., *Terrible Beauty: A Life of Constance Markievicz* (London, 1988).

O'Brien, W., *The Irish Revolution and How it Came About* (London, 1923).

Ó Broin, L., *Revolutionary Underground: The Story of the Irish Republican Brotherhood* (Dublin, 1976).

Ó Broin, L., *Michael Collins* (Dublin, 1980).

Ó Broin, L., *In Great Haste: Letters of Michael Collins and Kitty Kiernan* (Dublin, 1983).

Ó Broin, L., *W.E. Wylie and the Irish Revolution, 1916–1921* (Dublin, 1989).

O'Callaghan, J., *Revolutionary Limerick: The Republican Campaign for Independence in Limerick, 1913–1921* (Dublin, 2010).

O'Callaghan, M., *For Ireland and Freedom: Roscommon's Contribution in the Fight for Freedom* (Cork, 2012).

O'Callaghan, S., *Execution* (London, 1974).

O'Carroll, J.P. and Murphy, J.A. (eds) *De Valera and His Times* (Cork, 1983).

Ó Ceallaigh, S.T., *Seán T* (Dublin, 1973).

O'Ceirin, K. and O'Ceirin, C., *Women of Ireland* (Galway, 1996).

O'Connor, B., *With Michael Collins in the Fight for Independence* (London, 1929).

O'Connor, F., *The Big Fellow* (London, 1969; 1979).

O'Connor, J., *A History of Ireland 1795–1924* (London, 1925).

O'Connor, U., *A Terrible Beauty is Born: The Irish Troubles, 1912–1922* (London, 1975).

O'Donoghue, F., *No Other Law* (Dublin, 1954; 1986).

O'Donoghue, F., *Tomás MacCurtáin, Soldier and Patriot* (Tralee, 1971).

O'Donoghue, F. (ed.), *IRA Jailbreaks, 1918–1921* (Cork, 1971).

O'Donovan, D., *Kevin Barry and His Time* (Glendale, 1989).

Ó Duibhir, L., *Prisoners of War: The Ballykinlar Internment Camp 1920–1921* (Cork, 2013).

Ó Faoláin, S., *The Life of de Valera* (Dublin, 1933).

Ó Faoláin, S., *Constance Markievicz* (London, 1934).

Ó Faoláin, S., *De Valera* (London, 1939).

O'Farrell, B., *The Founding of Dáil Éireann* (Dublin, 1971).

O'Farrell, P[adraic], *The Seán MacEoin Story* (Dublin, 1981).

O'Farrell, P[adraic], *The Ernie O'Malley Story* (Dublin, 1983).

O'Farrell, P[adraic], *Seán MacEoin: The Blacksmith of Ballinalee* (Mullingar, 1993).

O'Farrell, P[adraic], *Who's Who in the Irish War of Independence and Civil War* (Dublin, 1997).

O'Farrell, P[eter], *Memoirs of Irish Volunteer Activity, 1917–1924* (New York, 1978).

Ó Fathaigh, P. (ed. T.G. McMahon), *Pádraig Ó Fathaigh's War of Independence: Recollections of a Galway Gaelic Leaguer* (Cork, 2000).

O'Halpin, E., *The Decline of the Union: British Government in Ireland, 1892–1920* (Syracuse, NY, 1987).

O'Halpin, E., *Head of the Civil Service: A Study of Sir Warren Fisher* (London, 1989).

O'Hegarty, P.S., *Sinn Féin: An Illumination* (Dublin and London, 1919).

O'Hegarty, P.S., *The Victory of Sinn Féin* (Dublin, 1924; 1998).

O'Higgins, K., *Civil War and the Events that Led to it* (Dublin, 1922).

Ó Luing, S., *I Die in a Good Cause: A Study of Thomas Ashe, Idealist and Revolutionary* (Tralee, 1970).

O'Mahony, S., *Frongoch, University of Revolution* (Killiney, 1987; 1995).

O'Mahony, S., *The Burning of the Custom House in Dublin, 1921* (Dublin, 2000).

O'Mahony, S., *The First Hunger Strike—Thomas Ashe, 1917* (Dublin, 2001).

O'Mahony, S., *Three Murders in Dublin Castle, 1920* (Dublin, 2005).

O'Malley, C., *The Men Will Talk to Me* (Cork, 2010).

O'Malley, E., *On Another Man's Wound* (Dublin, 1936; 1979).

O'Malley, E., *An Army Without Banners: Adventures of an Irish Volunteer* (Dublin, 1939).

O'Malley, E., *The Singing Flame* (Dublin, 1978).

O'Malley, E., *Raids and Rallies* (Dublin, 1982).

O'Malley, E. (ed. C.K.H. O'Malley), *Rising Out: Seán Connolly of Longford (1890–1921)* (Dublin, 2007).

O'Meara, M., *Bloody Sunday, 1920–1995: A Commemorative Booklet* (Dublin, 1995).

O'Neill, F. and Gallagher, T.P., *The Anglo-Irish Treaty* (London, 1965).

O'Neill, T., *The Battle of Clonmult and the IRA's Worst Defeat* (Dublin, 2006).

Ó Neill, T. and Ó Fiannachta, P., *De Valera* (2 vols) (Dublin, 1968–70).

O'Reilly, T. (ed.), *Our Struggle for Independence: Eye-witness Accounts from the Pages of An Cosantóir* (Cork, 2009).

O'Reilly, T., *Rebel Heart: George Lennon: Flying Column Commander* (Cork, 2010).

Ó Ruairc, P. Óg, *Blood on the Banner: The Republican Struggle in Clare* (Cork, 2009).

Ó Ruairc, P. Óg, *Truce: Murder, Myth, and the Last Days of the War of Independence* (Cork, 2016).

O'Sullivan, M., *Seán Lemass* (Dublin, 1994).

O'Sullivan, N., *Every Dark Hour: A History of Kilmainham Gaol* (Dublin, 2007).

Osborne, C., *Michael Collins, Himself* (Douglas, Co. Cork, 2003).

Osborne, C., *The Michael Collins Album: A Life in Pictures* (Cork, 2007).

Owen, F., *Tempestuous Journey: Lloyd George, his Life and Times* (London, 1954).

Packenham, F. (Lord Longford), *Peace by Ordeal* (London, 1935; 1972).

Packenham, F. (Lord Longford) and O'Neill, T.P., *Éamon de Valera, A Biography* (Dublin, 1970).

Packenham, T., *The Year of Liberty* (London, 1969).

Paret, P. (ed.), *Makers of Modern Strategy* (Princeton, NJ, 1986).

Pelling, N., *Anglo-Irish Relations 1798–1922* (London, 2003).

Phillips, W.A., *The Revolution in Ireland: 1906–1923* (London, 1923).

Phoenix, É., *Northern Nationalism: Nationalist Politics, Partition and the Catholic Minority in Northern Ireland, 1890–1940* (Belfast, 1994).

Pinkman, J.A., *In the Legion of the Vanguard* (Cork, 1998).

Polk, W.R., *Violent Politics: A History of Insurgency, Terrorism, and Guerrilla War from the American Revolution to Iraq* (New York, 2007).

Pollard, H.B.C., *The Secret Societies of Ireland: Their Rise and Progress* (London, 1922).

Price, D., *The Flame and the Candle: War in Mayo, 1919–1924* (Cork, 2012).

Price, D., *We Bled Together* (Cork, 2017).

Rees, R., *Ireland 1905–25, Volume I. Text and Historiography* (Newtownards, 1998).

Regan, J., *The Irish Counter-revolution, 1921–1936* (Dublin, 1999).

Regan, J., *Myth and the Irish State* (Sallins, 2013).

Regan, J.M. (ed. J. Augusteijn), *The Memoirs of John M. Regan, a Catholic Officer in the RIC and RUC: 1909–1948* (Dublin, 2007).

Riddell, Lord, *War Diary, 1914–1918* (London, 1970).

Ring, J., *Erskine Childers* (London, 1996).

Robertson, Sir W., *From Private to Field Marshal* (London, 1921).

Robins, J., *Custom House People* (Dublin, 1993).

Roskill, S., *Hankey: Man of Secrets* (2 vols) (London, 1972).

Ryan, A., *Comrades: Inside the War of Independence* (Dublin, 2006).

Ryan, B., *A Full Private Remembers the Troubled Times* (Hollyford, 1969).

Ryan, D., *Remembering Sion* (London, 1934).

Ryan, D., *Unique Dictator: A Study of Éamon de Valera* (London, 1936).

Ryan, D., *Seán Treacy and the Third Tipperary Brigade* (Tralee, 1945).

Ryan, D., *Michael Collins: The Invisible Army* (Tralee, 1968).

Ryan, L. and Ward, M. (eds), *Irish Women and Nationalism: Soldiers, New Women and Wicked Hags* (Dublin, 2004).

Ryan, L. and Ward, M. (eds), *Irish Women and the Vote* (Dublin, 2007).

Ryan, M., *The Tom Barry Story* (Dublin, 1982).

Ryan, M., *The Day Michael Collins Was Shot* (Dublin, 1989).

Ryan, M., *Michael Collins and the Women in his Life* (Dublin, 1996). [Republished as *Michael Collins and the Women Who Spied for Ireland* (Cork, 2007).]

Ryan, M., *Tom Barry: IRA Freedom Fighter* (Cork, 2003).

Ryan, M., *The Real Chief: The Story of Liam Lynch* (Dublin, 2005).

Scanlon, M., *The Dublin Metropolitan Police* (London, 1998).

Seibold, B.S., *Emily Hobhouse and the Reports on the Concentration Camps during the Boer War 1899–1902* (Stuttgart, 2011).

Seth, R., *Anatomy of Spying* (New York, 1963).

Sheehan, T., *Mrs Lindsay, Lady Hostage* (Dripsey, 1990).

Sheehan, T., *Execute Hostage Compton-Smith* (Dripsey, 1993).

Sheehan, W., *Fighting for Dublin: The British Battle for Dublin, 1919–1921* (Cork, 2007).

Sheehan, W. (ed.), *British Voices from the Irish War of Independence 1918–1921: The Words of British Servicemen Who Were There* (Cork, 2007).

Sheehan, W., *Hearts and Mines: The British 5th Division, Ireland, 1920–1922* (Cork, 2009).

Sheehan, W., *A Hard Local War* (Dublin, 2011).

Shelly, J.R., *A Short History of the Third Tipperary Brigade* (Cashel, 1996).

Short, K.R.M., *The Dynamite War: Irish-American Bombers in Victorian Britain* (Dublin, 1979).

Sigerson, S.M., *The Assassination of Michael Collins* (CreateSpace Independent Publishing, 2013).

Sinn Féin: A Century of Struggle (Dublin, 2005).

Smith, J., *Britain and Ireland: From Home Rule to Independence* (Harlow, 2000).

Smith, M., *The Spying Game* (London, 1996).

Smith, M.L.R., *Fighting for Ireland: The Strategy of the Irish Republican Movement* (New York, 1995).

Smith, N.C., *Dorothy Macardle: A Life* (Dublin, 2007).

Smuts, J. (ed. J. van der Poel), *Selections from the Smuts Papers* (7 vols) (Cambridge, 1973).

Stafford, D., *Churchill and Secret Service* (New York, 1997).

Steed, H.W., *Through Thirty Years, 1882–1922*, vol. II (New York, 1924).

Stephens, J., *Arthur Griffith, Journalist and Statesman* (Dublin, 1922).

Stewart, A.T.Q., *The Ulster Crisis: Resistance to Home Rule: 1912–1914* (London, 1967).

Stewart, A.T.Q. (ed.), *Michael Collins: The Secret File* (Belfast, 1997).

Street, Major C.J.C. [writing as 'I.O.'], *The Administration of Ireland, 1920* (New York, 1921; London, 1922).

Street, Major C.J.C., *Ireland in 1921* (New York, 1921; London, 1922).

Stubbs, R., *Hearts and Minds in Guerrilla Warfare: The Malayan Emergency, 1948–1960* (Singapore, 1989).

Sturgis, M. (ed. M. Hopkinson), *The Last Days of Dublin Castle: The Mark Sturgis Diaries* (Dublin, 1999).

Talbot, H., *Michael Collins' Own Story* (London, 1923).

Tansill, C.C., *America and the Fight for Irish Freedom, 1866–1922* (New York, 1957).

Taylor, A.J.P., *English History 1914–1945* (London, 1965).

Taylor, A.J.P. (ed.), *Lloyd George: Twelve Essays* (London, 1971).

Taylor, R., *Assassination: The Death of Sir Henry Wilson and the Tragedy of Ireland* (London, 1961).

Taylor, R., *Michael Collins* (London, 1970).

Thomson, Sir B., *The Scene Changes* (New York, 1939).

Townshend, C., *The British Campaign in Ireland, 1919–1921* (Oxford, 1975).

Townshend, C., *Political Violence in Ireland. Government and Resistance since 1848* (Oxford, 1983).

Townshend, C., *Britain's Civil Wars: Counterinsurgency in the Twentieth Century* (London, 1986).

Townshend, C., *The Republic* (London, 2013).

Travers, P., *Settlements and Divisions: Ireland, 1870–1922* (Dublin, 1988).

Travers, P., *Éamon de Valera* (Dublin, 1994).

Twohig, P.J., *The Dark Secret of Bealnablath: The Michael Collins Story* (Ballincollig, 1990).

Twohig, P.J., *Green Tears for Hecuba* (Cork, 1994).

Ua Ceallaigh, S. [S. O'Kelly, 'Sceilg'], *A Trinity of Martyrs: Terence MacSwiney, Cathal Brugha, Austin Stack. Anniversary Lectures Delivered at Sinn Féin Headquarters* (Dublin, 1947).

Urquart, D., *Irish Women's History Reader* (Dublin, 2001).

Valiulis, M.G., *Portrait of a Revolutionary: General Richard Mulcahy and the Founding of the Irish Free State* (Blackrock, 1992).

Van Voris, J., *Constance de Markievicz: In the Cause of Ireland* (Amherst, MA, 1967).

Vane, Sir F., *Agin the Government* (London, 1929).

Walsh, J.J., *Recollections of a Rebel* (Tralee, 1944).

Walsh, L.J., *On 'My Keeping' and in Theirs: A Record of Experiences 'On the Run', in Derry Gaol, and in Ballykinlar Internment Camp* (Dublin, 1921).

Walsh, M., *The News from Ireland: Foreign Correspondents and the Irish Revolution* (Dublin, 2008).

Walsh, M., *G-2: In defence of Ireland: Irish Military Intelligence 1918–1945* (Cork, 2010).

Walsh, O., *Ireland's Independence, 1880–1923* (London, 2002).

Ward, M., *Unmanageable Revolutionaries: Women and Irish Nationalism* (Dingle, 1983).

Ward, M. (ed.), *In Their Own Voice* (Dublin, 1995; 2001).

Waters, S. (ed. S. Ball), *A Policeman's Ireland: Recollections of Samuel Waters, RIC* (Cork, 1999).

Weinstein, J.M., *Inside Rebellion: The Politics of Insurgent Violence* (Cambridge, 2007).

Wells, W.B., *An Irish Apologia. Some Thoughts on Anglo-Irish Relations and the War* (Dublin, 1917).

Wells, W.B., *John Redmond: a Biography* (London, 1919).

West, N., *MI5: British Security Service Operations, 1909–1945* (London, 1983).

Wheatley, M., *Nationalism and the Irish Party: Provincial Ireland 1910–1916* (Oxford, 2005).

White, G. and O'Shea, B., *Irish Volunteer Soldier, 1913–1923* (Oxford, 2003).

White, G. and O'Shea, B., *The Burning of Cork* (Cork, 2006).

White, T. de Vere, *Kevin O'Higgins* (London and Tralee, 1948; 1986).

White, T. de Vere, *Ireland* (New York, 1968).

Wilkensen, P.K. and Bright Ashley, J., *Gubbins and the SOE* (London, 1993).

Wilkinson, B., *The Zeal of the Convert: The Life of Erskine Childers* (Washington, DC, 1974).

Willbanks, J., *The Tet Offensive: A Concise History* (New York, 2008).

Williams, T.D. (ed.), *The Irish Struggle, 1916–1926* (London, 1966).

Williams, T.D. (ed.), *Secret Societies in Ireland* (Dublin, 1973).

Winter, Sir O., *Winter's Tale* (London, 1955).

Wilson, D., *Mao Zedong in the Scales of History* (Cambridge, 1977).

Wilson, H. (ed. K. Jeffery), *The Military Correspondence of Field Marshal Sir Henry Wilson, 1918–1922* (London, 1985).

Woodcock, C., *Experiences of an Officer's Wife in Ireland* (London, 1921; 1994). [Originally published in *Blackwood's Magazine*, vol. 209, no. 1267 (May 1921).]

Wright, F., *Northern Ireland: A Comparative Analysis* (Dublin, 1988).

Yeates, P., *A City in Wartime, 1914–1918* (Dublin, 2012).

Yeates, P., *A City in Turmoil, 1919–1921* (Dublin, 2014).

Yeates, P., *A City in Civil War, 1921–1924* (Dublin, 2015).

Yeates, P. and Wren, J., *Michael Collins* (Dublin, 1989).

Youngblood, N., *The Development of Mine Warfare: A Most Murderous and Barbarous Conduct* (Westport, 2006).

Younger, C., *A State of Disunion* (London, 1972).

Younger, C., *Ireland's Civil War* (New York, 1969).
Younger, C., *Arthur Griffith* (Dublin, 1981).

PAMPHLETS, PAPERS, PERIODICALS

'General played tennis in IRA custody—remembering the past', *An Phoblacht*, 29 June 1995.
'The IRA and the Treaty', *An Phoblacht*, 17 April 1997.
'Rebuilding the Republican Movement', *An Phoblacht*, 29 July 1999.
'The East Clare election', *An Phoblacht*, 12 August 1999.
'Remembering the past: Molly O'Reilly', *An Phoblacht*, 7 October 1999.
'Erskine Childers', *An Phoblacht*, 29 November 1999.
'The Forgotten Ten', *An Phoblacht*, 11 October 2001.
'The missing piece', *An Phoblacht*, 27 March 2002.
'The burning of Balbriggan', *An Phoblacht*, 27 August 2010.
'Report of the Irish National Aid and Volunteers' Dependants' Fund', *Catholic Bulletin* (August 1919).
'Amazing adventures of the man who played hide-and-seek with the government', *Daily Sketch* (London), 24 August 1922.
Editorial, 'The helmsman gone', *Daily Sketch* (London), 24 August 1922.
'Organisation of flying columns', Organisation Memo No. 1, Óglaigh na hÉireann, 4 October 1920. (Reproduced in John M. MacCarthy, Witness Statement 883, Military Archives.)
'Interview with General Strickland', *Evening Standard*, 25 January 1921.
'De Valera 1882–1975', *Irish Times* (1976).
'An appreciation of Arthur Griffith', *Studies* (September 1922).
'Murdered officers' last journey', *The Times*, 25 November 1920.
'What causes reprisals', *Weekly Summary*, No. 9 (8 October 1920).

Acland, F., *A Report of a Fortnight's Tour in Ireland* (pamphlet, place of publication not given, 1920).
Acland, F., 'The Sinn Féin fellowships', *Westminster Gazette*, 29 April 1921.
Ainsworth, J., 'British security policy in Ireland, 1920–1921: a desperate attempt by the Crown to maintain Anglo-Irish unity by force', 11th Irish-Australian Conference, Queensland University of Technology, School of Humanities and Social Science, 25–30 April 2000.
Ainsworth, J., 'The Black and Tans and Auxiliaries in Ireland, 1920–1921: their origins, roles and legacy', paper presented to the Queensland History Teachers' Association, Brisbane, Queensland, 12 May 2001.
Asprey, R.B., 'The challenge of guerrilla tactics', *New York Times*, 13 July 1975.
Augusteijn, J., 'Review of M. Hopkinson: *War of Independence*', *American Historical Review*, vol. 108, no. 4 (2003).
Augusteijn, J., 'Political violence and democracy: an analysis of the tensions within Irish republican strategy, 1914–2002', *Irish Political Studies*, vol. 18, no. 1 (2003).
Barry, M.B., 'The Irish War of Independence as seen by the international press', *Irish*

Times, 3 January 2019.

Béaslaí, P., 'A comrade's tribute: the message of a hero's death', *An Saorstat*, 29 August 1922.

Béaslaí, P., 'How it was done: IRA intelligence', in *Dublin's Fighting Story 1916–21* (Tralee, 1949).

Béaslaí, P., 'The National Army is founded', *Irish Independent*, 5 January 1953.

Bell, J.B., 'The Thompson submachine gun in Ireland', *Irish Sword*, vol. 8, no. 31 (1967).

Bell, J.B., 'The shadow of the gunman', *Sword of Light: The Irish American Review*, vol. 1, no. 1 (1974).

Bell, J.B., 'Revolts against the Crown: the British response to imperial insurgency', *Parameters* (Journal of the Army War College), vol. 9, no. 1 (1974).

Bew, P., 'Collins and Adams, LG and Blair', *The Spectator*, 31 May 1997.

Bew, P., 'Moderate nationalism and the Irish Revolution 1916–1923', *Historical Journal*, vol. 42, no. 3 (1999).

Bielenberg, A., 'Protestant emigration from the south of Ireland, 1911–1926', lecture delivered at a conference on 'Understanding our history: Protestants, the War of Independence, and the Civil War in Cork', University College Cork, 13 December 2008.

Binder, G., 'On critical legal studies as guerrilla warfare', *Georgetown Law Journal*, vol. 76, no. 1 (1987).

Borgonovo, J., 'Revolutionary violence and Irish historiography', *Irish Historical Studies*, vol. 38, no. 150 (1996).

Bowden, T., 'Bloody Sunday, a reappraisal', *European Studies Review*, vol. 2, no. 1 (1972).

Bowden, T., 'The Irish underground and the War of Independence 1919–1921', *Journal of Contemporary History*, vol. 8, no. 2 (1973).

Bowden, T., 'Ireland: the impact of terror', in M. Elliott-Batemen, J. Ellis, and T. Bowden (eds), *Revolt to Revolution: Studies in the 19th and 20th Century European Experience* (Manchester, 1974).

Bowden, T., 'The IRA and the changing tactics of terrorism', *Political Quarterly*, vol. 47 (1976).

Bowman, J., 'De Valera on Ulster, 1919–1920: what he told America', *Irish Studies in International Affairs*, vol. 1 (1979).

Bowman, J., 'Sinn Féin's perspective of the Ulster Question: autumn, 1921', *Crane Bag*, vol. 4, no. 2 (1980).

Boyce, D.G., 'How to solve the Irish Question: Lloyd George and Ireland, 1916–21', in A.J.P. Taylor (ed.), *Lloyd George: Twelve Essays* (London, 1971).

Broom, J.T., 'The Anglo-Irish War of 1919–1921, "Britain's troubles—Ireland's opportunities"' (final draft), published in *That Fatal Knot: Compound Warfare* (Fort Leavenworth, Kansas: US Army Command and General Staff College Press, 2002).

Buckley, D., 'War of Independence: diary of Mayo events', *Cathair na Mart: Journal of the Westport Historical Society*, vol. 19 (1999).

Carey, T. and de Burca, M., 'Bloody Sunday 1920: new evidence', *History Ireland*, vol. 11, no. 2 (2003).

Carroll, F.M., 'All standards of human conduct: the American Commission on

Conditions in Ireland, 1920–1921', *Éire-Ireland*, vol. 16 (Fall 1981).

Casey, J., 'Republican Courts in Ireland, 1919–1922', *Irish Jurist*, vol. 5 (1970).

Casey, J., 'The genesis of the Dáil Courts', *Irish Jurist*, vol. 9 (1974).

Chartres, J. [writing as 'Edward Seaton'], 'The bloody English', *Irish Press* (Philadelphia), 7 January–15 April 1922.

Chartres, J. [writing as 'Fear Faire'], 'The English peril', *The Nation*, 26 March, 2 and 9 April 1927.

Chesterton, G.K., *What are Reprisals?* (pamphlet, undated, no place of publication).

Chesterton, G.K., *The Delusion of the Double Plan* (pamphlet, undated, no place of publication).

Childers, R.E., 'Military rule in Ireland', *Daily News*, March–May 1920.

Coleman, M., 'Women escaped the worst of the brutalities in the War of Independence', *Irish Examiner*, 27 November 2015.

Coleman, M., 'Violence against women in the Irish War of Independence, 1919–1921', in D. Ferriter and S. Riordan (eds), *Years of Turbulence: The Irish Revolution and its Aftermath* (Dublin, 2015).

Coleman, M., 'Compensating female Irish revolutionaries, 1916–1923', *Women's Historical Review*, vol. 26 (2016).

Coleman, M., 'Military Service pensions and the recognition and reintegration of guerrilla fighters after the Irish revolution', *Institute of Historical Research*, vol. 91, no. 253 (2018).

Coleman, S., 'The day we decided to sit down and fight', *Sunday Tribune*, 12 August 2007.

Collins, L., 'Michael Collins had a stalker', *Irish Independent*, 9 October 2005.

Comerford, M., 'Women in struggle', in P. McGlynn (ed.), *Éire Amach na Casca* (pamphlet, 1986).

Connolly, L., 'Sexual violence a dark secret in the Irish War of Independence and Civil War', *Irish Times*, 10 January 2018.

Conway, An t-Athair C., 'The Third Tipperary Brigade (1921–1923)', *Tipperary Historical Journal* (1990), 9–26; (1991), 35–49; (1992), 23–30.

Coogan, T.P., 'Collins' place in history stands the test of time', *Irish Independent*, 22 August 2002.

Corkery, D., 'Terence MacSwiney', *Studies: The Irish Jesuit Quarterly Review* (December 1920).

Costello, F.J., 'The Anglo-Irish War, 1919–1921: a reappraisal', unpublished Ph.D thesis, Boston College (1992).

Costello, F., 'King George V's speech at Belfast, 1921: prelude to the Anglo-Irish Truce', *Éire-Ireland*, vol. 22, no. 3 (1987).

Costello, F., 'The role of propaganda in the Anglo-Irish War, 1919–1921', *Canadian Journal of Irish Studies*, vol. 14, no. 2 (1989).

Costello, F., 'The Republican Courts and the decline of British rule in Ireland', *Éire-Ireland*, vol. 25, no. 3 (1990).

Costigan, G., 'The Anglo-Irish conflict, 1919–1921: a war of independence or systematized murder?', *University Review*, vol. 5, no. 1 (1968).

Counahan, G., 'The people backed the movement, 1920', *Capuchin Annual* (1970).

Coyle, E., 'The history of Cumann na mBan', *An Phoblacht*, 8 April 1933.

Cremin, M.R., 'Fighting on their own terms: the tactics of the Irish Republican

Army, 1919–1921', *Small Wars and Insurgencies*, vol. 26, no. 6 (2015).

Cronin, S., 'Connolly's great leap in the dark', *Capuchin Annual* (1977).

Cronin, S. *et al.*, 'Activities of the Ballingeary IRA 1920–1921', *Ballingeary Historical Society Journal* (1998).

Crowe, T., 'Life with a flying column, 1919–1921', *Tipperary Historical Journal*, vol. 17 (2004).

Cuenca-Sanchez, I., 'The dynamics of nationalist terrorism: ETA and the IRA', *Terrorism and Political Violence*, vol. 19 (2007).

Curran, J., 'Ireland since 1916', *Éire-Ireland*, vol. 1, no. 3 (1966).

Curran, J., 'Lloyd George and the Irish settlement, 1921–1922', *Éire-Ireland*, vol. 7 (1972).

Curran, J., 'The decline and fall of the IRB', *Éire-Ireland*, vol. 10, no. 1 (1975).

Curtis, L., 'Ireland', *Round Table*, vol. 20 (June 1921).

Curtis, L., 'The Irish boundary question', *Round Table*, vol. 57 (December 1924).

Curtis, L., *Ireland* (with introduction, 'The Anglo Irish Treaty and the lost world of Imperial Ireland', by P. Walsh) (pamphlet, Belfast, 1991).

Danzer, M., 'The political consequences of terrorism: a ccomparative study of France and the United Kingdom', Unpublished Master's dissertation, University of Bucharest (2019).

Davis, E., 'The guerrilla mind', in D. Fitzpatrick (ed.), *Revolution? Ireland 1917–1923* (Dublin, 1990).

Davis, R., 'Arthur Griffith', *Dublin Historical Society* (1976).

Davis, R., 'The advocacy of passive resistance in Ireland, 1916–1922', *Anglo-Irish Studies*, vol. 3 (1977).

Davis, R., 'The IRB: a natural outcome of Young Irelandism?', *History Ireland*, vol. 16, no. 6 (2008).

Dennis, P. and Grey, J. (eds), 'An art in itself: the theory and conduct of small wars and insurgencies', Australian Army Military Conference (2006).

Deasy, L., 'The Beara Peninsula campaign in the War of Independence', *Éire-Ireland*, vol. 1, no. 2 (1966).

Deasy, L., 'The Schull Peninsula in the War of Independence', *Éire-Ireland*, vol. 1, no. 2 (1966).

Deasy, L., 'The gallant Volunteers of Kilbrittain', *Bandon Historical Journal*, vol. 22 (2006).

Denning, Major B.C., MC, 'Modern problems of guerilla warfare', *Army Quarterly* (January 1927).

Dillon, G., 'The Irish Republican Brotherhood', *University Review*, vol. 2, no. 9 (1960).

Dolan, A., 'Killing and Bloody Sunday, November 1920', *Historical Journal*, vol. 49, no. 3 (2006).

Dolan, A., 'The shadow of a great fear: terror and revolutionary Ireland', in D. Fitzpatrick (ed.), *Terror in Ireland* (Dublin, 2012).

Donnelly, J.S.. Jnr '"Unofficial" British reprisals and IRA provocation, 1919–1920: the cases of three Cork towns', *Eire-Ireland*, vol. 45 (2010).

Dorney, J., 'How the Civil War "murder gang" tried to take over as judge, jury and executioners', *Irish Independent*, 20 August 2017.

Dorney, J., 'Women, the right to vote and the struggle for Irish independence', *Irish Story*, 9 February 2018.

Dowling, M., '"The Ireland that I would have": de Valera and the creation of the Irish national image', *History Ireland*, vol. 5, no. 2 (1997).

Doyle, E.J., 'The employment of terror in the forgotten insurgency: Ireland 1919–1922', unpublished MS dissertation, US Defense Intelligence College, Bethesda, MD (1969).

Draper, G.I.A.D., 'The status of combatants and the question of guerrilla warfare', *British Year Book of International Law*, vol. 173 (1971).

Duggan, G.C. [writing as 'Periscope'], 'The last days of Dublin Castle', *Blackwood's Magazine*, vol. 212 (August 1922).

Dwyer, T.R., 'The key to ending partition that Michael Collins couldn't turn', *Sunday Independent*, 22 August 1982.

Dwyer, T.R., 'Sectarian violence spreads across the North', *Irish Examiner*, 2 July 2012.

Dwyer, T.R., 'When the horror of war hits homes', *Irish Examiner*, 25 March 2013.

Dwyer, T.R., 'The biographer who unwittingly made Michael Collins gay', *Irish Examiner*, 25 June 2015.

Dwyer, T.R., 'The 1918 election that marked a turning point in history', *Irish Examiner*, 5 December 2018.

Dwyer, T.R., 'A momentous day as Dáil meets and first shots of War of Independence occur', *Irish Examiner*, 20 January 2019.

Evans, G., 'The raising of the First Dáil Éireann Loan and the British responses to it, 1919–1921', unpublished Ph.D thesis, Department of History, National University of Ireland, Maynooth (2012).

Fall, B., 'The theory and practice of counterinsurgency', *Naval War College Review* (April 1965).

Fallon, L., 'Forgotten allies: the Dublin Fire Brigade, 1919–1921', *An Cosantóir* (March 2019).

Fanning, R., 'Leadership and transition from the politics of revolution to the politics of party: the example of Ireland, 1914–1939', paper delivered to the International Congress of Historical Societies, San Francisco, 27 August 1975.

Fanning, R., 'Michael Collins, revolutionary democrat', *Sunday Independent*, 14 October 1990.

Fanning, R., 'Michael Collins—an overview', in G. Doherty and D. Keogh (eds), *Michael Collins and the Making of the Irish State* (Cork, 1998).

Fierro, M.R., 'British counterinsurgency operations in Ireland 1916–1921: a case study', unpublished MA dissertation, US Naval War College, Newport, RI (1997).

Fishel, J.T. and Manwaring, M.G., 'The SWORD model of counterinsurgency: a summary and update', *Small Wars Journal* (2008).

FitzGerald, D., 'Mr Packenham on the Anglo-Irish Treaty', *Studies: The Irish Jesuit Quarterly Review*, vol. 24 (1935).

Fitzgerald, T.E., 'The execution of "spies and informers" in West Cork, 1921', in D. Fitzpatrick (ed.), *Terror in Ireland* (Dublin, 2012).

Fitzpatrick, D., 'Irish people and policies', unpublished Ph.D thesis, University of Cambridge (1974).

Fitzpatrick, D., 'The geography of Irish nationalism: 1910–1922', *Past and Present*, no. 78 (1978).

Fitzpatrick, D., 'Ireland since 1870', in R.F. Foster (ed.), *The Oxford Illustrated History of*

Ireland (Oxford, 1989).

Fitzpatrick, D., 'Militarism in Ireland, 1900–1922', in T. Bartlett and K. Jeffery (eds), *A military history of Ireland* (Cambridge, 1997).

Fitzpatrick, D., '"Decidedly a personality": de Valera's performance as a convict, 1916–1917', *History Ireland*, vol. 10, no. 2 (March/April 2002).

Fitzpatrick, D., 'The price of Balbriggan', in D. Fitzpatrick (ed.), *Terror in   Ireland* (Dublin, 2012).

Fitzsimons, F., 'The Irish National Aid and Volunteers' Dependants' Fund', *History Ireland*, vol. 24, no. 3 (2016).

Flynn, C., 'My part in Irish independence: the statement of Cornelius Flynn' (ed. Philip McCarthy), *Bandon Historical Journal*, vol. 4 (1988).

Flynn, K.H., 'Soloheadbeg: what really happened', *History Ireland*, vol. 5, no. 2 (1997).

Foot, M.R.D., 'Michael Collins and irregular warfare', lecture to the Irish Military History Society (1969).

Foot, M.R.D., 'The IRA and the origins of the SOE', in M.R.D. Foot (ed.), *War and Society: Historical Essays in Honour and Memory of J.R. Western 1928–1971* (New York, 1973).

Foot, M.R.D., 'The Irish experience', M. Elliott-Batemen, J. Ellis, and   T. Bowden (eds), *Revolt to Revolution: Studies in the 19th and 20th Century European Experience* (Manchester, 1974).

Foster, R., 'We are all revisionists now', *Irish Review*, vol. 1 (1986).

Fox, R.M., 'Ireland, retrospect and prospect', *The Nineteenth Century*, vol. 102 (August 1927).

Freeman, P.A., 'The career of Michael Collins with special reference to the Treaty of 1921', unpublished Ph.D thesis, Bristol University (1963).

Gallagher, F., 'Literature of the conflict', *Irish Book Lover*, vol. 18 (May–June 1930).

Gardiner, A.G., 'Stop the terror', *Daily News*, 6 November 1920.

Gonne, M., 'The real case against partition', *Capuchin Annual* (1943).

Good, J.W., 'Partition in practice', *Studies*, vol. 11 (1922).

Gough, General H., 'The situation in Ireland', *Review of Reviews*, vol. 63 (1921).

Gray, C.S., 'The Anglo-Irish War 1919–1921: lessons from an irregular conflict', *Comparative Strategy*, vol. 26, no. 5 (2008).

Gregory, A., 'The boys of Kilmichael', *Journal of Contemporary History*, vol. 34, no. 3 (1999).

Griffith, A., *The Resurrection of Hungary: A Parallel for Ireland* (pamphlet, 1904).

Gubbins, Sir C., 'SOE and the coordination of regular and irregular warfare', lecture and discussion in M. Elliott-Bateman (ed.), *The Fourth Dimension of Warfare*, vol. 1 (Manchester, 1974).

Gunther, J., 'Inside de Valera', *Harper's Magazine* (August, 1936).

Gwynn, S., 'Ireland's Constitution', *The Nation*, 26 July 1922.

Gwynn, S., 'Dáil Éireann and the Irish Constitution', *Fortnightly Review*, vol. 113 (December 1922).

Hallinan, C.T., 'Ireland's role in the British Empire', *New Republic*, vol. 29 (9 February 1922).

Hammes, Col. T.X., 'The way to win a guerrilla war', *Washington Post*, 26 November 2006.

Hammond, J.L., 'A tragedy of errors', *The Nation*, 8 January 1921.

Hammond, J.L., 'The terror in action', *The Nation*, 30 April 1921.

Hanley, B., 'Terror in twentieth-century Ireland', in D. Fitzpatrick (ed.), *Terror in Ireland* (Dublin, 2012).

Hannon, K., 'Winifred Barrington', *Old Limerick Journal*, vol. 24 (Winter 1998).

Hare, Major-General Sir S., KCMG, CB, 'Martial law from the soldier's point of view', *Army Quarterly*, vol. 7 (October 1923 and January 1924).

Hart, P., 'Michael Collins and the assassination of Sir Henry Wilson', *Irish Historical Studies*, vol. 28, no. 110 (1992).

Hart, P., 'The geography of revolution in Ireland, 1917–1923', *Past and Present*, no. 155 (May 1997).

Hart, P., 'Operations abroad: the IRA in Britain, 1919–1923', *English Historical Review*, vol. 115, no. 460 (2000).

Hart, P., 'Peter Hart and his enemies', *History Ireland*, vol. 13, no. 4 (2005).

Hartline, M.C. and Kaulbach, M.M., 'Michael Collins and Bloody Sunday: the intelligence war between the British and Irish intelligence services', *CIA Historical Review Program* (2 July 1996; approved for release 1994).

Harvey, A.D., 'Who were the Auxiliaries?', *Historical Journal*, vol. 35, no. 3 (1992).

Hawkins, F.M.A., 'Defense and the role of Erskine Childers in the Treaty negotiations of 1921', *Irish Historical Studies*, vol. 11 (1970).

Hawkins, R., 'Dublin Castle and the RIC (1916–1922)', in T.D. Williams (ed.), *The Irish Struggle 1916–1926* (London, 1966).

Henderson, F., 'Irish leaders of our time: Richard McKee', *An Cosantóir*, vol. 5 (1945).

Hobson, B., 'The origin of Óglaigh na hÉireann', *An t-Óglách* (June 1931).

Hoffman, F.G., 'Neo-classical counterinsurgency', *Parameters* (Summer 2007).

Hopkinson, M., 'President Woodrow Wilson and the Irish Question', *Studia Hibernica*, no. 27 (1993).

Hopkinson, M., 'Review article: Biography of the revolutionary period: Michael Collins and Kevin Barry', *Irish Historical Studies*, vol. 28, no. 111 (1993).

Hughes, B., 'Persecuting the Peelers', in D. Fitzpatrick (ed.), *Terror in Ireland* (Dublin, 2012).

Huntington, S.P., 'Introduction', in F.M. Osanka (ed.), *Modern Guerrilla Warfare* (New York, 1962).

Issacharoff, S. and Pildes, R.H., 'Targeted warfare: individuating enemy responsibility', *New York University Law Review*, vol. 1521 (2013).

Jeffery, K., 'The British Army and internal security 1919–1939', *Historical Journal*, vol. 24, no. 2 (1981).

Jeffery, K., 'British military intelligence following World War I', in K.G. Robertson (ed.), *British and American Approaches to Intelligence* (London, 1987).

Jeffery, K., 'Intelligence and counter-insurgency operations: some reflections on the British experience', *Intelligence and National Security*, vol. 2, no. 1 (1987).

Jeffery, K., 'Colonial warfare: 1900–1939', in C. McInnes and Y.D. Sheffield (eds), *Warfare in the Twentieth Century: Theory and Practice* (London, 1988).

Jeffery, K., 'Ireland and war in the 20th century', Parnell Lecture, Magdalene College, Cambridge, 10 November 2003.

Jeffery, K., 'Some problems and lessons of the Anglo-Irish War in the twentieth century', in P. Dennis and J. Grey (eds), *An Art in Itself: The Theory and Conduct of Small Wars and Insurgencies* (London, 2006).

Jung, P., 'The Thompson machine gun during and after the Anglo-Irish War: the new evidence', *Irish Sword*, vol. 21, no. 84 (1998).

Kavanagh, S., 'The Irish Volunteers' intelligence organisation', *Capuchin Annual* (1969).

Keane, V., 'Republican and RIC casualties, 1919–1924, the Mayo connection', *Cathair na Mart: Journal of the Westport Historical Society*, vol. 21 (2001).

Kearney, R., 'The IRA's strategy of failure', *Crane Bag* (1980).

Kelly, J., 'We were framed', *Hibernia*, 31 July 1980.

Kelly, M., 'Nationalism's pilot light?', *History Ireland*, vol. 16, no. 6 (2008).

Kenneally, I., 'Press played pivotal role in the War of Independence', *Irish Times*, 15 November 2014.

Kenny, M., 'Michael Collins's religious faith', *Studies*, vol. 96, no. 384 (2007).

Kilcullen, D., 'Counterinsurgency *redux*', opinion paper by the Chief Strategist in the Office of the Coordinator for Counterterrorism, US State Department, Washington, DC (undated).

Kinane, P., 'My part in the War of Independence, part I', *Tipperary Historical Journal*, vol. 8 (1995).

Kinane, P., 'My part in the War of Independence, part II', *Tipperary Historical Journal*, vol. 9 (1996).

King, C.R., 'Revolutionary war, guerrilla warfare, and international law', *Case Reserve Journal of International Law*, vol. 91 (1972).

Kirby, D., 'The IRA and Manchester: how terror unit waged war on the city', *Manchester Evening News*, 20 January 2013.

Kissane, C., 'An eye for an eye: the IRA's campaign in 1920's Britain', *Irish Times*, 17 December 2017.

Kline, B., 'Churchill and Collins 1919–1922: admirers or adversaries?', *History Ireland*, vol. 1, no. 3 (1993).

Kostal, D., 'British Intelligence in Ireland 1919–1921: integration of law enforcement and military intelligence to support force protection', unpublished MS dissertation, US Joint Military Intelligence College, Bethesda, MD (2004).

Kotsonouris, M., 'The Dáil Courts in Limerick', *Old Limerick Journal* (Winter 1992).

Kotsonouris, M., 'Revolutionary justice: the Dáil Éireann Courts', *History Ireland*, vol. 2, no. 3 (1994).

Kotsonouris, M., 'The George Gavan Duffy Papers', *History Ireland*, vol. 8, no. 4 (2000).

Laffan, M., 'The Sinn Féin Party', *Capuchin Annual* (1970).

Laffan, M., 'The unification of Sinn Féin in 1917', *Irish Historical Studies*, vol. 17 (1971).

Laffan, M., 'Labour must wait: Ireland's conservative revolution', in P. Cornish (ed.), *Radicals, Rebels, and Establishments* (Belfast, 1985).

Larkin, F.M., 'A great daily organ: *The Freeman's Journal*, 1763–1924', *History Ireland*, vol. 14, no. 3 (2006).

Larkin, F.M., 'The Irish revolution's impact has been greatly exaggerated', *Irish Times*, 23 April 2018.

Lavery, B., 'Irish rebury 10 republicans hanged by British in 1920's', *New York Times*, 15 October 2001.

Lawlor, D., 'Why the Black and Tan stain has never washed out of the Irish psyche', *Irish Independent*, 9 May 2002.

Lawlor, D., 'The Black and Tans—nine things to know', *An Phoblacht*, 19 November 2016.

Lawlor, S.M., 'Ireland from Truce to Treaty, war or peace? July to October 1921', *Irish Historical Studies*, vol. 22 (1980).

Lawrence, T.E., 'The evolution of a revolt', *Army Quarterly and Defence Journal* (October 1920).

Lawson, Lieutenant General Sir H., *A Report on the Irish Situation* (pamphlet, London, 1921).

Lawson, Lieutenant General Sir H., *A Second Report on the Situation* (pamphlet, undated).

Lee, J., 'The challenge of a Collins biography', in G. Doherty and D. Keogh (eds), *Michael Collins and the Making of the Irish State* (Cork, 1998).

Lee, J.J., 'De Valera's use of words: three case-studies', *Radharc*, vol. 2 (2001).

Leeson, D., 'Death in the afternoon: the Croke Park massacre, 21 November 1920', *Canadian Journal of History*, vol. 38, no. 1 (2003).

Leeson, D., 'Imperial stormtroopers: British paramilitaries in the Irish War of Independence, 1920–1921', unpublished Ph.D thesis, McMaster University (2003).

Leeson, D., 'The "scum of London's underworld"? British recruits for the Royal Irish Constabulary, 1920–1921', *Contemporary British History*, vol. 17, no. 1 (2003).

Leiser, B.M., 'Terrorism, guerrilla warfare, and international morality', *Stanford Journal of International Studies*, vol. 39 (1977).

Leonard, J., '"English dogs" or "poor devils"? The dead of Bloody Sunday morning', in D. Fitzpatrick (ed.), *Terror in Ireland* (Dublin, 2012).

Leonard, P.B., 'The necessity of de-Anglicising the Irish nation: boycotting and the Irish War of Independence', unpublished Ph.D thesis, University of Melbourne (2000).

Levie, H.S., 'Review of *An International Law of Guerrilla Warfare: The Global Politics of Law-making*, by Keith Suter', *Maryland Journal of International Law*, vol. 9, no. 2 (1985).

Lloyd, J., 'Ireland's uncertain peace', *Foreign Affairs*, vol. 1027, no. 5 (1998).

Lowe, T.A., 'Some reflections of a junior commander upon the campaign in Ireland 1920 and 1921', *Army Quarterly* (1922).

Lowe, W.J., 'The war against the RIC, 1919–1921', *Éire-Ireland*, vol. 37, nos 3–4 (2002).

Lowe, W.J., 'Who were the Black and Tans?', *History Ireland*, vol. 12, no. 3 (2004).

Lynch, P., 'The social revolution that never was', in T.D. Williams (ed.), *The Irish Struggle 1916–1926* (Toronto, 1966).

MacAodh, S., 'IRA wipe out "G" Division', *An Phoblacht*, 6 September 2001.

MacAodh, S., 'Terence MacSwiney', *An Phoblacht*, 25 October 2001.

MacAodh, S., 'Murder in the Castle', *An Phoblacht*, 22 November 2001.

McCann, J., 'Burning of the Custom House', *The Kerryman*, 17 March 1938.

McCartan, P. (ed.), 'Extracts from the papers of Dr Patrick McCartan', *Clogher Record* (1964 and 1965).

McColgan, J., 'Partition and the Irish administration, 1920–1922', *Administration*, vol. 28 (1980).

McColgan, J., 'Implementing the 1921 Treaty, Lionel Curtis and the constitutional procedure', *Irish Historical Studies*, vol. 20, no. 79 (1997).

McConnell, J. and McGarry, F., 'Difficulties and opportunities: making sense of the Fenians', *History Ireland*, vol. 16, no. 6 (2008).

MacDonnacha, M., 'Partitionist states established', *An Phoblacht*, 5 December 2002.

McFate, M., Ph.D, JD, and Jackson, A.V., 'The object beyond war: counterinsurgency and the four tools of political competition', *Military Review* (January/February 2006).

McGarry, F., 'Keeping an eye on the usual suspects: Dublin Castle's "Personality Files", 1899–1921', *History Ireland*, vol. 14, no. 6 (2006).

McGarry, P., 'Flashpoints imminent in Ireland's Decade of Centenaries', *Irish Times*, 2 November 2018.

McGreevey, R., 'What really happened at Soloheadbeg?', *Irish Times*, 17 January 2019.

McGreevey, R. and Collins, S., 'Gunman believed to have killed Michael Collins was granted a military pension', *Irish Times*, 3 October 2014.

McGuigan, J., 'Michael Collins on file?', *History Ireland*, vol. 19, no. 4 (2011).

Machnik-Kékesi, G., 'Gendering bodies: violence as performance in Ireland's War of Independence (1919–1921)', unpublished MA thesis, Concordia University Montreal, Quebec 2017.

McInerney, M., 'James Ryan', *Irish Times*, 15–17 March 1967.

McInerney, M., 'Gerald Boland's story', *Irish Times*, 8–19 October 1968.

McInerney, M., 'Seán MacEntee', *Irish Times*, 22–25 July 1974.

Mack, A., 'Why big nations lose small wars: the politics of asymmetric conflict', *World Politics* (January 1975).

McKeane, I., 'Michael Collins and the media: then and now', *History Ireland*, vol. 3, no. 3 (1995).

McKenna, K., 'The Irish Bulletin', *Capuchin Annual* (1970).

McKillen, B., 'Irish feminism and national separatism', *Éire-Ireland*, vol. 17 (1982).

McLaughlin, T., 'The aftermath', *An Cosantóir* (April/May 2006).

McMahon, D., 'Michael Collins—his biographers Piaras Béaslaí and Rex Taylor', in G. Doherty and D. Keogh (eds), *Michael Collins and the Making of the Irish State* (Cork, 1998).

McMahon, Msgr J.T., *The Cream of their Race: Irish Truce Negotiations, December 1920– January 1921* (pamphlet, Ennis, 1970).

McVeigh, J., 'Constance Markievicz: aiming for the stars', *An Phoblacht*, 17 September 1998.

Maguire, C.A., 'The Republican Courts', *Capuchin Annual* (1984).

Mahon, Sir B., 'The Irish welter as I found it: an indictment of British methods', in W.G. Fitzgerald (ed.), *The Voice of Ireland* (Dublin, 1924).

Malouf, M., 'With Dev in America: Sinn Féin and recognition politics, 1919–21', *Interventions: International Journal of Postcolonial Studies*, vol. 4, no. 1 (2002).

Mangran, H.C., 'John Chartres', *Irish Independent*, 25 October 1935.

Mansergh, M., 'The freedom to achieve freedom: the political ideas of Collins and de Valera', in G. Doherty and D. Keogh (eds), *Michael Collins and the Making of the Irish State* (Cork, 1998).

Mansergh, M., 'Physical force or passive resistance? Soloheadbeg—vindicating a democratic mandate for independence', *History Ireland*, vol. 27, no. 2 (2019).

Markievicz, Countess C., 'Cumann na mBan', *Cumann na mBan*, vol. 11, no. 10 (1926).

Marnane, D.G., 'The War of Independence in Tipperary town and district, part one: chronology', *Tipperary Historical Journal*, vol. 21 (2008).

Maume, P., 'From deference to citizenship: Irish republicanism, 1870–1923', *The Republic*, no. 2 (2001).

Mawe, T., 'A comparative survey of the historical debates surrounding Ireland, World War I and the Irish Civil War', *History Studies*, vol. 13 (2012).

Merari, A., 'Terrorism as a strategy of insurgency', *Terrorism and Political Violence*, vol. 5, no. 4 (1993).

Merrigan, P. (ed. M. Bourke), 'Life with the South Tipperary Volunteers 1914–1921', *Tipperary Historical Journal*, vol. 18 (2005).

Mills, M., 'Seán Lemass looks back', *Irish Press*, 20 January–6 February 1969.

Mockaitis, T.R., 'The origins of British counterinsurgency', *Small Wars and Insurgencies*, vol. 1, no. 3 (1990).

Mockaitis, T.R., 'Resolving insurgencies', *Strategic Studies Institute* (June 2011).

Morgan, E., 'Ireland's lost action hero: Michael Collins, a secret history of Irish masculinity', *New Hibernia Review*, vol. 2, no. 1 (1998).

Mulcahy, General R., 'Conscription and the General Headquarters staff', *Capuchin Annual* (1968).

Mulcahy, General R., 'Chief of Staff, 1919', *Capuchin Annual* (1970).

Mulcahy, Dr R., MD, 'The development of the Irish Volunteers, 1916–1922', *An Cosantóir*, vol. 40 (Part 1: February, Part 2: March, Part 3: April 1980). [A paper read to the Irish Historical Society, 9 November 1978.]

Mulcahy, R., 'Michael Collins and the making of a new Ireland', *Studies* (Autumn 1976). [A paper read to the Irish Historical Society, 10 February 1976.]

Mulcahy, R., 'The Mulcahy tapes and papers', *History Ireland*, vol. 8, no. 1 (2003).

Mulcahy, R., 'Mulcahy and Collins—a conjunction of opposites', *History Ireland*, vol. 13, no. 2 (2008).

Murdoch, R., 'Robert Barton', *Sunday Press*, 26 September and 3 October 1971.

Murphy, B., 'The First Dáil Éireann', *History Ireland*, vol. 2, no. 1 (1994).

Murphy, Major H.L., 'Countess Markievicz', *An Cosantóir* (June 1946).

Murphy, J.F. Jr, 'Michael Collins and the craft of intelligence', *International Journal of Intelligence and Counterintelligence*, vol. 27, issue 2 (17 August 2010).

Murphy, M., 'Revolution and terror in Kildare, 1919–1923', in D. Fitzpatrick (ed.), *Terror in Ireland* (Dublin, 2012).

Murphy, Fr S., 'War of Independence seen as Catholic war on Protestants', *Irish Times*, 15 January 2019.

Murray, N., 'The rarely spoken about violence against women during the Irish revolution', *Irish Examiner*, 12 September 2017.

Nevinson, H., 'The Anglo-Irish War', *Contemporary Review*, no. 667 (July 1921).

Newsinger, J., 'I bring not peace but a sword: the religious motif in the Irish War of Independence', *Journal of Modern History*, vol. 13, no. 3 (1978).

Ni Chumnaill, E., 'The history of Cumann na mBan', *An Phoblacht*, 8 April 1933.

Noonan, G., 'Republican terrorism in Britain, 1920–1921', in D. Fitzpatrick (ed.), *Terror in Ireland* (Dublin, 2012).

Novak, R., 'Keepers of important secrets: the Ladies Committee of the IRB', *History Ireland*, vol. 16, no. 6 (2008).

Nunan, S., 'President de Valera's mission to the USA, 1919–20', *Capuchin Annual*

(1970).

O'Beirne-Ranelagh, J., 'The IRB from Treaty to 1924', *Irish Historical Studies*, vol. 20, no. 77 (1976).

O'Brien, G., 'The record of the first Dáil debates', *Irish Historical Studies*, vol. 28, no. 111 (1993).

O'Brien, P., 'Masters of chaos: British special forces during the Irish War of Independence', *An Cosantóir* (March 2019).

Ó Ceallaigh, S.T., 'Memoirs', *Irish Press*, 3 July–9 August 1961.

O'Doherty, L., 'Dublin Brigade area of 1920', *Capuchin Annual* (1970).

O'Donnell, J., 'Recollections based on the diary of an Irish Volunteer', *Cathair na Mart: Journal of the Westport Historical Society*, vol. 10, no. 1 (1990); vol. 11 (1991).

O'Donoghue, F., 'Irish leaders of our time: 2—Tomás MacCurtain', *An Cosantóir*, vol. 5, no. 2 (1945).

O'Donoghue, F., 'Irish leaders of our time: 12—Liam Lynch as OC 1st Southern Division', *An Cosantóir*, vol. 6, no. 1 (1946).

O'Donoghue, F., 'Guerilla warfare in Ireland', *An Cosantóir*, vol. 23 (1963). [A paper read to the Dublin Historical Society, 7 February 1963.]

O'Donoghue, F., 'The reorganisation of the Volunteers', *Capuchin Annual*, vol. 34 (1967).

O'Donoghue, F., 'Volunteer "actions" in 1918', *Capuchin Annual*, vol. 35 (1968).

O'Donoghue, F., 'The sacking of Cork City by the British', in G. Doherty and D. Keogh (eds), *Michael Collins and the Making of the Irish State* (Cork, 1998).

Ó Giollain, D., 'Heroic biographies in folklore and popular culture', in G. Doherty and D. Keogh (eds), *Michael Collins and the Making of the Irish State* (Cork, 1998).

O'Halpin, E., 'Sir Warren Fisher and the Coalition, 1919–1922', *Historical Journal*, vol. 24, no. 4 (1981).

O'Halpin, E., 'British intelligence in Ireland', in C. Andrew and D. Dilks (eds), *The Missing Dimension: Governments and Intelligence Communities in the Twentieth Century* (Urbana, IL, 1984).

O'Halpin, E., 'Collins and intelligence 1919–1923', in G. Doherty and D. Keogh (eds), *Michael Collins and the Making of the Irish State* (Cork, 1998).

O'Halpin, E., 'Counting terror: Bloody Sunday and the dead of the Irish Revolution', in D. Fitzpatrick (ed.), *Terror in Ireland 1916–1923* (Dublin, 2012).

O'Hannigan, D., 'The origin of the IRA flying column', *An Cosantóir*, vol. 6, no. 12 (1946).

O'Leary, N., 'An account from the Bureau of Military History: Ned O'Leary's account of the War of Independence in North Tipperary', *Tipperary Historical Journal*, vol. 23 (2010).

O'Luing, S., 'The "German Plot" 1918', *Capuchin Annual* (1969).

O'Mahony, R., 'The sack of Balbriggan and tit-for-tat killing', in D. Fitzpatrick (ed.), *Terror in Ireland* (Dublin, 2012).

O'Mahony, S., *Three Murders in Dublin Castle* (pamphlet, Dublin, 2000).

O'Malley, E., 'IRA raids', *Sunday Press*, 23 and 30 October, 6 and 13 November 1955.

O'Malley, C.K.H., 'Ernie O'Malley autobiographical letter', *Cathair na Mart: Journal of the Westport Historical Society*, vol. 9, no. 1 (1989).

O'Neill, D.J., 'The cult of self-sacrifice: the Irish experience', *Éire-Ireland*, vol. 24, no. 2 (1972).

Ó nEochaidh, É., *Liam Mellows* (booklet, undated, place of publication unknown).

Ó Riain, S., 'Dáil Éireann, 1919', *Capuchin Annual* (1969).

O'Riordan, M., 'The spy who grew up with the bold', *Irish Political Review*, vol. 25, no. 4 (April 2010).

O'Rourke, P., 'Remembering the past: FitzGerald, Murphy and MacSwiney', *An Phoblacht*, 2 November 1999.

Ó Ruairc, L., 'Did the Black and Tans run from the rifles of the IRA?', *History Ireland*, vol. 12, no. 2 (2004).

Ó Ruairc, P. Óg, 'Terror in Ireland', *History Ireland*, vol. 20, no. 3 (2012).

Ó Ruairc, P. Óg, 'Spies and informers beware', *An Cosantóir* (March 2019).

O'Sheil, K., 'Memories of my lifetime', *Irish Times*, 7–23 November 1966.

O'Shiel, K. (ed. F. Campbell), 'The last land war? Kevin O'Shiel's memoir of the Irish Revolution (1916–21)', *Archivium Hibernicum*, vol. 57 (2003).

Ó Snodaigh, A., 'General amnesty—1917', *An Phoblacht*, 13 June 1997.

Ó Snodaigh, A., 'Sir Henry Wilson executed', *An Phoblacht*, 19 June 1997.

Ó Snodaigh, A., 'Electoral success—the first step', *An Phoblacht*, 17 June 1999.

Ó Snodaigh, A., 'The Mansion House "Irish Assembly"', *An Phoblacht*, 8 July 1999.

Ó Snodaigh, A., 'Sinn Féin and Sinn Féin', *An Phoblacht*, 30 September 1999.

Ó Snodaigh, A., 'Usk jail death, 1918', *An Phoblacht*, 2 December 1999.

Ó Snodaigh, A., 'The Declaration of Independence', *An Phoblacht*, 13 January 2000.

Ó Snodaigh, A., 'Ireland's independence declared', *An Phoblacht*, 27 January 2000.

Ó Snodaigh, A., 'An Address to Free Nations', *An Phoblacht*, 3 February 2000.

Ó Snodaigh, A., 'The Democratic Programme', *An Phoblacht*, 9 March 2000.

Ó Snodaigh, A., 'The first Cabinet', *An Phoblacht*, 16 March 2000.

Ó Snodaigh, A., 'Press coverage for First Dáil', *An Phoblacht*, 30 March 2000.

Ó Snodaigh, A., 'Remembering the past: the 1917 IRA Convention', *An Phoblacht*, 27 April 2000.

Ó Snodaigh, P., 'The Thompson machine gun: a few notes', *Irish Sword*, vol. 22, no. 89 (2001).

O'Sullivan, P. and Lee, F., 'The execution of Field Marshal Sir Henry Wilson: the facts', *Sunday Press*, 10 August 1958.

O'Toole, F., 'The 1918 election was an amazing moment for Ireland', *Irish Times*, 8 December 2018.

O'Toole, F., 'The first shots of the "Tan War" in 1919', *Irish Times*, 16 January 2019.

Paret, P., *Internal War and Pacification. The Verdict.* Princeton University Research Monograph no. 12 (1961).

Perlman, J., 'Terence MacSwiney, the triumph and tragedy of the hunger strike', *New York State Historical Association*, vol. 88, no. 3 (2007).

Petter, M., '"Temporary gentlemen" in the aftermath of the Great War: rank, status and the ex-officer problem', *Historical Journal*, vol. 37, no. 1 (1994).

Phelan, S., 'Michael Collins's "killer" met him twice', *Irish Independent*, 2 October 2014).

Popplewell, R., 'Lacking intelligence: some reflections on recent approaches to British counter-insurgence 1900–1960', *Intelligence and National Security*, vol. 10, no. 2 (1995).

Power, G., 'Irish leaders of our time 8—Liam Lynch', *An Cosantóir*, vol. 5, no. 9 (1945).

Prisk, C.E., 'The umbrella of legitimacy', in M.G. Manwaring (ed.), *Uncomfortable Wars: Toward a New Paradigm of Low Intensity Conflict* (Boulder, CO, 1991).

Quinlan, A., 'The mother who turned IRA spy to save her son', *Irish Independent*, 25 November 2012.

Rains, G.J., 'Torpedoes', *Southern Historical Society Papers*, vol. 3 (May–June 1877).

Rast, M., 'Tactics, politics and propaganda in the Irish War of Independence, 1917–1921', unpublished Master's thesis, Georgia State University (2011).

Regan, J., 'Looking at Mick again—demilitarising Michael Collins', *History Ireland*, vol. 3, no. 3 (1995).

Regan, J., 'Michael Collins—the legacy and intestacy', in G. Doherty and D. Keogh (eds), *Michael Collins and the Making of the Irish State* (Cork, 1998).

Regan, J., 'Irish public histories as an historiographical problem', *Irish Historical Studies*, vol. 37, no. 146 (2010).

Reid, C., 'Stephen Gwynn and the failure of constitutional nationalism in Ireland, 1919–1921', *Historical Journal*, vol. 53, no. 3 (2010).

Reid, E.N., 'British intelligence operations during the Anglo-Irish War', unpublished Master's dissertation, Central Washington University (2016).

Richardson, M., 'Terrorism: trauma in the excess of affect', in R. Kurtz (ed.), *Cambridge Critical Concepts: Trauma and Literature* (Cambridge, 2018).

Roche, R., 'Events in Wexford—1920', *Capuchin Annual* (1970).

Roth, A., 'Gun running from Germany to Ireland in the early 1920's', *Irish Sword*, vol. 22, no. 88 (2000).

Ryan, L., '"Drunken Tans": representations of sex and violence in the Anglo-Irish War (1919–1921)', *Feminist Review*, no. 66 (Autumn 2000).

Ryan, M., 'Tom Barry and the Kilmichael ambush', *History Ireland*, vol. 13, no. 5 (2005).

Ryan, M., 'The Kilmichael ambush, 1920: exploring the "provocative chapters"', *History*, vol. 92, no. 306 (2007).

Ryan, M., 'The commander-in-chief's cap badge?', *History Ireland*, vol. 19, no. 5 (2011).

Ryan, R., 'The man who stood next to Collins's killer', *The Cork Examiner*, 5 November 1985.

Ryan, T., 'One man's flying column', *Tipperary Historical Journal*, vol. 4 (1991).

Ryan, T., 'One man's flying column, part 2', *Tipperary Historical Journal*, vol. 5 (1992).

Ryan, T., 'One man's flying column, part 3', *Tipperary Historical Journal*, vol. 6 (1993).

Seedorf, M.F., 'The Lloyd George government and the Strickland Report on the burning of Cork 1920', *Albion: A Quarterly Journal Concerned with British Studies*, vol. 4, no. 2 (1972).

Seedorf, M., 'Defending reprisals: Sir Hamar Greenwood and the "Troubles", 1920–1921', *Éire-Ireland* (Winter 1990).

Selth, A., 'Ireland and insurgency: the lessons of history', *Small Wars and Insurgencies*, vol. 2, no. 2 (1991).

Sharkey, S., 'My role as an Intelligence Officer with the Third Tipperary Brigade (1919–1921)', *Tipperary Historical Journal*, vol. 11 (1998).

Shortt, R., 'IRA activity in Westmeath during the War of Independence, 1918–1921:

part one', *Ríocht na Midhe*, vol. 16 (2005).

Shortt, R., 'IRA activity in Westmeath during the War of Independence, 1918–1921: part two', *Ríocht na Midhe*, vol. 17 (2006).

Silke, A., 'Ferocious times: the IRA, the RIC, and Britain's failure in 1919–1921', *Terrorism and Political Violence*, vol. 27, no. 3 (19 April 2016).

Simon, Sir J.A., 'Irish reprisals: Auxiliary Division's record', *London Times*, 25 April 1921.

Sitaraman, G., 'Counterinsurgence, the War on Terror and the laws of war', *Virginia Law Review* (2009).

Smith, S.C., 'General Templer and counter-insurgence in Malaya: hearts and minds, intelligence and propaganda', *Intelligence and National Security*, vol. 16, no. 3 (2001).

Snoddy, O., 'Three by-elections of 1917', *Capuchin Annual* (1967).

Stapleton, W.J. (Bill), 'Michael Collins's Squad', *Capuchin Annual* (1969).

Staunton, E., 'The Boundary Commission debacle 1925, aftermath and implications', *History Ireland*, vol. 4, no. 2 (1996).

Stewart, S., 'The difference between terrorism and insurgency', *Strategy* (26 June 2014).

Stover, J.D., 'Terror confined? Prison violence in Ireland, 1919–1921', in D. Fitzpatrick (ed.), *Terror in Ireland* (Dublin, 2012).

Stubbs, J.O., 'The Unionists and Ireland, 1914–1918', *Historical Journal*, vol. 33 (1990).

Sugg, W., 'British intelligence wiped out', *An Phoblacht*, 20 November 1997.

Sugg, W., 'Bloody Sunday', *An Phoblacht*, 27 November 1997.

Sugg, W., 'Christmas Week ambush', *An Phoblacht*, 16 December 1999.

Sweeney, G., 'Self-immolation in Ireland: hunger strikes and political confrontation', *Anthropology Today*, vol. 9, no. 5 (1993).

Sweeney, G., 'Irish hunger strikes and the cult of self-sacrifice', *Journal of Contemporary History*, vol. 28, no. 5 (1993).

Taber, R., 'The offensive and the problem of innovation in British military thought, 1870–1915', *Journal of Contemporary History*, vol. 13, no. 3 (1978).

Tery, S. (trans. M. Gaddis Rose), 'Raids and reprisals: Ireland: eye-witness (1923)', *Éire-Ireland* (Summer 1985).

Thomas, E., Nordland, R. and Caryl, C., 'Operation Hearts and Minds', *Newsweek*, 29 December 1992 and 5 January 1993.

Thornton, Commandant B.L., 'Women and the Army', *An Cosantóir* (November 1975).

Tierney, M., 'Eoin MacNeill: a biographical study', *Saint Patrick* (1964).

Townsend, C., 'The Irish railway strike of 1920—industrial action and civil resistance in the struggle for independence', *Irish Historical Studies*, vol. 21 (1978–9).

Townshend, C., 'Bloody Sunday: Michael Collins speaks', *European Studies Review*, vol. 9 (1979).

Townshend, C., 'The Irish Republican Army and the development of guerrilla warfare, 1916–1921', *English Historical Review*, vol. 94, no. 371 (1979).

Townshend, C., 'Martial law: legal and administrative problems of civil emergency in Britain and the Empire, 1800–1940', *Historical Journal*, vol. 25 (1979).

Townshend, C., 'Military force and civil authority in the United Kingdom, 1914–1921', *Journal of British Studies*, vol. 28, no. 3 (1989).

Townshend, C., 'The meaning of Irish freedom: constitutionalism in the Free State', *Transactions of the Royal Historical Society*, 6th series, vol. 8 (1998).

Townshend, C., 'In aid of civil power: Britain, Ireland, and Palestine 1916–1948', in D. Marston and C. Malkasian (eds), *Counterinsurgency in Modern Warfare* (Oxford, 2008).

Traynor, O., 'The burning of the Custom House—Dublin's fighting story', *The Kerryman* (1939).

Vickery, Lieutenant Colonel C.E., CMG, DSO, 'Small wars', *Army Quarterly*, vol. 6 (1923).

Walker, G., 'The Irish Dr Goebbels: Frank Gallagher and Irish republican propaganda', *Journal of Contemporary History*, vol. 27, no. 1 (1992).

Walsh, J.P., 'De Valera in the United States, 1919', *Records of the American Catholic Historical Society of Philadelphia*, vol. 73, nos 3/4 (1962).

Ward, A., 'Lloyd George and the 1918 Irish conscription crisis', *Historical Journal*, vol. 17 (1974).

Ward, M., 'The League of Women Delegates and Sinn Féin, 1917', *History Ireland*, vol. 4, no. 3 (1996).

Weeks, L. and O'Fathartaigh, M., *The Treaty: Debating the Irish State* (Sallins, 2019).

Whelan, B., 'Wilson was urged to support presence of Irish voice at Paris Peace Conference', *Irish Times*, 21 January 2019.

White, D., 'The Castle Document', *History Ireland*, vol. 24, no. 4 (2016).

White, R.W., 'From gunmen to politicians: the impact of terrorism and political violence on twentieth-century Ireland', *Journal of Conflict Studies*, vol. 27, no. 2 (2007).

Williams, A.F.B., 'A truce in Ireland', *Manchester Guardian*, 9 December 1921.

Williams, T.D., 'The Irish Republican Brotherhood', in T.D. Williams (ed.), *Secret Societies in Ireland* (Dublin, 1973).

Winter, Sir O., 'A report on the Intelligence Branch of the Chief of Police, Dublin Castle, from May 1920–July 1921', in P. Hart (ed.), *British Intelligence in Ireland, 1920–1921: The Final Reports* (Cork, 2002).

Yeates, P., 'Irish craft workers in a time of revolution 1919–1922', *Saothar*, vol. 33 (2008).

Yeates, P., 'Michael Collins's "Secret Service Unit" in the trade union movement', *History Ireland*, vol. 19, no. 3 (2014).

Yeates, P., '"Oh God, what did I do to deserve this?" The life and death of Detective Sergeant John Barton', *History Ireland*, vol. 24, no. 5 (2016).

Yeates, P., 'Was the War of Independence necessary?', *History Ireland*, vol. 27, no. 1 (2019).

Young, P., 'Michael Collins—a military leader', in G. Doherty and D. Keogh (eds), *Michael Collins and the Making of the Irish State* (Cork, 1998).

INTERNET RESOURCES

Department of the Taoiseach:
http://www.taoiseach.gov.ie/index.asp?locID=383&docID=511
List of members of the Irish Republican Army:
http://en.wikipedia.org/wiki/List_of_members_of_the_Irish_Republican_Army
National Library of Ireland: http://www.nli.ie/1916/

Noor R. Ampssler, 'Hearts and minds: Malayan campaign re-evaluated':
https://www.defenceviewpoints.co.uk/articles-and-analysis/hearts-and-minds-
malayan-campaign-re-evaluated

The Art of Guerrilla Warfare: www.scribd.com/doc/12858042/The-Art-of-Guerrilla-
Warfare

The Auxiliaries (Auxiliary Division of the Royal Irish Constabulary): www.theauxil-
iaries.com/index.html

Beginning of Guerrilla Warfare: https://youtu.be/SoAZS9HAptc

Colonel David Benest, OBE, 'British atrocities in counter insurgency':
https://www.militaryethics.org/British-Atrocities-in-Counter-Insurgency/10/

Bloody Sunday, initial press reports: http://www.gaa.ie/centenary/bloody-sunday-
archive/1920-initial-press-report-bloody-sunday/

Max Boot on the History of Guerrilla Warfare:
https://youtu.be/Mawx2BkIo8g
https://youtu.be/o_rB4TiwWrs
https://youtu.be/WxMCcqRc9C0
https://youtu.be/W7ah26QEdUI

Max Boot, 'Kick the bully: Michael Collins launches the War of Independence':
http://www.historynet.com/kick-the-bully-michael-collins-launches-the-
1921-irish-rebellion.htm

Ned Broy, the greatest spy of Ireland's freedom struggle:
https://youtu.be/E1IEl7NArLw

Michael Collins and the intelligence war:
http://www.generalmichaelcollins.com/life-times/rebellion/intelligence-war/

Michael Collins, Ireland's greatest:
https://www.youtube.com/watch?v=vV2gzXhz8o8

Michael Collins's last day: https://www.youtube.com/watch?v=0qb1c5NXtwA

Michael Collins, terrorist or freedom fighter:
http://www.bu.edu/phpbin/calendar/event.php?id=34747&cid=46

Linda Connolly, 'Did women escape the worst of the brutalities between 1919–
1921?': https://www.maynoothuniversity.ie/research/research-news-events/lat-
est-news/did-women-escape-worst-brutalities-between-1919-1921

Edwin Creeley, 'The idea of terrorism':
https://www.academia.edu/35833429/The_idea_of_terrorism

Stephen Donovan, 'The multiple functions of terrorism: how the IRA used terrorism
to resist British control while the British utilized terror to conquer the Irish
people': https://www.trentu.ca/deanundergraduate/documents/S.Donovan.doc

The English terror in Ireland: list of towns and villages ravaged by British troops or
police during the past twelve months:
http://catalogue.nli.ie/Record/vtls000506734

Ronan Fanning and Martin Mansergh, review and discussion of *Terror in Ireland*: RTÉ
Radio 1, *Off the Shelf*, 16 February 2013.

David Fitzpatrick on *Terror in Ireland*:
http://www.theirishstory.com/2012/05/17/david-fitzpatrick-on-terror-in-ire-
land/#.W_qkcThKjcs

Anthony Gaughan, 'Listowel police mutiny', Garda Síochána website, 1974:
http://www.esatclear.ie/~garda/listowel.html

Great Irish Journeys: Michael Collins: https://youtu.be/0qb1c5NXtwA

Guerrilla Warfare (IRA Handbook): https://youtu.be/IUQ6-dJYhi0

Guerrilla Warfare in the American Civil War: https://youtu.be/Y80nI8dDLL0

Guerrilla Warfare in the American Revolutionary War:
    https://youtu.be/Q87QfuqpOck

Che Guevara, *Principles of Guerrilla Warfare*:
    http://www3.uakron.edu/worldciv/pascher/che.html

Hang Up Your Brightest Colours: https://www.youtube.com/watch?v=jwNJ3aFZg44

Hidden History: The intelligence war in Dublin:
    https://www.youtube.com/watch?v=Q5eL4cL9Zt8&feature=em-subs_digest

Barry Keane, 'The IRA response to loyalist co-operation during the Irish War of In-
    dependence, 1919–1921': https://www.academia.edu/27954537/The_IRA_re-
    sponse_to_loyalist_co-operation_in_County_Cork_during_the_Irish_War_of_I
    ndependence

Fergheal McGarry, 'The War of Independence': https://www.qub.ac.uk/sites/irishhis-
    torylive/IrishHistoryResources/Articlesandlecturesbyourteachingstaff/The-
    WarofIndependence/

Mao Tse Tung (Mao Zedong), *On Guerrilla War*: https://youtu.be/owHCqjFL67Q

Carlos Marighella, 'The mini-manual of the urban guerrilla':
    https://www.marxists.org/archive/marighella-carlos/1969/06/minimanual-
    urban-guerrilla/index.htm

Frances Mulraney, 'Michael Collins denied Catholic pogroms in Northern Ireland':
    https://www.irishcentral.com/roots/history/michael-collins-denied-catholic-
    pogroms-in-northern-ireland

Brian P. Murphy, Niall Meehan: The Embers of Revisionism
    https://www.academia.edu/34075119/The_EMBERS_of_REVISIONISM_
    essays_in_full_

Eunan O'Halpin, 'Dead of the Irish Revolution':
    http://www.theirishstory.com/2012/02/10/eunan-o-halpin-on-the-dead-of-
    the-irish-revolution/#.XAwb8ttKjcs

Gordon Pattison, 'The British Army's effectiveness in the Irish campaign 1919–1921,
    and the lessons for modern counterinsurgency operations, with special reference
    to C3I aspects', UK Ministry of Defence:
    http://www.ismor.com/cornwallis/cornwallis_2009/6-Pattison-CXIV.pdf

Anne Schwenkenbecher, *Terrorism: A Philosophical Inquiry* (e-book): https://www.pal-
    grave.com/us/book/9780230363984

Shadow of Béal na mBláth: https://www.youtube.com/watch?v=k6Yv7zriFTw

Special Operations Executive: SOE Training Manual: https://ironwolf008.files.word-
    press.com/2010/07/the-wwii-soe-training-manual-rigden.pdf

Terror in Ireland in the War of Independence: https://ifiplayer.ie/terror-in-ireland/

Urban Guerrilla Warfare: https://youtu.be/nYWQkbz9JMs

Index